FILM DIRECTORS
ON DIRECTING

FILM DIRECTORS ON DIRECTING

John Andrew Gallagher

CONTRIBUTIONS TO THE
STUDY OF POPULAR CULTURE,
NUMBER 22

GREENWOOD PRESS

New York • Westport, Connecticut • London

Library of Congress Cataloging-in-Publication Data

Gallagher, John
    Film directors on directing / John Andrew Gallagher.
      p.   cm. — (Contributions to the study of popular culture,
  ISSN 0198–9871 ; no. 22)
    Bibliography: p.
    Includes filmographies and index.
    ISBN 0–313–26227–6 (lib. bdg. : alk. paper)
    1. Motion pictures—Production and direction. 2. Motion picture
  producers and directors—Interviews. I. Title. II. Series.
  PN1995.9.P7G35 1989
  791.43′0233—dc19   88–24648

British Library Cataloguing in Publication Data is available.

A paperback edition of *Film Directors on Directing* is available from Praeger Publishers
(ISBN 0–275–93272–9).

Library of Congress Catalog Card Number: 88–24648
ISBN: 0–313–26227–6
ISSN: 0198–9871

First published in 1989

Greenwood Press, Inc.
88 Post Road West, Westport, Connecticut 06881

Printed in the United States of America

The paper used in this book complies with the
Permanent Paper Standard issued by the National
Information Standards Organization (Z39.48–1984).

10 9 8 7 6 5 4 3 2 1

Copyright Acknowledgments

The author and publisher gratefully acknowledge permission to reprint material from the
following sources:

  Michael Cimino, reprinted with permission, *Millimeter Magazine*, copyright 1978; Stuart
Gordon, reprinted with permission, *Fangoria*, copyright 1987; Susan Seidelman, reprinted with
permission, *Rolling Stone*, copyright 1983; François Truffaut, Joan Micklin Silver, reprinted
with permission, *Grand Illusions*, copyright 1977; Ulu Grosbard, reprinted courtesy of *Films
in Review*, copyright 1981; Mark Rydell, reprinted courtesy of *Films in Review*, copyright
1982; John Milius, reprinted courtesy of *Films in Review*, copyright 1982; Franc Roddam,
reprinted courtesy of *Films in Review*, copyright 1983; Wim Wenders, reprinted courtesy of
Films in Review, copyright 1983.

To Mary Hickey,
with love and thanks

Contents

Preface and Acknowledgments   ix

John G. Avildsen   1

Tony Bill   21

Michael Cimino   37

Abel Ferrara   49

James Glickenhaus   57

Menahem Golan   75

Stuart Gordon   89

Ulu Grosbard   101

Anthony Harvey   115

Dennis Hopper   127

Ted Kotcheff   141

Adrian Lyne   159

John Milius   169

Alan Parker   183

Franc Roddam   195

Mark Rydell   209

Susan Seidelman   221

Joan Micklin Silver   231

James Toback   241

François Truffaut   259

Wim Wenders   269

Bibliography   279

Index   283

About the Author   301

Preface and Acknowledgments

This book is a collection of interviews with twenty-one filmmakers on the craft of directing, or, as the French say, "mise-en-scène"—literally, the placing of a scene. All the directors in the book, with the exception of the late François Truffaut, are currently active in the film industry, and further, have created compelling entertainments over the last two decades. The filmmakers include mainstream Hollywood talent like John G. Avildsen, Michael Cimino, Ted Kotcheff, Adrian Lyne, John Milius, and Mark Rydell, and acclaimed independents such as Abel Ferrara, Stuart Gordon, Susan Seidelman, and Wim Wenders, covering a range of genres from comedy and drama to action-adventure, horror, and science fiction.

The backgrounds of the filmmakers are as diverse as their movies. Tony Bill and Dennis Hopper, for example, were originally actors. Anthony Harvey graduated from the editing room to the director's chair. John Milius and James Toback were successful screenwriters. Ted Kotcheff, Alan Parker, and Franc Roddam directed television before moving into features. Ulu Grosbard was an assistant director in film and a director on Broadway, while Menahem Golan and James Glickenhaus double as studio heads. John Avildsen, Abel Ferrara, Stuart Gordon, Joan Micklin Silver, Susan Seidelman, François Truffaut, and Wim Wenders worked their way up from low-budget features.

The directors in this book offer an intriguing look into the mechanics of moviemaking, from the big guns who spend millions of dollars per film to the resourceful independents who must make do with considerably less financing. Among the subjects we discuss are influences and inspirations, choosing and preparing the screenplay, working with actors and crew, post-production, dealing with distributors, breaking into the business, and advice to aspiring filmmakers. I have tried to keep my editorializing to a minimum; ultimately, the directors speak best for themselves.

Each director is briefly profiled in a note preceding the interview. The note ends with a filmography, in chronological order, providing film title, year of release, distributor, and home video availability; short films are not included.

Many people helped me in the preparation of this book. I wish to express warm thanks to Marilyn Brownstein and William Neenan of Greenwood Press for their patience and assistance. Mark Patrick Carducci, a close friend and an accomplished screenwriter, kindly contributed his interview with Michael Cimino. When we were fellow film students at Boston's Emerson College publishing a film journal called *Grand Illusions,* my friend and colleague Sam Sarowitz participated in the interviews with John Avildsen, John Milius, and François Truffaut. A number of these interviews were originally videotaped by Ira H. Gallen, president of Video Resources New York, Inc., for our long-running Manhattan Cable TV program *Biograph Days, Biograph Nights,* and I thank him for his help, support, and friendship over the years. Mary Hickey lived with this book from inception to completion, and offered valuable suggestions, a wealth of knowledge about movies, and unfailing encouragement.

For help in arranging the interviews, I am grateful to some of the best publicists in the film industry—John Springer (François Truffaut); Diane Collins of M/S Billings Publicity (Abel Ferrara); Marty Montgomery of M/S Billings Publicity (Adrian Lyne); Bill Kenley of Paramount Pictures (Franc Roddam); Reid Rosefelt (Dennis Hopper, Susan Seidelman, Wim Wenders); Priscilla MacDonald, vice president of publicity of The Cannon Group, and Susan Hammer (Menahem Golan); Jonathan Marder and Associates (Stuart Gordon); Rachel Rosen, formerly of Tri-Star Pictures (Alan Parker); Corin Nelson of Tri-Star Pictures (Ted Kotcheff); Myrna Post (James Glickenhaus); and the late Marjery Hymowitz of MGM/UA (James Toback). For further helping to expedite interviews, I appreciate the cooperation of Joyce Wilson Fetherolf, assistant to John Avildsen; Kirsten Bates and her predecessor Jane Muset at Glickenhaus Film; and Debbie Leonard, assistant to Mark Rydell.

For the photographs of the directors, I wish to thank Mark Patrick Carducci (Michael Cimino); Michael O'Neill (Abel Ferrara); Sam Sarowitz (John Milius); Len Tavares (Anthony Harvey); Nathan Scott of Empire Pictures (Stuart Gordon); and Lilyan Sievernich of Gray City, Inc. (Wim Wenders). The other photographs in the book were contributed by the filmmakers, and drawn from the author's personal collection.

For permission to reprint interviews, I am grateful to Alison Johns, *Millimeter Magazine;* Jann S. Wenner and Susan Murcko, *Rolling Stone;* Robin Little, *Films in Review;* Tony Timpone, *Fangoria;* and Sam Sarowitz, my co-editor of *Grand Illusions.*

For assorted kindnesses during the course of this project, thanks to Dawn and John Altyn; Sal Campo; Tony Chaskelson; David, Janis, and Harrison

Chaskin; William Coleman; Laura Epstein; Frank Farel; David Fitzgerald; my parents, Vincent and Lee Gallagher; David Goodman; Niña Hickey; Michael Hirsch; Marc Hirschfeld; John Iula; Steve and Nava James; Lisa Levine Sarowitz; Benton Levy; Howard Lisch; Scott McQueen; Forrest Murray; Peter Newman; Nellie Nugiel; Mitch Pickman and World of Video, Manhattan; Peter Stein; James Tanner; Frank Thompson; Spence Waugh and Janet Wortendyke.

Finally, my special appreciation goes to all of the directors interviewed herein for their time and cooperation.

John A. Gallagher
New York City

FILM DIRECTORS ON DIRECTING

John G. Avildsen

Born in Oak Park, Illinois, in 1937, John G. Avildsen moved with his family to New York at the age of ten. He attended City College at night, working by day in the advertising business. After a two-year stint in the army as a chaplain's assistant, Avildsen moved into features as an assistant director, production manager, and cameraman, a technical training ground that served him well when he began directing low-budget movies. He photographed his first six features himself, often editing them as well, and later served as president of the New York cinematographer's local (IATSE Local 644). With Francis Coppola, Avildsen was among the first mainstream American filmmakers to edit his features on video.

Avildsen made his mark with the controversial hard hats vs. hippies drama *Joe* (1970), but although Hollywood beckoned, he continued to direct low-budget independent features like *Cry Uncle!* (1971) and *The Stoolie* (1972). In his first Hollywood feature, *Save the Tiger* (1973), Avildsen guided Jack Lemmon to an Oscar in the role of a frustrated middle-aged businessman. *Rocky* (1976) won Avildsen the Academy Award for Best Director, launched Sylvester Stallone to superstardom, and added a new batch of characters— Rocky Balboa, Adrian, Paulie, Apollo Creed—to American popular culture. The sports underdog motif was repeated with equal success in Avildsen's *The Karate Kid* (1984) and *The Karate Kid, Part II* (1986).

The director cities *Sweet Dreams/Okay Bill* (1971), *Joe, Save the Tiger, Rocky,* and *The Karate Kid* as his favorite films, and he has indeed been at his best when he has handled smaller, more personal projects that feature relative newcomers like Peter Boyle (*Joe*), Sylvester Stallone (*Rocky*), and Ralph Macchio (*The Karate Kid*) in the stellar roles.

The following interview was culled from two sessions with Avildsen in New York City, the first (with the assistance of Sam Sarowitz) in January 1978, and the second in February of 1988.

John G. Avildsen (from the author's collection).

FILMOGRAPHY

Turn on to Love (1969, Haven International).
Guess What We Learned in School Today? (1970, Cannon). HV: Paragon.
Joe (1970, Cannon). HV: Vestron.
Cry Uncle! (1971, Cambist). HV: Prism.
Sweet Dreams/Okay Bill (1971, Four Star Excelsior).
The Stoolie (1972, Jama).
Save the Tiger (1973, Paramount). HV: Paramount.
Fore Play (1975, Cinema General). Avildsen directed "Inaugural Ball"; other seg-
    ments directed by Bruce Malmuth and Robert McCarty.
W. W. and the Dixie Dance Kings (1975, 20th Century-Fox).
Rocky (1976, United Artists). HV: CBS/Fox.
Slow Dancing in the Big City (1978, United Artists).
The Formula (1980, MGM/UA). HV: MGM/UA.
Neighbors (1982, Columbia). HV: RCA/Columbia.
A Night in Heaven (1983, 20th Century-Fox). HV: Key.
The Karate Kid (1982, Columbia). HV: RCA/Columbia.
Happy New Year (1986, Columbia). HV: RCA/Columbia.
The Karate Kid, Part II (1986, Columbia). HV: RCA/Columbia.
For Keeps (1988, Tri-Star). HV: RCA/Columbia.
Lean on Me (1989, Warner Bros.).

AVILDSEN INTERVIEW

JOHN A. GALLAGHER: What sparked your interest in films?

JOHN G. AVILDSEN: My father always took home movies so I grew up
    looking at a camera, but I never had any desire to make movies when I
    was growing up. I had desire to dance and to act, but not to direct. I got
    into advertising and did that for about five years. Then when I got out
    of the army, Jack O'Connell, a guy I'd worked for in the advertising
    business, who had left advertising and went to work for Antonioni and
    Fellini, made his first picture, a thing called *Greenwich Village Story* (1961).
    I worked for him on that and said, "This beats working," so I got into
    it that way. After *Greenwich Village Story,* I tried to get another job in
    the movie business and couldn't. I went back into advertising for a year,
    got fired for making a Studebaker commercial that nobody wanted to
    pay for, and figured, "Well, if I'm going to work in the movie business,
    I'd better get out of advertising." I got a job as an assistant cameraman
    on a low-budget feature, made a couple of shorts, worked as an assistant
    director on *Black Like Me* (1964), then got a job as a production manager
    with Arthur Penn on *Mickey One* (1965). My first big job was on Otto
    Preminger's *Hurry Sundown* (1967).

JAG: Was Preminger as volatile as the stories go?

JGA: Oh indeed. At the same time he was very kind and gave me a lot of
    opportunities. He would carry on and rant and rave, but he could also
    be very sweet and turned out to be a good friend. I went to Louisiana

on *Hurry Sundown* as a "go-fer" and ended up doing the second unit directing. He only yelled at me once. We were down in Baton Rouge shooting in a courthouse. Burgess Meredith was playing the judge and the scene was about to be shot. "Quiet" had been called and I was whispering to a friend on the sidelines. Suddenly Otto spotted me and he said, (with accent) "Mr. Avildsen! Why is it that you write me letters that you want to work on my movies and then you come down here and talk?" I got nailed that afternoon, but that was rather mild. I saw him destroy a prop man who had schlepped two armfuls of pots and pans across a muddy Louisiana plantation field to see which one Otto wanted, and he just threw this prop guy on the ground and yelled at him. It was terrible. He would do this to actors. I remember there was an actor who came in for a screen test and when it was over, Otto said, "You call yourself an actor?" This guy flipped out, grabbed Otto, got him down on the floor and was about to punch him when Otto looked up and said, "What's the matter? You can't take a joke?" He was quite a character. I learned a great deal from him. He worked very well with the cameras. I didn't see a lot of evidence of the time he took in his work with the actors. I remember one scene late at night out in the swamps. John Phillip Law was going to drive up in an old truck with Faye Dunaway, in her first movie, and stop at this cabin in the woods. Just before they shot it, John looked at Preminger and said, "Refresh my memory, Otto. Where is it that I've just come from in this scene?" Preminger said, "Where you come from is not your concern. You come up and you start on the line, that's what you do!" That's one way of doing it, but I haven't embraced that technique.

JAG: What was Arthur Penn like on the set of *Mickey One*?

JGA: Arthur worked much closer with the actors. From my observation, he didn't work as closely with the camera as Preminger did. I had just worked for Otto before him so I could contrast the two. Arthur was much more involved in getting the best possible performance from the actors, which he does very well.

JAG: How did you get your first feature directing job?

JGA: Leonard Kertman was working in the mailroom of an advertising agency. He had never made a movie before, and he placed an ad in *Backstage* that said, "Wanted—Movie Director." I answered the ad!

JAG: The film was *Turn on to Love*, a "sexploitation" movie. What did that involve?

JGA: That was before the terms "porno" and "hardcore." Ladies' breasts were about as exciting as it got in a world without pubic hair. The language wasn't particularly exciting and the stories were usually pretty boring. Mine was really boring. It was a terrible picture. We did it in seven days for fifteen grand on five-year-out-of-date 35mm Tri-X film. A 16mm print was made up to cut. I didn't have anything to do with the cutting. *Turn on to Love* was pretty bad, but it did OK, made some money for the producer, and got me the opportunity to do the next one, *Guess What We Learned in School Today?*

JAG: How did you find Peter Boyle for *Joe*?

JGA: He sent me a picture. I saw a lot of pictures and I responded to his. I gave the different candidates for the part the speech in the bar where we first meet Joe damning the hippies. There was a line in the script that said, "You show me a welfare worker who's not a nigger lover and I'll massage your asshole." That was the written dialogue, and when Peter came to read "I'll massage your asshole," he looked at me and said, "I'm not queer!" I knew right then that he was the guy because that would be exactly the attitude a guy of his mentality would have. I wanted to go with him but the people who were producing it said no, he would be too young, nobody would believe that he had been in World War Two. I had to get somebody else. So I did, an older man, and a couple of days before we had to shoot, this other actor took a leak in the escalator at Bloomingdale's and slugged a saleslady, so I said, "Look, why don't we go with Boyle? I think you'll like him. He'll be all right." So we did. That whole picture was sort of a mistake inasmuch as the people who produced it, Cannon, had raised money to do another movie, and four weeks before they had to begin they realized it was a terrible script. I had just finished making another picture for them called *Guess What We Learned in School Today?* They came in and said, "Make us something right away because we don't want to make this, and if we don't make something in four weeks we have to give the money back." So I said that I had this outline Norman Wexler had written and that it would make a good movie. They said, "The guy's never written a script before." I said, "Well, he's a good writer, he's a playwright," and so forth. Really, out of desperation, they said, "OK, go ahead," and that's how it happened, strictly by accident.

SAM SAROWITZ: What was the budget on *Joe*?

JGA: $250,000.

JAG: How long did it take you to shoot?

JGA: About twenty-five days.

SS: It wound up being quite a box-office hit.

JGA: Thank goodness. The timing was incredibly successful. We shot that in January and February of '70 and in May the hard hats freaked out down on Wall Street over the Vietnam protestors and "hard hat" had become a national identity. The picture opened in July, so the timing couldn't have been better. I wasn't really that happy with *Joe* because I wasn't allowed to cut it. I always thought it was much more exploitive than it might have been. Also, the ending of it wasn't the ending it was supposed to have. If you recollect, the guy shoots his daughter and runs out of the house and we go out. That's how it ended. It was supposed to end a few minutes later when Joe walks out, sees what's happened, drops his rifle, and we go out on him where he's beginning to realize that this isn't the solution. This point isn't made, which is very distressing.

JAG: What kind of feedback did you get from *Joe*?

JGA: Mostly positive. People seemed to like it and could relate to it. I didn't get the reaction, "You must hate hard hats," or "You must hate hippies," which I was glad about because it didn't take either attitude, hopefully. In other words, it didn't try to judge. Of course, the way it was cut, the movie *was*, as I say, exploitive. But people seemed to like it. It sold tickets, which was the reality.

JAG: *Sweet Dreams* was actually made before *Joe*, but released afterwards.

JGA: Nothing happened with it originally, and then after *Joe* came out, I put in a more political soundtrack. Because *Joe* worked, they called it *Okay Bill* and it had a very limited release. *Sweet Dreams* is about temptation. This guy gets tempted sexually. He's married and has a kid and the movie shows how he deals with the temptation and how he and his wife resolve it and end up back together. It was an example of doing a film just the way I wanted it. We shot it silently, which is something I would do differently now. I told the producer that we would put the dialogue in the track later and it would be sort of impressionistic. Visually we had it together, then we got the actors together and improvised for days. Then I cut up those tracks and that's where the story came from. *Sweet Dreams* won some prizes and got some nice reviews, but never really found a distributor. We just got some interest to rerelease it and put it on video. I still know a lot of people who were in the film and are old friends and I've always wanted to do what we did in 1968, get those people together and come up with a story we could shoot now, using pieces of the film we made twenty years ago. I've been paying rent on the negative storage all this time.

JAG: When did you go out to Hollywood for the first time?

JGA: After *Joe*. Some people at Warner Brothers wanted me to do something. I remember going out there for the first time and walking around that place. I was very awed by it, walking down the halls with all the photographs of the different stars and movies that they'd had, and it made me realize why they used to call them dream factories. It was like a real factory, like a shoe factory with all the different model shoes that they made, and it was the first time that I realized that movies had numbers, and this was number so-and-so on a particular production schedule. I had the feeling at the time of an assembly line, and number 6075 had to be ready because it opened down the line. I was very turned off by the people I ran into at the time and turned down the deal. I came back to New York and made *Cry Uncle!* instead. It was only when I got the script for *Save the Tiger* that I went out there for the first time to work.

JAG: How did you get that job?

JGA: Jack Lemmon had committed to the script. He liked it very much and his advisers told him he ought to get a new, young director to do it. Somebody showed him *Joe,* which he liked, and I got a call about three o'clock in the morning. They had just seen it in Los Angeles, and they called me in New York and woke me up. He said, "Hey, this is Jack Lemmon. I loved your movie!" I said, "Terrific!" Then I went out to meet him and he was a terrific guy. I told him that I had always been a fan of his, but, if he chose me to direct it, I didn't want to see him in this one with all those Lemmon mannerisms that a lot of people enjoyed in his comedies. This thing was anything *but* a comedy. He said, "That's right, Slick. You keep your eyes open." That's what I did mostly. Every so often he'd do something and I'd say, "Well..." and he'd say, "You didn't like the eyebrow, right? Without the eyebrow, better?" I said, "Maybe without the eyebrow," and he said, "You got it." He was just a dream to work with. I tried to be very straightforward in the shooting of the movie. It was a good story, very sad and depressing, and I think that's one reason nobody bought a ticket.

JAG: The critics liked it. It won an Oscar for Lemmon.

JGA: The critical response was good but it sure didn't do anything at the box office.

JAG: Do you think that was because people didn't like seeing him in a role like that?

JGA: I think because people would rather come out of a movie feeling good instead of sad. *Save the Tiger* made you feel really lousy. It presented no hope. It may all be true, but I think people pay to see some hope, some fantasy.

SS: There was a trend for a while of downer movies, like *Midnight Cowboy* (1969) and *Easy Rider* (1969).

JGA: But even those were still sort of adventure yarns, whereas this could be the guy next door. A very unexciting character doing a very unexciting thing with his life. You got the idea that the country's made up of people like this, and things are getting so bad that a guy like this is committing felonies and the country's in trouble. I don't think anybody wanted to know that.

JAG: You did most of the pre-production on *Serpico* (1973). Did you have problems with Dino DeLaurentiis?

JGA: No, I had a lot of problems with Marty Bregman, who was the producer of the picture. Marty had a girlfriend named Cornelia Sharpe who was an actress. He wanted her to be one of the girls in the movie, and I thought she just couldn't act to save her life. He realized that I wasn't going to cast her, so she got the part and I didn't. If I had it to do over again, I would have done it differently, with more finesse.

JAG: You worked with Serpico?

JGA: Yes, I got to know Frank very well and spent time with him over in Switzerland. He really regretted that I wasn't able to do the picture because I thought it could have been better and much more inspirational, since Serpico was a very inspirational person. I don't think the picture captured as much of that as it might have. He's really an extraordinary person.

SS: Was the screenplay true to life?

JGA: Probably more so than not, but it was the attitude of the film. Again, it was exploitive, and didn't really get into what made him tick. He was a very funny guy. Only person I've ever seen who lit a fart. Ever see anybody do that? Yeah, he'd fart through his bluejeans, hold a match there, and a giant blue flame would leap out. He's a great mimic and a very funny guy. I remember around the time the movie came out he was back here and we were driving around one night. We stopped at a light and a guy walked across the intersection with a golf bag on his back, and Frank said, "Boy, you don't know how terrific it is to look at that guy and not wonder what's in his golf bag."

JAG: Did you see any of your work in *Serpico*?

JGA: Maybe a few things. The script I wanted to do was somewhat different than that. I guess I cast the cameraman, the art director, the sound man, and one or two people that I cast ended up in the film.

JAG: You're credited with an anthology film called *Fore Play*.

JGA: That was a sort of lark I did after the *Serpico* thing fell apart. It was a four-part comedy. Terry Southern was going to do one, along with Dan Greenberg, Bruce Jay Friedman, and myself. Each one was a little sex comedy. Mine was called "Inaugural Ball." From the time Johnson was in office I always wondered what if somebody kidnapped the President's daughter, and the ransom was that the President and the First Lady had to fuck on television to get their daughter back. The plot was that the Mafia had financed the President's campaign with the understanding that once he's in office he'd outlaw pornography so the Mafia could make more money selling it. Since the President wasn't moving quickly enough, they kidnap his daughter Trixie. We got Zero Mostel and Estelle Parsons to play the First Couple. While we were making it, Watergate was going on and it was very tough to stay ahead of that. Every day something more outrageous was revealed. It turned out all right. The other sections didn't. The one with Terry Southern never got made, so the idea was that the other two would be absorbed into the one that I did with Zero. We went back about a half a year later and shot some stuff with Zero where he's out of office, in a wheelchair, being interviewed by the BBC for their documentary program called "Going

Down in History." Eventually they retitled the movie *The President's Women*. We wanted to call it *All the President's Women*. It opened and played down South, didn't do very much. I don't think it ever played in New York at all.

JAG: How did *W. W. and the Dixie Dance Kings* come about for you?

JGA: I was broke and had to pay about eight inches of bills. The script had come to me when I was doing *Save the Tiger*. I liked the script that Tom Rickman had written but at that time Burt Reynolds was part of the deal and I said, "Forget it. I'll be happy to make it with Jimmy Caan." They said that Burt was part of the deal, so I said, "No, thank you." About a year or so went by and the script came back again with the same deal, a different studio and even less money this time. I had to do it or go to work. So I did, and it was a terribly painful experience. I found Reynolds very arrogant, untalented, very difficult to work with, so it was a really gruesome experience.

JAG: How was Art Carney?

JGA: A pleasure. Very nice guy. Jerry Reed was very good. He should have played W. W. The thing that the film taught me was that I could do something that I had no passion for, that my mechanics were such that I could make it work. There's some satisfaction to that.

JAG: Did you have any say in the cutting of the film?

JGA: I cut it and had it down about 90% of the way I wanted it. There were a couple of things the studio insisted on, the sequence of scenes, that I didn't like. The day came when it was time to show it to Reynolds. He liked it and I said, "Well, there's one scene that should go there and another that should go there." He said, "Yeah, that makes sense." I said, "You might mention it," and sure enough, the word came down from the brass to do that. So I had no control, I only had influence and it was because Reynolds agreed with the way I saw it that it ended up more or less the way I wanted it. If he hadn't, he would have said, "No, that's full of shit," and it would have been full of shit.

JAG: Did Sylvester Stallone test for that?

JGA: He came in and read. He seemed too urban. He had just done *The Lords of Flatbush* (1974) and he hadn't gotten the grease out of his hair. I couldn't see him in the South.

JAG: How did you get involved with *Rocky*?

JGA: I was going to do a picture in Malta of all places, called *Operation Bandersnatch,* but it ran out of money. My friend Gene Kirkwood was working at Chartoff-Winkler, and sent me a script called *Hell's Kitchen,* which Sylvester wrote before *Rocky,* a very good script that Sylvester directed himself with a new title, *Paradise Alley* (1971). It turned out somebody else owned *Hell's Kitchen,* so Gene sent me a script called *Rocky* about boxing. I said, "I hate boxing. I don't know anything about boxing and I think boxing's really dumb." He said, "Read it anyway." I read it, and on the second page, Rocky is talking to his turtles, so I found him a very engaging character. I said, "Sure, that's a sweet idea," so I went out and did *Rocky* with the idea that no more than six people would ever get to see it. Working with Sylvester was terrific. He's a very talented writer and actor. Evidently, they had considered Burt Reynolds, Jimmy Caan, and Ryan O'Neal for the part.

JAG: What was Stallone like on the set?

JGA: He's a great energy to have around. He always knew everybody's lines, always ready to do whatever had to be done.

SS: It was his pet project.

JGA: Sure. The crew didn't take him seriously. The producers didn't take him seriously. They were busy making *Nickelodeon* (1976) and they figured that was going to be their big movie. We had to make *Rocky* for a million bucks.

JAG: How did you come to cast Talia Shire as Adrian?

JGA: She came in and the chemistry between the two of them was very good. She looked right and she was playful, a real pleasure to work with.

JAG: How about Burt Young?

JGA: I wanted Burt in *Serpico,* as a matter of fact. The same guy that gave me my chance, Leonard Kertman, gave Burt his break. Leonard was making some low-budget movie after the thing I did for him. I think Burt was painting the apartment that the scene was going to be shot in, and some actor didn't show up, so Leonard said to Burt, "Look, will you come over here for a minute, . . . " and that's how it happened.

JAG: Burgess Meredith?

JGA: We were going to go with Lee J. Cobb as Mickey, but he wouldn't read for us. Then we were going to go with Lee Strasberg for a while. He read for us, but he was real tied up and could only give us a few days here and there. We were also going to use Kenny Norton as the boxer, but both he and Lee just had so many other things to do. I said, "Look, why don't we get somebody who doesn't have anything else to do, who'll give us their attention." The producers said "OK." I had met Burgess on *Hurry Sundown* and found him a very amusing fellow. I had him come in and he and Sly read a couple of scenes. I had them improvise the scene at the gym when we first meet Mickey. Rocky says, "What happened to my locker?" At the end of that scene, Rocky turns to walk away, and Burgess said, "Hey, kid. You ever thought about retiring?" Rocky says, "No," and Burgess said, "Think about it." I thought that was very funny and said, "Yeah, that's the spirit."

JAG: How did you come to shoot in Philadelphia?

JGA: Sylvester had lived in Philadelphia for a few years as a teenager. They didn't want us to go to Philly, they wanted us to make it in Los Angeles and make it look like Philadelphia. It was supposed to be set in the winter time, and I said, "How are we going to do that?" The producer said, "Well, I can see my breath around my pool in the morning in January."

I worked it out so we did the stuff in Philly non-union with Ralf Bode, the cameraman who shot my earlier stuff like *Joe* and *Cry Uncle!* I got my crew together that had done my low-budget pictures with me, snuck into Philadelphia, and shot there for five days then left. We later got caught by the union and had to pay a fine, but it was a lot less than if we had gone there and shot union.

SS: Did you look at any of the old boxing movies?

JGA: Yeah, and I realized how terrible all the boxing sequences were. They really looked phony in some of these films. First thing I said was, "If we're going to have boxing it better look real, otherwise people are going to giggle." I got them rehearsing and the first day we got into the ring Sylvester said, "I'll do this," and Carl Weathers said, "I'll do that," and I said, "Look, this is silly. I don't care what you guys do, but we gotta do it the same way every time, otherwise I'll never be able to cut it, and you're never going to be able to learn the moves. So Sylvester, why don't you write the whole thing out. You want a left, you want a right, you bounce against the ropes and we'll do that." He came back the next day and they started practicing that. It became like a ballet. It really paid off because everybody knew what was going to go on. When I was cutting the thing and I'd stop it on the machine, the glove would be an inch away from the guy's nose. They'd come very close and that's what made it look so real.

SS: You used the Steadicam extensively.

JGA: Garrett Brown's camera. It saved a lot of time and made it possible to get shots that otherwise we never could have done on that kind of budget. Bill Conti's music was also a big contributor to how successful the picture was.

JAG: The editing, too, especially the big fight.

JGA: That's when I decided to get into the damn union, because I did it all and didn't get paid for it, and someone else got the credit, so I figured the heck with that. So I finally got into the union for *Slow Dancing in the Big City,* both the cameraman's union and the editor's union. I do it myself, like I did on my earlier low-budget pictures. When I did *Save the Tiger* and *Rocky* I couldn't operate the camera and I couldn't cut the stuff myself.

JAG: There's a feeling of spontaneity in *Rocky.*

JGA: I always leave things open and don't say, "It's written this way and that's how it has to be." In the scene when Mickey comes up to ask for the job and Rocky says, "The hell with you," and he leaves, in the script the next cut was outside and Mick is walking down the street. Rocky runs out after him, which we'd already shot in Philly. We finished the scene and I said, "Wait a minute, we never see Rocky change his mind. We never see why it is he decides to go after Mickey. We've gotta see that." Sly said, "Jesus, how do we do that?" I said, "I don't know." We did a few takes where Rocky comes out of the bathroom, stands by the door and the shadows are on his face. We set up a mirror so we could see how far to open the door to see if the shadow was right. It was really boring. I said, "This stinks. Maybe you take a big breath and let all that frustration out." We did it and it was beautiful. Then the sound man said, "No good, my batteries were dead," which was very frustrating so we had to do it a few more times. We used pieces of different takes, but that was all improvised by Sylvester. When I cast I try to find people who have the knack for improvisation. I'll tell them when they come in to read, "Forget about the script. You know more or less what the scene's about, fake it." I'm attracted to people who come up with good ideas, so once they're cast I know they have that knack, and during rehearsal we keep trying to do that. Once it comes time to shoot we've narrowed it down so we know what's going to happen, but I like to rehearse a lot long before we shoot.

JAG: How did you approach the climactic fight?

JGA: We had four days to do all that stuff and I realized how enormous the job was. I worked with Bill Cassidy, a friend of mine who I used to be in the advertising business with, told him all the different shots I needed and he made up the storyboard. We made copies of it and gave it to everyone, made them realize how much had to be done. It was really an excellent logistics job to get this done in such a short amount of time. The makeup that Sylvester had to wear took an enormous amount of time. For instance, when he comes into the ring, we had about two thousand extras for one day. We had most of them before lunch because they were doing *Two Minute Warning* (1976) at the Coliseum next door and they had a much better lunch than we did, so most of the extras disappeared. When Sly comes into the ring we never see his face because his face looks like it did at the end of the fight. Once he was in the ring we shot the last round first, and then the fourteenth round because the makeup wasn't quite so severe. So we did the whole fight backwards. That was the first time I used a storyboard and it proved very beneficial. I did the same thing at the end of *Slow Dancing*. Normally I don't storyboard every day's shooting. I work out what I'm going to have to get during the rehearsal time for a couple of weeks before we shoot. During that time I'll figure out the set-ups and the cutting. We'll videotape the rehearsals and see the different angles, so when the time comes to do it, the shooting goes quickly because everyone knows what the shot is.

JAG: Many critics pointed out that *Rocky* is in the spirit of the Frank Capra movies.

JGA: Capra is a great hero of mine, and one of the things that attracted me to the script was that it had a positive attitude. The original ending of the picture had Rocky carried out of the ring and down the aisle. He reaches for the girl, pulls her up, and they go off. When it came time to shoot that sequence, the extras had carried off Apollo Creed. The assistant director came back and said, "We don't have enough extras to carry Rocky out." Sylvester heard that and said, "Wait a second, maybe Rocky just says goodbye to the guys in the ring and walks down the aisle himself, sees the girl, and they walk off." It seemed sort of poetic at the time so we shot it that way. Then as I was nearing the completion of the cutting and Bill Conti brought in the music he had written for the end, it was so stirring and inspiring. I said, "This is terrific but I haven't got the footage here to go with that." That was what got me to think Rocky stays in the ring and the girl runs through the crowd like a Clairol commercial. I convinced the producers I could shoot that in about six hours with twenty-five extras, so we went back and re-shot the end. I think it really made a big difference about how you felt at the end of it. I'd never seen the picture all the way through because we had a deadline to get it ready. I spent the last four weekends by myself putting that stuff together so it would be ready for the mix. We mixed it, and the last reel was a real tough one for us. There were so many tracks, and I wanted the music, the crowd, and the effects loud. The first time I saw the film was when we finished mixing that last reel. We took it over to the screening room where I had about one hundred friends to see it. They all freaked out, so that made me feel good. The producers said, "'What do you think?" Very sarcastically, after that response, I said, "I think it needs a lot of work." They said, "Well we do too," and I said, "Oy vey!" I realized my only hope was to get a lot more people to see it in this version right away and if they had the same reaction then maybe the producers wouldn't try and make it any better. I arranged for a screening at the big room at MGM that seated about five hundred people. About six hundred showed up and *they* all freaked out. It was at this point they said, "OK, we'll try it like this."

JAG: What was your reaction when the film won the Oscar for Best Picture and you won for Best Director?

JGA: I was there! I was very surprised and very pleased. Surprised because I never would have fancied myself in that club. I was figuring even if I didn't win it's OK because then I won't have to get up there, which I was quite terrified of doing. But once I heard my name, all that fear went away and I just felt terrific. It certainly was a rush. A lot of stuff came my way and I made a lot of poor choices and reeled with the impact of success through a number of turkey movies, and then got lucky again with *The Karate Kid*.

JAG: Had you intended to make *Slow Dancing in the Big City* right after you finished *Rocky?*

JGA: No, I was going to do *Saturday Night Fever* (1977). We must have been within three or four weeks from shooting when I had a disagreement with Robert Stigwood, the producer, about the script, so that was the end of that. I started looking for scripts again. *Slow Dancing* came my way and I was very taken by it.

JAG: You were always interested in dance?

JGA: Yeah, I had a fantasy I was going to do *The Gene Kelly Story* someday, so I'd always had an affinity to dance in the broadest aspects, but not to ballet, which is what we had in *Slow Dancing*. It wasn't so much the dance as it was the love story between this Jimmy Breslin sort of journalist and this modern dancer ballerina that drew me to the project.

JAG: How did you get involved with *The Formula?*

JGA: I read the galleys before the book came out. I couldn't understand it. I kept reading and going back and calling up Steve Shagan, the writer and producer. I found it a very convoluted plot and learned a very expensive lesson. I was betting that the movie wouldn't be made. They optioned my time to get the script and cast together. I said, "Sure, I'll give you the next sixty days," because I thought within those sixty days somebody would surely realize this thing was too complex and would turn it down. I would walk away with a fistful of dollars and not have to make a movie. I got caught. They made the movie.

JAG: Marlon Brando is always fascinating to watch. He was quite a casting coup.

JGA: He got paid every day in cash. We went up to Mulholland Drive to see him one afternoon and he was very cordial. We started talking about the story and he started telling us how he imagined this character who was patterned after an Armand Hammer type of oil magnate. He saw this guy as living out in the desert, a desert rat with big dish antennas, wearing rags because he was a recluse. He described this guy very eloquently. Steve Shagan was sitting next to me and I could sense this poor guy was dying. Brando was creating this totally different character. It was making no sense to me at all. Finally Marlon finished and I said, "I don't know. I see this guy as one of these people with a coat and vest on the cover of *Time* magazine. He's the Establishment. Why make him some kind of screwball?" There was a long pause and Brando said, "OK, I was just testing you." Once he signed on, he was a pleasure, a lot of fun and very funny.

JAG: Did Brando contribute bits of business like offering George C. Scott the Milk Duds, and hiding behind the shrubbery in his office?

JGA: They were both Marlon's suggestion. He was constantly coming up with things like that. Unfortunately, some of his best stuff in the scene where we meet him for the first time at the palatial estate where he's having breakfast was cut. That scene went on for a couple of minutes more where he was doing outrageous, hilarious bits, but David Begelman, the convicted felon who was running MGM at the time, didn't think it was funny.

JAG: On *Neighbors*, John Belushi was playing his part very much against type.

JGA: My original notion on *Neighbors* was to have Rodney Dangerfield play the part that Belushi ended up playing. He certainly was much closer to the age of the character that Thomas Berger wrote about in his novel. I had worked with Rodney for a few weeks on a screen test and he was great, playing it straight, not doing his stand-up, a very good actor. But there was no interest at the studio that he could sell a ticket. Belushi was also on my list because I thought *he* was a very good actor, but he thought I wanted him to play the other character, Vic. I said, "No, you've done that character a million times. Play Earl, stretch yourself as an actor. Play an older guy, you're a terrific actor." I don't think he really wanted to do that. He didn't want to appear that old and he wanted to keep the gag aspect of it rather than playing the straight part and playing against type. He had a lot of problems of his own going on at that time, so you never knew when he was going to show up, but sometimes he could be very charming and very sweet. Dan Ayckroyd was a real gentleman, a great pleasure to work with.

JAG: How did Belushi and Aykroyd relate to Cathy Moriarity? It was her first picture after her debut in *Raging Bull* (1980).

JGA: They were very patient with her and very supportive. She worked real hard, and I'm sure it was a lot for her to deal with because her rise had been instantaneous. She was very conscientious and I thought she did a good job.

JAG: *Neighbors* didn't perform at the box office.

JGA: I wish it had done better. I don't think I had any quarrel with the cut. It was a difficult picture to promote. Maybe they could have promoted it better, but thank goodness for video because it does give it an endless life. People keep commenting on it, people who didn't see it when it was in release, but saw it on tape.

JAG: *The Karate Kid* was a huge popular success.

JGA: Robert Kamen wrote a really good script, and wrote the Ralph Macchio/Pat Morita relationship very well. Ralph and Pat hit it off on a personal level, too. They had a lot of respect and affection for each other. We spent a lot of time rehearsing. I'd videotape rehearsals and we worked in a very informal and friendly atmosphere. That friendly atmosphere makes a big difference. If everybody's liking each other and having a nice time, the work that comes out the other end is always better because the energy is going to that instead of, "Is Charlie angry today?" or "Who's freaked out in the last twenty minutes?" Then all the energy is worrying about that rather than trying to make the movie and use the very few expensive hours you're given each day to shoot and get on film the best you can. It's tough to do and it takes a lot of concentration and cooperation because the time is so precious and there's so little of it.

JAG: How did you approach the choreography of the martial arts sequences in *The Karate Kid?*

JGA: From a fair distance so I wouldn't get hit! I was very lucky and got Pat Johnson, a martial artist and master of karate. Again, I know as much about karate as I do about boxing. Robert Kamen is a black belt and knows all about it. I listened and said, "That's a nice step. Can you do this and still be true to it? Would it make a nicer picture if you did that?" We worked together closely and rehearsed every blow for weeks and weeks, using the technique I learned on *Rocky*. You can't improvise these things. In the weeks prior to shooting, the actors on *Karate Kid* learned the moves like a ballet. When we came to shoot, it would look as good as it could given the time that we had, and nobody would get hurt. I'd also be able to figure out the best angles to shoot the various kicks and punches in order to make them look convincing.

JAG: *The Karate Kid, Part II* was a natural continuation

JGA: Bob Kamen and I spent a lot of time working on the script. I was very pleased with how it came out and had a great time in Hawaii shooting it.

JAG: *Happy New Year* had a very limited release.

JGA: Yes, it was released by the CIA. It was a secret release! It was released primarily to qualify for video sales. *Happy New Year* was an orphan of changing regimes at Columbia. When David Puttnam came in he didn't feel the picture had any potential. When it was released for about a minute and a half, it got some very good reviews that surprised everybody. I'll give you an illustration of how out to lunch they were in hustling this movie. It concerns Harry Winston's and a jewelry heist in Palm Beach, Florida, which is synonymous with money and society. In the movie we see Peter Falk getting off the train and there's a sign that says "West Palm Beach." That's where the train station is. Then the taxi goes across Lake Worth and into Palm Beach, so obviously the story takes place in Palm Beach, plus Palm Beach has a certain panache about it and conjures all sorts of images. In the advertising for the film, they say, "See what happens when two guys go to West Palm Beach"! Nothing happens when two guys go to West Palm Beach and nothing happened with the movie either.

JAG: Were you happy with the film itself?

JGA: Not particularly. It was based on a movie that Claude Lelouch wrote and directed in 1973, a French film starring Lino Ventura. It had very moderate success and certain critical reaction. What gave it any notoriety was that it dealt with the feminist movement in 1973. This criminal type falls in love with a girl from the other side of the tracks. He gets caught and is put away for six years and she waits for him. Hard to believe, but romantic, and the attraction was that they were so different and opposites attracted. He gets out and discovers that while he was in jail she was living in his apartment in Paris and keeping company with some guy. This destroys him and his friend says, "Look, things are different now. Girls do what guys do. It's a different world than when you went into prison." He finally forgives her in a miserly way. It appealed to me because it seemed to be about forgiveness, and Peter Falk is terrific, so I figured we could come up with a good script using the same basic story and update it, setting it in America. We had three terrific scripts written by three very good writers. Peter unfortunately rejected all of them. He really wanted a translation of that French movie, which basically is what we got. We tried to jazz it up a bit, but it's not one of my favorites.

JAG: What attracted you to *For Keeps?*

JGA: The opportunity to do a love story. I always liked Molly Ringwald. The story itself seemed to be about something that's unusual. I had to do something because there was going to be a cut-off period when people stopped making movies in anticipation of the Directors Guild strike that never happened. So those were the factors.

JAG: You've been cutting your films on video. What does that process entail?

JGA: I use the video editing in conjunction with the 35mm film. I'm never concerned about the video being shown because the 35mm film is cut to conform with what I've done on video. The dailies are transferred onto VHS and broken down in a particular order. For example, on cassette one I'll have the master shot, on cassette two I'll have the closeup of the person looking to the right, and on another cassette I'll have the closeup of the person looking left. I pop in the masters, transfer that onto the cassette that I'm building, pop in the closeup, get that done, then pop in the next shot. It's real fast. I'm not looking for trims and I'm not pasting the stuff together. You just press a button to get a preview of what it's going to be like. If you don't like it, you adjust it until you like it, then you hit the button and go on to the next shot. You don't have to keep track of everything like on film. The whole movie fits into a couple of bookcases, whereas you need rooms and rooms for the 35mm film. I think you do a better job because you're not spending 90% of the time physically cutting the film and taping it together, mounting it again and having the machine eat it.

JAG: You work with one of the industry's top sound editors, Dan Sable. How does the video process affect the sound editing?

JGA: Dan and I first worked together on *Neighbors* and since then he's computerized his sound effects and has a terrific system. He's able to press buttons and get stuff on a track. It's real quick. When I'm working on the video I'm just cutting picture and dialogue and I don't get into the sound effects. I'll cut a scene, send it to the cutting room, and they'll conform the work print to the tape. Then they'll make me a tape of that and send it to me. Once the picture is cut I'll start refining on the film itself, but by then it's 90% done.

JAG: What kind of resistance did you face in joining the editors and cinematographers unions?

JGA: The reason I cut *For Keeps* here in New York was that I applied for membership in the local in Los Angeles and was turned down; the reason being that in their contract, one of the clauses says that none of their members will perform more than one function on a film. If you're the editor, you can't be the assistant editor, and if you're the assistant you can't also be the apprentice. I ran into the same problem with the camera local in New York. They had a similar provision. I wanted to operate the camera in addition to directing the movie. They made the same objection but eventually it was voted down. There again, if you're the camera operator, you can't be the assistant, and if you're the loader you can't be the director of photography. They can make rules that govern their particular category, but it means if I wrote the picture I can't photograph it. I got nowhere with this argument in Los Angeles and they refused me membership. Since I was already in the local in New York we cut it here. I think they're afraid all the directors will start cutting their own pictures. I don't think that's a concern that has any reality. It's not that it's so difficult, but I think most directors don't want to bother and they're used to working with an editor and often have one they enjoy working with. I always did it myself because I started that way, and also figure that no one will stay up as late as I will covering my blunders. The cutting process is the last chance to save the movie, so I've always done it myself. When I first started doing this I was working on industrial films for an advertising agency. I'd make these movies for Clairol, IBM, Shell Oil that ran anywhere from a few minutes to an hour to get their salesmen excited about whatever it was they were trying to get excited about. I was hired to direct these things and I hired myself as cameraman and editor. It was a great learning process and a lot of fun. There was very little supervision and you could use whatever music you wanted. I figured I was a more attractive commodity to the buyer if for the same bucks you got three jobs instead of one.

JAG: Do you have any theories about working with actors?

JGA: The trick is to get good ones who are intelligent, have chemistry, can improvise, are sympathetic to the story. More often than not I would prefer to go with an unknown. It depends on the story and the circumstances, but certainly with the new face it's more of a trip for an audience to see this new face and not have all the preconceived notions. They're also much less expensive and they don't have the mannerisms, they don't have the ego, they don't have all the excess baggage a lot of stars carry around with them. The big star can be a big headache. I think one of the reasons *Joe* was so successful was that you never saw Peter Boyle before, and the audience figured he must be the character. Same thing with *Rocky*. You really hadn't seen Sylvester before, so it was easy to get absorbed by the story because it wasn't Paul Newman.

JAG: You're planning a sequel to *Joe* and a movie about the Guardian Angels.

JGA: The *Joe* sequel is written by Vincent Patrick, who wrote the novel *The Pope of Greenwich Village*. Peter Boyle will be in it. We're trying to get our script for *Guardian Angels* in a final stage and I'm very excited about that. Getting to know Curtis Sliwa and his wife Lisa was a great treat. Before I got involved I had been reading about them and liked the concept. My younger son Jonathan had joined the Angels and I learned more about it from him, so by the time Curtis approached me and said, "Would you do a movie about the Angels?" I was primed. It'll concern Curtis when he was a young boy and all the various influences that converged to make him the very unique man that he is, and how the Guardian Angels were formed, their trials and tribulations. I'm doing both movies with Cannon.

JAG: What kinds of movies did you like when you were a kid?

JGA: My favorite movie is an English picture called *Stairway to Heaven* (1945). I remember seeing that as a kid and liking that a lot. *It's a Wonderful Life* (1946) was another, and *An American in Paris* (1951). They were all "up" type movies. I would go to see a Bergman film out of a sense of duty rather than to go and have a nice time.

JAG: Didn't Martin Scorsese work on one of your first films?

JGA: Yeah, he was a "go-fer" on the first short that I did, a thing called *Smiles*, and Roy Scheider was the leading man. Marty was very intense and eager.

JAG: What qualities do you think make a good film director?

JGA: From my experience, the more you know about the mechanics of the business, the better your chances are, especially if you're going to get your chance on a low-budget. The more you know about the nuts and bolts of it, the more likely you'll be able to do the thing for the money you've got. I did a lot of industrials that I shot, cut, and directed, and they proved to be a great learning ground. If you've got something like that behind you, you've got it a lot easier. Having sympathy with the actors and allowing them to give you what they have to give makes sense. Picking a story that you can do for the time and the money you've got also makes sense. If you've got a couple of hundred thousand dollars, don't make a Civil War epic.

JAG: What kind of advice would you give to aspiring filmmakers?

JGA: Get into the insurance business. Seriously, you've got to be able to afford to survive the dry periods. It's very hard. There are a lot of people with more credits and more experience out there scrounging for jobs.

My advice would be to do what I did, because that's my only frame of reference. Work on other productions and gain knowledge from that. Editing offers an awfully good vantage point to observe. You'll learn this guy got himself into a corner because he didn't have this shot. When your turn comes you'll be sure to get that kind of shot. You get a sense of perspective, composition, lenses, direction. You learn a lot because you see what the editor is stuck with. Keep your ears open as to ways you may be able to get your own picture made, even if it's only a five- or ten-minute film, because it's much more impressive to show somebody what you've done than to tell them what you would do if you had the chance. I always figure that the last film gets you to the next one.

(1978, 1988)

Tony Bill

Tony Bill brought fifteen years of filmmaking experience as actor and producer to his first feature as director, the charming *My Bodyguard* (1980), an intelligent department from the usually mindless youth market fare. Born on August 23, 1940, in San Diego, California, Bill attended Notre Dame and ventured to Hollywood to seek summer employment as an actor. In a scenario straight out of a movie, he landed a starring role as Frank Sinatra's younger brother in Bud Yorkin's version of Neil Simon's *Come Blow Your Horn* (1963). He continued to work with interesting directors—Ralph Nelson on *Soldier in the Rain* (1963), Francis Coppola on *You're a Big Boy Now* (1966), John Sturges on *Ice Station Zebra* (1968), Sydney Pollack on *Castle Keep* (1969), Carol Reed on *Flap* (1970), and Hal Ashby on *Shampoo* (1975). He joined forces with Michael and Julia Phillips to form Bill-Phillips Productions, and after an initial picture, the unreleased *Deadhead Miles* (1972), the company produced such films as *Steelyard Blues* (1973), *Taxi Driver* (1975), *Hearts of the West* (1975), and *The Sting* (1973), which won an Academy Award as Best Picture.

With *My Bodyguard*, Bill shifted his focus to directing, with television films *Love Thy Neighbor* (1984) and *2½ Dads* (1986), the unsuccessful tearjerker *Six Weeks* (1983), and the extraordinary *Five Corners* (1988). The first produced screenplay by John Patrick Shanley, *Five Corners,* maintains a precarious balance between humor and tragedy, relying on Bill's expert direction of a cast of relatively unknown performers.

I interviewed Tony Bill in 1983, prior to the release of *Six Weeks,* and again in 1988 as *Five Corners* was opening in New York.

FILMOGRAPHY

My Bodyguard (1980, 20th Century-Fox). HV: CBS/Fox.
Six Weeks (1983, Universal). HV: MCA.

Tony Bill (courtesy of Cineplex Odeon Films).

Love Thy Neighbor (1984, 20th Century-Fox TV).
2½ Dads (1986, Walt Disney Productions).
Five Corners (1988, Cineplex Odeon). HV: Cannon.

BILL INTERVIEW

JOHN A. GALLAGHER: *Come Blow Your Horn* must have been a heady
  experience for you.
TONY BILL: It was wonderful, like being dropped in from Mars into a
  new world. I had no experience whatsoever in the movie business. I had
  never met a famous person outside of a few academics. I had never been
  on a soundstage or seen a movie made. I never had a basic concept of
  who these people were that I was working with. Even Frank Sinatra was
  somebody who I only knew of slightly. It was great to be welcomed and
  cared for by all of these people as I was. That may well be where my
  compulsion to have a pleasant experience comes from, because it was
  such a wonderful time and a terrific family. I still see Bud Yorkin, Norman Lear, and Howard Koch from that movie, and I still feel like they're
  my foster parents.
JAG: What was your dramatic training prior to that film?
TB: Nil, outside of the experience of working as an actor in college productions at Notre Dame for three of the four years I was there. My
  schooling in the movies has never really been training except as it applies
  to on-the-job training. I learned by doing, not by studying.
JAG: How did you get cast in *Come Blow Your Horn?*
TB: I came to Los Angeles to get a summer job acting in the movies. I felt
  it was one of the few skills that I had that they pay you to do. The other
  things I know how to do, people don't care about or pay you for. Naively,
  I felt being from San Diego I should go to L.A. and get a job in the
  movie business. As it turned out, that's just what I did. The first person
  I met was the producer-director Leo McCarey to whom I had an introduction from my dean at Notre Dame. Leo McCarey was very kind to
  me and sent me to the William Morris Agency, where I met an agent
  named Steve Yates, who in turn took me to Paramount to audition for
  a job. The job, however, happened to be starring in a movie. It was just
  a bigger and better job than I had hoped for, although I can't say it came
  totally out of the blue because I sort of expected to get a job starring in
  a movie. You always want to get the best job that you can, and that was
  the best job I could think of.
JAG: You made three films with Frank Sinatra—*Come Blow Your Horn,
  None But the Brave* (1965), *Marriage on the Rocks* (1965). Is it true that he's
  a "one-take" actor?
TB: He works fast. In my case on *Come Blow Your Horn*, I only remember
  him as generous enough under those circumstances to do another take if

it was to my benefit, if the director said, "I'm not really happy with Tony in that take, let's do another one." I don't ever remember him saying, "Nah, he was good enough," so I never suffered from that syndrome.

JAG: In your second film, Ralph Nelson's *Solider in the Rain,* you appeared with Steve McQueen and Jackie Gleason. What are your memories of making that film?

TB: Frankly, I recall that I felt uncomfortable because I felt that Steve McQueen was so in control of the picture. It was an early experience for me working with big stars. On my first movie with Sinatra, I was inexperienced enough that I probably didn't notice as much as I should have noticed, and I was protected enough by Bud Yorkin and Norman Lear in that whatever power plays or whatever disagreements or whatever battles that were fought between them and the star, if any, were outside of my purview. I never encountered it. But on my second movie, I learned what it's like to be on the set during those encounters. Ralph Nelson was being pushed around a lot by Steve McQueen, by virtue of McQueen's new-found stardom. He had just become a big star off of the John Sturges pictures *The Magnificent Seven* (1960) and *The Great Escape* (1963), but it was an early stardom for him. It was sort of typical of what happens. I watched it happen over the next twenty-five years. Early stardom is a horrible thing. A lot of people come to stardom too soon in their lives and they're just simply too young. Other people come to it with a lot of bad baggage which they start unloading on undeserving people. Then a few people really wait for stardom and work a long time for it, and it sits rather well with them. But on that picture, he was really in control. It was one of the first and only pictures I've been associated with where you had actors who hated each other and had to work together, Steve McQueen and Jackie Gleason. They didn't get along together quickly. It was that problem which is not uncommon, where a star will say, "Don't call me until you're ready to shoot." Well, that's fine if you only have one star, but if you have two stars, one of whom has been in the business for a long time and gets wind of that, then he says, "Well, don't call me until Mr. McQueen is on the set." It's like a Mexican stand-off. I learned a lot about the harsh realities of star behavior and egos on that film.

JAG: You had an interesting role in Coppola's *You're a Big Boy Now* as Peter Kastner's worldly friend. Were there any intimations of Coppola's later brilliance?

TB: It's hard for me to say because I had known Francis for several years before *You're a Big Boy Now.* I had met him because it was being discussed that I would star in a movie that he wrote while he was a student at UCLA that someone else was going to direct called *Pilma, Pilma.* It was about a misunderstood kid in college, his father's a musical conductor, so I think it had some autobiographical overtones. Francis and I met each other, got to know and like each other very well, as did our wives, so we hung out together a lot. As a matter of fact, I gave him the book *You're a Big Boy Now* from which the movie was written, which was one of the first experiences I had as a producer that encouraged me to do it really and truly for myself, and officially. I had originally wanted to play the lead. That was why I gave Francis the book. I thought I would enjoy that part, but I also suggested Peter Kastner to him because I had seen a little Canadian film he was in called *Nobody Waved Goodbye* (1965). So that was an early stage of my nascent efforts to do something creative in the movie business. I've always thought that Francis was a very talented guy and I was telling my friends, "Hey, I've got this friend I think you ought to meet, he's a talented writer and director," because I had seen *Dementia 13* (1963). There have been quite a few people I've met early in our lives who I've discerned that taste or talent in.

JAG: What do you remember about the veteran British director Carol Reed on *Flap?*

TB: He was very skilled in cutting in the camera. He knew exactly what he needed of each scene and was able to come on the set and say, "We're only going to shoot from this point to that point, then we're going to move the camera and shoot from this point to that point." He was very skilled in that manner, and a very kindly man. I never felt that the picture stood a chance because I never had any great faith in the script, but I looked forward to work on the picture with Carol Reed, Anthony Quinn, Victor Jory. I tried to choose my jobs as an actor to not so much advance my career as an actor, because I was never really interested in that quality of it, but to have the experience of working with people of taste, talent, and accomplishment—actors, cameramen, directors, producers, writers.

JAG: You worked for John Sturges on *Ice Station Zebra*.

TB: I learned from hanging around him how unforceful you need to be. You don't need to yell at people. You don't have to run around like you know everybody's job. John Sturges was a director who sat there in his director's chair and very calmly and quietly said, "Let's try that again."

JAG: Sydney Pollack's *Castle Keep* is an excellent, underrated war movie.

TB: It's one of my favorites of the ones I've acted in. That was one of the most poignant and powerful experiences of my life. Again, I've come away from it with a lasting affection for and with most of the people connected with it. The producer, John Calley, gave me my start as a producer, and Sydney has always been an advice giver. I still see Patrick O'Neal as often as possible.

JAG: Why was *Castle Keep* such a meaningful experience for you?

TB: When you go off to some strange and wonderful place like the middle of Yugoslavia with a bunch of people for five months, if it's a good experience, you become a family. That was a nice part of making that movie. Also, it was a movie that required a lot of improvisation. Everything went wrong all the time. It was a script that was being constantly worked on, and it constantly presented terrible challenges, especially to Sydney. So in a sense, it's my kind of movie. It's not a paint-by-numbers movie. It's very oblique, a little odd. The experience was my kind of experience and the product was my kind of movie.

JAG: How did you make the move into producing?

TB: On *Come Blow Your Horn* I decided that becoming a movie star was not my goal. As a matter of fact, Bud Yorkin and Norman Lear gave me an office and encouraged me to bring them ideas for producing movies, one of which later became a very successful movie, *The Sterile Cuckoo* (1969), that someone else did. All of these things encouraged me to do for myself what inadvertently in some cases I was doing for others. It really came about from a personal relationship and contact with John Calley, the producer of *Castle Keep*. He knew my proclivities to produce, have ideas, and put things together. I had an acquaintance who was a student at the American Film Institute who had never written a screenplay, but who instinctually I felt had it in him to do so. I went to John Calley and I said, "I'd like you to meet this guy Terry Malick, who I think could write a screenplay. We have an idea for it. It's very original, based on some records of truck driving music I've collected over the years." This was in an era when country music was from outer space as far as the movie business was concerned. Terry wrote the script and it became a movie called *Deadhead Miles,* my first production. It was the most disastrous production a producer could possibly experience, in that Paramount deemed it unreleasable. It was never distributed in any general manner.

JAG: At what point did you form your production company with Michael and Julia Phillips?

TB: Around the time of *Deadhead Miles* I had met another young writer just out of UCLA named David Ward, who had written a script that I was impressed with called *Steelyard Blues*. Although I felt it had a lot of problems as a script and limited potential as a movie to get made, I was very impressed with the talent it exhibited. I asked him if he had another idea for a movie and he said, "Yeah," and told me a little five-minute idea, which was *The Sting*. I was so enthusiastic about the idea for *The Sting* and the talent he'd shown in *Steelyard Blues,* I set about to try to option *Steelyard Blues* and commission *The Sting*. I never had any money as an actor so I needed some financial partners to split the cost. I came across Michael and Julia, who were interested in investing in a project or two, and who were interested in getting into the movie business. I don't think Michael had ever been on a set, maybe Julia hadn't either. Julia was working at First Artists in New York, so we pooled our resources, optioned *Steelyard,* commissioned *The Sting* and several other scripts. Later we optioned *Taxi Driver,* so that was born of that need.

JAG: How did *The Sting* come to be made by Universal?

TB: David finished the script and we gave the script to Redford, who we had hoped would become involved. Redford made a kind of uneasy commitment, which is to say, "Yeah, I'm pretty interested." We then took it to various studios, among them Universal. Our approach to Universal was through Richard Zanuck and David Brown, who had been very kind to us on *Steelyard Blues.* We had produced it at Warners, where they were executives for a time. We felt that as a kind of "thank you" gift to them, instead of handing it to Lew Wasserman ourselves, we'd let them hand it to him. About 90% of *The Sting* was done on the Universal back lot. The costume designer, Edith Head, was under contract to Universal, and the crew was inherited from the Universal roster.

JAG: *Taxi Driver* was a low-budget film for a major studio.

TB: *Taxi Driver* was done for just a little over $2 million. That was Michael's baby. Michael Phillips is singularly responsible for everything that a producer could be responsible for on that film. My involvement was simply as a co-purchaser of Paul Schrader's script.

JAG: During this period you also acted in Hal Ashby's *Shampoo.*

TB: From Hal Ashby I further became convinced that one does not need to be a screamer or a yeller or a bully on the set in order to do a good job as a director. It was terrific, and I had a good time. When I think about the directors I've worked with, just talking now, I realize how terrifically varied those films are. I tried to work as an actor along the way with directors from whom I had something to learn, whether it was Reed, Sturges, Coppola, Ashby, Pollack, Bud Yorkin, Ralph Nelson. On the other side of that Ralph Nelson equation is how you get along with people who are at each other's throats or acting too big for their britches.

JAG: What prompted you to direct?

TB: I had always wanted to direct a movie. For me, *My Bodyguard* was a test of several things. It was a test of whether I had learned anything over the years I had been in the movie business, like a test in school. Had I learned anything? Had my life added up sufficiently in terms of my experience that I could direct a movie? That was one test it represented for me. The second test was should I stay in the movie business because I wouldn't want to stay in the business without moving to directing, and I didn't really know if I could stay in the movie business given my limited tastes. When I say "limited," I mean they are limited to the exclusion of car chase movies, spaceship movies, sports movies, or what I call "food fight movies," that is, movies about young people that include tits and ass, dumb gross-out jokes, food fights, boogie-ing, trendy looks at today's youth. *My Bodyguard* had none of those staples of the youth market film. I really felt if I couldn't get that movie made and if having made it, the movie wasn't successful, that it would either not be well enough directed therefore I had failed, or it hadn't been embraced by the public, which means the public isn't interested in my tastes, I would have seriously considered getting out of the movie business. *My Bodyguard* represented those two tests of my tastes.

JAG: It was also a relatively low-budget film.

TB: It was probably one of the cheapest films made that year by a major studio. It was brought in for under $4 million. I rather doubt I would ever direct a movie that was burdened by an excessive, oppressively heavy budget. I really feel the weight of that money on my shoulders.

JAG: How did you find Matt Dillon for *My Bodyguard*?

TB: Matt was the first guy I met. We hired Vic Ramos to do our casting and Vic had found Matt on a previously cast picture, *Over the Edge* (1979). Vic said, "Before we start casting this picture, there's a kid I think you ought to meet." I met him and I never had a second choice.

JAG: How about Chris Makepeace?

TB: Chris was actually suggested by Jessica Harper, who had seen him in a little movie called *Meatballs* (1979). She knew that I was casting *Bodyguard* and said I should check out the kid in this movie. I did and I just liked his looks. Again, there was no second choice for him, or in fact for anybody on that film.

JAG: I understand Martin Mull's role was expanded.

TB: Yeah, a bit. I wanted to have a father and son relationship that I hadn't seen in a youth market film. Not that it was any effort for me because it's so offensive to me, but I wanted to stay away from the clichéd image of old Dad. It seems like Dad always has gray hair, doesn't understand kids or remember what it was like to have been one, let alone act like one. I liked the idea of a father who still does things a kid does, and who is still kind of a kid himself, flirting with girls, making silly jokes, looking through a telescope. I feel so oppressed by the images of movies that I saw when I was growing up, few as they were, because I never really went to movies or watched television. Still, I look around me and I see how movies have shaped our image of what we should be, and disappointed us when we weren't in that image, so I like to go against the cliché of parenthood, or whatever it is in films, whenever possible.

JAG: Did 20th Century-Fox consider doing a sequel?

TB: Fox and the Melvin Simon Company had the right to do a sequel if they wanted, and to offer it to me first. They developed a pilot for a television series which they were obliged to offer me, but I turned it down.

JAG: On your second feature, *Six Weeks*, you stepped into the project very late.

TB: I had eight weeks to prepare a script that I'd never read. Polygram had started pre-production on another movie starring Dudley Moore, which they decided to cancel at the eleventh hour and substitute *Six Weeks*. They called me on a Friday and said, "We've got this script, we've got Dudley Moore obligated, we've got a start date and a stop date. We have to start in eight weeks and we've got to finish eight weeks later. Can you do it?" I couldn't say, "Yeah, if . . . " It had to be a simple yes or no. I said, "OK, let's go for it." The big challenge for me was almost a technical one. Can you make this movie? It was written for winter time in New York. The picture was shot in L.A. with only a week in the middle of the Christmas season in New York to get everything we needed there, so it was a real three-ring circus just to get around town and get the job done. As soon as I knew I was going to do the movie, I called everybody that had worked on *My Bodyguard* and said, "Can you ride again?" Fortunately, almost everybody could.

JAG: How was your relationship with Dudley Moore?

TB: I think of directing as being divided between being an audience and being a helper. With Dudley, I didn't need to be much of a helper. I was an audience. Orson Welles once said, "A director is someone who presides over the accidents." That was pretty much what I enjoyed doing with Dudley, working with him and presiding over the accidents, the accidents being his repeated bursts of inspiration and talent.

JAG: You have an affinity for working with young actors, like the cast of *My Bodyguard* and Katherine Healy in *Six Weeks*.

TB: For me, there's a great pleasure of discovery in opening up someone on film in any role who has never been there before. I think that's probably traceable to my own beginnings in the movie business where I started out starring in a movie. I suspect that someone digging deep enough could find out that I'm just repeating the same experience again and again, whether it's with new writers, directors, producers, or actors, and maintaining that exhilarating feeling of being the new kid in town. I still feel like that.

JAG: What initially appealed to you about John Patrick Shanley's screenplay for *Five Corners?*

TB: Virtually all the films I've developed, produced, or directed have been original screenplays. I've never made a movie from a play or a book, so I'm always on the lookout for the same thing in all screenplays—originality, uniqueness, or boldness. I like scripts that are not like other movies that I've seen or scripts that I've read. I like films that are not derivative and that are personally informed, either by the writer's tastes or experiences. What appealed to me about *Five Corners* was what appealed to me about every script from *The Sting* to *My Bodyguard*. It's fresh, it's special, it's new, it's not like other movies. That's what I look for.

JAG: *Five Corners* is a daring film, the kind of picture that I don't think a major studio would have financed.

TB: I don't think they would have, either. I think it would have been turned down by everybody. *My Bodyguard* was turned down by everybody too, so I'm sort of used to it.

JAG: The movie happened rather quickly from the time you read the script to production.

TB: I read the script, called up, wrote a check and optioned it virtually overnight. After that it took about a year to get the movie started.

JAG: *Five Corners* is HandMade Films' first American film.

TB: It's their first American release and the first one they've financed. I would say that HandMade was pretty much long distance geographically in London, as well as practically speaking for most of the film until we finished shooting, then they had their comments about the cut, but it was pretty much a hands-off operation once we got started.

JAG: Once again, you've made a low-budget movie that looks big-budget.

TB: It's about as cheap as you can make a film in the mainstream today. It's a real movie populated with Screen Actors Guild members, a NABET crew, catered by a real catering company, so it was made in that sense like a $20 million movie. It only cost $5 million, largely because my producer, Forrest Murray, and myself, said we'd make it for $5 million. We like to feel we'll do what we say we're going to do.

JAG: It's also a period film.

TB: It's tough. It's a New York movie, shot all on location, set in 1964, with a lot of nights, and a very large speaking cast, so all of those things were major challenges to bring it in on budget.

JAG: With those kinds of pressures, how do you keep it from getting crazy?

TB: The only way to keep a movie from getting crazy is to not be a crazy person. I like to think of myself at the very least as a very professional and responsible filmmaker. If I say I'm going to make a movie for a certain price, which is basically what I say when I go into business with anybody, I make that movie at that price, and make the same movie that we all started to make, the same script we all started with, at the money we said we'd make it for.

JAG: How do you go about creating an atmosphere for the actors?

TB: You don't have to create that much of an atmosphere. You just have to prevent it from becoming the wrong atmosphere. You have to avoid letting it devolve into something it shouldn't be. It's easy to have a happy set, it's easy to have actors that are welcomed to be creative and a crew that is contributing to the spirit of the film and not just doing their job, because that's what everybody wants and that's what everybody gravitates toward. It's when you start impeding that atmosphere and start imposing an ego on it that things go wrong. In effect, it's really letting it happen as opposed to making it happen.

JAG: Do you rehearse much prior to shooting, or do you wait until you're on the location?

TB: I don't like to rehearse mainly because I really can't get much out of
 The idea of rehearsing a scene that say two or three people are going
play on an empty set is just too difficult for me. Until an actor sees

it for real and can think, "Gee, look at all these things I have to play with," the things that the art director, prop master, or director thought to put on the set, it's pretty hard to rehearse because the rehearsal you might have undergone when you're working in an empty room goes out the window when you get on the set and find out there's table and chairs where you didn't think there was going to be one, or nothing where you thought something was going to be. I like to rehearse on the set with the actors under battle conditions of the reality of what's happening.

JAG: Do you find the actors respond better to that?

TB: For the most part actors do. Some actors feel that they need and want rehearsal time. I haven't come up against a situation where an actor so needed pre-shooting rehearsal that I felt they or the movie suffered because they didn't have it. Maybe some day I'll do a movie in which somebody says, "I just can't go to work without a week's rehearsal," so we'll find a way to do that. Basically, directing for me is solving the problems that you're presented with. It may be an actor problem, a location problem, or it might be that you get up in the morning and you have a weather problem. None of these things is insurmountable and they're all gonna happen. I don't have a method. My method is to do what's best for the actors.

JAG: What kind of preparation did Jodie Foster have for her Bronx accent?

TB: She worried about her accent. We found somebody who specializes in accents and we brought him out one day to work with her. In an hour or so, he said, "She's got it," and she did. Again, there's a problem you face and you deal with it however you can. In an hour, she got it fine. If it required her having somebody on the set throughout the picture, that would have been fine, too, but that was the solution to the problem.

JAG: John Turturro is outstanding as the psychotic Heinz, yet you also feel sympathy for his character.

TB: Turturro's character is a pretty amazingly violent and simmering personality. If you look at this picture cynically, you might see this guy has no redeeming values and he's a psychopath. But within the script there is the room, and John brought to it a humanity that most bad guys in the movies don't exhibit. That's based among other things on the notion that the prisons of this country are filled with terrible guys who've done terrible things, but outside that prison there's somebody that they love. There's a wife or kid somewhere, somebody that loves them, who sees something in them that the judge and jury will never see, a compassion or a feeling. They're not just murderers, they're not just bad guys. I'm happy to say that Turturro's character reflects that philosophy of mine that every bum on the street or every bad guy in prison was somebody's little boy.

JAG: Gregory Rozakis gives a very quirky and off-beat performance as the detective who talks about Indians in the Bronx.

TB: He was the star of Kazan's *America, America* (1963). The first few days of shooting we did a lot of the detective scenes. In a sense I worried more about that than anything else in the movie because it set the tone for the other performances. It walked a tight rope. I wondered, "Is it too much, is it too far out?" Gregory didn't know it, but he was sort of the trial horse for the tone of the picture. He was great.

JAG: The drama in *Five Corners* is balanced with the humor of the Elizabeth Berridge and Carl Capatorto characters, roles that could easily have slipped into caricature.

TB: That was another challenge, to balance the humor with the pathos and shocking aspects of the film. Again, it's reflective of my view of life, which is that the most horrible moments have their humorous asides, and the funniest moments have touching asides in real life. Nothing is always straight.

JAG: How did you approach the elevator sequence?

TB: That was a scene in the script that I didn't feel could be shot. It had to be, but I didn't know how. It was scripted in a different way than how it plays in the movie, but ultimately the idea of the scene, which is that somebody had to get out of the elevator and become endangered, had to be played out. We had to make it up in its detail as we went along, because you just can't simply control the situation the way you want to as a filmmaker. It couldn't be storyboarded. Basically it was invented out of the scene that was originally written. It was very tough to shoot. We had to have three elevators rising and falling in unison, controlled by somebody on the inside who couldn't see what was happening on the outside, populated by only a few people on the top of the elevator who were in danger. It was a real location, real actors on top of real elevators.

JAG: You doubled the Bronx in Astoria, Queens. How was the neighborhood's cooperation?

TB: They really got into the movie. They invited us over for dinner. We put some of their kids in the movie. We integrated ourselves very well into the neighborhood and vice versa. They were very tolerant of us, shooting all night on a roof for a week, disrupting the neighborhood as a film company does. They were mighty kind. We only had one case of a guy in the neighborhood, who was a pretty crazy guy to begin with. One night he got miffed that we were shooting right outside his window, which I would have been too, but he responded pretty crazily.

JAG: The 1964 setting is interesting because it adds another layer of meaning to the film, showing how the civil rights movement sociologically affects this white working class neighborhood.

TB: Without any one of us knowing it, we touched upon an aspect of what has come to be current events with the whole Howard Beach incident. In this movie, a white guy says to a black guy, "You couldn't walk through my neighborhood without a bunch of guys like me coming out and beating you up." Suddenly, twenty years later it came true. It's been interesting to watch the parallels in contemporary American racist attitudes raising their ugly heads when we were just making a movie about an historical moment.

JAG: For the main title, you chose the poignant Beatles tune "In My Life." Even though George Harrison was one of the film's executive producers, you had to go elsewhere for rights.

TB: As far as I know, The Beatles don't own any of their music and you have to go through Michael Jackson to get it. The other irony is that George, who was a total supporter of this movie throughout, actually didn't want us to use the Beatles tune. He felt that it would appear to be self-serving and self-advertising. He was real leery of using it. I said, "It really fits the film," and like the generous and professional executive producer that he is, he said, "If you really believe that's the right thing for the movie, fine." But ironically, many people may yet feel that it's George Harrison's choice to use his tune when in fact it's over his objections that we used it.

JAG: James Newton Howard composed a very effective score for the film.

TB: James was a suggestion, again, not a demand, from George Harrison and his pal Ray Cooper, who works at HandMade in London, and who is a great musician himself, a percussionist. When it came time to do the score, I said I had some people in mind, and asked, "Do you have anybody in mind?" Not a bad question to ask Ray Cooper and George Harrison. They said, "Yeah, there's this guy that's just starting out who's only done one score and maybe you ought to check him out." I did, liked him, and thought, "Why not?" I was very happy with what he did for the movie. I wanted a real movie score, not a nostalgia score. There are only two or three pieces of period music in the movie, like "The Times They Are A-Changin'," which comment on the movie a little bit. I wanted something that made it a real "movie-movie."

JAG: How did you work with your editor Andy Blumenthal?

TB: He's got good taste, which is really what an editor represents. Andy has been working on one film or the other of mine since the first film I directed, a half-hour 16mm film of *The Ransom of Red Chief,* based on the O. Henry story and starring Harry Dean Stanton and Joe Spinell. Andy was the assistant editor on that. I felt that it was time for Andy to be the chief on *Five Corners,* so he was the editor, and happily so.

JAG: You've described *Five Corners* as a "writer's film." That's very unusual.

TB: I feel that John Patrick Shanley deserved that credit. It's Shanley's first screenplay. It pre-dates *Moonstruck* (1987). It's the first movie that he ever had anything to do with and I felt he was owed the tip of the hat that most writers don't get. Again, as I've said, I've dealt exclusively with original screenplays in my filmmaking career, and writers often get buried under the credits of their director or the stars.

JAG: You've directed several television movies.

TB: I think I've done a good job on the three or four things I've done for television and the people who've asked me to do them have been pleased, but my method of working is hard for them to take, which is to say it's not formulaic. It's improvisational to a certain degree and not standard television stuff. For example, on *2½ Dads* I got my friend Georges Delerue to do the score, but the people at Disney who were financing the film, which was intended as a pilot, were afraid to use Georges Delerue, one of the great living composers. I'm comfortable doing television the way it needs to be done, which is fast and on schedule and on budget, but I'm a little too loose for what they're used to.

JAG: You directed a *Fairie Tale Theatre* episode for cable.

TB: "The Princess and the Pea" with Liza Minnelli, Tom Conti, and Tim Kazurinsky. Among the reasons I wanted to do that was to accommodate what was for me a new technique, three-camera video. It's a whole other ballpark of directing, but I got used to it pretty quickly. I had wonderful help from the crew. I did something stylistically unusual. I dressed all the sets and props in black and white, and only the actors were natural. It gave it an interesting look as a fairy tale come to life.

JAG: *My Bodyguard, Six Weeks,* and *Five Corners* reflect your interest in the human condition.

TB: I'm not particularly skilled or interested in what I would call hardware movies. That's outside of my range of interest and experience. By default, if nothing else, I'm interested in movies about people, or at least to a great degree about people's lives and their interrelationships. That interests me a lot.

JAG: What qualities would you say are essential to the job of directing movies?

TB: I think everybody has different qualities that they bring to the job, but as a producer or as an actor I certainly have enjoyed most and benefited most from working with directors who embody the qualities of patience, human kindness, calmness, joy, and having fun doing your job. There's another school of thought that subscribes to the notion that great art comes out of this crucible of pain, suffering, and human conflict on the set. I just don't subscribe to that in my work, and so for me, the most important quality is the ability to lighten up, have a good time with your work and enjoy working with the people on the film. For me the process is the product. I don't really have a big stake in the success of a film in a personal way as much as I do have a stake in the process of making it. A movie takes a year of your life if you're working fast, from the moment you begin to know you're going to make the movie through pre-production, production, post-production, and the machinations of releasing it. You can't guarantee that a film will be well received critically, and you can't guarantee it will make money or that it will be well received by the public. But as a director, the headiness I feel, the power of the director, is that you can guarantee that the year will be a well-spent year of your life and that's almost my entire interest in making a film. Part of that well-spent year, by definition, is that you do the best work you can do, but not at the expense of enjoying spending the time doing it.

(1983, 1988)

Michael Cimino

Michael Cimino is a 1963 graduate of Yale University who entered film-making as a director of documentaries and industrials before turning to screenwriting as a way to break into feature directing. His first film, *Thunderbolt and Lightfoot* (1974), came about through the insistence of Clint Eastwood, who wanted Cimino to direct him on the strength of his rewrite of *Magnum Force* (1973), the second *Dirty Harry* film. *Thunderbolt and Lightfoot* was not critically well received, but has since attracted a loyal following. Jeff Bridges was Oscar-nominated for Best Supporting Actor, an early spotlight on Cimino's obsessive interest in character and performance.

The next few years were spent writing and doing pre-production work on a half-dozen original and adapted screenplays, but again and again Cimino was frustrated in his attempts to put any of them before the cameras. Then, rather quickly, *The Deer Hunter* (1978) came together for him. An extremely ambitious film, it was one of the first attempts by an American filmmaker to depict and confront the horror of Vietnam. *The Deer Hunter* was one of the most important films of the Seventies, and won Academy Awards for Best Picture and Best Director. Cimino now had the clout to begin a long-cherished film, *The Johnson County Wars,* which mushroomed into the epic *Heaven's Gate* (1980). Reams have been written on that ill-fated venture, most notably Steven Bach's *Final Cut,* yet despite its excesses, *Heaven's Gate* is full of stunning images and has begun to live down its notorious reputation through cable TV and homevideo screenings. For his next two pictures—*Year of the Dragon* (1985) and *The Sicilian* (1987)—Cimino turned to the crime genre.

This interview with Michael Cimino by Mark Patrick Carducci took place on the set of *The Deer Hunter* in Mingo, Pennsylvania, in July 1977. Carducci spent three days with the production unit, waiting for his opportunity to speak at length with Cimino: "On the afternoon of the second

Michael Cimino on the set of *The Deer Hunter* (photo by Mark Patrick Carducci).

day he came over to me and suggested we do the interview during the ride back to the Holiday Inn we were quartered in that evening. When Cimino turned around to look for cinematographer Vilmos Zsigmond to frame and light the next set-up, he could not find him. An outburst of creative temperament had transpired between Vilmos and the script girl while Cimino and I spoke, and Vilmos had walked off the set in anger. For a moment, Cimino seemed lost. His gaze weakened and for an instant he appeared near exhaustion. I sensed it might be best to take a walk outside, and did so. But before going out I glanced back. Cimino had climbed behind the massive Panavision camera and was himself framing an upward-angle closeup. At that point he was alone on the set, the only man in the room."

FILMOGRAPHY

Thunderbolt and Lightfoot (1974, United Artists). HV: CBS/Fox.
The Deer Hunter (1978, Universal). HV: MCA.
Heaven's Gate (1980, United Artists). HV: MGM/UA.
Year of the Dragon (1985, MGM/United Artists). HV: MGM/UA.
The Sicilian (1987, 20th Century-Fox). HV: Vestron.

CIMINO INTERVIEW

MARK PATRICK CARDUCCI: I understand that you were not initially decided on a career in film.

MICHAEL CIMINO: No. I was really more involved with the plastic arts—architecture, art history. That's what I had done most of my undergraduate and graduate work in. It wasn't until after I got out of school that I decided I wanted to become more involved with film. It was kind of an abrupt thing.

MPC: What made you begin writing?

MC: Joann Carelli, the associate producer on *The Deer Hunter,* actually talked me into it. I'd never really written anything before. I still don't regard myself as a writer. I've probably written about thirteen or fourteen screenplays by now but I still don't view myself that way. Yet, that's how I make my living.

MPC: Is *The Deer Hunter* a personal work?

MC: As it happens, the screenplay is very personal. When I was growing up I had a number of very close friends who were Russian Jews. I was influenced a great deal by them. Certain things stayed with me. For instance, I was best man at one of their weddings, a Russian Orthodox wedding. There is a wedding very similar to that one in the film. When I was writing documentaries and industrials I came to Pennsylvania for U.S. Steel. That was my first look at a steel mill and I spent quite a lot of time there. That also made an impression on me. Lastly, I served in the army as a medic attached to a Green Beret unit that was taking advanced medical training in Texas, and I got to know and like those men very much. All those things are a part of *The Deer Hunter* script.

MPC: Is this the first opportunity you've had to draw upon your own life as source material?

MC: No, I would say that *Thunderbolt and Lightfoot* is similar to *The Deer Hunter* in that respect. The things that interest me are present to a degree in both films. *Thunderbolt,* however, masquerades more easily as a less personal work.

MPC: How long did *The Deer Hunter* screenplay take to complete?

MC: It went fairly quickly once I began it. A peculiar set of circumstances attended the start of the project. I had spent a year and a half at Paramount working on something called *Perfect Strangers*, an original, a love story with a political background. By way of easy description it bears some resemblance to *Casablanca* (1942), involving the romantic relationship of three people. Someone called it a romantic *Z* (1969). I was very close to doing it. In fact, we'd already shot two weeks of pre-production stuff, but because of various political machinations at the studio, the project fell through. This was just before David Picker left. He was the producer. There were internal difficulties, that's all. Nevertheless, I'd spent a year and a half of my life on something. It had been a difficult time. My father passed away while I was writing the screenplay. I kept working, spending the next two and a half years writing something I liked very much with Jimmy Toback. It was called *The Life and Dreams of Frank Costello*, based on the man some people have called the founder of the modern Mafia. We got a good screenplay together but again, the studio, 20th Century-Fox in this case, was going through management changes and the script was put aside. Almost simultaneously, I finished an original called *Pearl* for Fox. It's almost a musical, based on the life of Janis Joplin. I was working with Bo Goldman on that one and we were doing a series of rewrites. I also had an agreement with United Artists to adapt *The Fountainhead*. All these projects were in the air at once. I postponed *Fountainhead* until we had a first draft on *Pearl,* then after meetings with Jimmy began *Frank Costello*.

MPC: You seem to write quickly.

MC: Sometimes. Other times it's quite slow and painful. *The Fountainhead* was that kind of script. The book itself was almost 800 pages and just reading it takes a considerable amount of time. Also, making it a contemporary story meant that there was a lot of new work that had to be done. It was very time-consuming. Plus when you work from a book with that kind of reputation you put more pressure on yourself. *Silent Running* (1972) was very quick. *Thunderbolt and Lightfoot*, the first rough draft, I remember quite clearly doing in six weeks. I polished it over the next two months. *Costello* took a long time because *Costello* himself had a long, interesting life. The selection of things to film was quite hard.

The Deer Hunter, and here I'm talking very rough first draft, took seven or eight weeks.

MPC: Do you normally work out the script in detail in your head before committing it to paper?

MC: Sometimes. But I don't claim to be a trained writer. I learned about writing principally from studying acting. I probably learned more about it there than any place. I just can't draw a general conclusion from your question.

MPC: Wouldn't you say it's beneficial to know where you're going before you get too far into it?

MC: Ummm . . . I suppose. I suppose that's a reasonable thing. Sometimes I have a vision of the whole thing. That's happened. But in many cases it hasn't. Often, one just plunges in and flails around in the dark, trusting one's instincts and intuition. Both are valid ways to work.

MPC: What was it like collaborating with John Milius on *Magnum Force*?

MC: We really didn't work together. It was John's initial script, not mine. He wrote what amounted to a first draft, which he couldn't finish because he'd gone off to direct *Dillinger* (1973). I was asked by Clint Eastwood and Warner Brothers to pull the script together. At first I said no. I didn't feel used to the genre. But they were very persistent and finally I took it on with the understanding that I don't turn in any pages, I just turn in the script when I'm finished. That's the deal I've made on everything I've written so far.

MPC: Do you establish your own personal quota?

MC: There have been days where I've felt really great completing five pages. But I'm usually slower than that.

MPC: Why did you choose Vilmos Zsigmond as your Director of Photography on *The Deer Hunter*?

MC: I think he's an extraordinary cinematographer. His reputation is there. We're trying to do a very difficult thing on this picture—shooting summer for winter. We're also working in real places. In the eastern United States alone we're shooting in seven cities just to create the look of one small town. There have been times when we weren't able to move the camera fifteen degrees in either direction. We've got interiors and exteriors two and three hundred miles apart. We've had to strip trees, brown grass, defoliate huge areas. To take the long way around in answering your question about Vilmos, I felt that given all of these things, we needed somebody special. Once again, Joann Carelli was the one who suggested Vilmos to me.

MPC: Have you and he worked out a visual attitude for the film?

MC: Yes. I would call it highly stylized. Some might call it naturalistic, which it is not. It's only natural in the sense that we're shooting location.

MPC: Zsigmond is noted for a very low-key, muted kind of lighting style.

MC: We've gone for more than that. There's a whole approach to the way of shooting, especially of exteriors. I happen to like large exteriors, exteriors that have scope. I like a sense of figures in a landscape, of seeing the size of the landscape in relation to the people. If it's a large landscape, as big as a steel mill that's twelve miles long, then I want to see the scale. It becomes an element of the film with its own dramatic presence. Not to show it would be to waste it. Vilmos and I talked at great length about going for that.

MPC: How heavily are you relying on Zsigmond for composition?

MC: Because of my background I've always been very concerned with that. For instance, when it comes to the design of the sets, I get extremely specific.

MPC: The Welsh's Bar set is something amazing. What a sense of reality.

MC: I don't know how carefully you've looked at it, but if you study it closely you'll see that there are practically no parallel lines in it. It's designed that way to enhance the notion of age, of the warping of the wood in a building as it gets older and older. This is true of the beams in the ceiling, the moldings, door frames, everything.

MPC: Have you scripted your angles and framing, or are you giving Zsigmond some latitude in these areas?

MC: On the first screenplay I ever wrote I tried to lay out the way it would be shot. In my view it's a mistake. When you sit down to write a screenplay, in most cases you haven't even seen the locations yet. All you're doing is cutting yourself off from the possibilities of things you might find. Anything that limits you before you start is a mistake. It's quite mysterious, anyway. What I mean is, when you write a film, you envision a place that is a composite of things you know. Then you go out and somehow find that place. It exists, it's waiting for you, and if you're persistent enough, you will find it. I've only found a couple of cameramen whose way of seeing things coincided with my own. Once you've found someone like that you can stand back and become more involved with other things, especially performance. You can work with the actors. The first day of shooting required a large set-up with hundreds of extras and all the principals. It was then that I knew I was right about Vilmos. We were on the same wave length.

MPC: I've been told you're a few days behind schedule. What effect is this having on you and the cast and crew?

MC: Naturally, you always care about being ahead or behind. It's nicer to be ahead. You work as hard as you can every day and try and maintain a certain level of quality. It becomes a daily battle.

MPC: Francis Coppola has said that the actual shooting of a film is the most trying time for him. Do you find this to be true?

MC: I would say so. When you're writing there's much more control. You only deal with your own energy level. While shooting you must deal with the energy level of a hundred people and not everybody is up at the same time. It's up to the director to keep willing it through. George

Cukor said, "Never tire, never wilt." You've got to keep fighting for quality. That's Bobby DeNiro's attitude as well. He feels there's always room to improve, there's always a way to do it better. He attempts to fill every moment and that's what should always be striven for, particularly in a picture like this, which is about people, their relationships and the nature of courage and friendship. There's a great deal going on between the characters. I've got eight or nine first-rate actors, all of whom must receive attention. It's a great relief to have Vilmos, to have an area I'm completely comfortable with. Between me, Vilmos, and Bobby, all of us pushing for perfection, things can be very trying. It can wear people down. A crew likes to move at a certain pace—quickly. You try to move as quickly as possible but there are times when you simply cannot do that. And it's in those very moments that it's easiest to let go. You can succumb to the pressure of having all those people standing around. You can panic and allow them to be the overriding factor. Of course, you must always maintain a certain responsibility to budget and schedule as well. It's very hard.

MPC: Parts of *The Deer Hunter* take place in Vietnam. You apparently feel Americans are ready to confront that war in their entertainment.

MC: I think it's time. I'm sure, for instance, that Francis' *Apocalypse Now* (1978) will be a hugely successful film.

MPC: I read recently that one of the reasons *Apocalypse Now* has been so long in the making is that in working with generals and other army personnel, Coppola's ideas about the mentality of those men were challenged. What began basically as an anti-war tract suddenly lost its focus as certain myths he held to be true were exploded.

MC: That's interesting because it's one of the points of *The Deer Hunter.* People ascribe certain political leanings to combat troops like the Green Berets, which in fact most of them don't have. Many guys join those kinds of outfits for the adventure or other non-political reasons. After going through the formidable training they have to endure, they naturally develop bonds with one another which then become the primary thing. War becomes a question of protecting your friends, people you care about. Their combat experience has more to do with that than anything else. If I had to go into combat tomorrow, I'd want to go in there with guys like that, not a bunch of weekend warriors from some National Guard unit.

MPC: You've chosen Peter Zinner as your editor, an editor on Coppola's *The Godfather* (1972) and *The Godfather Part II* (1974). What challenges do the two of you face?

MC: This will be an unusual picture from that standpoint. Many of the exterior scenes are done in long, uninterrupted master shots.

MPC: Why is that?

MC: Part of the reason is to preserve the relationship between the characters and their environment, to remove those interruptions that prevent you from feeling that relationship. Most editors hate it because it locks them into using the shot. There's no way they can alter it. This makes it all the more important for me, as the director, to concentrate on the performances. They can't be altered, either. When you've got five or six people in a single shot like that, each performance needs to be right. It's not easy to shoot this way, but when it works it's quite exciting.

MPC: Will the Vietnam sequences, which you are filming in Thailand, be shot or lit differently from the footage taken in the States?

MC: It will be very different. There will be more abrupt cutting. And just being in Thailand will impose differences in our visual style, since the light and colors of the place are not the same.

MPC: Who are some of the directors whose films you respond to most?

MC: I admire Francis' films very much. I must say I have a great feeling for Sam Peckinpah's work. Even in films of his that people don't much admire, I find there's always a certain humanity, a concern for people.

MPC: Then you must have liked *Junior Bonner* (1972).

MC: I thought it was wonderful. I really love that picture. Sam understands about life and death. He's one of the few American filmmakers who does. There's a scene in *Pat Garrett and Billy the Kid* (1973) where Slim Pickens gets shot. He's sitting on a rock at the edge of a lake and his wife is sitting on another rock across from him. He's dying. There are no words, but it's a magnificent scene. The unspoken understanding between the two of them is beyond description. Or take the scene in *Junior Bonner* on the back stairs behind the bar between Robert Preston and Ida Lupino. I was terribly moved by it. In even the least of Sam's work there are moments like that.

MPC: What European directors would you cite?

MC: Godard, certainly. There was always some new direction he was going in. Visconti, for the same reason. Fellini, particularly the early films. Back to American directors, John Ford was a strong influence. His films have real emotion. And I love Vincente Minnelli's work—his attention to detail, especially in the musicals. There are so many I can't single them all out. Then there are some brilliant American still photographers who I feel a great affinity for, men like Walker Evans and Robert Frank. They've captured this country in much more vivid ways than our filmmakers have. Eugene Smith, for instance, documented the city of Pittsburgh in still photographs. When I think about it I realize these men have been a stronger influence on me than the films I have seen. I haven't seen any American films that communicate the very special nature of certain portions of this country. It's what moves me to find locations like the ones we're shooting in now, to get those images in a film.

MPC: Are you much concerned with how your finished films are received?

MC: A part of me worries about that, I suppose. The part of me that is connected to deal-making, those elements that go into getting the money up for this kind of thing. I would like *The Deer Hunter* to be a successful, mass appeal film. That would be nice. But I do not think about that possibility on a daily basis. The actual work is too hard. Stravinsky said, "When you work you look down, you don't look up." So you put down one brick at a time and eventually you'll find yourself on top of a building. Also, you try and learn what is hardest in life to learn—a way to extract a measure of enjoyment from the doing of the thing. But if all one does is look up, one can become discouraged. Surely if one worries every day about what will be happening six months from now, the results you'll be getting every day will suffer. As regards an audience's reaction, my major concern is closely related to the film itself. Are things clear? Are the things the actors are doing understandable? Are their intentions clear? You know, you can reach a point while writing a script where you become lost and you wonder whether the script makes any sense at all. It's then that you must keep going. If the idea is sound to start with, you will get past that point. To use a famous phrase Clint Eastwood uses, "You must will it through." That's the only way.

MPC: Have you made any changes or new discoveries in the screenplay of *The Deer Hunter* since filming began?

MC: One of the things we were all surprised at was the love which has developed between Bobby's character and Meryl Streep's character. It's become marvelous, much more vivid than I'd imagined it. What did this was seeing how well the two of them play together. They're so good, so exciting.

MPC: Does DeNiro "feed" other actors or does he derive energy from them?

MC: It's a mutual process. Bobby uses everything, where it's applicable; and, by virtue of the way he works, he sets a certain tone which sparks things.

MPC: It is true you wrote the lead role with him in mind?

MC: No, it is not. I don't do that. The chances of getting a particular actor are always quite remote. I make a conscious effort not to form a pre-conception of the character in this respect. I like to stay wide open.

MPC: There are writers who believe that casting in your mind's eye while you write helps you write more easily.

MC: I've never found it to be of any help. The only thing I can say that has helped me in writing is the experience of studying acting. That was and is enormously helpful. I would like to know a hundred times more about acting than I do. You never really feel you know as much as you should and yet there comes a time when you have to just jump in and do a thing. That's true in every field today. Unfortunately, we no longer have a master and apprentice system, as once existed. The opportunity to perfect one's craft from the ground up is largely non–existent.

MPC: I understand what you mean. Look at the scarcity of good animators today or the scarcity of good matte painters.

MC: And that's true in acting as well, which makes someone like Bobby so rare. He is a craftsman, a professional. He believes that acting is something to work at, that a special performance is not entirely an accident. Bobby lives that. He's his own best example.

MPC: There's a story I've heard from guys in various crews that Gordon Willis is largely responsible for the success of the first *Godfather* film. I can't buy that.

MC: I suppose that's a case of the conductor thinking he composed the score after conducting it a few times. The whole business of making a movie is a rather strange affair. To bring a project to the point where it can be shot can involve literally years of effort. You write something, struggle and sweat over it, cast it, and then people like the cameraman, crew members, and the editor come in and work on it. They are very lucky. They work only on the projects that go, only seeing the tip of the iceberg. The writer-director lives with a particular project for a couple of years before and a couple of years after them. To him it represents a major chunk of his working life. Gone are the days when a guy like Victor Fleming could do *The Wizard of Oz* and *Gone With the Wind* in the same year (1939). Each of those things would take five years apiece today. It's a bittersweet thing. In the end, I have no idea why anyone would want to take *The Godfather* away from Francis.

MPC: To read some of the reviews of your own *Thunderbolt and Lightfoot*, many critics seemed to want to take that picture away from you.

MC: Very few of them realized that *Thunderbolt and Lightfoot* was a first feature. It was passed over, written off as just another Clint Eastwood movie. This put my ego out of joint a little bit, but I got over it. In Europe, for some reason, the critics were able to see past that easy characterization. In England, particularly, I felt very good about the way the film was received. They show it at the National Film Theatre all the time. It was also very gratifying when Jeff (Bridges) got his second Academy Award nomination for his role. It meant that, within the industry at least, people had seen the picture and appreciated it.

MPC: *Silent Running,* for all its problems, was certainly a signpost in the light of the current resurgence of interest in science fiction cinema. When did effects genius Doug Trumbull enter the project?

MC: Doug was the first person involved. He developed the original premise, which was not finally what the film was about. Doug's was a straightforward, simple story about a guy who runs a space shuttle, who gets fired from his job, and out of revenge takes off with the ship. The screenplay had gone through drafts at the hands of a whole line of writers and they were already committed to building the sets when the producers called me in. They flew me to California and I was holed up at the Bel Air Hotel for two weeks working out a new story.

MPC: Many people think of science fiction as frivolous at best, idiotic at worst.

MC: I didn't think of *Silent Running* as science fiction. My storyline had a strong enough premise that it could have been set anywhere. That's one of the problems with most filmed science fiction—they depend too much on the liberties you can take with the genre. Science fiction really requires incredible discipline because you set the ground rules yourself. My concern was with writing material that didn't use the fact that it was science fiction like a crutch. Unfortunately, after I left they decided to rely more on the technology, the special effects, and the gadgets.

MPC: For me the film's major flaw lies in the extremity of Bruce Dern's action in killing his fellow officers in order to preserve the last of Earth's forests.

MC: That was the problem. My contribution to *Silent Running* was in providing the notion of the forests, saving the forests. But you have to know that the other guys were career men. Things like promotions were real to them. The survival of the forests didn't mean anything. In the finished film their blasé reaction is almost gratuitous, making Dern's action seem unmotivated. It was supposed to be indicated that they had been disconnected from things like trees for so long that they no longer cared. Not that they were unthinking, unfeeling individuals, but that they'd simply lost contact. This tragedy was to have fueled Dern's action. He was to have killed them as much in a rage against them as against a world, a system that could come to such a pass.

MPC: You are now directing your own screenplays. Would you ever again consider writing material for others to direct?

MC: I don't know the answer to that. I really don't. Who knows? Maybe I'll surprise myself.

(1977)

Abel Ferrara

Abel Ferrara has carved a niche for himself as the American cinema's resident urban hipster, making dark, violent neon nightmares, latter day action *noir* informed by his gritty street sense. His first feature, *Driller Killer* (1979), made on a shoestring budget, was a brutal tale of a struggling artist, (played by Ferrara) who goes berserk when a rock band moves into his building and drives him crazy with loud, round-the-clock music. *Ms. 45* (1981) cast Zoe Tamerlis as a mute woman who is raped twice (once by a low-life again played by Ferrara), then turns into a nocturnal vigilante in an ironic twist on this normally macho genre. *Fear City* (1985) also had a sordid subject, with a psychopath terrorizing Times Square strippers. Ferrara refined his kinetic style with television work for producer Michael Mann on *Miami Vice,* and especially the highly acclaimed pilot for *Crime Story.*

Ferrara's most accomplished film to date has been *China Girl* (1987), an updated *Romeo and Juliet* story set in New York's Little Italy and Chinatown. Stunningly photographed by Bojan Bazelli, *China Girl* is the perfect synthesis of Ferrara's earlier, low-budget films and his slick TV movies, with a new element of romance added to the director's flair for fast-paced action and strong visuals. *China Girl* was the official American entry at the 1987 Taormina Film Festival in Sicily, and also played the Deauville Film Festival and the Edinburgh Arts Festival.

The following interview with the native New Yorker took place in Manhattan shortly before *China Girl*'s theatrical release.

FILMOGRAPHY

Driller Killer (1979, Rochelle Films). HV: Magnum.
Ms. 45 (1981, Rochelle Films). HV: IVE.
Fear City (1985, Chevy Chase Distribution). HV: Thorn-EMI/HBO.

Abel Ferrara (photo by Michael O'Neill).

Crime Story (1986, Michael Mann Productions/NBC).
China Girl (1987, Vestron). HV: Vestron.

FERRARA INTERVIEW

JOHN A. GALLAGHER: *China Girl* is a reworking of the *Romeo and Juliet/West Side Story* plot transposed to an Italian boy and a Chinese girl in downtown Manhattan. What was your concern in revitalizing this formula?

ABEL FERRARA: To take the basic story and work it into the reality of the community. The Chinese and Italian situation is much different than Verona, or the Sharks and the Jets. *China Girl* is Little Italy 1987, so once we set it there, it's a new story.

JAG: In the film, the conflict is between the youths of Little Italy and Chinatown. The Italian dons and the Chinese elders are at peace.

AF: The power structure is united, and when the kids discover that, it's a great political awakening. The Chinese and the Italian kids have been brought up to hate each other. They never realize the racism that they're instilled with is just another tool being used to oppress them in that society. It's the older generation that is oppressing that strata of kids. The film is about their realization of that—their political awakening.

JAG: *China Girl* cost approximately $5 million, but it looks like twice that amount.

AF: Yeah, it looks like a fortune. Still, $5 million is a lot of money. It can go a long way, depending what you do with it.

JAG: You filmed entirely on location in Little Italy and Chinatown.

AF: The neighborhood was supportive all the way. It's more or less our neighborhood. We don't live exactly on Canal Street but we shoot downtown. The community wanted the film there. Everyone was open to it. Everyone got the feeling we weren't taking a negative side to it. The relationship between the Chinese and Italians in reality is pretty good.

JAG: Did you have problems with crowds?

AF: When you shoot nights, the crowd thins out around three or four in the morning. That's one of the benefits of night shooting, as crowded as you think Little Italy and especially Chinatown would get. Mott Street's pretty quiet at four in the morning. If there's a crowd, we deal with it. It's part of filmmaking in New York. But we weren't shooting a period piece. People *can* be in the shot. The story is taking place now, so basically the community or whoever is there is part of the film. Some people you clear. Some people you hope come by, y'know, you're hoping for a crowd. Free extras.

JAG: Was it difficult shooting in the feast?

AF: No, it wasn't. It was all intercut, some of the feast, some set-ups. We even created a mini-feast.

JAG: It looks like the crew was right in the thick of the feast.

AF: That's the magic of cinema.

JAG: On *China Girl,* you had a number of crew members who've worked with you on most of your films—the screenwriter, Nicholas St. John, production manager, Mary Kane, creative consultant and dolly grip, John McIntyre.

AF: Everybody knows each other. They know what's expected of everybody. When you get on the set, it's not, "Joe, meet Mary. Mary, meet Dolores." The "how" or "what to do" is on everybody's mind. They all know what the responsibilities are at a particular moment. It's more fun working with your friends.

JAG: Bojan Bazelli's cinematography is magnificent. *China Girl* is his first American feature.

AF: He's brilliant. I found him just by pure luck. Jimmy Lemmo, who shot *Fear City* and *Ms. 45,* went off and directed a film, so I was stuck with no D.P. I looked at a lot of tapes. It got hairy for a while. We were a week away from shooting, then I saw a little piece of something that Bojan had done in Europe. He was at the Czech Film School. I saw one shot and thought, "He's got it." We brought him in right before the show, meeting him cold, but it really worked out well. Since then he's done *Tapeheads* (1988), *Pumpkinhead* (1988), and he's doing Paul Schrader's new film, *Patty Hearst* (1988).

JAG: James Russo has a strong role in *China Girl.*

AF: Tell him that! He doesn't think he's in it enough. He does have a good part. The brother's the classic part in that story. Jimmy is great, *Once Upon a Time in America* (1984), *Extremities* (1986). I've known him a long time.

JAG: You also got an excellent performance from Richard Panebianco, a young actor with no prior film experience.

AF: Richard's sixteen years old. He lives the life. He's a wild kid. He's a young kid, that's the thing. You gotta deal with a sixteen-year-old, and sometimes that's difficult. He really understood the role. His father owns a restaurant in Little Italy, so even though he's from Brooklyn he has a lot of the Lower East Side in him. He showed *us* the way. He really had a grip on his part.

JAG: What's your philosophy in staging action scenes?

AF: Action always comes off better. I mean, cinema more or less *is* action. Camera starts moving, people start moving, the energy gets up, it's more dangerous. Everybody's blood starts pumping a little bit harder and then the shots come flying quickly. Then it becomes real movies.

JAG: Do you storyboard your action?

AF: I have one storyboard artist I get along with pretty well, Matt Golden, so we bring him in and he and I do a lot of drawings that sometimes we use and sometimes we don't. The cinematographers I've worked with are not big on storyboards. You can draw all you want, because we'll come in with these great shots, only they're done in two-dimensions, man, and you're shooting three. The cameramen are not too crazy about storyboards. They like to work it out on the set. You gotta shoot to the location. You gotta shoot to the movement of the night. You gotta feel what really is happening, not what you come expecting to happen or what you want to happen.

JAG: *China Girl* played a lot of festivals before it opened in theatres. The *Variety* critic who saw it at Cannes gave it a rave.

AF: I wrote that one myself. Yeah, Cannes was alright. The French get off on our films. For me it's more fun going to a movie theatre with people who actually pay to see the film, because then they have a contract with us. They're paying us and we're playing for them. They're not getting paid like a critic to come up with a response, so they have all options open to them. They can walk out or react to it. You pay your money and you dig it for ninety minutes. It's more of a gut reaction. The people who go to movies on that level aren't so bogged down by who made it or who's in it. They get down more.

JAG: You made some changes in the film after Cannes.

AF: We added a scene in the middle because Nicky St. John wanted to change a scene where they meet in the alley and the cops come. We re-worked that. Vestron was uptight about a clip I used from Sam Fuller's *Steel Helmet* (1951), so that was a hassle. I conceded that and went out and shot a new music video clip myself. Also, it was the first time I did a Dolby stereo track, a very expensive and time consuming process. Once we got the reaction at Cannes, Vestron was ready to give us a lot of money to do more. We also were able to get the Run-DMC/Aerosmith song "Walk This Way," thanks to Jimmy Ienner.

JAG: A Dolby track requires a lot more pre-mixing.

AF: Yeah, it's a nightmare kind of thing if you really want to do it right.

JAG: You had an excellent supervising sound editor, Greg Sheldon.

AF: He's great. He did a killer job. To really do what Greg wanted to do and get it exactly right on the budget we had is really a number. Once you make the commitment to it, you gotta go all the way. The first mix we were just jammin'. But we went back and worked it some more.

JAG: How was your experience with Vestron?

AF: They were around. They were more around when they saw the film done. They always liked the script a lot. They were very supportive, but when they saw the film, that kind of freaked them out. But they were alright.

JAG: Nicholas St. John has written all your features.

AF: Nicky and I have grown up together. He's been with me since the beginning. It's basically the same team from when we were kids.

JAG: You must have an almost telepathic communication by now.

AF: It's more like telephonic communication by now. AT&T is our third partner. Talk about storyboards, Nicky gives you a shot-for-shot script.

He's also a great re-writer. He's good on a set also. He's there with the actors running it down, ready to do changes and rock and roll.

JAG: How do you work together?

AF: It changes from film to film. We're always working on ideas. Because we started so young we have a backlog of all the things we want to do. We work on something, put it away, come back to it, come up with a different idea. We work on two or three different things at a time, then whatever happens that makes a film be financed, we focus in. *Ms. 45* was a situation where he just gave me the entire script, shot-for-shot, line-by-line. I didn't even known that he was working on it, and he didn't even know if it was a good idea.

JAG: Your first feature, *Driller Killer,* is a horror cult film.

AF: It's a comedy.

JAG: It's not as explicitly gory as a lot of horror films.

AF: It's more explicit than *Ferris Bueller's Day Off* (1986). Back then, *Halloween* (1978) and *Texas Chainsaw Massacre* (1974) were big movies. It was a different era.

JAG: You also played the title role, under the name of Jimmy Laine.

AF: That's my *nom-de-act.* That was really an independent movie, shot on weekends. But we had to finance it; there was a script. In the end, whether the film costs $100,000 or $30 million, it's the same deal. You gotta take the idea and present it to the capital. Either you get it or you don't. Fortunately we got the money for *Driller Killer.* Unfortunately for the audience. Fortunately for me.

JAG: What did you finally bring it in for?

AF: Under $100,000.

JAG: *Ms. 45* got some good notices.

AF: Some bad, too.

JAG: What were the negative reactions?

AF: I don't want to repeat them. I don't want to hear them again.

JAG: How do you feel about *Ms. 45* now?

AF: Yeah, y'know, it's cool.

JAG: *Fear City* had a limited release.

AF: *Fear City* was a big-budget movie that got caught up in the politics of the financing. Sometimes in these situations it's in the best interest of everyone that the film doesn't come out, if you know what I mean. Good cast. Tommy Berenger, Billy Dee Williams, Melanie Griffiths, Rae Dawn Chong.

JAG: You've done some television work, directing for Michael Mann on a couple of *Miami Vice* episodes and the pilot for *Crime Story,* which are stylistically similar to your features. Do you have to modify your technique for television?

AF: Michael's into the same basic groove. He's going after the same things, so it's easy to lock into his style.

JAG: When you work on a hit series like *Miami Vice,* how do you deal with actors like Phillip Michael Thomas and Don Johnson, who play the same characters week after week. How do you direct Don Johnson?

AF: With a baseball bat. Just kidding. They're doing their thing. Directing a TV show is like directing the middle of a movie. You're coming into an ongoing situation. You just jump in and rock and roll for a week. Real fast schedule. It's like playing chess against the clock. Can you do this scene in two hours? Then do it in forty minutes. No matter how fast you go, you're behind.

JAG: Did you have more leeway on the two-hour *Crime Story* pilot?

AF: *Crime Story* was major. Chuck Adamson wrote it, same guy who wrote the *Miami Vice* episodes I did. I sat in on meetings. Dennis Farina and Adamson were partners as cops. Farina's Torello character is Adamson's life story. Farina plays Adamson. I helped on the script but they had worked on that project a long time before I got there. Michael really had a vision of what he wanted to do. It was travelling around in his mind. I dig TV. It really turns me on to be able to get into people's homes like that.

JAG: What films impressed you when you were growing up?

AF: I just saw a great film last night I saw as a kid and really liked, and hadn't seen since then, Anthony Mann's *The Naked Spur* (1953) with Jimmy Stewart and Janet Leigh. I grew up in the beginning of the Technicolor age, big movie theatres in the Bronx, super wide screen. Those were my earliest recollections. The films that got me and still do are the ones that really move you emotionally. Different points of your life it's different things. At one point it was horses and Indians, especially living in New York City. Other times it was intellectuals on Parisian streets.

JAG: What are you working on next?

AF: We're gonna do *The King of New York.* Nicky just finished the script. It's about a gangster who comes out of prison and takes over the drug trade in the city. He uses the money to build a hospital in East Harlem, gives hotel rooms to the homeless, feeds the poor. So you can imagine the opposition he's up against.

JAG: Is that set up anywhere?

AF: Set up in our mind.

JAG: What do you need to be a good director?

AF: Patience, a loud voice, and a good pair of boots.

JAG: A baseball bat?

AF: Sometimes.

(1987)

James Glickenhaus

In *The Soldier* (1982), *The Protector* (1985), and *Shakedown* (1988), James Glickenhaus has perfected the time-honored movie tradition of the chase, with logistically complex, stunt-laden sequences that have earned him a place as one of the world's premier action directors. The ski pursuit over the Alps in *The Soldier*; the New York harbor boat chase and helicopter stunt in *The Protector*; and the Times Square scramble, Coney Island rollercoaster stunt, and airborne finale in *Shakedown* rank with the best action scenes of a James Bond film.

Glickenhaus was born on July 24, 1950, in New York City, and attended University of California Santa Barbara, Antioch College, and Sarah Lawrence. After a failed first feature, *The Astrologer* (1979), Glickenhaus surveyed theatre owners throughout the southern United States and crafted his second feature, *The Exterminator* (1980), to exhibitor demands. The result was a huge box-office hit both in the United States and abroad, and the director was able to follow up with action pictures of ever increasing budgets and more extensive set pieces. Critics have been harsh to Glickenhaus' movies, but audiences around the world have embraced them for their non-stop action and thrills. In 1987, Glickenhaus merged with Shapiro Entertainment to produce and distribute features for the international market. To his achievements as writer, producer, and director, Glickenhaus has added the role of studio executive.

I interviewed Jim Glickenhaus in January 1988, as he was editing his first film for Shapiro Glickenhaus Entertainment, *Bluejean Cop,* retitled *Shakedown* after its domestic acquisition by Universal Pictures.

James Glickenhaus (courtesy of Mr. Glickenhaus).

FILMOGRAPHY

The Astrologer/The Suicide Cult (1979, Interstar/21st Century). HV: Continental.
The Exterminator (1980, Avco Embassy). HV: Embassy.
The Soldier (1982, Embassy). HV: Embassy.
The Protector (1985, Warner Bros.). HV: Warners.
Shakedown (1988, Shapiro Glickenhaus/Universal). HV: MCA.

GLICKENHAUS INTERVIEW

JOHN A. GALLAGHER: When did you first get interested in movies?

JAMES GLICKENHAUS: I was about eight years old, I always loved movies. When I was a kid, it was the glorious days of "B" movies. Your mother could give you a buck, you'd take a bus into White Plains. The films were fifty cents, so you'd have a quarter to go and a quarter to get back, maybe another dollar for popcorn and a coke. Every weekend they would have a different double feature. Those were the days of Roger Corman movies like *House of Usher* (1960) and *The Pit and the Pendulum* (1961), and Sergio Leone's *Colossus of Rhodes* (1960). Those were the first films I saw.

JAG: When did you first pick up a movie camera?

JG: I went to a high school in New York City called Fieldston that had a very good art department. It was the beginning of underground film-makers, 16mm in those days. We started with Bolex 16's, which were great, hand-cranked cameras. You could do a twenty-minute take, you could do an in-camera fade. That's really where I started making short films, and we learned as we went.

JAG: Your first feature was *The Astrologer,* an extremely low-budget film.

JG: It was about $65,000. It was 1977 when that was a lot of money. We shot ninety days in 35mm Panavision. It was based on a novel, and the premise was that all of the astrologers that exist in the world were extraordinarily ignorant about science. They would say, "Look at this chart. Here's where the planets are." They're wrong. They really have no idea where the planets are. This famous scientist says, "So many people believe in astrology, could it possibly be true?" He uses modern astronomy and computers, and finds out that against all odds, it does have some validity, and it does have the ability to predict when very unusual people and conditions exist. Basically, he foretells the Second Coming of Christ, and then goes looking for the event.

JAG: What was the fate of the film?

JG: It was basically unwatchable. It had seventy-two minutes of dialogue. It wasn't undistributable, interestingly enough. If you could cut a trailer, which we were able to do, and you were willing to put up the money for prints and advertising, you could travel around the country with it.

We used to make prints, ship them as excess baggage on the airline, rent a Hertz car, drive to a small town in Texas, take out $10,000 and agree to buy television ads, and lo and behold, you could distribute anything. It was before video, when people still went to "B" movies. It was the same thing that the video market has now become. On a Friday night, people would show up, and if they didn't tear up the theatre, the guys would give you the film rental and you'd be on to the next town. I took *The Astrologer* can by can around the whole southern United States, all through Texas, Louisiana, Mississippi, Georgia, Florida. In doing that, I really got a feeling as to what people in the audience did and didn't like. I talked to a lot of theater managers and I got the idea then for writing a more commercial script, which became *The Exterminator*.

JAG: That must have been an invaluable experience, since most novice directors really don't have a feel for the marketplace.

JG: It's incredible. We go to film school, study the classic films, sit in a classroom and discuss them. You live in a city like New York or Los Angeles and you get some vision of how the world is. Well, the world is nothing like that. In the film business in 1977, tremendous amounts of film were in drive-in movies, Southern movies that never saw New York City but were doing enormous business.

JAG: Like *Smokey and the Bandit* (1977).

JG: There you go. Whole companies were doing that, like Roger Corman. The interesting thing is that these people were using young filmmakers who later went on to become extraordinarily famous. We all know who worked for Corman—Bogdanovich, Coppola, Jack Nicholson, Dennis Hopper, Peter Fonda, Bruce Dern, Robert DeNiro.

JAG: *The Astrologer* had an alternate title.

JG: Yeah, after many years of me distributing it, another group of people, 21st Century, came in and tried to distribute it. They retitled it *The Suicide Cult*. They tried to capitalize on the Jonestown Massacre. I really didn't have much to do with it. They released it and did a surprising amount of business with the damn film; 21st Century has since gone bankrupt. The rights have reverted back to me, however, I have not commercially exploited the film since the rights for 21st Century have expired, nor do I plan to.

JAG: Did 21st Century ever try to hype *The Suicide Cult* as "From the director of *The Exterminator*"?

JG: They tried, but I was fairly adamant about it and didn't allow them to do that. I really did not want to rip people off. It's not that I wasn't proud when I made *The Astrologer*, but I didn't want people to be tricked into seeing it. So they had those restrictions, but they still went out and tried all of that. They went even further when they released it in England on video. They tried to make it look like it was my new movie. I was a little pissed off.

JAG: *The Exterminator* was based then on your experience of meeting the exhibitors and consciously setting forth to make a commercial movie.

JG: It was two-fold. I had gone to the Cannes Film Festival with *The Astrologer* and had the unpleasant experience of literally making no sales except for one to Canada. In talking to the foreign distributors and watching movies over there I got an idea as to what films were selling foreign. The key to the foreign market in those days was to make a film that needed very little translation, because in an international market, and I think this is still true, people don't like to read subtitles or hear dubbing, and the nuances of language that mean something in the United States, the double entendres and in-jokes, don't translate well. They want visual action.

JAG: That's why comedies don't travel well overseas.

JG: Exactly. The original *Exterminator* script literally had no dialogue. The final film had something like twenty-two lines of real dialogue, plus ad-libs and things like that.

JAG: *The Exterminator* was remarkable for being a low-budget action movie filmed on the streets of New York.

JG: When we started, we had in mind that we'd make it for around $850,000. We wound up spending $2 million. We didn't go over budget per se, we decided to increase the budget. We shot the Vietnam sequence after we had virtually finished the movie. The Vietnam sequence cost us $400,000. As we looked at the footage and we liked the film, we kept putting in more and more money trying to make it as good as we could. We then mixed it in Dolby stereo, we did some fancy sound effecting, we got the music composer Joseph Renzetti, who had just won an Academy Award for his adaptation of *The Buddy Holly Story* (1979). We recorded some original songs for the movie. We kept stepping up the budget once we saw we had a good product.

JAG: You shot the Vietnamese sequence at Indian Dunes, California, which was later the site of the tragic *Twilight Zone* (1982) accident.

JG: It was in the exact same spot, it used the exact same special effects guy. It was a little coincidental. No one got hurt, though, on *The Exterminator*.

JAG: In *The Exterminator*, many people swear that they actually saw the hand go through the meat grinder.

JG: I've seen reviews where people have written that they saw this happen. None of that happened in the film. You see a guy get lowered into this stainless steel bin and you actually see chopped meat coming out of the bottom of it, but there's nothing else. Actually, in the United States, the MPAA made an enormous trim, so I don't even know if the chopped meat is in the U.S. version. It definitely is in the original version, but that original version has not played anywhere in the world except for Japan. That's the only place they have not censored it an iota.

JAG: What kinds of changes are in the Japanese version?

JG: Only about forty-seven seconds more. When we first showed the film to the MPAA, they took the position that there's no way this film can ever be shown theatrically; forty-seven seconds later of cuts, they showed the film. We had a lot of arguments with them. In one scene in the massage parlor, they maintained that behind Bob Ginty on the wall was a gay pin-up showing a guy with a semi-erect penis. We then freeze-framed the shot, blew it up, and in fact it was not a semi-erect penis. What they were referring to was his leg. Then we had this infamous day with them when they implied that we were implying that they didn't know what a penis looked like. As a compromise, we actually took some Vaseline, put it on the lens of an optical printer, and if you look at the film you'll see in the corner that there's a blurry dot where this photo was. It's totally absurd. They made us trim the beheading. In the original version, the beheading lasted a lot longer and it was a lot harder to watch. Quite honestly I had never intended that it be left in totally. I had gone over the top on purpose to know that I would have to cut. They made us trim it, but I think a bit too much. In the original version it's a lot nicer. In another scene, there was a burnt body on the bed and someone off-camera made a comment about smoking in bed, which I thought was pretty good. We had to excise that because they thought the body was too disgusting. If you want to see the original version you've got to buy the Japanese videocassette of the film.

JAG: You had an interesting cast in *The Exterminator* for an action exploitation movie.

JG: We were trying to get some respectable names for that film. That's why we got Samantha Eggar and Christopher George. Both of them were consummate professionals, very helpful and a lot of fun. I had an enjoyable experience with the whole cast. If you look at *The Exterminator,* there are a lot of people, like Bob Ginty and Steve James, who went on to do enormous amounts of work. Steve's an interesting case in that he had come in to read for the part of a bartender. In the original script, the exterminator's friend was Puerto Rican, not black. We were looking for Puerto Rican actors to play the part. Steve auditioned for the bartender and we really liked his reading. I liked it so much I rewrote the script to make Ginty's friend black so that it could be played by Steve James. That's how that all started with Steve, and I used him again in *The Soldier.*

JAG: *The Exterminator* started Steve James' acting career; he had been a stuntman before that. He has a very natural quality that really came across in the movie.

JG: He humanized the film and that whole character, and that's why we changed it. Ginty has also gone on to do dozens of these kinds of films.

JAG: How did you come to cast Bob Ginty?

JG: We cast him in an interesting way. We had originally cast Joseph Bottoms. Although it had not been released yet, Bottoms was coming off a Disney film called *The Black Hole* (1979), which everybody thought was going to be a monster and a half. He had also been huge in *Holocaust* (1978). We made this deal with him and I thought he was a very good choice for it. We were looking for someone who was not like Charles Bronson in the sense that we wanted someone who was more all-American looking, so that you could believe that you could be the exterminator, not that Bronson and Clint Eastwood aren't great. They're fantastic, but I wanted to make a different kind of statement. We signed, sealed, and delivered the deal with Bottoms because we thought he was going to be such a big star. We had given him an astronomical percentage of the profits. His agent calls at the end of the day he's supposed to show up for wardrobe fittings and he says, "You know, we've been thinking about it. The Disney film was so big and they want to do more films with him. His image in *The Exterminator* is very hard and we think the price we negotiated is this and that, and we need $10,000 more." I hung up. The guys calls back and tells me we were disconnected. I said, "We weren't disconnected. I hung up. This is total crap. We had a deal, you're reneging on the deal. I don't talk to people who renege on a deal." He said, "What are you talking about? You start shooting next week. You have no choice." I hung up again. We pushed shooting back a week and started looking around. I had seen Ginty in *Coming Home* (1978) and the TV series *The Paper Chase*, so I said, "Let's take a shot." I would say that agent and Bottom's decision not to show up probably cost him several million dollars. It's unbelievable how much money they would have made had we gone through with him on *The Exterminator*.

JAG: The movie was truly a sleeper. How do you account for that?

JG: One thing was that no one knew anything about the movie and it came totally out of left field. When we went to Cannes, they didn't know who I was, they really didn't know who Ginty was. Samantha Eggar and Chris George were somewhat names, but no one knew what to expect. In addition to which, a month before Cannes we had taken out a four-page color insert in *Variety* with some pretty spectacular stills of the Vietnam section and some action scenes. People said, "What is this?" They hadn't heard anything and then they saw these stills. Later on, one of the television stations refused to run the commercial for the film because they thought we had stolen footage from *Apocalypse Now* (1979)! At Cannes we had taken out about $150,000 worth of double page color ads of the guy getting blown up, with the ad line, "If you're lying, I'll be back." People thought we were either nuts or we had the goods. Also, at Cannes we were one of the first people who rented a regular movie theatre. Traditionally up to that point, everyone just went to these dinky little screening rooms that were very uncomfortable. Four or five distributors would sit there, and it wasn't a way to watch a movie. I said, "Look. For the world premiere of this film, I want to see it in a regular theatre." We rented the theatre and I went down and passed out free tickets to everyone on the street I could find at Cannes—kids, teenagers. This was another thing you didn't do. The distributors were used to going to screenings very calmly, having plenty of room to spread out. They didn't want to sit with the hoi-polloi. The room held about six hundred people, and probably a thousand showed up. A free ticket to street people at Cannes was pretty exciting. There was no room for the distributors, so there were big fights. People were standing and screaming. In the midst of all the shouting, I started running the film. It was wild. From that moment on, it became evident that we had something that was special. The Vietnam scene, and especially the beheading, was amazingly intense, and I also think that people had no idea what they were going to see. You have a lot of very fancy people who never expected anything like this. When the head came off, there was some guy who stood up and tried to leave the theatre to throw up. He passed out on top of four or five people, who immediately thought he had a heart attack and started screaming. People were yelling, "He had a heart attack!" and an ambulance came. I locked the door of the projection booth and paid the projectionist off to keep rolling and not turn on the house lights. There were cops pulling people out, people screaming "Sit down!" because they wanted to see the film. It was a wild screening.

JAG: The distributors must have started bidding then and there.

JG: It was crazy. We had a situation where people were trying to buy the film in the lobby. We went home that night on purpose. The next morning I went to the Carlton Hotel about eight o'clock. The night before I had asked our foreign sales agent what would be a good price for the Japanese rights. She said $150,000 would be a great price. At the Carlton that morning, there were people standing outside in the hallway. A gentleman came in and said, "We represent Joypack in Japan. We know a lot of people want this film, but we want you to tell us a price that if we say yes, we get the film for Japan and you don't go out in the hall and play our number off someone else." I said, "Fine, $500,000." The guy said "Done," and that was it. From then on I knew there were no rules in the business and anything could happen. Within about four hours we had sold out the entire world except for the United States, which we eventually sold to Avco Embassy.

JAG: When the picture opened in New York it did great business.

JG: *The Exterminator* was one of the first films that had the video box showing clips from the movie outside the theatre. It also was in the right place at the right time. Avco Embassy spent money and did a terrific campaign, but it was the last days of "B" movie theatres when people still went out to the movies, before video. It was also at a time when no one had traditionally done business on a Jewish holiday, which was when it opened. Kids were off, and it did more business on that week in New York than had ever been done in the history of the film business during that week. It was number one in the charts for about two weeks, which was amazing for that type of film.

JAG: Were you involved in the sequel, *The Exterminator II (1984)?*

JG: Not really. I had the rights to the property and after a series of misadventures I wound up licensing those rights to Cannon Films through the original producer, Mark Buntzman.

JAG: How did your next movie, *The Soldier,* come about?

JG: After *The Exterminator,* I got a call from a French guy who said, "I'll finance your next film. I'll send you a first class ticket, meet me in Paris." I went over to Paris and he said, "Here's the deal. I'll finance your next film but you have to write a film that takes place partially in Germany because I have a German investor. Have you ever been to Germany?" I said, "No." He said, "Here's my American Express card. Fly around Germany and let me know if you can write this." I got on a plane, went to Munich, walked around, I went to the concentration camps, which was an amazing experience, and then I flew to Berlin and walked around. I said, "Yeah, I can write something. I have some ideas." He said, "Great." I wrote *The Soldier.* He was going to finance it. Then the guy evaporated in a sense. He lost his financial backing. We had been in preproduction and had spent about $300,000. Worse than that, when his checks stopped coming in and he was saying the money's in the mail, I started funding the picture, so I was personally on the hook for about $291,000. I went to Lenny Shapiro, who was vice president at Avco Embassy at the time, and I said, "Lenny, this film's gonna fall apart next week. I need $5 million to make it. It's a good picture, here's the situation." Lenny and I got in a car and went over to a restaurant where he knew Frank Capra, Jr., president of Avco, was having dinner. We walked up to his table and said, "Look, Frank, you gotta do this by Monday." Frank read the script, called the parent company of Avco Embassy and said, "We made money on *The Exterminator.* This is his next film," and they green lighted the film.

JAG: Your script was inspired by John McPhee's book *The Curve of Binding Energy.*

JG: In that book he talked about the incredible laxity that we show regarding plutonium, which is the most toxic substance in the world. A gram of plutonium could poison everyone in the world. In Buffalo, literally sitting behind a chain link fence, were tons of plutonium. McPhee made an interesting point. The chances of someone like Khadafy making a hydrogen bomb are frankly zero. The technology that you need to make an atomic weapon is really much more complex than you think. I know you always read about high school kids that make them in their basements, but it's a little more complicated than that. You need the capability to machine stuff that can withstand incredible pressures, which is very difficult to construct. However, the chance of taking plutonium and jacketing it in conventional explosives and blowing it up—that you can definitely do. His point was that these fucking trucks drive down the highway with pounds of plutonium and no guard, and someone can steal them. Now, the truck that we made in *The Soldier* that was hijacked in the film was exactly the kind of truck that they transport plutonium in, and it even says it on the side of the truck. The only difference is that in real life they have no armed guards. They just have a truckdriver! I put in the armed guards, otherwise people would think this is stupid. The other thing that was concocted for the movie was breaking into the missile silo, but it was based on a statement that a computer operator who had designed the Strategic Air Command's control had made that you could hack it and you could get in.

JAG: The logistics on *The Soldier* were enormous.

JG: We were in Israel, Egypt, Berlin, Paris, the Alps, London, Montreal, Philadelphia, New York City, and Buffalo, New York. It cost about $4.2 million in cash. Embassy would claim it was about $5 million, but they add a nice fee for themselves.

JAG: How do you do a picture of that scope for that kind of money?

JG: To be honest with you, I don't know. It was 1982, which has a lot to do with it. The other thing was we were just very clever. We really were very specific in what we wanted to do. We did an enormous amount of pre-production. I wrote scenes that took place around existing locations. This is the main difference in what I did in those days. I didn't just write a script. I would go and look at a chair lift somewhere and say, "God, this is a very exciting ski area." I knew that they would let us film there and I'd write a sequence around it. That's how we came to blow up the cable car in St. Anton. I saw a picture postcard of their cable car and said, "Wow, that would be kind of neat. Let's blow it up."

JAG: A sequence like that must be very heavily storyboarded.

JG: Yeah, it was, but it was more that it was very heavy pre-production. Boyce Harman, the line producer, and I made many trips to Austria when there weren't three hundred people standing around wondering what to do. We just took our time to figure it out step by step, inch by inch. Boyce was absolutely the one who was able to put all those little elements together to make it happen.

JAG: Tommy Lee Jones was your original choice for the lead.

JG: He wanted to do *The Soldier*. Embassy said, "OK, we'll use him but we'll only pay him X dollars." He had an offer from NBC-TV to do the Gary Gilmore story, *The Executioner's Song* (1982). I met him in Los

Angeles and he felt that the NBC deal would give him more cash, plus NBC would let him direct some television. He wanted us to step up and at least match the money, but Embassy wasn't willing to do that. They also felt that Ken Wahl, who had been excellent in *The Wanderers* (1979) and *Fort Apache, The Bronx* (1981), was going to be a big star because he was in this Bette Midler film *Jinxed!* (1982). They were not quite right about that, but Ken was actually a very nice guy. I think he was a little bit wrong for the film only because he was too young. My original concept was that this guy was the top CIA agent and I think he needed a little more age than Ken. That's no reflection on Ken. He was just physically too young.

JAG: *The Soldier* was also successful at the box office.

JG: Absolutely. The foreign on *The Soldier* was actually much bigger than *The Exterminator*. The U.S. was not as good as *The Exterminator* but we got caught in a change of studio administration. We started *The Soldier* in discussions with Bob Rehme, who was president of Avco Embassy at that time, left to go to Universal, and now is chief executive at New World. When Bob left for Universal, *The Soldier* flowed through to Frank Capra, Jr. When Jerry Perenchio and Norman Lear bought the company they fired Frank, Lenny Shapiro, and everybody, so it went through three changes of regimes. Traditionally when this happens it's a total disaster for the film. In fairness to Norman Lear, I don't think he ever would have made a film like *The Soldier*. They had paid something like $20 million for the company; $5 million of it was the film *The Soldier*, and they didn't want films like this. They kind of let the people release it, but it was a tough time. They really didn't have their hearts and minds in it. Quite honestly, the people in the company who were responsible for this kind of film were being fired right and left, so it wasn't the most optimum time.

JAG: *The Soldier* is full of huge stunt sequences. What kind of coverage do you use on these kinds of scenes?

JG: As many as seven cameras and as few as four or five. That was always the most interesting thing to me, the multiple cameras, where would you place them, what lenses, what speeds you run the cameras at. That was a lot of fun. The game has changed. There was a lot of slow motion in *The Exterminator* and *The Soldier,* and to some extent in *The Protector,* although by then I was beginning to take it out. In *Shakedown,* there's virtually no slow motion. That style was begun in earnest by Sam Peckinpah and we were just copying him. It worked very well a number of years ago but it's become a little tiresome now. More modern action films have less slow motion and it has a little more impact. We'll probably go back to slow motion five years from now.

JAG: How did you come to direct *The Protector?*

JG: Tom Gray at Golden Harvest gave me a call and said they had Jackie Chan, an enormous star in Southeast Asia who wanted to work again with an American director. He had made *The Big Brawl* (1980) for Robert Clouse and in *The Cannonball Run* (1981) he had nothing more than a cameo. Chan had seen my films, liked them, and wanted to work with me. Golden Harvest asked if I would be willing to come to Hong Kong and do a film with Jackie. I didn't want to just go and make a Hong Kong karate film, but I was interested in working for Raymond Chow, the head of Golden Harvest. I mean, he made *Enter the Dragon* (1973), one of the greatest action films ever. I asked if I could write something that took place in Hong Kong and New York. They called me back and said, "Here's the deal. Whatever you can pre-sell the film for in Cannes, that'll be the budget for the film. You can write anything you want, do anything you want. How's that for a deal?" I said, "Fine," shook hands, went to Cannes, pre-sold it for about $5.6 million, and that was the budget. I wrote *The Exterminator* because I wanted to, but with both *The Soldier* and *The Protector* it was, "Go here, write around this."

JAG: Did you have a language problem with Jackie Chan?

JG: Jackie does not speak any English. You can have a conversation with him in English and you think he understands you, but his grasp of English is very minimal. When he spoke in the film, he was really parroting. It was very difficult. I had to write very simple dialogue. When I'd direct him I would say the line and give him the nuance, and he would try to imitate me. It was tough for Danny Aiello because he's a very inventive actor, a guy who plays off other actors. All in all, I think Jackie came out very well for a guy that doesn't speak English.

JAG: He plays straight man in the film to Danny Aiello.

JG: I enjoyed that very much. I think I was moving a little bit away from ultra-violence and much more into action, which I think you have to do today. *Shakedown* has even more of that. It's more of a movie than the other films have been.

JAG: How was your experience shooting *The Protector* in Hong Kong?

JG: Fantastic. Hong Kong is one of the most interesting places in the world. If I was young and single I'd move there. There's so much opportunity to make movies and money, economic expansion, twenty-four-hour-a-day life. There are some very good crews, plus we brought some people from the United States. Raymond Chow is a terrific guy and his staff is great.

JAG: In *The Protector,* you staged one of the most spectacular stunts I've ever seen, the cigarette boat/helicopter chase in New York Harbor.

JG: That was another logistical nightmare. We had to get OK's from something like fourteen agencies from the Port Authority to the FAA, the Staten Island Ferry, the police, the Coast Guard. But it can be done. No one wants to let you do anything like that, but they all don't want to be the one that publicly says no. The key is to get them all in a room, explain what you want to do, and answer all their questions on safety. That's a very interesting example because we had to do that twice. The first time we tried to do it the special effects guy made a mistake, hooked up the battery hot and blew up the boat prematurely and erroneously. Our answer to everybody was, "Hey, the worst thing that could have happened, happened, and guess what? Nobody got hurt." Therefore, we were in fact doing something right and they let us do it again. We had an incident on *The Soldier* where a helicopter crashed. It was shot out of the sky. We set off the special effects explosion too early, the pilot changed his speed when he shouldn't have, and it was a pure accident. The helicopter flew into the ground. The main thing was we had come up with safety procedures on our own that ensured that nobody was hurt. The helicopter had virtually no fuel in it, it was flying twenty-five feet over the ground, there was no one underneath it. It was a long lens telephoto shot so it was a half mile away from people. Everything that could have gone wrong went wrong. We did about $491,000 worth of damage to the helicopter, but nobody was hurt and that's the point. If you use proper planning, you really don't have to hurt anybody. If you do these stunt films, eventually someone is going to break an ankle, and that's happened, but I certainly don't think we've ever put anybody in a life-threatening position. We've never had a serious accident on any of the films.

JAG: What happened with the domestic distribution on *The Protector?*

JG: We premiered the film in Cannes. Warner Brothers loved it, picked it up for the United States and a few foreign territories that were left over, then claimed they couldn't find a hook to release it. I think what happened was a hole developed in their schedule because another of their films, *The Clan of the Cave Bear* (1986), did not turn out to be everything that they wanted. I think they had a theatre date and they rushed the opening. They only had two weeks to make the spots, and as far as I was concerned, they were terrible spots. They were mystified. They said, "We like the picture but we can't get people in." I said, "Well, that means the advertising is wrong." I was very disappointed in their handling of the film.

JAG: The picture ultimately made money.

JG: It made a lot of money. It did incredibly well in the foreign market, especially Japan. It was bigger than *Beverly Hills Cop II* (1987) in Japan.

JAG: In all of your films you take great care in post-production.

JG: Post-production is always very important to a film. Whatever you shoot, if you mix in Dolby sound and get the top sound effects editors and mixers, and go for good music, it's always going to be better. You make an enormous difference in a picture doing that, so I'm always interested in having the best post we possibly can.

JAG: *Shakedown* is your most ambitious film to date. What is the premise of the film?

JG: On some levels, it's a flip of *The Exterminator*. The film starts off in Central Park. We see a black crack dealer making a sale to someone dressed in bluejeans, who you later discover was an undercover cop. There's something wrong with the scene but you don't know exactly what. At the last minute we pull away from the scene and you learn that there has indeed been a shoot-out. We come back on the scene—there's money and drugs, bodies on the ground. A young black dealer is charged with killing this cop. The hero of our film is played by Peter Weller, who plays a legal aid lawyer who was a hippie in the Sixties, really thought he could change the world, is totally disillusioned, about to go for the big bucks and marry the rich girl whose father owns a fancy firm, and he'll become a Yuppie. On his last day as a legal aid lawyer he's sent to Riker's Island prison to interview this guy. The dealer says, "Yeah, I'm selling drugs in the park. This white dude comes up to me, takes out a gun, says give me your money, so I shot him, but he never said he was a cop." Weller says, "I'm supposed to believe that and convince a jury?" The dealer says, "Hey. I'm a lot of things but I don't lie to my lawyer. That dude was a bluejean cop." When Weller leaves Riker's, he thinks, "What happened to me? I used to believe people were innocent. Now I'm sure they're guilty." He goes to 42nd Street, where a friend of his, played by Sam Elliott, is an undercover cop whose wife has just thrown him out and he's living in the balcony of a Times Square movie theatre. Weller asks, "What's a bluejean cop?" Sam says, "Where did you hear that?" Weller says, "One of my clients." Sam says, "Well look at it this way. I wear Wranglers, but the guys I arrest wear Sergio Valente. You take a cop, making an average salary of $28,000 a year, and he's arresting people making $28,000 a day, and that's the problem." There begins a Serpico-esque journey through New York City.

JAG: *Shakedown* is based on a real incident.

JG: Yeah, an incident that happened in the park, a shooting made me think about this. The drug dealer said exactly those words. My immediate reaction was, "Oh, this guy's lying. He's just selling drugs and he killed the cop." I used to care about things, I used to think things mattered, I used to believe in truth and justice, and now I've become a nouveau-fucking-Reaganite, and what happened to me? This is wrong. So that was the genesis of *Shakedown*. *The Exterminator* really started from a true incident of a Columbia University student who on graduation day was mugged in the elevator and left paralyzed for life. I remember the outrage I felt about that. Then I began thinking, "Jesus, the next day I'm going to be carrying on with my life, the *New York Times* will carry on with its life, and I'm never going to see mention of this guy again." That was the rage that became *The Exterminator*.

JAG: What kinds of stunts did you stage in *Shakedown?*

JG: There were three major sequences. We derailed a full-sized, real Coney Island rollercoaster. We did a big sequence in Times Square where Sam shoots at a bad guy, jumps out onto a theatre marquee, it crashes onto

42nd Street, Sam lands on top of a passing bus, falls off onto a group of Hell's Angels on motorcycles, commandeers a motorcycle, chases the bad guy who has commandeered a police car. That's an exciting scene. The third one is at the end of the film where a bad cop and a drug dealer are escaping to Costa Rica in a $20 million business jet, and in an act of desperation Sam and Peter chase them out onto the runway in this convertible Turbo Porsche. The car drives under the wing at 145 miles per hour. The plane lifts its nose off the ground and Sam grabs onto the nose cone as the plane takes off. He then shoots the hydraulic lines so they can't retract the wheels, shoots out one of the engines, all with Manhattan and the Statue of Liberty in the background. He puts a hand grenade into the wheel well, the plane turns around, screeches into LaGuardia, and comes in for a landing. At the last minute Sam jumps into the water, the plane lands, and it blows up. That was a really major sequence.

JAG: Boyce Harman has been your line producer on *The Exterminator, The Soldier, The Protector*, and *Shakedown*. How would you describe your working relationship?

JG: Boyce has enabled me to put my films on the screen in the sense that he's done the business, he's figured out the logistics and enabled me to do what I want to do, so it's been very good. It works and we keep on doing it.

JAG: How do people react when you and Boyce want to do your seemingly impossible action sequences?

JG: For example, the Times Square scene in *Shakedown*—people said, "You won't be able to do it. The city will never let you shut it down." We did it. We shut down 42nd Street between Eighth and Ninth Avenue for five nights between midnight and five in the morning. It's an incredible action scene. No one has ever done that and I don't know that anyone else will. There are a lot of people when confronted with "Why not?" and they're told "You can't do it" just say "OK." I'm a person who will *always* ask "Why not?" You can do anything safely, you can do anything if you use your head, and it doesn't have to cost a trillion dollars.

JAG: Now you're not only a writer-producer-director, you're a movie mogul.

JG: A mini-mogul! It came about in the way that Bertolt Brecht said, "What is the robbing of a bank compared to the founding of a bank?" I just realized that at a certain point, if you're going to finance films, for very little money more you can own a distribution company and really hold onto some of the money that movies generate. I wanted to be able to say to my investors, "Not only do you have a chance to make money from the film, but you can own some of the distribution." I've teamed with Lenny Shapiro to form Shapiro Glickenhaus Entertainment. I go back with Lenny to the Avco Embassy days with *The Exterminator* and *The Soldier*. We're a fully integrated company. We can honestly provide a couple of services. We can finance and distribute films, but I think the most important thing is that on the production side we're a group of people who have stood in the rain and made movies. While I may give you some input, I'm not the kind of guy who asks you, "Why are there grease pencil marks on the workprint?" I also know that you have to let people make their own mistakes. I think the main thing with a film is even if there's a problem with it, if it comes from a single voice, it has a chance of working, but if there are too many cooks, it's classic, too many films get destroyed. The new company also enables me to be what Roger Corman used to be, in the sense that if I find a young director, writer, or producer, if I can sell the films and at least know that I'm going to break even, I can afford to let people make their films and become a studio. When I made *The Astrologer*, the whole thing cost $65,000. With interest, *Shakedown* is $14 million. You're not going to get a kid out of film school and give him $14 million, but there has to be a mechanism to give these people the ability to make films, and that's what I want to try to become and try to do. We've already done a couple of films with people who had a few films to their credit. We've done *Maniac Cop* (1988) with Bill Lustig, *Black Roses* (1988) with John Fasano, and *Lethal Pursuit* (1988) with Gary Gibbs. We're looking every day at more directors and more projects and trying to roll some of this money back into it.

JAG: Do you have a method to your screenwriting?

JG: I come up with an idea, something I want to do. I take a Bic pen and a yellow pad and try to write as much as I can. Then I usually put it away for four or five months and I think the movie in my head. Every night when I go to sleep I try to watch the movie and then I get more and more of it. When I go to foreign markets, I announce a title, start selling it, and people say, "What's it about?" I start telling them, and in the pitch, I can get a handle on what parts they like, and the parts where I see them wandering I excise. One fine day, it just comes.

JAG: The critics in America have been less than kind to your films.

JG: I think anybody that says they don't care what a critic says is stupid. Obviously you care, and it bothers you if somebody says they're junk. On the other hand, living well is the best revenge. The first review of *The Exterminator* in *Variety* said that I'd made the classic mistake of making an action film with no action. That's just wrong. I have gotten occasional good reviews, for example, *The Washington Post* said that the ski scene in *The Soldier* was one of the most spectacular ever shot and compared it to some of the things that Spielberg had done. In Europe I've gotten very good press. You have to have a little bit of the attitude of Bob Dylan in the sense that it's for myself and my friends, my stories I tell, and you can't take any of it personally. My films are not me. There's a wonderful ephemeral thing that happens when films get made. I don't know where the stories come from, I don't know where the ultra-violence comes from. It's a part of all of us. Even the person who says they can't stand it cracks their eyes to look. The only thing I don't like about critics is when they personalize it and make judgements about you as a person. Also, I find it curious that you take a guy like Clint Eastwood, who was making spaghetti Westerns, and then one magic day he became an *auteur* in the minds of some critics. I've always liked Eastwood. I liked him then, I like him now.

JAG: How has the homevideo market affected the feature film business?

JG: I think it's become the new "B" movie market. It's a wild thing. You're a kid, it's Friday night, you have twenty bucks, you rent five movies. You're renting a box, a cover, a title. It's a terrific opportunity to finance and distribute low-budget films. It's revolutionized the business. When I made *The Exterminator,* Avco Embassy had an output deal with Fox Magnetic Video. They said to me, "If we fold these videocassette rights into the Fox deal, you get $25,000 one-time payment." I said, "What's video?" They said, "No one knows. We think it's all bullshit. First of all, the machines cost a lot of money, and the cassettes cost eighty bucks. Who's gonna buy them?" No one thought about rental. But $25,000 is $25,000, so I said, "Ask them for $30,000." Fox said it was too much, so I happened to have retained those rights. Those rights have netted me over one million dollars. No one knew! And it's a brand new world with the ability to get films into people's homes and to have the convenience to watch them when they want to. If the phone rings they can put the tape on pause. One of the hardest things I have to do is to fight for distributors to still release films theatrically foreign. There are a lot of them who don't. There are a lot of them who don't even want to talk about it. In the old days, video was not even a consideration. Now, the video companies are the new theatrical companies foreign. I recently had a vacation in Bermuda with my wife and kid. We were talking to a cab driver about what I did, and he said, "You know, there's not a movie theatre in Bermuda anymore." The theaters deteriorate, they become noisy, raucous kids go and the older people don't. They rip the place up and that's the end of it. With video, there are no more movie theatres in a place like Bermuda. Homevideo is a blessing, but it's also a terrible liability. We can't just become people that make films for video, because then no more big films will get made.

(1988)

Menahem Golan

Menahem Golan is best known as the energetic head of The Cannon Group, and while he does serve as Cannon's Chairman of the Board, Golan is also an accomplished director, with twenty-five films to his credit. Born in Tiberias, in what is now Israel, on May 31, 1929, he studied theatre at London's Old Vic and attended New York's City College before starting his filmmaking career working for Roger Corman on *The Young Racers* (1962). He directed his first feature, *El Dorado,* in Israel the following year, and with Yoram Globus, formed Noah Films, a company that produced nearly forty films over the next fifteen years. Golan grew to become the pre-eminent filmmaker in Israel, helming such movies as the musical *Kazablan* (1973), the Isaac Bashevis Singer story *The Magician of Lublin* (1979), and the action-adventure *Operation Thunderbolt* (1977), based on the dramatic Israeli raid on Entebbe, which earned an Academy Award nomination as Best Foreign Film.

In 1979, Golan and Globus bought controlling shares in the faltering Cannon Group, and with a combination of chutzpah and a knowledge of the international market, built the company into a formidable production and distribution operation. Cannon was able to entice a wide range of major Hollywood talent into its fold, and despite industry predictions, has managed to stay in business through some less-than-profitable seasons, balancing its release slate with action films like the *American Ninja* series, and prestigious projects like *Runaway Train* (1985) and *Otello* (1986).

Throughout it all, Golan has continued to direct a variety of movies, including *The Delta Force* (1986), an action film in the tradition of *Operation Thunderbolt* based on the terrorist hijacking of a TWA jet; the Sylvester Stallone vehicle *Over the Top* (1987); and Golan's pet project *Hanna's War* (1988), the true story of Hanna Senesh's World War Two exploits.

Menahem Golan (courtesy of The Cannon Group).

This interview was held in February 1986 in New York, with an update in 1988 as Golan was completing the final mix on *Hanna's War*.

FILMOGRAPHY

El Dorado (1963, Noah Films).
Trunk to Cairo (1967, American International).
The Girl from the Dead Sea (1967, Noah Films).
Tevye and His Seven Daughters (1968, Noah Films).
Fortuna (1969, Noah Films).
What's Good for the Goose (1969, National Showmanship).
Margo (1970, Cannon).
Lupo! (1970, Cannon).
Highway Queen/Queen of the Road (1970, Noah Films).
Katz and Karasso (1971, Noah Films).
The Great Telephone Robbery (1972, Noah Films).
Escape to the Sun (1972, Cinevision). HV: Monterrey.
Kazablan (1973, MGM).
Lepke (1975, Warner Brothers). HV: Warners.
Diamonds (1975, Avco Embassy). HV: Embassy.
The Ambassador (1976, Noah Films).
Operation Thunderbolt (1977, Noah Films). HV: MGM/UA.
The Uranium Conspiracy (1978, Noah Films).
The Magician of Lublin (1979, Cannon). HV: HBO.
The Apple (1980, Cannon).
Enter the Ninja (1981, Cannon). HV: MGM/UA.
Over the Brooklyn Bridge (1984, Cannon/MGM-UA). HV: MGM-UA.
The Delta Force (1986, Cannon). HV: Media Home.
Over the Top (1987, Cannon/Warner Brothers). HV: Warners.
Hanna's War (1988, Cannon).
Three Penny Opera (1989, Cannon).

GOLAN INTERVIEW

JOHN A. GALLAGHER: How did you put *The Delta Force* into production so quickly?

MENAHEM GOLAN: I was in Hollywood when the TWA plane was hijacked, and I felt the atmosphere in the street—the feeling that America should take a stand, go in there, and release the hostages immediately using the Delta Force, which is the elite army organization trained for such situations. But then President Reagan went and changed the third act for me, and I had to invent a new third act. I wanted to give the people the feeling that something was being done—to satisfy that hunger for heroic action. In a way, I was following in my own footsteps. When I did *Operation Thunderbolt* about the Israeli raid on Entebbe, I was living in Israel, and I remember the excitement that all of us there felt when the Israelis saved the hostages. I was sure that the same thing was going to happen in America. Like any other American, I was frustrated. I wanted to see an immediate rescue, but it didn't work out that way. Then I thought to myself, "I must bring a movie to the screen fast for the public which, like me, want to see things end differently." *The Delta Force* came together very quickly. We started shooting on the eighteenth of September 1985. We chose to shoot in Israel because, for me, it's the obvious place to shoot any Middle East location. We recreated the Algiers airport at the Jerusalem airport, and used Ben Gurion Airport outside Tel Aviv for the Beirut airport. We also shot secretly in Athens, because the government there was not sympathetic to this project. By the first of December, we had the movie in the can, and six weeks later we had a print. Now we're opening in 1,750 theatres around the country, which is a very wide release for Cannon.

JAG: That's an extremely swift post-production schedule.

MG: If you're an experienced director, you know what you need to shoot, you know what you want in the cutting room, and it works. I believe that working on a movie twenty-four hours a day with complete concentration can actually improve its quality. In 1960, Roger Corman did a movie—shot it, cut it, and made a print—in forty-eight hours. It became a classic horror film, *The Little Shop of Horrors*. It became so successful in fact, that it was later made into a hit stage musical, which in turn was remade as a big-budget movie in 1986.

JAG: *Operation Thunderbolt* was a kind of blueprint for *The Delta Force*.

MG: When we did *Operation Thunderbolt*, we did a lot of research into the feelings of the people sitting on that hijacked Air France jetliner. I had sixteen people who had actually been on that plane working as extras in the movie, and that gave it a lot of authenticity. I also had officials in the Israeli government, including Shimon Peres, recreating their real life roles in the crisis, documentary style. It's exciting to make a movie so directly connected to historical fact. Of course, you have to watch yourself all the time and be careful not to intrude on anyone's privacy. And, of necessity, you have to invent or modify some details. But even fictional characters or incidents must convey the essential reality of what happened. The interesting thing about this approach is that today, when people in Israel talk to me about the rescue, Entebbe for them *is Operation Thunderbolt*—and in a way, they're right. The people in the movie *are* the same people who were really there. This *is* exactly how Jonathan was hit. This *is* how the passengers were rescued. But the power of films is such that, even if a movie is not 100% historically accurate, the movie *becomes* popular history. Oddly enough, when TWA was giving us problems during the early phases of production, they were concerned about how they would look in the film. I asked them what they were so worried about. They kept on saying, "We know that five years from now, the

TWA hijacking will be remembered not as it was, but how it is shown in your picture. The movie will be the historical document. Everything else will be forgotten." If you think about it for a moment, you realize it's true. You read newspapers, and they wind up in the next day's trash, but a movie stays there. It goes to video, it goes to television, and it plays for years and years to come. It becomes a part of history. So TWA was scared. To mollify them, I changed the name of the airline company from TWA to ATW, "American Travel Ways." Then, last week, when they saw the movie, they were so happy that they came to me again and asked if I could change the name back to TWA. I said, "It's too late. I shot it with the ATW logo, and I'm not going to reshoot those scenes!"

JAG: A lot of kids today seem to think that Robert Redford and Dustin Hoffman cracked the Watergate case because of the film *All the President's Men* (1976).

MG: Exactly, because movies are such a powerful medium. You forget that maybe history was a little different. Filmmakers romanticize history, take dramatic license, and people forget the real facts. For them, the "real facts" become the illusion they see on the screen.

JAG: In *The Delta Force*, you have an all-star cast with a wide range of acting styles—Lee Marvin from the old school of instinctive actors, a personality star like Chuck Norris, and Method actors like Martin Balsam, Shelley Winters, and Susan Strasberg.

MG: I think the stressful environment, the fact that we shot on a 707 with no air conditioning, sitting there in intense heat on the runway in Israel for twelve hours a day gave everybody a feeling of reality. It went beyond acting—they actually suffered during shooting. Chuck Norris learned a lot working with Lee Marvin; we talked about it a lot during shooting. He found qualities within himself as an actor that he never knew he had. We made sure we had a really good actor in every small but important character part. We also cast against type—George Kennedy as a warmhearted priest from Chicago instead of a tough guy or fighter, Robert Forster as an Arab. We stayed away from conventional casting, except for Shelley Winters as an elderly Jewish woman who had been in a concentration camp.

JAG: Forster gives a fantastic performance as the terrorist.

MG: I agree. I brought him to Israel a few weeks before shooting and had him work with an Arabic teacher. We went into the Arab streets and marketplaces. We created a feeling for him. The script was actually written while we were shooting. We felt we were doing something important, and that we should be very careful with it. We had two units going all the time, and I was jumping from one unit to the other. Fortunately, all the actors were really involved; I've never seen actors so involved in a movie. They weren't just sitting in a hotel when they weren't shooting.

Lee Marvin was out there on the set day and night. It was kind of a Method way of making a movie. The actors were involved in each other's scenes. We always were discussing scenes. Everyone cared about the movie as a whole. I'm very proud of this movie. There was a real excitement on the set, and I hope the audience will feel the same excitement in the theatre.

JAG: Two of the younger Delta Force members, Steve James and Bill Wallace, more than hold their own with the veterans.

MG: They're both very good actors, and they both got their first big breaks with Cannon, Steve with *American Ninja* (1986) and Bill with *America 3000* (1986). I think they both have beautiful screen personalities, and they are developing those personalities with Cannon. You'll see them doing some more movies with us. I have some ideas for Steve James because I think, in fact I'm sure, he can be a movie star. Hollywood is just so full of talent, I wish I could give everybody a part!

JAG: *The Delta Force* theme music by Alan Silvestri is appropriately rousing.

MG: I brought Alan to Tel Aviv. He was sitting with us on that plane. In Hollywood, you don't take a composer on the set. Alan spent a week with us in Israel, and that gave him a chance to absorb the atmosphere. He sat in the cutting room with our editor, Alain Jakubowicz, a wonderful editor, and by the time we came back, Alain had already had most of the themes ready for me. He was very much a part of the making of this movie.

JAG: In addition to being in charge of The Cannon Group, you also have a long list of directing credits.

MG: Besides *The Delta Force* and *Operation Thunderbolt*, I did *The Magician of Lublin,* which was the first film based on a book by Isaac Bashevis Singer. I also did a musical called *Kazablan* in Israel, and *Highway Queen,* about prostitution in Israel, believe it or not. The thing is, even though I'm a studio head, I'm also a moviemaker, and not just a director. I love dealing with other directors, and they are happy to work with us. When we came to Hollywood in 1979 and started to produce films at Cannon, the first thing we did was to give above-the-line credit to directors. Hollywood was not accustomed to doing business that way. Until we arrived, it wasn't "A John Frankenheimer Film," it was "A Zanuck-Brown Production." In other words, in the Hollywood system, the producer used to take the credit for making the movie. He was ostensibly the king, ruler, and creator of the moviemaking process, which I don't believe is true. A good producer assembles the elements of a movie; he does not create the movie. A movie is putting images together, telling a story, creating an emotion, and that is done by writers, directors, editors, cameramen, actors, and movie composers. They are the creative people who make the movie. In France, Italy, Israel, it has always been like that. Money and budget do not dictate the creative aspects of a movie. I think over the years Hollywood became stale with the power it gave to producers, because the producers were the people who could assemble a big project with big stars and a good director. We came to Hollywood from Europe and Israel, from another kind of moviemaking world, where filmmakers had greater creative freedom. That's why you see directors the stature of Robert Altman, Andrei Konchalovsky, John Cassavetes, Franco Zeffirelli, Jean-Luc Godard, Jerry Schatzberg and Hector Babenco coming to us now. Stars and writers also are coming to us because they're hungry for this freedom in Hollywood. It helps us to make better quality pictures, without losing our commercial base in what people call our "exploitation" films.

JAG: Your bread-and-butter pictures like *Breakin'* (1984) and the *American Ninja* series give you the opportunity to make films like *Otello* (1986) and *Fool for Love* (1985). Darryl Zanuck let William Wellman make *The Ox-Bow Incident* in 1942 knowing his studio would never make a dime with it, but because he wanted the prestige.

MG: It's not just prestige. Cannon is able to dictate the selling of a movie to a distributor. That's the power we have in foreign markets. We came to America to make American movies that could be sold to independent distributors around the world. As a kid, I was raised on American motion pictures. I was educated and Americanized by the American cinema. I lived in a little town called Tiberias in Israel. We had one cinema, and I was in it every Saturday night. It was like a rule—there was no Saturday night I was not in the cinema. I also went there Wednesday afternoons for the matinees, and if a movie didn't make it to Saturday, I'd go on Thursday. I saw everything. It was bread and butter for me. Ninety-nine percent of the movies we saw were American. Why? Because Hollywood had the major stars, and Hollywood gave the people of the world a vision of a different kind of life that lifted us out of the dreary life the century had given so many of us. That cinema was practically controlled by the major film companies in Hollywood. Like other kids in millions of other cinemas, I lived the American life vicariously through the movies. I've said before that America became an empire due to motion pictures. Americans didn't have to send soldiers to conquer little Tiberias on the Sea of Galilee! It was the motion picture that grabbed all the kids on Saturday nights. We were there fist-fighting to get a ticket to watch Humphrey Bogart, Gary Cooper, James Cagney, you name them. I remember in the Forties and Fifties, during the terrible years of the war, movies were our only entertainment. I remember buying my first pair of jeans—something I had seen in a movie. I remember pouring oil on my hair when I was going to a party on a Friday night because I saw Elvis Presley do that to *his* hair. The new dance where you lifted a girl away from your chest during the earliest days of rock 'n' roll—America gave us that, too. When I became a filmmaker, I already knew all about that power.

In the first fifty years of the movie industry, there were just eight major companies—Paramount, MGM, United Artists, Columbia, 20th Century-Fox, Disney, Universal, and Warner Brothers—and no new distributors broke into the world market, because the system was locked and blocked. An American film could come to Tiberias only through the exchange office of a United Artists or a Paramount. That's the only way movies came over there. What happened to Italian movies, German movies, French movies, Indian movies? The people making and marketing those films were frustrated. They hardly got a screen because they couldn't compete with the American studios' power. *They* didn't have Humphrey Bogart and Gary Cooper. Every cinema wanted, and still wants, American movies. Yoram Globus and I grew to become local moviemakers in Israel, and we immediately jumped over to distribution. We couldn't buy an American movie, and we knew that if we didn't have an American movie, if we only had a French movie, for example, we would play only on Thursday night, not Saturday night. You couldn't get a theatre. It was almost an unfair competition. Then a generation of new distributors came up, distributors who bought French movies just as the New Wave was arriving. Suddenly everybody wanted to see the new French cinema, the Italian neo-realistic cinema, the cinema of DeSica, Fellini, and Pietro Germi. These great international filmmakers came to international audiences almost by default, through distributors who had no other choice, distributors who couldn't get an American movie. When Yoram and I started to make movies, we understood that. We started to go to the festivals at Cannes and Milan, and we learned that if we wanted to have our place in the world cinema, the old saying applied—"If you can't beat 'em, join 'em." We had to go to Mecca, and Mecca for us was Hollywood. When we came to America, we said, "We're going to make big American pictures." We were going to build our company by making American movies with good production values, good stories, and big stars. We were going to be involved with the creators of quality movies in America, and we were going to bring those movies to the world not through the major studios, but through Cannon. "Create your own product and sell it to the independent"—that was the idea. All of a sudden when we came to Cannes, you saw a line of distributors taking numbers like in a barber shop to meet with Yoram and me. We became popular there because we brought them what they could never get before, a good commercial American film to compete for a Saturday night date in their own countries. Once we had that power, we could have been swallowed up by Hollywood and become like everybody else. We didn't want that. Instead, we brought a European sensibility with us to Hollywood, a creativity and a sense of doing something better. When Taiwan, for example, wanted to buy our *Death Wish 3* (1985) or *American Ninja,* we would say to the local distributor, "Sorry, but you have to take John

Cassavetes' *Love Streams* (1984) first, or you don't get Charles Bronson."
In other words, we started to sell tomatoes with cucumbers, apples with
oranges. We sold films in packages, which forced the first Cassavetes
screening in Taiwan. Before that, Cassavetes couldn't get a screen there.
He couldn't even get talked about in Taiwan, because all you saw in the
cinemas there were martial arts movies. How could you expect kids in
Taiwan to be interested in seeing something better; more intelligent films
with higher aspirations? They do have universities, you do have people
who are eager to see something new, but those new films weren't getting
into their cinemas. The distributors were scared, but we forced the issue.
We gave away the Cassavetes picture for practically nothing. And now
in Taiwan they *have* to see an Altman movie or Zeffirelli's opera *Otello*,
because otherwise they know they're not going to get Charlie Bronson
or Chuck Norris. This is something we're proud of, and something we
do take credit for. Check in the international market, and you'll see that
Cannon is slowly elevating not just the level of quality in motion pictures,
but the audience level as well. Of course, we have not stopped making
action pictures, because then we would not have the leverage to sell the
better films. I also think that the quality of our action movies is improving
because now we are working with better directors. Even our ninja movies
are improving. The stories are a little more thoughtful, and the acting is
better. We're all learning from movie to movie, and we're all developing
together, because The Cannon Group is a family of moviemakers who
are free to do things which are much more challenging than before.

JAG: You're also giving directors multi-picture contracts like they did in
the old studio system days.

MG: I believe you need stability. I don't like this game of musical chairs
being played by the people who run the studios in Hollywood, where
they're all busy protecting their seats. How does Hollywood work today?
Today's moguls are not real moviemakers. They're bankers and lawyers.
You don't have moguls today like Sam Goldwyn and David Selznick,
inspiring men who were always striving to make exciting cinema and
true entertainment. You don't have people like that today because they
became Coca-Cola, which now owns Columbia. I have nothing against
Coca-Cola. I love Coca-Cola, but they're not real moviemakers. I think
the heads of studios today should be creative people, people who were
editors, directors, screenwriters, cameramen. Basically, that's what
Yoram and I are. We are trying to make movies that don't have to make
commercial sense when you first plan them. Protect yourself by pre-
licensing. Don't delude yourself that every movie will bring in $200
million. Strive for some continuity from film to film, which means cul-
tivating a group of filmmakers you believe in and working with them
in a creative manner. Once we find somebody we can work with, a
creator, a real moviemaker like Andrei Konchalovsky, we like to keep

them with us. We adopted Chuck Norris because I think Chuck is developing into a major star. His acting abilities are getting better from movie to movie. He will keep the excitement with Cannon for the next ten years. He has an office on our premises, and he's sitting there with writers developing material for himself and others. Zeffirelli also has a deal with us. He loves to work with us. John Frankenheimer shot Elmore Leonard's *52 Pick Up* (1986) for us in Pittsburgh. He told me, "You know, Menahem, for the first time I feel the excitement of making a movie that I used to feel when I first got out of college. I know when I start a movie that it will be the same studio management when I finish it. That hasn't happened to me for more than five years." Even if I have an argument with a filmmaker, we both know we're still on the same side. William Friedkin came to me and said, "Can I have a place at Cannon?" and I said, "Yes, come in, do what you want. What film do you want to do?" There is a real challenge there. He can come in with any crazy idea he wants, something he's dreamed of but never dared to take to any of the major studios. *Runaway Train* was Konchalovsky's dream, but the project had been around for a long time. Akira Kurosawa wrote it more than fifteen years ago. Let's go back to when we started making American movies, with *That Championship Season* (1982) by Jason Miller. Jason had wanted to do that film for years. It was difficult, and it's not the most obviously commercial movie. But if you really try to limit your risk, try to cut the overhead, try to cut the bullshit, you can make an exciting movie at a reasonable price with a filmmaker who has the freedom to go beyond the usual creative and budgetary constraints.

JAG: You've been producing a number of sequels at Cannon, like the *Death Wish* films, the *American Ninja* series, *The Exterminator II* (1984).

MG: Sequels have become an important part of moviemaking. It's the same with novels. You get to know a character, you fall in love with him, you want to know what he's doing now. You don't want to part with the character. That applies to James Bond, Superman, the *Star Wars* (1977) sagas, the Indiana Jones films—all sequels based on the same hero people initially got involved with. The audience is on friendly terms with James Bond, Superman, and Indiana Jones. When they go to the theatre, from the very first shot on the screen, they know him. They are part of his life, and they want to see his story continue. Some critics sneer at sequels, but I think they're an important part of the moviemaking process.

JAG: You recently directed *Over the Top* with Sylvester Stallone.

MG: Yes. We do not have any fixed rules at Cannon. We'll pay one actor a fortune, and with another we'll fight to get him for practically nothing. It depends on the project and the actor. Because we come to them with challenging material, we often get stars to cut their salaries by half. For instance, that's how we did *Grace Quigley* (1985) with Katharine Hepburn and Nick Nolte, and *The Naked Face* (1985) with Roger Moore. In order to do better material, they're willing to forego their usual salary. I'm saying that the stars are rich enough, and they don't work enough. A moviemaker or an actor with a real creative drive wants to be in front of the camera or to have a script in hand every day of his life. For an actor, the moviemaking process takes ten weeks of shooting, and maybe four weeks of costuming and discussions with the director. But a great star can only do one or two movies a year because of the commercial system and the way he's protected by agents, managers, and lawyers. In the time it takes for them to read the script and prepare a contract, a year passes! And what do all those big stars do during all that time? They play tennis and they go to psychiatrists and they get divorced. That's their business, but they're not dealing with their art, and if you're clever enough, if you get to them with material they like, you can get them. Now, Stallone; we came to Stallone during the period when his career was skyrocketing with the *Rocky* movies, which always use violence. Stallone feels he can do well in other kinds of films, but he is afraid to lose audiences when he steps aside and does a different, better movie like *F. I. S. T.* (1978). He created a new word—"Rambo-ism"—in 1982 with *First Blood,* which again dealt with physical violence. So when I found a script that had to do with more humane elements, a melodrama of conflict between a man and society, not shooting his guns, not using his fists, I knew I'd get his interest. *Over the Top* came into my hands a few years ago. It's a love story between a father and a little boy who is taken away from him by the Establishment, and how he fights for the boy. Although it has to do with arm wrestling, which fits Stallone, it is not violent. It's a sport, a hobby. He's a gambler who uses arm wrestling to raise money to fight for his son. The screenplay was wonderful. He wanted to do it very much, but then came all his lawyers and protectors. They said, "Stallone? You have to pay a fortune." The number which was quoted, which everybody knows, and I'm not afraid of telling it, was $12 million. Everybody said to me, "What are you, nuts or something? Paying Stallone $12 million to make a movie?" So we decided to do something nobody had ever done before—option him. Take an option on his life, as a human being, as an actor, for six months. I think this is creative producing. We optioned him for six months for half a million dollars, which meant that if we failed to raise the money for the film during that time, we'd lose $500,000. But Stallone wanted to do the film very much, and we wanted to do the film with him. So we went out to the international markets and festivals, out to our distributors and buyers, people who could never get a Stallone film on their home screens, announced the fact that we had him, and quickly saw that even if the picture cost $25 million, we'd make a profit before we ever began to shoot the movie. That's how popular he was. Still, it was a big risk at the time we first took the option. This was before *Rambo: First Blood Part II* in 1985. Then came *Rambo*, and suddenly every major company was offering us a huge amount of money to sell them the project. We did a deal with Warner Brothers for domestic distribution, which was the first time Warners ever approached a company like ours. Part of the deal with Warners was also for them to co-produce *Cobra* (1986) with us and Stallone. It was a big thing for Cannon to have such a big commercial star in our "stable." So I directed the movie *Over the Top*. It was a different kind of Stallone. Up until then, my encounters with him had been very good, but I was dreading the first day of shooting. After all, he's a very strong personality. One thing I can tell you from all the meetings I had with him, though, is that the man is very professional. He understands what he can do and what he cannot do. He was finishing the last draft of the screenplay at the time.

JAG: You started out in the business working for Roger Corman on *The Young Racers* in 1962.

MG: That probably was my best school. I really admire Roger. Although he is known for his exploitation films in Hollywood, he is a true film-maker. Like many others in this business, he loves what he's doing. He really is a cinema animal. He is a producer who, again, does not want to waste money, who wants to do every one of his films logically. Young people love his films. Sometimes he creates very good movies. Most of the time his movies are just run-of-the-mill, but American cinema should be grateful to Roger Corman. Look at the people who went through his "school"—Coppola, Bogdanovich, Bob Towne, Scorsese, Jack Nicholson. I learned a lot from him on *The Young Racers*. I wrote Roger a letter after I finished some film courses here in New York at CCNY. He wrote me back immediately and said, "If you can pay your way and get to Monte Carlo on June 10, and you pay for your own hotel and food and don't expect me to give you money, you can help carry the camera and you'll work on a movie." Eventually he made me his driver and gave me a hundred dollars a week. Then one Sunday morning he had to change his schedule. He said that by the next morning, Monday, we had to shoot the driver getting the winner's wreath. Where do you get a beautiful wreath made on a Sunday? Nobody could find one. By the afternoon, he was frustrated, and he absolutely had to shoot the next day because he had arranged for a big crowd to be there. He said, "Menahem, you are an Israeli, and I know sometimes when Israelis are under stress, they know how to solve problems. If you bring me a wreath by tomorrow morning, I'll make you my assistant and I'll give you ten bucks." I didn't sleep that night. I wandered around town looking for flower shops. I looked up addresses. They were all closed. Finally I found a coffee shop where they gave me the address of a florist. I went to his home and Sunday night at midnight I brought him back to his flower shop. At eight o'clock the next morning, I was on the set with that wreath, and

I got promoted. I became Roger Corman's assistant. It was one of the greatest days of my life. Francis Coppola was working on the movie as a sound man. They bought a Nagra recorder, one of the first ever made. Nobody knew how to use it. Coppola surely didn't know, but he was the sound engineer on the film. Every night Francis was sitting there writing his first script, which later became *Dementia 13* (1963). I told Roger I had a script based on a play about the underworld in Jaffa called *El Dorado* that I wanted to make. I told Roger that for $30,000, he could own a movie for the whole world. I didn't even dream I'd need more! I didn't understand budgets yet. He signed a little letter with me and said, "OK, when you finish working for me on *The Young Racers,* you're going to Israel to shoot your movie, and I'll give you $30,000." Coppola looked at it and said to Roger, "Are you an idiot? For $30,000, I'll make you a good American horror movie." Roger said, "Do you have a script?" and Francis said, "Of course!" But of course he didn't, and that night he started to type. He typed *Dementia 13* for two consecutive weeks. He finished it so quickly that my script wasn't even translated into English from Hebrew yet, so Roger couldn't read it. So he took my $30,000 and gave it to Coppola. Francis had the nerve to offer me one point to work on his movie for no money! I said, "Francis, we are the best of friends, and I'm sure we'll meet again in the future. But I'm going to go do my own film." It was a very exciting time. As I say, it was a school for emerging talent. Robert Towne was working with us. We wandered all over Europe making our little movie about racers. The Campbell brothers, Bill and Robert, were in the film, along with Luana Anders, who I understand is now writing and directing. Floyd Crosby was the cameraman. He had shot *High Noon* (1952). Because of that experience on *The Young Racers,* I took him to shoot *Sallah* (1963), our first Oscar-nominated movie. Ephraim Kishon directed it, I produced it, and we discovered Chaim Topol, who later became *The Fiddler on the Roof* (1971). Those were definitely exciting days for the young, growing filmmakers of the future. It gave me an understanding of the kind of freedom one needs, the kind of excitement you have to have to create exciting movies.

JAG: It was guerilla filmmaking.

MG: That's right. That's a good name for it.

(1986)

JAG: *The Delta Force* was quite successful in the international market.

MG: Yes, and there will be a sequel with Chuck Norris, *The Delta Force II: Operation Crackdown,* directed by Chuck's brother Aaron, who just did *Missing in Action III: Braddock* (1988) for us.

JAG: *Hanna's War* has been a long-time dream of yours.

MG: For twenty-three years. It's a true story based on Hanna Senesh's life. During World War Two, she was trained as a commando to parachute into Nazi-occupied territories and help create a partisan resistance to Hitler. In a world of hatred, Hanna was defiant, a determined and tenacious spirit. Her youth and her innocence impelled her to risk her twenty-four-year-old life for her fellow Jews. The name of Hanna Senesh should be as well known to the world as Anne Frank's. I acquired the rights to her story from the family, her mother and brother, who live in Israel. I acquired the rights for the first time twenty-three years ago. It's a very expensive film and I couldn't put it together, so I lost the rights. I wanted to do *Hanna's War* because it represents my heritage as a Jew. Hanna would not stand by as the Jews were perishing in Hitler's death camps. *Hanna's War* is my way of showing the world what these innocent heroes went through on this unbelievable mission. It's not just a great war story. It's a story of the human spirit, and I always felt her story was connected to my life and my heritage. Three years ago, I re-acquired the rights, and also to three books about Hanna. I wrote the last seventeen drafts of the script myself because I knew exactly what I wanted in this film. I shot it in Hungary and Isarel, spending a year and a half in production the second half of 1987. We'll open it at the 1988 Cannes Film Festival, and it's going to be Cannon's most important film for the coming year. I'm very proud of *Hanna's War*. It's a culmination of all my years of experience making movies, both as a director and a producer.

JAG: How do you balance running Cannon with directing films?

MG: I don't have any other occupation or hobby. I do this twenty-four hours a day. I have a very good partner, Yoram Globus. We're in communication on a daily basis wherever I am. I was in Budapest and Israel for four months shooting *Hanna's War* and I talked to Yoram every day on the phone. He ran the life of the company. I'm not alone here. I'm involved in many other projects with writers and directors, and all my life I've been working like that. I'm a work machine. I'm a workaholic!

(1988)

Stuart Gordon

Re-Animator (1985), *From Beyond* (1986), *Dolls* (1987)—the films of Stuart Gordon are marked by his imaginative direction and macabre sense of humor, along with stunning special effects and consistently fine acting. The Chicago–born filmmaker has brought an impressive background to his horror and fantasy product, having founded Chicago's acclaimed Organic Theatre Company in September, 1969. Under Gordon's direction, Organic Theatre developed and debuted such plays as *Bleacher Bums*, which became the longest running show in Los Angeles theatre history; *E/R Emergency Room*, later the basis for a CBS-TV series; and David Mamet's *Sexual Perversity in Chicago*, which was adapted into the feature film *About Last Night* (1986).

Gordon's first feature film, *Re-Animator*, based on a short story by H. P. Lovecraft, has already become a horror classic. A jury of leading French film critics named *Re-Animator* the best science fiction, horror, or fantasy film of the 1985 Cannes Film Festival and Market, and it was invited to the London Film Festival, which has rarely screened such grisly fare. Gordon followed with another Lovecraft adaptation, *From Beyond*, a horrific fairy tale, *Dolls*; and a large-scale sci-fi epic, *Robojox* (1988).

My interview with Stuart Gordon took place in New York in August, 1986. He had already completed *From Beyond* and *Dolls*, and was in the early planning stages of *Robojox*.

FILMOGRAPHY

Re-Animator (1985, Empire). HV: Vestron.
From Beyond (1986, Empire). HV: Vestron.
Dolls (1987, Empire). HV: Vestron.
Robojox (1989, Empire). HV: Vestron.

Stuart Gordon (courtesy of Empire Pictures).

GORDON INTERVIEW

JOHN A. GALLAGHER: How did your background with the Organic Theatre help your film work?

STUART GORDON: We borrowed very heavily from movies in the kinds of plays we did. A lot of times the Organic reviews would say, "This is a movie being done live on stage." We used movie effects on stage and people weren't used to seeing that happen. So I guess I've been making movies for years. I just haven't been putting them on film. I do feel that the technical side of moviemaking is the easiest thing to pick up, and I'm lucky in the background I had at Organic because I think the hardest thing is the script and working with actors. In theatre, you realize pretty quickly that the whole show is the acting. The actor has a tremendous amount of power. By flickering a light, a good actor can convince you a planet is blowing up on stage. If the acting is good, you'll go along with the simplest effect. I still think good acting is the best special effect.

JAG: Your films have a very effective blend of comedy and horror.

SG: I think that comedy works really well with horror. It's like salt and pepper. You need both spices. But I would never want the comedy to get in the way of the scares or vice versa. What I really like to do is build some tension and then let the audience release it with a laugh and then start up again.

JAG: The audience seems to care about the characters in your movies.

SG: I think it's crucial to a horror movie, or *any* movie, that you like the people. You care about them and when something bad happens to them it upsets you. So many horror movies don't give a shit about anybody and then you're just watching the technical side and the effects. I think the effects are just there to aid the acting and if the audience is with the characters you don't have to spend hundreds of thousands to do an effect. The acting and the script are the key ingredients. If you've got those together, everything else will be forgiven.

JAG: What movies influenced you?

SG: Definitely *Psycho* (1960). I still think that's the scariest movie ever made. One of my all-time favorite movies is *The Bride of Frankenstein* (1935). If we do a sequel to *Re-Animator*, we'll call it *Bride of Re-Animator*. I like the original *Alien* (1979) a lot. I wasn't crazy about *Aliens* (1986). I didn't think it was scary. For me, what was so great about the initial film was you didn't know what it was you were up against and every time you saw it, it was something else. With the sequel, you know exactly what it was and all the mystery was gone. It just became *Rambo* (1985). It could have been Viet Cong or anything, just a shoot-em-up. If I were going to do the sequel to *Alien*, I would have to have a new alien in it. I think *Aliens* fell into a trap that happens with a lot of sequels. The marketing philosophy is just give 'em more of the same. So instead of one alien, it's a hundred aliens. Just make it bigger and do everything the same. The one thing I liked about the movie was the forklift, because it was new. My feeling is when you start to do sequels and remakes of good movies, you're already falling into a no-win situation. What I would want from a sequel would be a similar feeling. Since I thought *Alien* was such a scary movie, I would hope the sequel would be scarier. I felt that way about *Return of the Jedi* (1983), that it was basically *Star Wars* (1977) done over with more money.

JAG: How did *Re-Animator* come to be made with Empire?

SG: It was an arrangement between Empire and the producer of the film, Brian Yuzna. In exchange for post-production facilities, Empire would have the right to distribute the film. Initially, Empire was taking a back seat, and then as we started shooting it and they saw the dailies, they got more involved. They made some suggestions and gave us more than was in the original bargain. They ended up letting John Buechler work on the effects, although both Tony Doublin and John Naulin did a great job. It was one of those projects where it was the more the merrier. They also suggested we get Mac Ahlberg as the Director of Photography, and that turned out to be a very good decision.

JAG: What was the budget and schedule on Re-Animator?

SG: *Re-Animator* cost about one million dollars and we shot it in Los Angeles in four weeks, a real fast shoot. With both *Re-Animator* and *From Beyond* we were able to rehearse before we started shooting. My background being theatre it was really essential to me to have time for the actors where that's all you're thinking about. Especially when you're dealing with effects, your concentration has to go to all the technical things and the actors are left alone. So the fact that the actors knew what they were doing before we started shooting made it all work.

JAG: Did you shoot *Re-Animator* on location or on a set?

SG: Most of it was done on a stage. I did a lot of research and visited several morgues taking pictures. The set is based on the brand new Cook County Morgue in Chicago. I had visited the old morgue, which had this creepy, decrepit look, and when I went back to get some pictures it had been torn down and they'd built a new one.

JAG: The Al Capone Memorial Morgue?

SG: Yeah, right! The guy that ran it wanted to do a whole exhibit of famous Chicago murders but he got overruled by the city council. He's quite a character. He originally told me that if I wanted to shoot *Re-Animator* in the real morgue, I could, and he would even allow me to use real corpses.

JAG: Can you imagine, under the hot lights?

SG: The old morgue smelled like a cat had died and after you left you had that smell with you for two weeks. The new morgue is very futuristic with a ventilation system that changes the air every thirty minutes. We ended up basing our set on the new morgue with its hi-tech look since we've seen the creepy old morgue in so many movies. In *Re-Animator* and *From Beyond* we had medical advisors who made sure our doctors and nurses were doing everything correctly and gave it a real sense of believability. My concern when you're doing a fantasy film is that there has to be some basis in reality. If you're gonna expect an audience to go off and believe something, you have to give them a real world first. If things get too crazy, they'll throw their hands up and say, "This is nuts!"

JAG: In *Re-Animator*, how did you get the re-agent to glow?

SG: The stuff really does glow. It's called Luminol and it's used in flares. It comes in tubes in a glass capsule. You break the glass and it glows. We could only find it in these plastic tubes so we had to break open hundreds to get enough for the movie. We did a test with it and found it really photographed well. It looks like an optical effect in the movie but it was really done live. In *Re-Animator*, that's the only leap of faith that you're asking the audience to make, which is to believe this stuff can bring the dead back to life. Everything else is as believable and real as we could make it.

JAG: How did you get the sound of the crazed cat?

SG: They took an actual cat's screech and put it through these machines, lowered the pitch, and raised the sound to give it an unearthly quality.

JAG: The way you make the dead walk in *Re-Animator* is jerky and awkward, as though if a dead person actually got up, that's the way they'd walk.

SG: Again, it was talking to doctors. One of the things I really appreciate about Lovecraft is that he really did his homework when he wrote these stories. He wasn't just some horror writer coming up with these weird ideas and writing them the next morning. In the story, "Herbert West, Re-Animator," he explains what kinds of chemicals would be used in the serum. In doing research I found there is work really being done that is identical to what West is trying to do in *Re-Animator*. The doctors' point-of-view is that this is not horrible but life-extending. They used to believe that when your heart stopped you were dead, and now they've got adrenalin and electro-shock and all sorts of ways to bring the heart back after it's stopped. Why not be able to do the same thing with the brain? In the movie they talk a lot about the six-minute limit and brain death. That is something that people are trying to break now. There's a lot of work being done with people who fall into icy water and are literally clinically dead for half an hour, then get revived and there is no brain damage. The same thing with *From Beyond*. All this stuff about the pineal gland that Lovecraft had in his original story is all turning out to be true. I talked to some people doing pineal research, which is now a very hot topic. Lovecraft came upon this in the Twenties and it's taken over fifty years for the scientists to catch up with him. A lot of the ideas we threw into the script turned out to be correct. The idea that the pineal gland might be the key to curing mental disorders like schizophrenia is something we put in the movie and found that yes, this research is being done. Lovecraft really was a science fiction writer, more than a horror writer. Everything has a scientific basis in his work. One of the big questions about Lovecraft was he did not believe in the supernatural, but he did believe in science. There's a great Arthur C. Clarke quote—"Magic is unexplained technology"—and that's where I think Lovecraft is working.

JAG: How did you determine the visual look of *From Beyond*?

SG: The biggest problem was how we should create this other world, the beyond. Lovecraft gives you a few hints in the story with violet and purples, but what Mac Ahlberg ended up doing on the photography was almost like *The Wizard of Oz* (1939). The scenes that take place in the real world are almost black and white, but when we go into the beyond, there are suddenly these intense colors.

JAG: What was the budget on *From Beyond*?

SG: About two and one half million, because we shot it in Italy. The value there was such that if we shot the picture in the United States it would have cost fifteen million. The technical expertise there is tremendous. Our art director, Giovanni Natalucci, had just finished doing *Once Upon a Time in America* (1984) and *Ladyhawke* (1985). The crew had worked with Sergio Leone and Federico Fellini. It's a great value there for a fraction of what it would cost here.

JAG: *Re-Animator* was released unrated, but I know you really had to battle with the Motion Picture Producers Association to get an "R" rating on *From Beyond*.

SG: There are no rules. It's unlike the old Hays Office where you used to know exactly what was allowed and what wasn't. If you had a woman's garter belt showing, you knew you were in trouble. With the MPAA, they're the first to tell you that they are not censors. They are basically there to let an audience know what to expect when they buy a ticket. They have these ratings, but it's all based on how these six people feel about the film they're watching and what they call the "cumulative effect." There are certain areas of concern: sex, violence, drugs, foul language. When they first saw *From Beyond* they said, "You have ten times too much of everything, and there's no way we're ever gonna give you an 'R.' " At first I was depressed because it was as if they were saying the whole concept of this movie was unrateable, that it was too disquieting to be rated. I argued that this is the way horror movies are supposed to be, that audiences will feel cheated if they're not scared to death. I ended up making very small trims, not removing any sequences. This actually ended up making the movie stronger. In a way, it left more to the imagination and gave you just enough of the idea of what was going on, and to see enough to get your mind spinning so the audience didn't have enough time to study an effect and figure out how it was done, or look for seams on the prosthetics. After resubmitting time and again to the MPAA, I think they got used to the shocks. Our last message was to cut one frame from a scene, so we really got down to fighting over frames. There's an R-rated version of *Re-Animator* that was done without my involvement that is like an episode of *Masterpiece Theatre*. All it needs is Alistair Cooke to introduce it. They've cut out anything they thought would be objectionable to anyone and put back in all the expositional scenes I'd cut because they really weren't necessary to tell the story. It's very talky, very little action.

JAG: Do you storyboard?

SG: Definitely. My background before I started working in theatre was commercial art. I had been an apprentice in a commercial art studio for six months and hated it. I stopped drawing. Working in movies gave me a good opportunity to draw and I used that drawing ability to do the storyboards for effects sequences. I only do boards for the effects scenes though. I'll storyboard the way I'd like to see it done in the best of all possible worlds. Then I'll show it to the effects guys and they'll suggest any changes to make it easier or even possible, but usually I'll shoot pretty much what I draw.

JAG: How is your working relationship with Dennis Paoli, the co-writer of *Re-Animator* and *From Beyond*?

SG: We go all the way back to high school. We had a comedy group together and we used to write sketches and perform them. It was a summer job. Dennis and I are real simpatico. I think he has a real feel for character and comedy, as well as understanding how horror movies work.

JAG: How did you like shooting *From Beyond*, *Dolls*, and *Robojox* at Empire Studios in Rome?

SG: Great. Dino DeLaurentiis originally built this enormous soundstage on the outskirts of Rome called Dinocitta. John Huston did *The Bible* (1966) there, and movies like *Barbarella* (1968), *Cleopatra* (1963), *Romeo and Juliet* (1968), and *The Taming of the Shrew* (1968) were shot there. It's fun to take a little tour because they still have remnants, like a piece of Barbarella's spaceship. The soundstages are bigger than anything at Cinecitta. In fact, I haven't seen anything in Los Angeles bigger than these stages. When Dino left Italy they were taken over by the government for non-payment of taxes, and were seldom used until Empire bought them. *From Beyond* and *Dolls* were the first pictures made there under the Empire aegis. The house in *From Beyond* was built next to this ancient temple Dino built for *Red Sonja* (1985). Empire left the *From Beyond* set standing, so they have the Old Dark House set, and they'll do the same with *Robojox* so they'll have a standing futuristic set. Charlie Band announced he wants to do a Universal Studios-style tour. The Italian press call it "Horror-land," but we dubbed it "Bandland."

JAG: How involved is Charles Band in your Empire films?

SG: Very involved. He chose the story *From Beyond* and always wanted to be kept abreast of all the various changes in the script. He visited the set a lot. He keeps his hand on things but never interferes. He's a very positive force. He's quite a good director. My only regret is that he hasn't directed more pictures. His picture *Trancers* (1985) was terrific. His father, Albert, was on the set of *From Beyond* as a producer and his experience was really invaluable. He's worked with John Huston on films like *The Red Badge of Courage* (1951), and he's directed some great films himself, *I Bury the Living* (1958) and *Face of Fire* (1959). He's done a lot of work in Italy so he knew the best way to utilize the crew's talents. Empire is very much a family. It's not like these big studios where you have to go through committees before you reach the top. You can just go and sit down with Charlie Band and he'll either like something or he won't, and if he likes it, the next thing you know you're making the movie. One thing he always says is, "There's no such thing as a development deal at Empire. There's no time for it." You either make the movie or you don't, and usually it has to be ready in two weeks! Now we're getting bigger budgets and longer schedules. *Robojox* is seven million, the biggest budget Empire's ever had.

JAG: What are the plans for *Bride of Re-Animator*?

SG: We've come up with three or four different ideas for plots. Trying to outdo the first movie is the name of the game. I think eventually there will be one. We just have to decide what the story is we're going to tell, although with the title *Bride of Re-Animator* we have to focus on Meg Halsey, Barbara Crampton's character.

JAG: How would you describe *Dolls*?

SG: It's a horror movie fairy tale. I viewed it as a version of "Hansel and Gretel," which is a very frightening story about abandoning children, although the storyline is more akin to *The Old Dark House* (1932). It's about some evil toymakers who turn people into dolls, and then send these dolls out to murder, so you have an army of homicidal dolls running around this house. The effects for *Dolls* are primarily stop motion animation by Dave Allen, who did *Young Sherlock Holmes* (1985).

JAG: What kind of research did you do for *Dolls*?

SG: I had been reading a lot of Bruno Bettelheim, particularly his book *The Uses of Enchantment*, which discusses the importance of fairy tales. He really debates these people who say fairy tales are too violent. His attitude is that it's a scary world out there, and fairy tales are a way children are prepared for that world. We're taught in fairy tales that yes, there are monsters and horrible things that can happen to you, but if you are brave, strong, and good and don't give up, you can succeed. He feels those lessons are important and to minimize it takes the whole punch and point out of fairy tales. The idea of doing a movie that rather than toning down those elements really plays them to the limit was something I found very interesting. When I came upon Ed Naha's treatment at Empire, I got turned on by the whole thing.

JAG: *Robojox* is your largest undertaking to date.

SG: It's about this futuristic society where nations settle their differences with gigantic robots battling it out, piloted by these robot jockeys representing their entire country. They sit in the head of the robot and are a combination of warrior and astronaut, the best of the best. Their nation's fate rests on their shoulders. These battles take the place of football games as well as warfare. It's like the Super Bowl every time these guys come out. I think it's an interesting metaphor. It's set in a post-nuclear era, although it's not *Mad Max* (1979). It's one hundred years after nuclear war. The world has rebuilt itself to some degree, but things are still pretty shaky. People have decided they're never going to allow another war, so now international disputes are settled in these battles.

JAG: What was the inspiration for *Robojox*?

SG: The idea occurred to me from looking at the illustrations on the boxes of those Japanese robot toys, with the maintenance crews scrambling over these giant robots. It's a ready-made fantasy that no one has really tapped into yet. It's just waiting for a chance to be up there on the screen, not in the form of an animated cartoon, but live action where the sense of size could really be created. Kids are already enjoying the robot toys and playing on their own, but now we'll be able to use the magic of moviemaking to create the illusion of these metal giants. It's a great fantasy for a kid to have that kind of power and size. Initially Empire was skeptical about the kind of budget we'd need, but eventually they got intrigued by the idea. The effects are similar to *Dolls*, only in reverse. With *Dolls*, Dave Allen creates the illusion of things being small, and in *Robojox* he's doing things huge, but it's basically the same set of stop motion tricks that are being used. There are some great battle scenes, as well as what I feel is missing from a lot of science fiction films, the human story. I don't want the people in the film to be like the robots. There has to be some real flesh and blood emotions that the audience can relate to. The idea is to let the audience drive the robots and let them play with these giant toys. It has to measure up to pictures like *The Empire Strikes Back* (1980), a movie that will appeal to children, but that parents can enjoy as well, a real family experience.

JAG: You're planning another Lovecraft picture.

SG: Yeah, *Lurking Fear*, a Lovecraft story set in the Twenties in upstate New York's Catskill Mountains. It's about a family that has degenerated into ape-like cannibal creatures through in-breeding. They've burrowed these tunnels underneath the mountains so they have secret passageways.

Whenever there's a thunderstorm, which is fairly common in this region, it drives them absolutely berserk and they go running around tearing people apart and dragging them into the tunnels. The thing I find most interesting about it is that the hero of the story is H. P. Lovecraft himself, who'll probably be played by Jeffrey Combs. We're talking about Barbara Crampton as a fast-talking Twenties reporter, like Glenda Farrell or Joan Blondell.

JAG: Crampton and Combs also starred for you in *Re-Animator* and *From Beyond*.

SG: My background being theatre, I'm used to working with a company of actors, and I really like that approach for film, especially doing movies as crazy as the Lovecraft series. You don't want to spend all your time trying to explain to somebody why something is important or why they should do something that seems ludicrous. Barbara and Jeffrey know that if they work with me I'll ask them to do all sorts of odd things. I really like the idea of doing a series of Lovecraft movies that have an ensemble company in them, sort of like the old Roger Corman Poe movies with Vincent Price. Jeffrey Combs is my Vincent Price!

JAG: What is *Berserker*?

SG: We just found out we're going to have to change the title. There's another movie called *Berserker* coming out. This guy called up and said, "Excuse me, we're calling our movie *Berserker*." I said, "OK, we'll call ours *The Real Berserker*." We originally wrote it for Arnold Schwarzenegger. He came and saw *Re-Animator* and really liked it. Afterwards we were talking and he said, "Write me a horror film. I'd love to make one with you." Dennis Paoli and I came up with this idea about an athlete who's been taking steroids and finds out what the side effects are. He has a choice—he can stop taking them and die, or he can be a berserker. So he becomes a monstrosity, completely out of control. We sent it to Arnold and his manager sent us a message saying that Arnold doesn't want to play a monster, he only wants to play heroes. What I tried to get across was this guy *is* the hero, someone the audience really sympathizes with being put in this terrible situation. The idea was to let Arnold really show some new sides of his acting ability. To have Arnold Schwarzenegger be in jeopardy for a change, to have him betrayed by his own body, would really be interesting. I think the problem with a lot of his movies is that you're never worried about him. You're just waiting for him to tear the other person to pieces.

JAG: What appeals to you about working in genre pictures?

SG: The thing that was great about the Organic Theatre was that we did all kinds of plays. I'd like the same thing to be true about my movies. One of the great things about genre movies is that as long as you follow the rules of the genre you can do anything you want and say anything you want. There's a tremendous amount of freedom. I got into a conversation with a friend that the horror films are really the subconscious of the movies. Even in the Fifties when things were very repressive in mainstream movies, the horror films were dealing with the fears and concerns that people were afraid to talk about, films like *Invasion of the Body Snatchers* (1956) and *The Thing* (1951). I find it very liberating to work on horror films, especially at Empire where I've never been censored by anyone. In fact, I'm encouraged. They say, "This isn't weird enough!"

(1986)

Ulu Grosbard

One of America's top theatre directors, Ulu Grosbard has also made several outstanding motion pictures featuring superior acting talent in some of their finest roles—Patricia Neal and Martin Sheen in *The Subject Was Roses* (1968); Dustin Hoffman in *Straight Time* (1977); and Robert DeNiro and Robert Duvall in *True Confessions* (1981). Born in Antwerp, Belgium, on January 9, 1929, Grosbard came to America with his family as a child to escape Hitler's conquering troops. He attended the University of Chicago and the Yale Drama School, and gained early film training as an assistant director on Elia Kazan's *Splendor in the Grass* (1961). He continued to work as an assistant director on Robert Wise's *West Side Story* (1961), Robert Rossen's *The Hustler* (1961), Arthur Penn's *The Miracle Worker* (1962), and as a unit manager on Sidney Lumet's *The Pawnbroker* (1965).

Grosbard made his directorial mark on the stage with his productions of Arthur Miller's *The Price* and *A View from the Bridge*, and Frank Gilroy's *The Subject Was Roses*. When *The Subject Was Roses* was transferred to the screen, Grosbard won critical accolades for his direction. He has continued to balance stage plays like David Mamet's *American Buffalo* and Woody Allen's *The Floating Light Bulb* with such films as *Straight Time*, *True Confessions*, and *Falling in Love* (1985).

The following interview is based on sessions with the director in his Broadway office in 1981 and 1987.

FILMOGRAPHY

The Subject Was Roses (1968, MGM). HV: MGM-UA.
Who is Harry Kellerman and Why Is He Saying Those Terrible Things About Me? (1971, National General).
Straight Time (1977, Warner Bros.). HV: Warners.

Ulu Grosbard (courtesy of Mr. Grosbard).

True Confessions (1981, United Artists). HV: MGM–UA.
Falling in Love (1985, Paramount). HV: Paramount.

GROSBARD INTERVIEW

JOHN A. GALLAGHER: Your films all deal with characters in crisis and people under stress. How conscious an effort has that been?

ULU GROSBARD: I've always been fascinated by watching role reversals, beginning during the war watching daily life suddenly being infringed upon by stressful situations, and watching how people behave under that condition. The experiences of those times left a permanent impression on me and had a very decisive influence on me as a person. Oddly enough, I've never really done anything directly related to that time. It's a fascination I've retained but I'm not consciously aware of that. I don't look for that specifically in my work.

JAG: Your pictures also present heavily emotional situations—the family in *The Subject Was Roses*, the fraternal conflict in *True Confessions*, the married people in *Falling in Love*—yet the performances are always very restrained. How do you achieve that?

UG: It very much has to do with working with good actors and going for the truth in behavior, the way people act in real life, recognizable behavior, not imitating a histrionic display of emotion which I think is more true of actors that don't know any better than it is of real people. I think if you watch the way people behave in life in situations of real accidents under real stress, there is frequently restraint. Granted, there are times people scream out or go berserk, but I think when people are experiencing real emotion they try to control those emotions. Traditionally when you look at the same event in a theatre, it's being pumped up with emotion. There's only a tradition of theatricality on stage and on film that leads to screaming and carrying on at the expense of what *should* be going on. I think it's automatically true of good actors that they know that.

JAG: What do you expect from a film producer?

UG: I've had a number of good experiences. On *True Confessions*, Bob Chartoff and Irwin Winkler were at United Artists dealing with the studio. They were running interference, not that there was much interference from the studio, but they provided me with a situation where I could concentrate all my energies on getting the production done properly. I was a production manager myself, so once I have a good production manager, in this case Jim Brubaker, between the two of us the day-by-day production is something that I don't need much help with. What's very helpful is a producer that has enough clout to get you access to the people you need, take care of the studio so there's no politics involved, and have some insight with their comments and do it not out of ego, but because they have a genuine opinion. If they're intelligent people, you can benefit from it. There's a value to the producer knowing when to be of help and when to leave you alone. Chartoff and Winkler were smart. They were astute. They knew what to do and what not to do. They knew when to do it and when not to do it. I have run into a situation where a producer's ego runs rampant, and it's at the expense of the project. I walked away four weeks from the shooting because I didn't want to deal with the producer. What was happening was destructive. I went to the studio and said, "Hey, it's not going to work."

JAG: You worked as an assistant director and production manager on some important films in New York during the early Sixties—*West Side Story*, *The Hustler*, *Splendor in the Grass*, *The Miracle Worker*, *The Pawnbroker*.

UG: I didn't work that much with Robert Wise on *West Side Story* because I only did a couple of weeks on the New York location as a third assistant director. I spent a good deal of time with Elia Kazan on *Splendor*, Arthur Penn on *Miracle Worker*, and Bob Rossen on *The Hustler*. Usually the second and third assistant gets hired by the first assistant director. It's his prerogative to hire his own assistants. There's a lot of paperwork involved in those jobs, and you make sure the actors are there on time. I was working with Charlie Maguire and Don Kranze on *Splendor*, and Larry Sturhahn on *Miracle Worker*. Charlie later was in charge of production at Paramount for a long time. I hadn't seen him for years until I directed *Falling in Love* for Paramount. I'm very fond of him. He's a very capable guy. Now he's with George Lucas in San Francisco.

JAG: What was your impression of Robert Rossen on *The Hustler*?

UG: Rossen knew what he was doing. He was very good with the actors and it was evident on a day-to-day basis.

JAG: How about *The Miracle Worker*?

UG: Patty Duke was incredibly talented. Those rehearsals were breathtaking. Both she and Anne Bancroft were extraordinary. Arthur did a lot of takes of some of those key scenes. Patty had such an amazing instinct for what she was doing.

JAG: You were the production manager on Sidney Lumet's *The Pawnbroker*.

UG: I spent five or six weeks setting up the locations in Harlem. With Lumet, the thing you learn is preparation. He's just a wiz. He's intimidating. It's like he had a computer before computers existed! He's one of those guys who on the twenty-sixth day of shooting could remember the third set-up on the third day of shooting!

JAG: What did you learn from Elia Kazan on *Splendor in the Grass*?

UG: How to run a relaxed set, how to use your time working with the actors while things are being set up, how to improve your staging. His ability to create an atmosphere on the set was something that stood out for me. There's enough pressure no matter what you do, and the ability to relax oneself so the actors can be relaxed is a key thing a director should be able to do.

JAG: How do you create that atmosphere on the set?

UG: You're being pulled in a million directions with a thousand questions about yesterday, today, tomorrow. You have to try to do the same thing behind the camera that the actors are doing in front of it. If you've worked with the actors before it helps set an atmosphere of trust. Part of it is who you are to begin with. If you're a very tense person it'll be much harder for you to do so. The key is to relax yourself so you can listen, hear, and respond. You're on the spot, yet you have to find a way to be open to what's going on. In a funny way, because it is so serious, you have to make light of it. You have to create the illusion that you can take time when you know time is very precious. Sometimes you have time, sometimes you don't. You may be under pressure to get out of a set. You don't have what you want, the actor knows he doesn't have what he wants. What you can't do is begin to rush or create the sense of rush. The clock will tick in its own objective way. It's what happens psychologically in the same five minutes. In the same five minutes, you can act as if you have a half hour or you can act like you have thirty seconds. All you accomplish if you rush is getting everybody tense. Less gets done than if you just do what you have to do and not worry about whether it's a half hour or a minute.

JAG: How was your experience working with Arthur Miller on the theatre productions of *A View from the Bridge* and *The Price*?

UG: I didn't work with Arthur that much on *View*. He came to see the production, but on *The Price* I worked with him closely for about eight months. I enjoyed working with him. He's very open and receptive. He was very undoctrinaire, rewrote, cut out. He was very easy to work with, contrary to what one might assume. If something made sense to him he would listen and just do it. Unlike some of his other plays, I think he was discovering *The Price* as he went along. He knew that he had the curtain but he didn't know how he was going to get there. He didn't know what was going to happen along the way. He hadn't laid out the writing of the plot and it was a process of true discovery for him.

JAG: Your first feature film was the screen version of your Broadway success *The Subject Was Roses*, written by Frank Gilroy and produced by Edgar Lansbury. How did you adjust to the transition?

UG: Since I worked on sets, I had a great knowledge of production, and the more you know about production, the more you can anticipate and not be at the mercy of circumstances. I had also been a director in the theatre, working with actors. As far as the camera, I was getting, and still get, help from the cinematographer, or the assistant director sometimes, too. It was still very hard. I've since overly compensated by not wanting to do plays into films. If I want to do a play I'll do it on stage. There's an element of frustration in that the better the play, the more it fights film, whereas I consider film as having a uniqueness as a medium. What you can do is direct it intelligently so you're not losing the points that you made on stage, so the play on film has an equivalent impact. It'll never have the same impact because you're missing the directness, tension, and interplay you get from live actor to audience. It's frustrating in a sense because the structure of each scene in a play is very different from the structure of a screenplay. Screenplays are built differently. They're sequences. It's not beginning, middle, and end of each scene with entrances and exits like you have on stage. The organic structure is much different.

JAG: Martin Sheen was in the original play as well as the film. How did you find him?

UG: He was one of the guys who came in to read. He improvised very well. I went to see him in some Broadway farce. I hadn't cared for the direction of the play and the whole thing looked rather dismal to me, but he had such a life when he improvised and read that he was by far our best choice. I was very happy with him. He and Jack Albertson developed a wonderful relationship as father and son that they retained throughout the run of the play.

JAG: Patricia Neal, who played the mother in the film, was coming off a long illness when you cast her.

UG: It was a big gamble Gilroy, Lansbury, and I took. We went to see her in London. She was suffering from a form of aphasia and had not worked in a long time. Aphasia is not like you forget something, but suddenly the word isn't there. But she was extraordinary. She was like a great race horse. You put her on the track and she just went for it. She was remarkable. I mean, the whole picture was shot in forty days here in New York.

JAG: Your next film, *Who is Harry Kellerman and Why Is He Saying Those Terrible Things About Me?* was unsuccessful.

UG: It's a hard call. I thought it was very special in the sense I thought there were some wonderful things in it. It's difficult when you have the main character of a very successful person with spiritual and psychic problems and you're trying to reach an audience. They have enough problems trying to make a living and pay the bills! There's a distancing effect involved. Another problem was that we had a schizophrenic character. It was based on a brilliant short story by Herb Gardner, and Herb did the adaptation.

JAG: What was the genesis of *Straight Time*?

UG: It's a complicated history. Dustin Hoffman was originally going to get Hal Ashby, then that didn't work out and he was going to direct it himself. When he called me, he had been doing the pre-production with the idea of directing it himself. He had done some casting, picked a number of the locations, and went up to San Quentin for a couple of days in pre-production and shot twenty thousand feet of film. I think that was the turning point when he decided it was more than he wanted to handle. The problem was, he had gone through five scripts. When I came on he had the first sixty pages of a script by Michael Mann written under Dusty's direction. I thought it was just the story of a junkie and there was no point of view. It was lost in the scenes, with no overview. There was no arc to the story. I didn't think there was a movie to be made. In those days when I was trying to make a decision whether or not to jump into it, there was another big problem in that they only had four million dollars, Dusty had guaranteed the budget with his own money, and they had already spent more than a third of it.

JAG: How did you get from that tenuous stage to an acceptable script?

UG: I went back in reverse order through all the scripts until I got back to the first draft that had been written by Alvin Sargent. It was a 175-page script, but in it I suddenly saw a story that I wanted to tell. Although it was obviously unwieldy, overwritten and much too close to the novel, I called Alvin and we sat down and tried to cut it down. He was already working on *Ordinary People* (1980), under pressure, and way behind on that, but at least we got it cut down to 120 pages. But then of course there were big gaps. There were characters cut out, there were jumps. When I had come out there, a full shooting crew was sitting around on payroll and nothing was being shot, so I took two weeks to cast the rest of the picture and rework the script. I just said, "We may as well start shooting. It's gonna cost as much as not shooting." It was an insane situation. As we went along, we had to fill gaps in the script and change things, and when you change "a," you have to change "b." Literally what we would do was improvise the next day's scenes at night, using Alvin's script as a reference, and as we made changes try and find the logic of it. The point of a scene hadn't been decided upon, but very often it was similar to what had been written. You had to keep shifting because there were other points being made. Then I would edit in and rehearse it in the morning and we'd shoot. I'd also be scouting locations at night and on weekends, working on the script. It was an incredible experience.

JAG: Is Dustin Hoffman as much of a perfectionist as he's portrayed in the press?

UG: There's a difficult line to draw between a perfectionist and a compulsive repeater. Perfectionism implies that you know what you want at the other end and are satisfied when you get there. At times I think he is a perfectionist, and at times he compulsively wants to repeat things without knowing whether he's gotten there or not, so I think it's not always perfectionism.

JAG: I think he gives one of his best performances in *Straight Time*.

UG: I think so, I must say. I thought he was wonderful. It was very hard and he contributed enormously to the script. Once he got hold of that character a couple of weeks into the shooting, he had great instincts about it.

JAG: What happened with the film ultimately?

UG: It's a sad story, and part of it was Dusty's responsibility. Warners was very high on the picture when they saw it cut. Dusty and I had a big falling out toward the last couple of weeks of the picture. Technically and legally, he had the right to final cut. I had agreed to it. On *Harry Kellerman*, Herb Gardner and I had had the cut. I just didn't want to make an issue out of it because he was in such bad shape when I came on the picture. He then went to do *Agatha* (1979), and when he took the part it was supposed to be a four-week role. It turned into a twelve-week part, so he wanted Warners to postpone the picture so he could do some improvements on *Straight Time*. Warners wouldn't do it, so he started to bad mouth the picture and in effect, sued Warners, the distributor, and First Artists, the producers, on *Straight Time* and *Agatha*, because he got into a big fight with them on *Agatha* too. Two weeks before *Straight Time* opened he publicly announced he was suing them for preventing him to exercise his final cut on the picture. So they lost heart in *Straight Time*, in a sense, because they were embroiled in a big mess with him. Both John Calley and Frank Wells were very high on *Straight Time*. I'll never forget when they first saw the film. They had heard about the problems and this and that, and they had sort of written it off, and they were stunned. They changed gears a few weeks before the picture opened, when the suit came out, and threw it to the wolves. In spite of that, it got some wonderful reviews.

JAG: How did you get involved in *True Confessions*?

UG: I had originally read the book and liked it a lot. I heard that Bob Chartoff and Irwin Winkler had acquired the rights to the book, and about a year later happened to notice they had a screenplay written by John Gregory Dunne and Joan Didion. I was looking around for a project, and I hadn't found anything I really wanted to do, and the book came back to me. I remembered how much I liked the whole feel of it, the story, and mainly the theme. I called my agent, and as it happened, he had just gotten a copy of the screenplay from the producers. I read it and had some reservations but I thought basically it was something I would be interested in. I set up a meeting with the producers first and I told them what I felt, where I felt the work needed to be done. Oddly enough, they had thrown out a lot of stuff from the book that I thought was important to the story and I thought they would say, "Well, who are you? Who needs your advice?" But that seemed to interest him. They set up a meeting with John and Joan and we went through the screenplay again. After it was over, they said they were interested and that's how I got the job. We actually did three other drafts before we went into pre-production, then in the course of shooting we worked every week, practically every Sunday. I must say, it was a terrific collaboration.

JAG: The film is framed by a sequence that shows us the brothers' poignant reunion as old men.

UG: The first draft did not have the bracket. I felt it was vital to the body of the story from a frame of reference, to see the reconciliation of the brothers, and where it is Des ends up. Without the bracket you have no perspective on the story. It's there in the book, actually. It's a tricky thing. I felt it was important not to just pick up where you left off, because you've got practically 110 minutes in between. You'll find one thing though—stylistically you can do anything as long as it's emotionally correct, as long as it's honest.

JAG: How did the casting of Robert DeNiro and Robert Duvall as the brothers come about?

UG: Robert Duvall was my first choice for the part of Tom. At first he had doubts, but then he said yes. I felt I couldn't consider DeNiro because he was doing *Raging Bull* (1980) and I knew I wasn't going to be able to get him to read the screenplay. The demands were so specific for the part of Des. The actor had to be somewhat younger than Duvall, he had to be somebody who could convincingly play a priest, he had to have a street background, and he had to be a first-rate actor. Aside from DeNiro, the other guy that came to my mind was Gene Hackman. I've always wanted to do something with him. He's an old friend and a wonderful actor. He turned it down, and it was open season. There's no one I seriously considered that I was happy with. I kept trying to go after DeNiro, and *finally* he did read it. This was in the period when he was gaining weight for *Raging Bull*. We had met a few times over the years. He liked the idea of Duvall, he liked the idea of the part, and I think he knew my work. The chemistry of Duvall and DeNiro really worked out marvelously. They like each other and they respect each other's work.

JAG: DeNiro played Monsignor Desmond Spellacy with his usual precision.

UG: The foundation for DeNiro was the Mass under the title sequence. I got the church where we were going to shoot and I surrounded him with three actual priests. He learned the Mass and he got into it three times a week for about eight weeks before he had to come on the set. It's a brilliant performance. His choices are just wonderful. He had a particularly difficult job, because he's playing a priest who during the course of the story is really more of a businessman than a priest. Des is an operator. When DeNiro and I discussed wardrobe, the kind of shoes he would wear, the haircut, almost inevitably his instinct is unerringly right. He had a sense of it, even his walk, and the very subtle physical things he does. DeNiro is a very intelligent man, and a rather private person. He's very friendly, but private. It's an interesting combination. He is meticulous in many areas and I am too. He has a sense of truth about behavior that is a joy. He is the kind of actor, like Duvall, who really does work for the same thing I want to go after, so that one is genuinely on the same wave length. There was never any real disagreement. DeNiro's instincts are unerring most of the time in terms of going for a choice that is not necessarily a flashy choice, but the true choice. That made it very easy, and when you put good actors together to work with each other, it makes life happy and easy on the set because they feed each other.

JAG: You had worked with Duvall in the theatre on *View from the Bridge* and *American Buffalo*.

UG: I've worked with him over a period of twenty-five years, from the start of my career. With Duvall it's like shorthand. He's very intuitive. He'll use very few words, and it'll be right on the money. When he accepts a part it's because he's got a bead on it. You just give him leeway and encourage him to go with it and trust his instincts.

JAG: He has a beautiful moment in the film when he discovers Brenda's corpse at the city morgue.

UG: The only thing you can do with something that's so delicate is you cannot talk about it. You don't want to articulate with that personal moment. You just leave the actor alone. You just walk through the mechanics of it and you shoot it. Then if something is missing, then you talk. You're calling on something so personal. A good actor will find him own way to relate to it and a great actor will do what Duvall did in that closeup—that vulnerability in the eye, that moment of hesitation just before he lifts the sheet.

JAG: How did you stage the scene at the testimonial in which Duvall attacks Charles Durning?

UG: I find a lot of fights in film to be stagey. I can tell they're staged. I didn't rehearse the fight in *True Confessions*. I got four cameras, one on DeNiro, one on Duvall, one on Durning, one master shot. None of the extras knew, nobody was told, only the principals. I had picked an area where they were free to move, and Duvall just walked over to say his lines. Durning didn't know precisely how Duvall was going to handle it. He knew Duvall would be ripping the sash off and going for him, that's all. Durning would be going for Duvall after that, and DeNiro's job was to stop Duvall from going at him again. When the fight broke out, you had genuine reactions from the extras. They actually thought there was a real fight between the actors. It was absolutely electric, because the actors didn't know it was going to happen.

JAG: How did you approach the period setting of late Forties Los Angeles?

UG: It's very tempting to get carried away with period detail. It was a great concern to me. I didn't want to do period for period's sake. I wanted it to be a "contemporary" period film. Put the camera where the point is made, then get in and get out when you've made the point. Don't look to be fancy, because the focus is on the story. Period detail calls attention to itself, and I wanted it to be part of the texture of the frame. You want to subordinate the visual look and the camera to telling the story. *True Confessions* is a film of relationships, not action. It's the relationship between the two brothers, the Cain and Abel aspects of it, that kind of rivalry. Des has it all going for him and seems to be the winner. Tom is the black sheep. The irony of it is the undoing of one brother by the other and how it ends up really being an act of salvation.

JAG: After *True Confessions*, you returned to Broadway to direct Woody Allen's play *The Floating Light Bulb*.

UG: He really surprised me, not that I really thought about it. It's funny, I said "Yes," and then I thought to myself, "What am I getting into?" Woody is enormously respectful. He never talked to the actors. He was absolutely ruthless with his own stuff. If a line wasn't working I'd have to stop him from cutting it out. If he wasn't satisfied with something he'd walk into another room at the rehearsal hall and come back with four alternatives. He would say to me, "OK, pick the one you like best. If you're not satisfied with any, pick the one you like the best and I'll work off that." I mean, it was instant. I was really amazed. I've worked with some really good writers, but his quickness and his fertility were incredible. He's a very hard worker, very demanding of himself, and a joy to work with.

JAG: What was the genesis of *Falling in Love*?

UG: DeNiro called me and said, "Read this thing. What do you think?" We both were yes and no. He sent it to Meryl Streep because they had wanted to work together again. Finally we decided, "OK, let's go ahead." That was really a project that came out of the blue. I thought it would be interesting for DeNiro to do, and that's why I think he was attracted to it. He's the one who really got it going. It was not a very strong, specific character like the ones he had played in *The Godfather, Part II* (1974), *Taxi Driver* (1976), and *Raging Bull*. It was away from that, a straight romantic lead. I loved working with him and Meryl on it.

JAG: It must be a pleasure to work with artists of that caliber.

UG: Oh, boy! You bet. It spoils you.

JAG: What was your rehearsal arrangement on *Falling in Love*?

UG: We rehearsed while the screenwriter, Michael Cristofer, was rewriting scenes, so it was done a couple of days a week over a period of a few weeks. I would take a week or two with DeNiro, Meryl, Michael, and I getting together to read the script, discuss it, and do rewrites. Actual rehearsal we'd try and do over the weekends during the shooting, not very far in advance. I hear that Sidney Lumet rehearses a screenplay like a play. He takes two weeks and literally gets the actors on their feet and runs through the whole film, which is amazing to me. He lays it out with furniture and props. I would think it would be an interesting thing to do. It certainly works well for him and helps the actors a lot. I've never done that. We sit around the table and read the script, get input from the actors and writer, and get a sense of the relationship between the characters and a sense of the story, where things feel false, where things could be more concise.

JAG: How did you approach the scene of Meryl Streep's breakdown at her father's funeral?

UG: She asked for some preparation and then she did it. We only did it twice because she was drawing on something that was very personal. There was no question that I had what I needed in two takes.

JAG: You built the entire interior of the Metro North train on a soundstage at Empire Studios in Long Island City.

UG: We had to. We looked at real trains but there was no way of making it work. We wouldn't have been able to move around.

JAG: Peter Suschitzky, who also shot *The Rocky Horror Picture Show* (1975) and *The Empire Strikes Back* (1980), would seem an unlikely choice to photograph *Falling in Love*.

UG: I wanted to use New York realistically but with a soft romantic edge to it. A couple of the American cameramen who I considered, like Vilmos Zsigmond, were not available. It struck me that Peter would be somebody who could bring that quality and I thought he did. He has a strong sense of light.

JAG: How did the film do?

UG: Not well. It wasn't received well critically. I think they expected something much heavier from DeNiro and Meryl, a different kind of story. There was disappointment here, but it was very well received in Europe. But here it was very mixed reviews.

JAG: What is the value of a casting director to you?

UG: There are some casting directors that can be enormously helpful, especially when the director of the film is not that knowledgeable about actors, because the casting person can expose him to actors whose work he's not aware of. I happen to know a lot of actors, but even so when you come to a specific part that you're having trouble with, you need help. If you're looking for someone who's eighteen years old in a part, you have the world at your disposal. It's hard when you're looking for somebody in that age group. With people in their thirties and forties, you're pretty much dealing with known quantities, and it's just a matter of sorting out who's right and wrong. But when you're dealing with younger parts, a casting director can be of enormous value if they're good at what they do.

JAG: Do you generally pre-determine camera angles when you're preparing a script, or do you work that out when you're working with the actors?

UG: It varies depending on the shots. If it's a scene in an office like this, I will not pre-determine. I'll think it through and know there are certain things I don't want to do. I'll take care to arrange the set, arrange the furniture so I don't get boxed in and that will determine to some extent where the actors can or cannot go. But I'll wait until they rehearse the scene before I'll determine where I put the camera. On the other hand, there are action scenes where you want the camera to be in a very specific set-up to make the point of the scene. In a scene with actors, frequently an actor will position himself in a way that you never anticipated, and if you do it diagrammatically, you will come up with something far inferior than if you waited to work with the actors.

JAG: Throughout your directing career, you've been able to maintain a position as an individualistic director, rather than a hired hand.

UG: It has to do with the scarcity of material you find yourself responding to. It's hard to find good scripts that I have a personal response to. They're simply not easy to come by. Clearly, I'm not in a unique position. It's just tough to come by stuff that translates well to the screen, and is also meaningful to me. Look at the films that are made, and how few of them amount to anything. I don't think those films are made because people don't know the difference. I think they're made out of the need for actors, directors, producers, studios having to go to work, sustaining and keeping your craft alive, making a living, having a sense of purpose. You see it happen all the time, and you find yourself struggling with the problem of "How long do I stay out of work?" It's a problem for everybody. When you see a film, you often find yourself thinking, "How did this guy end up in this piece of material?" You know them, you know they're intelligent, but when you've been around long enough and read enough screenplays, it's simply that there's not that much good material to go around.

JAG: Does that apply to the stage as well as movies?

UG: Absolutely. Good plays are even harder to come by. By their very nature, plays are a stricter and more demanding form than screenplays. Finding a play that will survive the rigors of New York is very difficult. As a form, screenplays are looser, closer to the novel in terms of the range you can have in film. Movies can range from photographed stage plays to totally non-linear stories. Most fall somewhere in between, in well-defined genres, because those are the ones the studios feel have a chance to sell. The cost of production being what it is, and for the studios to survive as corporate entities, they look for films with a recognizable market, action or comedy. Once in a while, a studio executive with some guts who's doing well will take a shot because he likes the material personally, even though they know it's chancy. They may break even or even lose money, but they want to do it because they feel it's something they believe in, because of a relationship with a star or a director who wants to do it. There are all those variables that enter into what is chosen, but basically a screenplay is selected for its mass appeal to an audience. In my own experience, very rarely have I seen a script where I say, "This is a remarkable piece of material," and it's not getting done because it's obviously not commercial. For example, Charlie Eastman has written a number of remarkable screenplays that have never gotten done. One of them was bought by Warren Beatty, who sat on it for years. That's exceptional, though. That rarely happens.

(1981, 1987)

Anthony Harvey

The roll call of fine actors in Anthony Harvey's films is indeed impressive—Peter O'Toole, Faye Dunaway, George C. Scott, Joanne Woodward, Glenda Jackson, Dirk Bogarde, Liv Ullmann, Martin Sheen, Michael Moriarty, Bette Davis, Nick Nolte, and especially Katharine Hepburn. Harvey calls Hepburn "a remarkable person and a great friend," and has directed her in *The Lion in Winter* (1968), for which she won an Academy Award; the Emmy-winning *The Glass Menagerie* (1973); and the black comedy *Grace Quigley* (1984). The director's affinity for actors stems from his beginnings in his native England. He was born in London on June 3, 1931, and as a teenager played Vivien Leigh's brother Ptolemy in *Caesar and Cleopatra* (1946). He won a scholarship to the Royal Academy of Dramatic Art, then moved into film editing, becoming one of England's top cutters on such pictures as John and Roy Boulting's *Private's Progress* (1956) and *I'm Alright, Jack* (1959); Bryan Forbes' *The L-Shaped Room* (1962) and *The Whisperers* (1965); and most importantly, Stanley Kubrick's *Lolita* (1961) and *Dr. Strangelove* (1964).

Harvey's directorial debut, *Dutchman* (1967), won him industry recognition at Cannes, and attracted the attention of Peter O'Toole, who insisted he direct *The Lion in Winter*, the twelfth-century historical drama with O'Toole as Henry II and Katharine Hepburn as Eleanor of Aquitaine. The picture earned Harvey the prestigious Directors Guild of America Award. Harvey has continued to direct such critically acclaimed features as *They Might Be Giants* (1971) and *Eagle's Wing* (1979), as well as outstanding television films like *The Glass Menagerie*, *The Disappearance of Aimee* (1976), and *The Patricia Neal Story* (1982).

I interviewed Tony Harvey in March, 1988, in New York City.

Anthony Harvey (Photo by Len Tavares).

FILMOGRAPHY

Dutchman (1967, Continental).
The Lion in Winter (1968, Avco Embassy). HV: Embassy.
They Might Be Giants (1971, Universal). HV: MCA.
The Glass Menagerie (1973, David Susskind/ABC).
The Abdication (1974, Warner Bros.).
The Disappearance of Aimee (1976, Tomorrow Entertainment/NBC). HV: USA.
Players (1979, Paramount). HV: Paramount.
Eagle's Wing (1979, International Picture Show). HV: Media Home.
Richard's Things (1981, New World). HV: Embassy.
The Patricia Neal Story (1981, Lawrence Schiller Productions/CBS). Co-director
        with Anthony Page.
Svengali (1983, Robert Halmi Productions/CBS). HV: USA.
Grace Quigley (1984, Cannon). HV: MGM/UA.

HARVEY INTERVIEW

JOHN A. GALLAGHER: Your initial background was acting.

ANTHONY HARVEY: My stepfather, Morris Harvey, was a fine and
    distinguished actor in London in the Twenties and Thirties. He wrote,
    produced, and acted in revues for Andre Charlot and C. B. Cochran. In
    1929 he came to New York and worked with the Shuberts. As a small
    boy growing up in London I was very much exposed to a theatrical
    background. One of my first recollections is the enchanting memory of
    sitting on Jack Buchanan's shoulder at the Savage Club and watching the
    Coronation in 1936. A few years later I was chosen to play Ptolemy in
    Caesar and Cleopatra (1946) with Vivien Leigh. I started the film when I
    was about fourteen and completed the part when I was fifteen. I returned
    to do some retakes and they couldn't fit me into my clothes. I had to be
    photographed from the neck up. It was during the war, and a buzz bomb
    actually hit Denham Studios where we were filming. *Caesar and Cleopatra*
    was the most expensive film the Rank Organization made. From a small
    boy's point-of-view it was absolutely riveting, especially the whole tech-
    nical side of the sets and cameras. I remember going to the stage next
    door and climbing up this enormous set where Mickey Powell was film-
    ing *Stairway to Heaven* (1945). I also remember Noel Coward visiting
    our set. It was a dazzling experience and by that time it was in my blood.
    I decided there was nothing else I wanted to do. I won a scholarship for
    the Royal Academy of Dramatic Art. My ego was soon dashed when I
    went into summer stock as an assistant stage manager and played juvenile
    leads for five pounds a week, which was then the Equity minimum. After

three months I realized I was an absolutely hopeless actor and wasn't going to be an Albert Finney. So that was that!

JAG: How did you move into editing?

AH: I landed a job in the Crown Film Unit, which made documentaries. I was an assistant in the library department. I would run film backward and forward on the Moviola, a remarkable way to learn about film. I also worked in a lab developing newsreel films, but I accidentally pulled a wrong switch and an entire negative was ruined. They said, "Goodbye! Out!" I didn't have a week's notice! All this time I was writing to the Boulting Brothers, John and Roy, for whom I had great admiration. They made brilliant movies—*Brighton Rock* (1947), *Seven Days to Noon* (1950). After nagging at them, I was finally given a job as an assistant editor. At twenty-five, an early age for a film editor, they gave me a chance to cut *Private's Progress*.

JAG: You worked for the Boultings on film after film at the Shepperton Studios.

AH: It was an amazing experience that rarely happens in 1988. It was teamwork, with Peter Sellers, Dickie Attenborough, Ian Carmichael, Roy and John Boulting. We'd work pretty late hours and we'd all meet for a drink at a pub on the way home from the studio. We truly were a team— the actors, the director, art department, cameramen, editing. It's something that has gone out of the film industry today, the great joy of doing it all. It also gave you enormous incentive to work because it was a glorious experience. Camaraderie and above all humor were a great part of it. Today it's all just become one big business.

JAG: What was your reaction when you were made an editor?

AH: Roy Boulting has always been a fine editor in his own right. I was very lucky. You weren't just out there in the cold. Roy and John were generous enough to give one enormous help.

JAG: How did you approach cutting comedy?

AH: When you're cutting comedy, you can't wait for laughs by leaving a pause. You can't think, "I'm going to get a big laugh here." I remember a critic's screening of *I'm Alright, Jack* in the West End. For some ghastly reason, which is still true today, a film is shown to the critics at ten in the morning. There was dead silence. When it opened that night to the public, the roof blew off. Cutting comedy is one of the best experiences for an editor. The timing of a cut can kill a laugh. You hold a shot for too long or you cut away just at the moment you're getting a laugh, and BOOM! . . . the laugh's gone. I spent my first six or seven years cutting comedies for the Boultings—*Private's Progress*, *I'm Alright, Jack*, and a wonderful film with Terry Thomas and Peter Sellers called *Carlton-Browne of the F. O.* (1959). One of the great rules about comedy is when you're shooting on the floor, you can't have the production crew laughing behind the camera. Comedy is a deadly serious business. Laughter behind the camera should never be encouraged.

JAG: You then cut an intense drama, *The Angry Silence* (1960).

AH: That was produced by Bryan Forbes and Richard Attenborough, directed brilliantly by Guy Green. It was made on a shoestring and really took off. I went on to work with Bryan on *The L-Shaped Room* and *The Whisperers*, both of which he directed.

JAG: You also worked with director Anthony Asquith on *The Millionairess* (1960).

AH: It was a Metro-Goldwyn-Mayer production with Peter Sellers and Sophia Loren. There was practically no editing in it. It was one of the first CinemaScope films made in England and almost every scene was designed to be shot in one master take. At that time, people were afraid to cut in CinemaScope because they were nervous about the shape of the screen. It was beautifully photographed by Jack Hildyard, but was far from Bernard Shaw's original play *The Millionairess*.

JAG: How did you get involved with Stanley Kubrick?

AH: Kubrick came to England around the time I was editing *The L-Shaped Room*. I had seen *Paths of Glory* (1957) several times and was deeply affected by it. I wrote to Stanley and asked him if he would consider me as an editor. He invited me to see him and I had at least four or five interviews. He gave me the MI-5 treatment—"What kind of hours do you work? What time do you go to bed? Are you married? Do you go on holidays?" He wanted somebody who was going to be there seven days a week, twenty-two hours a day, and indeed I did work very long hours for him. But, my God, what a great experience! He's a fascinating, funny, brilliant, eccentric fellow. I wouldn't have missed working with him for the world.

JAG: *Lolita* was the first film you cut for him.

AH: Kubrick said something at that time that I found to be very good advice. When an actor is giving an extraordinary performance you don't always need to make a conventional cutaway to see somebody else reacting. An audience imagines that reaction for themselves. I think to *not* cut is the one golden rule of editing. Cut only when an actor flubs a line or something goes wrong technically. There was a wonderful documentary, *The Unknown Chaplin* (1987), made by Kevin Brownlow and David Gill, and it showed how Chaplin would rehearse endlessly so he wouldn't have to cut. This is particularly true in comedy.

JAG: On *Dr. Strangelove*, did the script change much from pre-production to post-production?

AH: It was a brilliant script, but it was that curious thing that happens when you put a film together from a wonderful blueprint of a script. I remember when we saw the first cut. As with all first cuts, you want to slit your throat, and everyone runs off in different directions looking for a knife! The first cut didn't work. It was completely reassembled. The balance from one scene to another is such a delicate thing that sometimes it can't really be put on paper.

JAG: Did you have preview screenings of *Dr. Strangelove*?

AH: No, but with the Boultings and Martin Ritt on *The Spy Who Came in from the Cold* we would invite friends to a screening and seeing a film with an audience for the first time you can then rely on your own instincts for what works and what doesn't work to improve the cut. Sitting in a cutting room for weeks and weeks with an editor, you can get terribly close to a film and lose perspective. The first and last time you have any perspective is when you see the first cut.

JAG: How was your experience with director Martin Ritt on *The Spy Who Came in from the Cold?* The film has a very naturalistic tone, quite unlike other Sixties spy movies.

AH: Marty's a gritty New York character, a tough exterior, but deeply sensitive underneath. The film wasn't your usual kind of James Bond spy picture. It was a very dark, realistic, brilliantly written John LeCarre novel. By its very nature, you couldn't use the fast cutting of a slick Bond film. You wanted that feeling of wet, raining, sleazy gutters. It needed a different treatment. The material dictated the cutting and the long, slow dissolves.

JAG: How did you come to direct your first feature, *Dutchman*?

AH: In many ways, Kubrick encouraged me to become a film director. Stanley said to me, "You know, Tony, you've become quite impossible. You've become the Peter Sellers of the cutting room. You'd better get out and direct before you drive me mad." Later, in New York, I saw a remarkable play by Leroi Jones at the Cherry Lane Theatre called *Dutchman*. I had dinner with Leroi Jones and he gave me an option on it. I returned to London and my colleagues thought, "Is Tony absolutely insane? Doing a film about a murder on a New York subway?" The film ran less than an hour, but to my real astonishment, I ended up with John Barry writing the score, Gerry Turpin lighting it, Shirley Knight and Al Freeman, Jr. acting in it. Great credit must be given to the producer, Gene Persson, who raised the money in hundred dollar lots. I was cutting *The Whisperers* at the time and Bryan Forbes said, "Go off for a week and direct the film." I'd cut *The Whisperers* during the day and rehearse *Dutchman* at night. We shot the film in one week at Twickenham Studios. We were not allowed to shoot in New York's subway system because Mayor Lindsay said we were encouraging violence in the subways, as if there wasn't enough already!

JAG: How were you able to shoot so quickly?

AH: It was shot in black and white with three cameras. I got a blueprint for a New York subway, and although we really didn't have an art director, we had a brilliant set decorator and he copied the blueprint. We built on the smallest stage at Twickenham. We moved the camera slightly to give it a feeling of movement. Gerry Turpin used these lights to give it the effect of passing reflections in the subway, a nightmarish feeling. I wanted to shoot it like a newsreel, very grainy, and simulate a steamy New York heat wave, a desperate feeling.

JAG: Did you work fifteen-hour days?

AH: You couldn't because of those goddam English tea breaks! But the production unit was great and I shot long, ten-minute takes. Since I had three cameras, I had a good selection of angles to go to in cutting.

JAG: *Dutchman* was a very controversial film for its time, especially the strong language.

AH: Yes, the language was very rough, but Al Freeman was so skillful in the way he handled the dialogue that it was never offensive.

JAG: After the intimate, low-budget *Dutchman*, you were hired to direct the large canvas of *The Lion in Winter*.

AH: Peter O'Toole saw *Dutchman* and asked me to do a thriller which didn't materialize. A few months later he was set to do a film called *The Ski Bum*, which again didn't materialize. There was financing available to do *The Lion in Winter*, from the James Goldman play, and Peter flew to Hollywood to see Katharine Hepburn. They went down to a West Hollywood theatre to see *Dutchman* at three in the morning. Hepburn said, "I don't understand what this movie has to do with *The Lion in Winter*, but if you trust him, let's go ahead." It was timing and luck, being in the right place at the right time. You can be the most talented character and never make it because of timing. There are so many extraordinary people in this industry who've never had a career because of luck and bad timing.

JAG: *The Lion in Winter* is one of the few historical films that so completely capture the feeling of period.

AH: The script had so much humor, charm, and energy. I wanted to get the feel of the twelfth century, that terrible feeling of cold, dirt, and isolation. People lived very uncomfortably during that period of time, and there was a great deal of misery. They would light a fire in these enormous rooms but they never felt really warm. I didn't want the picture to look like a typical Hollywood historical epic, but a dark and realistic vision of what it must have been like to live in the twelfth century. I showed Douglas Slocombe, a brilliant cameraman, a Breughel painting to illustrate what I wanted the film to look like. We filmed on location in Ireland, France, and Wales in real castles with a fantastic cast of actors— O'Toole, Hepburn, Anthony Hopkins, Nigel Terry, John Castle, Timothy Dalton, Jane Merrow. It was one of those rare times when everything worked. There was an infectious quality of giving. Some films become agony, but on *The Lion in Winter* it was great from day one.

JAG: How was your experience with Katharine Hepburn?

AH: I'd seen Hepburn films all my life and I was somewhat worried about working with such a legend, but she had the capacity to make everyone feel comfortable, including the younger actors. We had a two-week rehearsal period, which broke down those barriers and we became a family.

JAG: Did you vary your approach in directing experienced actors like O'Toole and Hepburn with the newer performers?

AH: Not really. Each actor needs enormous love, affection, and encouragement, and the greater the actor, the more they need you to be dead honest. I know this myself from my early days as an actor. They need you to trust them so that they can trust themselves. I think it's an infectious thing. I found, rather to my astonishment, that Hepburn likes to challenge you and test you the first week or two.

JAG: What kinds of tests?

AH: Interpretation of a scene. For instance, in the mirror sequence she wanted to play it strong, while I felt she should play it more vulnerably. I shot around the scene because I didn't think it was going to work Kate's way. I said, "I don't bloody well agree with you so I'm going to stick to this." We were both very stubborn. Finally Kate did it the way I thought it should be played and it was then that we started to be friends. I think many actors test you out, and you better be damn good and have the right answers. Great actors need strong directors. Hepburn has such power on the screen. When she's dead simple, it's devastating. As a matter of fact, actors' instincts are generally quite extraordinary.

JAG: With your background in editing, how did you work with the editor on *The Lion in Winter*, John Bloom?

AH: It was very much teamwork. John did a fine job. I'd never worked with him before, but I cut *The Spy Who Came in from the Cold* in the next room to where he was cutting *Georgy Girl* (1966). While cutting *The Lion in Winter*, I wouldn't look over his shoulder. I don't believe in that. I'd come in and say, "This is brilliant" or "This is lousy." You can't suffocate people, whether they're editors, actors, or cameramen, but somehow you try to guide them to what you're after.

JAG: What appealed to you about James Goldman's script for your next film, *They Might Be Giants*?

AH: Like *The Lion in Winter*, his script had such hope, humor, life, and originality. It was also a good love story. Unfortunately, Universal didn't believe in the film, even though it got some fine reviews.

JAG: George C. Scott has a reputation for being difficult.

AH: He has that reputation but I found him a joy to work with, a wonderful fellow, always great on the first take, full of boundless energy.

JAG: How did *The Glass Menagerie* come about?

AH: I was in Sweden with Liv Ullmann making *The Abdication*. After two weeks Liv had to return to California to start *The New Land* (1973) with Gene Hackman. I had a few months off. Hepburn called me up and said we had the chance to do *The Glass Menagerie*. I took the crew from *The Abdication* to London and filmed it there. Again we had a week of rehearsal, not so much to block things out, but for the actors, Hepburn, Michael Moriarty, Joanna Miles, and Sam Waterston, to get to know each other, instead of being strangers on the first day of shooting.

JAG: Do you plan your coverage on the set or in rehearsal?

AH: I don't think you can see how it works until you really see how an actor looks on the set. You can plan things sometimes in the loneliness of your hotel bedroom, but then the whole thing goes out the window the next day.

JAG: You've directed Liv Ullmann twice, in *The Abdication* and *Richard's Things*.

AH: She's a magical actress. She has such capacity within a scene to create emotion, whether it's tragedy or comedy. On a silent reaction, she can visibly change from a warm, affectionate creature to a pale, trembling psychotic.

JAG: *The Disappearance of Aimee* was a well-received TV film.

AH: That was really a challenge, working in Denver, Colorado, very long hours, from six in the morning to nine at night, with two fine actresses, total opposites, Faye Dunaway and Bette Davis. We shot it in fifteen days. Edith Head designed the clothes. It was an interesting story, still enormously topical with what's happened in evangelism today.

JAG: How would you compare Bette Davis and Katharine Hepburn?

AH: They both arrive an hour before anyone else. They know every line of dialogue before the first day of shooting. It's this wonderful professional training in Hollywood, years of George Cukor, years of William Wyler, years of a very disciplined way to work. They're both from New England, but they've taken different paths. They both have endless humor, which I think is slowly disappearing from the human race. Humor is so important to everything. If you don't have it, God help you.

JAG: *Eagle's Wing* is a beautiful-looking Western.

AH: It was based on a story by Michael Syson, with a script by John Briley, who wrote *Gandhi* (1983), with strong actors in Martin Sheen, Sam Waterston, Harvey Keitel, Stephane Audran. We filmed in a haunting location in Durango, Mexico, miles from anywhere. It took three hours to get to the place. It's really the story of an obsession, an action film, a visually exciting subject beautifully photographed by Billy Williams. It's almost a silent picture. It had practically no dialogue. It was quite a challenge, something I'd always wanted to do, a film which doesn't rely on words. It was a unanimous success in London, both critically and financially, but still has not been released in the United States, due to little faith on the part of the distributor.

JAG: You shared directing chores on *The Patricia Neal Story* with Anthony Page.

AH: He did the English segments, while I did the Hollywood scenes. I was attracted to it simply because I wanted to work with Glenda Jackson and Dirk Bogarde. You're on very delicate ground when you're dealing with characters who are still living because you say to yourself, "Can you really be truthful?"

JAG: Nick Nolte and Katharine Hepburn made an interesting team in *Grace Quigley*.

AH: Hepburn needs a strong leading man. Hepburn and Tracy were unbeatable. She worked wonderfully opposite actors like Humphrey Bogart, Cary Grant, and Peter O'Toole.

JAG: When *Grace Quigley* opened in London, it got some brilliant reviews from critics like John Russell Taylor and David Robinson, but then Cannon re-edited the film.

AH: I wish Cannon would have left well enough alone. Two years of negative, destructive publicity also hurt the film, and audiences came to the movie with a pre-conceived idea. It was a desperate experience for me, and impossible to explain to anyone. Gossip has killed a great number of fine pictures before the public can see them for themselves.

JAG: What do you want an audience to get from a movie?

AH: Ideally I'd like them to be enlightened and entertained. You should go to a movie and laugh or be totally swept away and deeply moved. It makes you feel good when you come out of the cinema with renewed hope. That's why *Moonstruck* (1987) is great, beautifully directed and acted. You come out of it feeling good.

JAG: What qualities do you think are important in film directing?

AH: Your energy and concentration. Also, trust is very infectious, and people will work terribly hard and very long hours in the best way if you believe in *them*. It's good when you can work with the same glorious crew again and again. When I've made films in England, I've worked with sound mixer Simon Kaye, and cinematographers Douglas Slocombe and Geoffrey Unsworth. In America, it's been sound man Bill Daly and cameraman Larry Pizer. I've worked with editors John Bloom and Jerry Greenberg, and on the last few pictures I've worked with the same assistant director, the outrageous and unique Mike Haley. Once they know you, and they know the insanities and madness that film directors sometimes have, they can say with great humor, "Oh, there's Tony again. It doesn't matter, he'll be alright tomorrow!" With a crew you know, you can have a sense of humor and laugh at yourself. It's important to have that trust. When you're on location away from home, it's remarkable to have a team of people who want to give you the best they can, who all want to make a terrific movie. I feel close to technicians because that's how I started my career. It's very important to think of them as your family, and that feeling spreads to the actors.

(1988)

Dennis Hopper

In the course of our interview, Dennis Hopper related a comment made by his daughter. "Dad," she said, "You may not be remembered for a lot of things in film, but there's one thing you will be remembered for. You've said 'man' more than any other actor in the history of motion pictures"... to which Hopper added, "Hey man, can you dig it, man? You know what I mean, man?" Hopper's screen persona has surely been that of the dope-smoking, alienated Sixties maverick, but he will also be remembered for leading Hollywood into the Seventies with his landmark directorial debut *Easy Rider* (1969), a youth movie made for and by young people.

Hopper was born on May 17, 1936, in Dodge City, Kansas; one of his earliest memories is watching a caravan of Warner Brothers stars led by Errol Flynn arrive in town to promote *Dodge City* (1939). Fifteen years later, Hopper was under contract to Warners as one of their most promising young actors, co-starring with his close friend James Dean in Nicholas Ray's *Rebel Without a Cause* (1955) and George Stevens' *Giant* (1956). He also appeared in three films for Hollywood veteran Henry Hathaway, an important influence on his eventual directing career—*From Hell to Texas* (1958), *The Sons of Katie Elder* (1965), and *True Grit* (1969). In the same year he played opposite John Wayne's Rooster Cogburn in *True Grit*, Hopper starred in, co-authored, and directed *Easy Rider*. That film's unexpected success led to Hopper's quirky *The Last Movie* (1971), about a film crew on location in Peru. It failed to find an audience, and Hopper kept working as an actor for a range of fine directors in such films as Wim Wender's *The American Friend* (1976), Henry Jaglom's *Tracks* (1977), Sam Peckinpah's *The Osterman Weekend* (1983), Francis Coppola's *Apocalypse Now* (1979) and *Rumble Fish* (1983), and took over the direction of an independent film in which he was starring called *Out of the Blue* (1980).

Dennis Hopper and cinematographer Laszlo Kovacs on the set of *The Last Movie* (from the author's collection).

This interview took place in February 1983, prior to the New York premiere of *Out of the Blue*. Since that time, Hopper's acting career was bolstered in 1986 with performances in David Lynch's *Blue Velvet* and David Anspaugh's *Hoosiers* (for' which he was Oscar-nominated for Best Supporting Actor), and his directing career had a major resurgence in 1988 with *Colors*, a searing study of Los Angeles youth gangs, and the thriller *Backtrack*.

FILMOGRAPHY

Easy Rider (1969, Columbia). HV: RCA/Columbia.
The Last Movie (1971, Universal).
Out of the Blue (1980, Discovery Films). HV: Media Home.
Colors (1988, Orion).
Backtrack (1989, Vestron).

HOPPER INTERVIEW

JOHN A. GALLAGHER: You started in the business as a young actor under the old Hollywood studio system at Warner Brothers. What were the pros and cons of that school?

DENNIS HOPPER: It was good in a way. I went into it in *Rebel Without a Cause* with Nick Ray and James Dean, and *Giant* with George Stevens, Dean, Elizabeth Taylor, and Rock Hudson. I was eighteen years old, so that was an incredible introduction, a little different than your average Hollywood experience. Francis Coppola has tried the system again with Zoetrope, having people under contract, trying to build them into stars. Francis lost the studio in Hollywood but he still has the one in San Francisco. I think that's a very interesting concept on a business level, building sets on a studio soundstage. I've totally gone against that in the movies I've directed, because I believed in Godard and Truffaut saying, "Lock all those people in the studio and let's go shoot in the streets. We don't need a soundstage because the whole world is a soundstage. We don't need to do period things, we can do things in our own clothes." As far as a place to learn, boy, the studio system was a place to learn. It was a factory. You learned how to work and what was demanded of you. I was under contract, so they made me go in and dub foreign films into English. I did screen tests. For example, Fred Zinnemann was making a movie, *The Old Man and the Sea* (1958), with Spencer Tracy. For three weeks, while he was looking for a young boy and an actress, I would play Spencer Tracy's part off camera in these screen tests. You would do all those kinds of things. That was the one thing about the studio system. You learned the business if you wanted to. You could go watch George Stevens editing *Giant*, you looped foreign films, you had the opportunity to learn about wardrobe and props. You learned the basics of the business and the kinds of things you say by rote, like, "Alright, let's get ready, we're gonna make a take. Lock it up!" I had an acting class at Warners which James Garner and a lot of other people would come to. There were these great old-time directors like Raoul Walsh and William Wellman on the lot. Wellman was doing a thing called *Lafayette Escadrille* (1958), which he was a member of. It was the group that went over in the First World War and fought against the Germans in France before the U.S. was really in the war. I wanted to be in that picture badly, but I didn't get in. I did work with Lewis Milestone, who had done *All Quiet on the Western Front* (1930). I did lots of television, *Sugarfoot*, *Maverick*, *Gunsmoke*, *Wagon Train*. I did a very good *Cheyenne* with Clint Walker. I did a great *Studio One* with John Frankenheimer. I'd like to see some of those again. You had to do a lot of shit, but you learned a lot too.

JAG: Nicholas Ray directed you in *Rebel Without a Cause*.

DH: We worked as a unit. He got you into your part. He was a very fine director. He lived in my house in Taos for about a year and a half when he had some problems, then he came back East and taught at a university. Later we did *The American Friend* together, which Wim Wenders directed. Nick played the painter, and I say, "You've changed the blue," and he says, "How the hell would you know?" Then Wim did *Lightning Over Water* (1980) with him.

JAG: So much has been written about James Dean. You and he were very close; what kind of influence did he have on your life?

DH: He had a big influence on me. Every time I smoke a cigarette too short, I think of him. I said to him, "Boy, you really smoke your cigarette short." I have some stock answers to this because I've been asked so many times, so it's hard to really get down. I saw a man act. When I was nineteen years old, I thought that I was one of the best actors in the world, or at least on the way to being one. Watching him on *Rebel Without a Cause*, he was doing things that were so far over my head that I couldn't even comprehend. On the chickie run I grabbed him and threw him into the car and said, "You got to tell me what you're doing because I don't understand what you're doing. Should I go to New York and study at the Actors' Studio? What should I do?" He said, "Don't go to New York and study. Just do it. Don't show it, do it." I said, "What do you mean, 'Do it, don't show it'?" He said, "Well, you know, if you're smoking a cigarette, don't act smoking the cigarette, just smoke the cigarette when you feel like it. The simplest things will become very difficult but just do them, don't show them. If somebody opens the door and you turn to look and they got a gun in their hand, you may get up and make a joke, but you're scared as hell. You say, 'What are you doing here?' but you gotta see the guy and you gotta see the gun, and then you gotta react, however that is. It doesn't have to be the same every time. You can say that a lot of different ways. First thing though, you gotta hear the door. The door opens, the guy's got a gun, and you can say to the guy, 'You're scaring the hell out of me' however it comes out. That's not to be supposed, how you're going to react to it. So you do something *not* to show it. The simplest things like smoking a cigarette or drinking a cup of coffee will become very difficult, and then pretty soon you'll forget about it and things'll start happening." So he gave me a little advice and tips like that. Another time he said, "Everybody tries to think like, 'OK, I'm alone in a room,' but in point of fact I'm not alone in the room even though it says in the script I'm alone in the room, because there's a director, a cameraman, lighting people, grips, a continuity person writing down whether or not I'm matching the shot because I'm smoking a cigarette, so I'm not really alone in this room. But until I accept the fact that there are other people in this room, and accept as reality that there is a camera here, then there's the possibility of me being alone in this room." Let's say for example there's a script girl writing things down. I just took a drag off this cigarette and I'm talking to you. She just wrote down that I took a drag off this cigarette. That means when they come around and do my over-the-shoulder shot, uh-oh, I just put my hand over here, so not only am I going to have to match the cigarette, I'm going to have to match my hand too. Meanwhile, I'm talking to you and saying, "Do you know what the weather's like outside? It's snowing. The plane's not going to be able to come in. The deal's off. Now, you know what that means, doncha? Doncha?" and as I say that I'm pointing at you. The script girl just wrote down that I'm pointing. It's using a simple reality that you can find humorous. If you're in a restaurant, you can look all over, you can look over there at him, you can look over there at her. The audience doesn't know what you're looking at. Depending on what kind of scene it is, whether I'm angry at you, or explaining something to you, or whether I find it humorous, I still have to reproduce everything again because they're going to do the two-shot, the closeup, and the master shot, and it's got to match. That's a simple, moment-to-moment reality. These are simple things that Dean taught me that were very valuable. The most valuable was to be able to use what's around you rather than shutting out the people on the set. Instead of saying, "OK, we are now alone," or "We are now in a restaurant," it's, "No, actually we're filming this and that's what it is." Those kinds of things I learned a lot from Dean.

JAG: Technical things that have to do with film acting.

DH: Yeah. After doing *Giant* I came and studied with Lee Strasberg. He used to have us on the stage and he would say, "Look at us because we're real and you're real, we're real and you're real," so it's not that much different than stage acting. You have to accept the fact that there is an audience out there, that you are on a stage, before you can get into any kind of reality at all. It's the old story of the drunk coming in the middle of a performance and trying to find his seat. If you're doing a comedy you can use that as a humorous thing rather than letting it stop your performance and bother you. If you're in a tragedy you can use that guy coming in here and think, "He's screwing up my performance." You're doing *Death of a Salesman* or whatever and you're saying those lines, but there's a drunk out there looking for his seat and you use that in some way. The difference is accepting the reality of the circumstance of where you are because you're in an imaginary given circumstance anyway. You're acting, and it's just learning to use the reality of what's going on around you to help reinforce you rather than hinder you. Also, at that moment that I threw Dean into the car, he asked me why I wanted to be an actor. A lot of it comes out of a love/hate relationship with your parents and wanting to prove something. His was his mother dying when he was very young. He used to go to her grave and he used to cry on her grave, "Why did you leave me? Why did you leave me? Why did you leave me?" and that turned into "I'm gonna show you, I'm gonna show you, I'm gonna show you, I'm gonna be something, I'm gonna show you, I'm gonna do something, I'll show you, I'll show you." That we had in common. It's not a thing of "I'm going to impress this audience," or "I feel powerful because I'm on this stage, I'm controlling people's minds." It has nothing to do with any of that crap. All it has to do with is the fact that to work in the way that Dean did and Montgomery Clift did and Brando does and I've tried is that you're working with your subconscious. It's Stanislavsky whether you go to Stella Adler or Sandy Meisner or Lee Strasberg, who was my teacher. To trick your subconscious through subconscious means is like impossible. In other words . . . my father died, OK? My conscious mind is saying my father died, which is a reality this last year. I can say, "My father died," but it doesn't have an emotional thing. To have an emotional thing, I have to wipe everything out, get into a state where I can relax. I have tension in my brow and I can feel it so you have to shake out your tension. See where your tension points are in your body and get a place where you try to wipe everything from your mind. You don't think of anyone in particular. Then through sense memory, which is not pantomime, you try to remember, "What was I wearing, can I see anything? Is there anything I can touch? What was I touching?" . . . so then you do the lines. Someone says, "Your father's dead." "What do you mean? You're kidding me? My father's dead?" . . . (TEARS FORM IN HOPPER'S EYES) . . . I've never tried that one. It's too close anyway. You're tricking your subconscious. It has to come from the clothes you're wearing, the heat, the cold. It has to come from one of your senses. Your sight, your smell, your taste, your hearing.

JAG: Music does that too. Hearing a certain song can take you to another time and place.

DH: Absolutely. Once you've gone through a sense memory into an emotional memory, at that point, it's always the same object. It's always the same sound or the smell or the taste or something you saw that will spark it off. It'll always be the same thing. But you've got to trick yourself into not hearing. You've just got to hear it . . . (TEARS FORM AGAIN) . . . and you've got to be able to shut it off, man . . . (HE SNAPS HIS FINGERS) . . . so you can be doing something else. But it'll always be the same sound, the same smell, the same thing. But they wear out. Stanislavsky described it as like opening a box. He said that you have a golden box. You open that box and let out an emotional memory. But they wear out like a guy telling a joke at a party. Someone says, "Hey, tell that joke. It's a really funny joke." So you tell it and everybody laughs. Pretty soon, somebody says, "Hey, will you tell them this joke," and you say, "OK." You tell it pretty good and some people laugh. About the fifth time, you say, "Why don't you tell the joke? You know it by now. I don't really feel like telling it." They say, "No, no, no, you tell it better." You tell the joke and it falls flat. It's not so funny anymore. Emotional memories wear out, so you have to constantly regenerate your senses. You have to keep your touch, smell, taste, sight, and hearing really acute, which makes you totally bananas.

JAG: Your second film with James Dean, *Giant*, was directed by George Stevens, who was famous for getting lots of coverage.

DH: They used to say, "He shoots every corner of the room." No matter how small the part, whether you had one line or not, he would shoot every corner of the room. There was a lot of matching to be done with him. Dean used to come in to watch me without my knowing it.

JAG: Was an old Hollywood professional director like Henry Hathaway aware of these acting concepts?

DH: No, but I learned a lot from Henry Hathaway. Strangely enough, when I was directing *Out of the Blue*, I used a lot of the things. But no, he wasn't aware of them. There was this concept of me as being a rebel. I mean, I guess I was a rebel, but it wasn't that I was angry. It was just that I was trying to change the system of the school marm approach to things of "You say a line reading this way, you pick up the coffee cup now, you put it to your lips on this line, you put it down on this line. You turn this way and you say the line, 'Hello, how are you?' not 'Hi, how ya doing?' It's *got* to be this way." But I found something out on the first picture that I did with Hathaway, *From Hell to Texas*. I was bad in that movie. I felt out of place after I saw it. I felt I was in another picture, and that's not good. A picture's a picture, and a director's the director. The next time I worked with him, seven years later on *The Sons of Katie Elder*, I took his direction and tried to justify it and did, and I was much better in that film. Once you direct a film you gotta respect the fact that the director *is* the director, and as I say, I learned a lot from Hathaway.

JAG: He was a tough guy.

DH: He was a mean man on the set and a nice man to have dinner with. He hardly ever moved his camera so he wouldn't lay dolly track or anything. He'd ask you to make really weird moves that were so uncomfortable. He wanted *you* moving, not the camera. We used to have debates about that. He couldn't explain that to you, so he'd scream and yell, chomping his cigar, "Get those fucking people out from behind the goddam fucking wagon before I get my fucking gun and kill 'em! What the fuck are they in the fucking shot for! Get that shitty ass horse out of there!" It was just a totally crazy scene, but he was wonderful.

JAG: *Easy Rider* had a tremendous impact on young people as well as the movie business. The poster of you on your bike flashing the finger became a symbol for the Sixties.

DH: I saw it on a nuclear aircraft carrier in Monte Carlo on July 4th, 1976. Henri Langlois had asked me to open the second Cinématheque in Nice. I went and they took me into where they push the buttons for the bombs with the two keys, and there was the poster with me giving the finger right on the nuclear aircraft carrier. That was banana cakes. You have to realize how much change movies make. In Los Angeles at the end of *Easy Rider*, they screamed "Kill the pigs!" and in New Orleans they applauded when we were shot, so however it goes around. *Easy Rider* didn't revolutionize the movie business. They patted me on the back and they were very nice to me, and it made Bert Schneider, Bob Rafelson, Peter Fonda, Jack Nicholson, and myself some bread. Good bread.

JAG: I've always thought of *Easy Rider* as a Western.

DH: I think of it as a Western also. The campfires, the strangers come ridin' in to town, same as if they were on horses, only we had motorcycles. And I think it's an excellent movie, and it has some firsts in it. Like it's the first time that a movie was made where you used found music rather than having a score written for a film. It was a symbolic movie and the country was burning down at the time. It showed that you could smoke a marijuana joint and not go out and kill a bunch of nurses, you know what I mean? It introduced cocaine and I don't know about that, but it seems to be popular. But as far as revolutionizing the movie business, no. The movie business is built on a structure. I wasn't doing them a favor by making a movie for $340,000 when their low-budget was $1.2 million. Their tax structure was set up in such a way that I wasn't doing them a favor. As a matter of fact, I was stabbing them in the back, but nobody told me the game. I mean, you gotta tell somebody the game, you know, when they're from Dodge City, Kansas. I thought I was doing them a favor. I was doing the people I named a favor. It spawned a lot of films. A lot of people got a chance to direct because they figured if Dennis Hopper could do it, anybody can do it. A lot of bad films came out of that, too, but also a lot of very excellent films like *Mean Streets* (1973) and *Badlands* (1974). Those films were just squelched and put away.

JAG: Letting thirty-year-olds direct movies was unheard of.

DH: The directors were all in their seventies. Sixty was young! They were young directors! It was a change of time. I go to Hollywood now and my peer group are now sitting behind the desks and the system hasn't changed. They had long hair and they were my friends, they still are my friends. It doesn't mean I should expect them to give me jobs because they're my friends, however, the structure is still the same. It's still put all the eggs in one basket. If you make a picture for one million dollars, you can't steal one million dollars. I don't know if they steal money, you know what I mean, but I don't know that they don't, but I think so. I saw Roger Corman on television the other night and he said that the films that he made for those low–budgets at AIP [American International Pictures] just couldn't be done like that anymore, or wouldn't be worth doing anymore because the structure of the studio system couldn't financially allow it to happen.

JAG: At the same time as *Easy Rider* was in post-production, Henry Hathaway cast you in *True Grit*.

DH: I was editing the film and I told Schneider that Hathaway wanted me to be in *True Grit*. Schneider said, "Go do it. It's an eight-day part." I said, "You've gotta be kidding." He said, "I'm not kidding. I won't touch the picture." So I did the part and came back. Then Henry Jaglom, Jack Nicholson, and Bob Rafelson came in and recut the restaurant sequence. I had been editing thirty-two hours of film for months, and the restaurant scene was about twenty minutes longer than it is now, so Henry, Jack, and Bob came in and helped out on *Easy Rider*. I'm glad they did.

JAG: How did you get along with John Wayne on *True Grit* and *The Sons of Katie Elder*?

DH: He kept running around with his .45's everytime something happened, saying, "Where's that Commie Hopper? I'm gonna blow his brains out!" I got along with him pretty well. Mike and Pat Wayne are still friends of mine. I don't see them very often because I don't live in that part of the country. But hey, Duke was Duke, man, you know, he won the war in Iwo Jima! I mean, what are you gonna do, you know? I liked him. These guys like John Ford, Hathaway, Wellman were all tough, ornery guys. Stevens was no pussycat. He told Jack Warner to go back to his office and get off the set. He didn't go sit in Warner's office, so he ain't gonna be on Stevens' set. These guys were tough, and they made tough Westerns. Think of Ford's and Hathaway's and Wellman's outdoor Westerns. A lot of them came up through the labor departments, through construction. There'd be no jobs and they'd be snuck in through the backs of trucks into the studios and be scab laborers and start as carpenters, work their way into wardrobe and props, so they knew the business from the bottom up.

JAG: How was your experience working with Francis Coppola in *Apocalypse Now*?

DH: First of all, I came to the Philippines to do Colby, who was the CIA agent who had been corrupted and joined Brando's troops. I only had ten lines. I met the boat and I said, "Oh, he's up there." I said, "I'll do this part but I want one line with Marlon Brando." They said they thought that could be arranged. They closed down the whole production when Brando came down. Brando and Francis went off on a houseboat and came back a week later. The part of the photographer didn't exist originally. But in the book the movie was based on, *Heart of Darkness*, there was the Russian Jew in the tattered clothes that's going around like the Tarot card fool thinking that Kurtz is a great man and has a great idea. He's this babbling guy who tries to explain Kurtz. The tattered clothes became the camouflage uniform and the Tarot cards became the cameras. He has all the secrets of the world, he just can't remember how to use them anymore! Francis would come in with a small white piece of paper, typed from top to bottom with suggested dialogue. I'd look at it and they'd lay the dolly track. A regular camera load lasts ten minutes, and Francis had a special twenty-minute camera magazine made. When I bring them in from the boat, we did thirty-eight twenty-minute takes! Finally Francis said, "For God sakes, we've done thirty-seven takes and you've done them all your way! Would you just do one for me, Hopper, could you do one for me!" I said, "For Christ sakes, Francis, I shot *Easy Rider* for $340,000 and played Gabby Hayes to Fonda's Gene Autry! Look at you sittin' in that chair! Alright, I'll do one for you!" They printed all thirty-eight and he sent it off to one of his six editors. I just worked for Francis again in *Rumble Fish*. Francis' genius is really in his technology. It's very valuable what he's doing with video and applying it to film, and where he's headed. I hope he can continue. He's doing everything now from what we call The Silver Fish. He's got editors and three screens in there. He can talk to the set and he's got these little monitors everywhere. It's very sophisticated. In *Rumble Fish* I play Matt Dillon and Mickey Rourke's father. Mickey's great, and a great guy, too.

JAG: You acted for Henry Jaglom in *Tracks*, a low-budget movie that was shot mostly on the run.

DH: Was it ever! Going into a railway mail car on a moving train I think is against the law, you know what I mean? Jaglom would say, "Go on in there and run around!" I said, "Man, I'll get shot in there. These people carry guns." "Just go in there!" He's great. He's one of the true maniacs and I love him. I'd work for him anytime.

JAG: He takes a lot of chances.

DH: And you take them with him! But he's great. Now, he's somebody who makes his own films and they're personal films, and he goes right on making them. *Sitting Ducks* (1980) and *Can She Bake a Cherry Pie?* (1983) were successful, but *A Safe Place* (1971) and *Tracks* weren't, but he goes on making his films and that's really important. There are very few people in that position that can afford to do that, and I'm certainly glad that he can.

JAG: I worked on *Can She Bake a Cherry Pie?*, and he operated in a very improvisational manner.

DH: He would push you into scenes where you didn't even know what he was doing. He'd say, "Just put on your army uniform." I said, "Well, what do I do then?" He said, "Put on your army uniform! Don't talk about it! I don't have time! I'm losing the light! Just put on your army uniform!" We're on a train somewhere in the United States, so I rush in, put on my uniform, and he says, "Now get in there!" and he pushed me into a room with Barbara Flood, who's now going to wash and brush my hair. I'm there not having any idea what's going to go in the scene. However, he scripted a script that was so thorough that you knew your character and you knew how your character was going to react, and he primarily knew how you were going to react to the situation. There were no rehearsals. Paul Glickman was the cinematographer on that and he did an amazing job.

JAG: *Tracks* was one of the first films to deal honestly with the effects of the Vietnam war.

DH: It certainly was before *Coming Home* (1978), *Apocalypse Now*, and *The Deer Hunter* (1978). It shows a lot in festivals in Europe. It'll be around through the years. Jaglom definitely has a place. There are very few *auteurs* . . . is that a word? Authors, let's says authors rather than *auteurs*. There are very few filmmakers who really make their own films and that's partly because it's very difficult for people to give you financing who say, "Go ahead, you've got full autonomy and final cut. Just deliver a film."

JAG: You also worked with Sam Peckinpah on *The Osterman Weekend*.

DH: I've known him for years. I love him. Depends how much he drank and how he gets the drinks, but he's a really strong director. He was a writer originally. He wrote the pilot for *The Rifleman*, and I was the guest star on the pilot, though I never worked again on the series, 'cause I died. I died, not the series. Sam wasn't directing it, but he was taking me aside and directing me on the side, so that's when we first met. We've seen each other through the years, but this is the first time I've really worked with him in a film that he's directing. It was a great experience. I play Dr. Tremayne, who's suspected of being a KGB agent whose wife is sort of a nympho exhibitionist who he supplies with cocaine. It's an interesting part.

JAG: You directed the independent low-budget film *Out of the Blue*, which I felt is a black comedy.

DH: Hmmm. Would you like to explain that?

JAG: It has such a crazy, dark view of the family unit.

DH: It's the classic mother/father argument with the child trying to get them together and get some attention. Black comedy. It seems very real to me, but come to think of it I guess it *is* black comedy.

JAG: How did you get involved in the film?

DH: I came up to Canada to play the father. A husband and wife team had written the script, and he was directing it. It was his first directorial job, and Paul Lewis, the executive producer, had been my production manager on *Easy Rider* and my producer on *The Last Movie*. I met the director and went on the set once, stayed in my dressing room for a couple of weeks. Paul Lewis kept coming to me and saying, "You've got to come and see the rushes, nothing's working. It's not gonna make it." I said, "Paul, look, I'm sure he has a concept, and who says you're a judge of an artist?" He said, "Believe me, this guy's not an artist, you've got to see this stuff." I said, "I'm not gonna see it until I work. I'm not going to bother him on the set and see what he's doing." A couple of weeks went by. On a Friday night we were in a restaurant and Paul said, "Come in the toilet, I want to talk to you." He said, "Your money's in escrow in the United States. I'm leaving the picture." I said, "Wait a minute. How much film do you have?" He said, "We've shot two and a half hours." I said, "Let me see it tomorrow." I looked at it and there wasn't anything usable. It was sad, really bad. It was off the wall. I talked to the director and to some of the people who put the money up for the film, and I took over the film that night. The next day I started rewriting the script and rewrote the whole script one week at a time. I shot the film in four weeks and two days, and edited it in six weeks. I changed the whole story. Originally, it was a case history of Cindy Barnes, narrated by Raymond Burr. The father was killed by the daughter, and Raymond Burr saves the mother and daughter at the end. The girl wasn't into punk music. The story started on the day Elvis died. Can you imagine two women hearing on the radio that Elvis has died? Bursting into tears? I don't know, I think I'm a pretty good director but that's over my head, you know what I mean? So all that changed. The mother wasn't using drugs, and Burr now only has two scenes in the picture. Narration is not my school of filmmaking. I decided to have the ending where they all go bye-bye, because I didn't see that it was the father's fault or the mother's fault or the daugher's fault. I just thought it was a situation that seemed to be untenable. It's also symbolic of the way I feel, unfortunately, that the family structure in this country is falling apart and disintegrating.

JAG: *Out of the Blue* is the antithesis of the classic family structure of a John Ford film.

DH: And yet I love John Ford and I love his movies. If I was more successful I could say this with a lot more confidence, but if he were making films today, that might be the family structure that he might be seeing also, not necessarily in that way, but he was working at a time when the family unit was much more of a reality and it was a very strong part of the United States.

JAG: Did you screen *Out of the Blue* for the majors when it was finished?

DH: They saw it. Jack Nicholson really liked it and he showed it to Warren Beatty. They decided they'd take it to Paramount and show it to the head of the studio and see if he would distribute it. This was before *Reds* (1981) came out. But I guess Paramount just didn't want to put their name on it. I can understand that. If I was the head of a big corporation like Gulf and Western, I don't know. You know, what if one of the stockholders says, "Who in the hell is responsible for putting our name on this picture?" I don't know what they thought of it, but they didn't distribute it. The film was very successful in Europe. It was in competition at Cannes in 1980, one of the twenty-two films in competition. We made it in Canada, and Canada refused to put their name on it as an official entry. Rather than raising the Canadian flag and playing the national anthem of Canada, they came out and announced this was a film without a country, it was a Dennis Hopper film. I guess a lot of people would say, "Wow," and get a great ego boost out of that, but to me it was such a downer. I just didn't understand it. The whole life of this film has been very strange.

JAG: At this point you've directed three films—*Easy Rider, The Last Movie,* and *Out of the Blue*. How does the Hollywood establishment view these films?

DH: I don't really know. They don't offer me jobs as a director. To give a guy like me full autonomy and final cut, I'm sure they look at that as a little risky. Also, I haven't really presented them a script they can read and they can say, "This is something we'd like to do." I don't think they question my talent as a director. They may question my commerciali-bility.

JAG: Your films as director have been better appreciated in Europe.

DH: That's because they believe in the true filmmaker. A director knows that you don't make a film alone. You've got a lot of people that make this film, the camera people, grips, electricians, sound people, the editors, on and on. You don't make it alone, but it *should* be one person's decision and one person's thought that goes up on that screen. It should be that person's edit and it should be that person's film. It should be "A Film by. . . ."

(1983)

Ted Kotcheff

Variety is the hallmark of Ted Kotcheff's work, a diversity that he attributes to his early years in live television in Canada. His range has been displayed in a spectrum of genres, including action movies (*First Blood, Uncommon Valor*), farce (*Switching Channels*), the Western (*Billy Two Hats*), and especially social drama (*Two Gentlemen Sharing, Outback, Split Image*), and social comedy (*The Apprenticeship of Duddy Kravitz, Fun with Dick and Jane, North Dallas Forty*).

Born on April 7, 1931, in Toronto, Canada, Kotcheff directed five features before attracting Hollywood's attention with his adaptation of his friend Mordecai Richler's novel *The Apprenticeship of Duddy Kravitz* (1974). He has since proven particularly adept at directing strong screen personalities— Richard Dreyfuss in the title role of *Duddy Kravitz*, Jane Fonda in *Fun with Dick and Jane* (1977), Nick Nolte in *North Dallas Forty* (1979), Sylvester Stallone as John Rambo in *First Blood* (1982), Gene Hackman in *Uncommon Valor* (1983), and Burt Reynolds and Kathleen Turner in *Switching Channels* (1988).

The following interview took place in New York before the release of *Switching Channels*, while Kotcheff was completing post-production on *The Winter People* (1989).

FILMOGRAPHY

Tiara Tahiti (1962, Zenith International). HV: Almi.
Life at the Top (1965, Columbia).
Two Gentlemen Sharing (1969, American International).
Outback (1971, United Artists).
Billy Two Hats (1972, United Artists).
The Apprenticeship of Duddy Kravitz (1974, Paramount). HV: Paramount.
Fun with Dick and Jane (1977, Columbia). HV: RCA/Columbia.

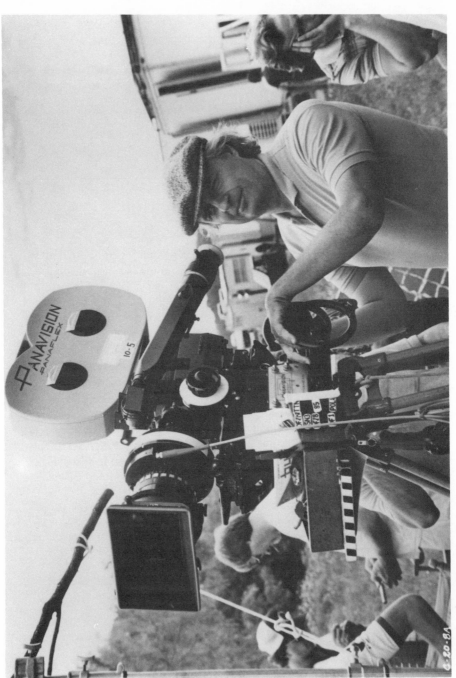

Ted Kotcheff on the set of *Split Image*.

Who Is Killing the Great Chefs of Europe? (1978, Warner Bros.). HV: Warners.
North Dallas Forty (1979, Paramount). HV: Paramount.
Split Image (1982, Orion). HV: Embassy.
First Blood (1982, Orion). HV: Thorn-EMI.
Uncommon Valor (1983, Paramount). HV: Paramount.
Joshua Then and Now (1986, 20th Century-Fox). HV: Key.
Switching Channels (1988, Tri-Star). HV: RCA/Columbia.
The Winter People (1989, Nelson Entertainment/Tri-Star).

KOTCHEFF INTERVIEW

JOHN A. GALLAGHER: What was your entree into film directing?

TED KOTCHEFF: If you had asked me at twenty-one what I was going to do, and someone said, "You're going to become a film director," I would have laughed in your face. It was the last thing on my mind. Don't laugh—I wanted to be a poet. Our generation was still in the grip of the last shadow of that Fitzgerald/Hemingway romanticism about going to Europe, so I went to Europe along with a lot of others. By accident, however, I was short of money and I went to work in a television station, the Canadian Broadcasting Corporation in Toronto. It was before they went on the air. Like every other young man who's arrogant and thinks he knows more, I used to watch these directors directing drama. I was a stage hand, and I'd say, "This guy doesn't know what he's doing. I can direct it ten times better." Someone called me on it and I started to direct television drama when I was twenty-four.

JAG: Was this live?

TK: Yes, the days of live television.

JAG: Were they as golden as they've been reputed to be?

TK: Like I said to somebody, there's no drug that can give you a high like directing live television drama because of the sheer adrenaline level. I wouldn't go to sleep for three days after I came off the set. I remember working on one of the first shows I did called *On Camera* that had as its theme music Charlie Chaplin's "Smile" from *Modern Times* (1936). Ten, nine, eight, your stomach's churning, seven, six, five, four, three, hit the music, fade up one! Super the titles! Cue, cue, cue! It went on like this for an hour. Dissolve twenty years. I'm sitting with my wife in a restaurant having a nice meal and I start getting these terrible pains in my stomach. What is it? I hear "Smile" on the Muzak! To this day it gets me going. But what training live television was for all of us. There's a whole generation of people that came out of live television: Sidney Lumet, John Frankenheimer, Arthur Penn, Franklin Schaffner. It was great because I directed a one-hour play every four weeks for two years. You directed everything—period, romance, satires, drama, comedy. People have told me one of the things that characterizes my work is versatility.

Well, that versatility was generated in television because you tried everything. I like variety, I must say. I don't like being pinned down. If I had to point to my favorite style, I would point to social comedy. That's what I like doing most, films like *The Apprenticeship of Duddy Kravitz*, *Fun with Dick and Jane*, *North Dallas Forty*, those films that have social comment built into them.

JAG: Your first feature was *Tiara Tahiti*.

TK: I think that film is best forgotten! It could have been a really interesting comedy. It was an Evelyn Waugh-style satire on class. James Mason and John Mills were in the army in World War Two, with Mason upper class and Mills aspiring. They meet again in Tahiti. James Mason is kind of a beachcomber, so this playing out of class attitudes is enacted in this ridiculous, totally inappropriate setting of Tahiti. It could have been funny, but unfortunately I was too inexperienced. I was too young, still in my twenties. I bungled it.

JAG: You had two veteran actors in Mason and Mills.

TK: James Mason was one of our great cinematic actors. I've never seen anyone with such economy of means. I'll never forget filming this great scene between James and John, a long uninterrupted dolly shot. John Mills was brilliant in the scene. It was a pyrotechnical display of a man getting drunk over a period of four minutes. He got drunker and drunker. It was really his scene. James did absolutely nothing, it seemed. The whole crew applauded John Mills at the end of the take. Next day in dailies, you could only see James Mason on the screen. You'd say, "What's he doing? He did nothing in front of us!" He was truly that great cinema actor who has that *je ne sais quoi*, whatever it is. They seem to be doing very little in front of the camera but the next day you can't get your eye off them.

JAG: Your second feature, *Life at the Top*, was a sequel to *Room at the Top* (1959).

TK: That was a hard act to follow. *Room at the Top* was one of the great British films of the Fifties and Sixties. It was directed by a good friend of mine, Jack Clayton. The sequel was written by Mordecai Richler, who wrote *Duddy Kravitz* and *Joshua Then and Now*. As a beginning director it's difficult getting assignments. I was skeptical about doing a sequel to such a distinguished film. Still, I thought it had its chances, and again, that was a kind of social comedy, a very interesting comment on English society in the Sixties.

JAG: *Two Gentlemen Sharing* received a good deal of acclaim.

TK: I think that was the best film of what you might call my British period. It was an examination of the West Indian community in London and the white attitudes towards that community. It was an interesting film because it had a negative statement. It said that whites and blacks can't get along, mainly because we have too many misunderstandings, too many illusions and myths about each other. It was fortunately written by a black man, Evan Jones, who became one of my best friends, but people were a bit puzzled by the ending. At the time, everybody felt, "All whites and blacks will always get along," and people wanted an upbeat statement about the brotherhood of man. I haven't seen it recently, but it got very good reviews and went to the Venice Film Festival, where it did very well.

JAG: *Outback*, about a schoolteacher who interacts with rough outdoor types, took you to Australia.

TK: I think that *Outback* and *Duddy Kravitz* are the two best films I've made so far. It was made prior to the outbreak of the great Australian film movement. Interestingly enough, Peter Weir was an observer on that film. Fred Schepisi and other directors have been very kind to me and said that *Outback* was a great inspiration to them because there had been no films made in Australia, and suddenly they realized that Australian subjects were worthy of cinematic exploitation and investigation, and inspired them to do the films they went on to do, so that was very nice. I think *Outback* is a very strong, powerful film, and I'm very proud of it.

JAG: *Billy Two Hats* was a Western shot in Israel, again with a social statement, this time about the mistreatment of the American Indian in the 1880s.

TK: United Artists in London were in charge of that film and for a variety of financial reasons it had to be outside of America. I thought that the Spanish locations had been exhausted, so we went to Israel. Also, the producer was Norman Jewison, and he was shooting *Jesus Christ, Superstar* (1973) in Israel at the same time. We happened to be within 150 miles of each other, so he could drop in periodically. It was a wonderful script by Alan Sharp, who also wrote *Night Moves* (1975), almost like a parable. There's a quotation from the Bible that says, "Two are better than one. If one shall fall, the other shall pick him up." *Billy Two Hats* was a story about the necessity to have somebody that you love and is there to support you when things are bad.

JAG: How was your experience with the star, Gregory Peck?

TK: He's a consummate cinema actor. I learned a lesson that astonished me at the time, and still surprises me about even the most experienced film actors. If a stranger came on the set and Gregory stumbled over a line for a second, that was it, finished for the day, because once he would stumble, then he would stumble again. I said, "What's the matter, Gregory?" He said, "That person walked on the set," so I banned all visitors from the set. Later on he said to me, "This is what's going through my head. Inevitably you stumble, and then this stranger is saying, 'Look at Gregory Peck being paid all that money and he can't even learn his lines.' Once I get that idea in my head, I stumble again, and once I stumble again, I keep stumbling." The other idiosyncrasy I love Gregory for is that he had to have the reality of the thing before him. I was doing a closeup of Gregory at the end of the day, and the sun was going down. I had to get off. We were shooting in a distant ravine somewhere in the Negev Desert. He's supposed to be watching an Indian riding along the top of the mountains. I said, "Gregory, we're going to do this closeup. This is where you see the Indian riding along the top of the mountains." He said, "Fine." I said to the crew, "Quick, the sun's going down. Camera ready. Action!" Gregory said, "Wait a minute, Ted. Where's the Indian on top of the mountain?" "Gregory, the sun's going down, I've got fifteen minutes for the shot." "I can't do the shot without the Indian on top of the mountains." "A.D., put an Indian on top of the mountain!" That was the way he achieved reality. He couldn't operate outside himself. Some actors don't even want the other actor there when they're doing their closeups, but Gregory had to have the whole thing played out. He said, "That's when I know I'm being real and not being phony." He was a lot of fun to work with, and a wonderful man, too.

JAG: What was the evolution of *The Apprenticeship of Duddy Kravitz*?

TK: Mordecai Richler is my best friend. We've known each other thirty, forty years, forever it seems. When I finally decided to become a film director, I went to London. Mordecai was aspiring to be a novelist. Although we're both Canadians, we met in the south of France. We liked each other immediately and came to share a flat in London. During that time he wrote *The Apprenticeship of Duddy Kravitz* while we were sharing this apartment. I was one of the early people, if not the first one, to read the manuscript. I read it in 1959 and said, "One day, Mordecai, I'm going to be a big time director and I'm going to make a film out of this novel." We all laughed at the absurdity of any such notion, because first of all there was no Canadian film industry to support such a film, and who's going to give this *pischer* the money to make this film anyway? I always had it in the back of my head and I tried it in the Sixties after I'd directed a couple of films, but during the Sixties people didn't want to make period films, and they especially didn't want to make period films about Jewish boys growing up in Montreal. There's always been a bias in Hollywood about the depiction of Jewish subjects. Finally, when the Canadian Film Development Corporation was set up in Canada during the late Sixties and early Seventies to finance Canadian films, I was able to get the money out of the Canadian government. I still couldn't get any private money from any distributors when I made the film because people said, "Oh, it's so parochial, Jewish boy in Montreal, forget it." It was obviously a film that was very personal to me. First of all, although it's based on a novel written by my best friend, that novel incorporates a lot of my own experiences. Since we're very good friends, Mordecai and I would chat endlessly about our boyhoods. Inevitably, like any good writer, he sucks-in certain details and puts them in, so the film was very personal, and also a very important film for me. I always thought I would do my best work going back to the world that I knew, the world that I had grown up in. I feel the strength of *Duddy Kravitz* is that there's nothing in there anybody can challenge me on. Nobody can say, "That's not the way it was." Oh, yeah? I was there. I know that's what it was like. I know how it smelled. I know how Duddy sweated. I worked in a Jewish summer hotel. I worked in dressmaking and did what Duddy did with the belts. A lot of the details came out of my own life. I feel a lot of the authenticity and verisimilitude it achieves is because of that. Also, because Mordecai Richler is my best friend, I wanted to do this novel the best I could. I hadn't seen the picture in a long time, then saw it again recently, and I was absolutely amazed by how good Richard Dreyfuss is in the film.

JAG: Had you seen Dreyfuss in John Milius' *Dillinger* (1973)?

TK: I'd seen him in that, but I didn't remember him. He's got about a minute and a half where he plays Baby Face Nelson. He's really over the top in that film. I was very fortunate in that I had Lyn Stalmaster, one of the legendary Hollywood casting directors. I had worked with him on *Billy Two Hats*. In spite of our budget I sent our script down to him and asked if he would advise me. I'd been all over Canada, into New York, but I couldn't find anybody. Lyn read the script and he phoned me immediately and said, "This is an amazing script. There's only one person to play it and that's Richard Dreyfuss. You won't have heard of him." I said, "You're right." Lyn said, "Do you remember seeing *Dillinger*? He's in that. He was born to play this part." I went down to Los Angeles and Richard walked in. I thought Lyn Stalmaster had gone out of his mind. I'd always seen Duddy as a kind of reflection of oneself. Once upon a time I was a thin, nervous, edgy, ambitious, aspiring young man, more in the tradition of dark-eyed Polish and Russian Jews. I saw Duddy in that way. Richard's slightly pear-shaped, and he's a German Jew with blue eyes and gray hair. At first I was shocked because he was not the picture I had in my mind whatsoever, but as soon as Richard opened his mouth and read those lines with that incredible emotional intensity, I said, "My God, now I know Lyn was right," and I cast him.

JAG: Did you face any criticism from the Jewish community because of the film?

TK: Certain of my friends excoriated me. A fellow Canadian director asked me how I could make such an anti–Semitic film. I know Mordecai suffered tremendously from that. There's a scene in the bath house where Joe Silver advises Duddy because he's depressed, he's killed this man in his business. Joe Silver says, "You know, I came this close to going to jail, but my partner went instead because I was smarter than he was." A lot of Jewish people felt nervous sitting there watching this. It was Mordecai's opinion and mine too that you shouldn't treat anybody as a special case.

You just say the truth and say that's what it's like and that's what people are. I always found Duddy very sympathetic. That was the thing that Richard did so wonderfully, which was always my intention, that Duddy should engage your sympathies. You should understand the network of causes and relationships that make him behave as he does. As one of the characters says, "Why do you run around as if you had a red hot poker up your ass all the time?" That was the purpose of the film. Why *does* he run around like he has a red hot poker up his ass? The picture was really an explanation of that behavior. He does some pretty nasty things. He cripples his friend and he forges checks, but by the end of it I hope that you understand why he was doing what he was doing, and out of that understanding would come some kind of feeling for him.

JAG: You've planned a continuation of Duddy's story.

TK: Originally, Mordecai and I always thought of *Duddy Kravitz* as a trilogy. We wanted to do the second part with him later in life and the third part with him in the middle years of his life, but I guess we're going to skip two and go directly to three with Richard. But that will be down the line in the next two or three years.

JAG: After *Duddy Kravitz*, Hollywood came calling.

TK: They did even though the picture was a mild financial success. It did have a lot of critical attention, and several of the companies were interested in me. I'd been living in England for seventeen years at that time, and finally I left London and moved to Hollywood as a result of all these invitations to make films there.

JAG: Your first Hollywood movie was *Fun with Dick and Jane*.

TK: I loved that. Mordecai worked on the script, and some of the mordant humor is his. There were also two very good writers who worked on it, Jerry Belson and David Giler, people who are social observers too. At the time there was a recession going on. George Bernard Shaw had written all these plays about people who had out of desperation and financial pressure committed criminal acts like prostitution just in order to survive. It was a very Shavian theme at the turn of the century. That's how the picture was at the beginning, and I said, "No, this theme is too old. What's funny, what's going on, is that people want to maintain their class status. They don't want just to survive, they want to stay where they are. Upper middle class people don't even want to move down one notch." That's what I thought was fresh about the picture. The characters that George Segal and Jane Fonda play commit criminal acts so they can stay exactly where they are, and they're not going to accept being cheated on the dream they had struggled so hard to realize.

JAG: That was an important film for Jane Fonda.

TK: It was her first part after her long hiatus with her political activities regarding the Vietnam war, her first American movie in years. It created a lot of problems for us because there was still a great deal of bitterness toward her. This was 1976. It precluded us from getting a lot of locations. We'd apply to some location, like the aerospace factory that George Segal's character is involved in. People would say, "Who's in it?" We'd say, "George Segal," and they'd say, "Oh, great. We'd love you to come down. Anybody else?" We'd say, "Jane Fonda." "No picture with that traitor is going to come into my place!" and the phone would slam. A lot of that went on. There was still a lot of strong feeling. But she's a great comedic talent. I think she should do more comedy.

JAG: Your next picture, *Who Is Killing the Great Chefs of Europe?* was a comedy about food and murder.

TK: I think that picture would have succeeded better if it had been brought out today with our obsession with food. It was a bit ahead of its time in terms of the audience. Comedy has a very strange status in filmland. I'm very pleased that one or two comedies like *Moonstruck* finally crept into the 1987 Oscar nominations, which is very unusual. People sneer at comedy and think it's very low-level activity when really comedy is the most difficult thing to do, no question, hands down. I can speak here because I've directed dramas and action pictures. *First Blood* is the easiest thing to do. Any action picture is a snap. There's no dramatic depth you have to explore, and secondly, you're not looking to make people laugh. The next most difficult thing is drama, and the hardest by far is comedy. There's no middle ground of success with comedy. You can't be 80% successful with a joke. Either a joke works 100% or it's zip. With drama, if it's 80% moving, you're OK, but if a comedic scene doesn't work you're dead in the water. If it doesn't make an audience laugh, you have nothing going for you. You understand the style with drama. You always have the appeal to your own personal experience. You say, "Yes, that's accurate, that's inaccurate." You have some measuring stick by which to operate when you're directing drama. With comedy, sometimes the humor is generated after the shooting, in the editing, so on the floor you can't even see what it's going to be. The other thing is that comedy is a stylized medium because it has to carry jokes which are totally unreal. You have to discover some kind of style which will carry jokes. You have to be careful, and it's one of my tendencies, not to go too far, not to go into farce if it's not going to be a farcical film. You're always walking this tightrope and any moment you're liable to fall off one side or the other. You're either too serious or you've gone too far. Oscar Wilde had that great line when he was dying, supposedly. Someone said to him, "Dying must be hard, Oscar." He said, "No, dying's easy. Comedy's hard." I always admired Billy Wilder. When I was an aspiring director I wanted to be Billy Wilder. I love that kind of sophisticated Lubitsch humor. Billy Wilder really got short shrift in Hollywood. He got an Oscar for doing a serious film, *The Lost Weekend* (1945). Until

The Apartment (1960), he never really got the respect he should have. The comedies that he was doing were much more complicated and difficult than what a lot of other directors were doing.

JAG: Some of Wilder's comedies have a dark side to them, like *The Apartment* (1960) and *The Fortune Cookie* (1966).

TK: That's another thing about comedy. It doesn't function unless there's some meanness in it. It's gotta have a barb that makes it stick, otherwise it doesn't work.

JAG: With *North Dallas Forty*, Nick Nolte was first recognized as an actor instead of just a sex symbol.

TK: I think Nick is one of our finest cinema actors and one of the best that I've ever worked with. He works with great depth. He's one of those actors who instinctively know at what level to put a directorial comment. For example, if I said to him, "Nick, you look at this girl with this man over there and you feel a real pang of jealousy," Nick has this instinct to put it down several layers where it belongs and where it happens, whereas certain actors put jealousy right across their forehead too obviously. With Nick, a lot of other things are going on top of it, so it manifests itself exactly the right way. That's always pleasing to a director because you're using shorthand. You can't go around saying, "No, no, what you should be showing is this." Filmmaking is an expensive business and you're always under tremendous pressure to get out of it. You hope when you say things like that to an actor he can digest it and know how to make itself manifest, and Nick has that great capacity, which is wonderfully satisfying for a director. He makes it very clear and yet at just the right level of clarity, not sending telegrams. He is also a man of tremendous dedication and professionalism. I really loved working with him. We haven't worked since but we often look for material to do together. This was a big project for him. He was a fan of the book. When I was offered the film, Nick came with the package. *North Dallas Forty* was one of the few scripts that I wrote myself. I just never could get a satisfactory script from any writer. I knew exactly what I wanted, so I wrote the script myself, but Nick had a lot of contributions to make.

JAG: Were there any problems with the Dallas Cowboys organization about the depiction of professional football?

TK: Not really. Peter Gent wrote the book and there was no question what it was. Pete also worked on the screenplay after I got through with it and gave it authentic dialogue. I don't know how these people talk in the locker rooms. Pete Gent played for the Cowboys as a wide receiver and tight end for six years. He's an amazing man. Here he was a great football player, and yet he has all the sensibilities of a novelist, so he was a perfect man to write about this world with depth and feeling. There's no question it was a highly autobiographical novel about the Dallas Cowboys, and there was no point to obfuscate the issue and muddy it all up by pretending it was something else. It wasn't, so I just went for it and said, "Here's what it's about, this man's feelings and experiences with the different members of the team."

JAG: *Split Image* is an underrated film about religious cults.

TK: I started from scratch on that one. Peter Guber came to me and asked if I'd be interested in making a film about a person who's sucked into a cult. Indeed I was. I thought it was a very resonant subject when you figure there are about three million young people involved in one cult or another in America today. Why is this happening? What are they looking for that's missing? What values are they searching for? They're not deriving satisfaction from our society. The subject allowed you to examine everything that's going on around us. It was full of endless possibility and really attracted me for that reason. I worked on it for two years and the film disappeared practically without a trace. It's a subject that American people don't want to hear about. It's a scary subject. Parents don't want to see a film about kids disappearing into a cult like that. People would just rather avoid it than examine it.

JAG: James Woods gives such a manic, off-beat performance as the deprogrammer.

TK: Traditionally that part would have been played by a savior figure, a man who comes in and saves the boy from the cult, but I wanted to make him a much more ambiguous figure. You're never sure just what his motives were, was he self-interested in trying to exploit the situation, so he was a much more interesting man. Finally he was genuinely interested but he had a lot of other motivations as well.

JAG: David Morrell's novel *First Blood* had been around for some time before you were able to make it into a movie.

TK: I got involved around 1975 or 1976, when Robert Shapiro was president of Warner Brothers. He had been my agent before that. The property had been worked on by a variety of writers and directors. I think Martin Ritt had been involved at one point. When Bob came to Warners he said, "There's a very interesting book that hasn't been adequately scripted. Would you read the scripts and book and see what you feel about them?" I read the book and liked it tremendously. I thought it was a wonderful cinematic subject because it was very sparse in dialogue. My pictures tend to be rather heavily dialogued, coming from a literary tradition as I do. *First Blood* seemed to me to be totally visual, with hardly any dialogue. At the heart of it, I thought it had a very strong motif, almost like the Frankenstein story. The hero is this incredible engine of violence that has been created, and now that it's no longer needed he's come back to haunt us, always ready to start again. He had no place in American society anymore. Another thing I liked was Rambo attacking an American town exactly the way he would attack a Vietnamese town. That's what he used to do. I thought the whole image at the end of experiencing what it was like for these people to attack a Vietnamese town was a very strong vision. For all these reasons I was attracted to it. Finally, Warners decided not to make it, because it was 1976 and they felt the audience would prefer to forget about Vietnam. At that point, any film about Vietnam was taboo. They also felt it was too violent. People would periodically ask me if there was any film I would like to make and I'd say, "Yes, there's a script over at Warners." Finally, these two independent financiers, Mario Kassar and Andy Vajna, who were starting a small company called Carolco, asked me the same question. This time they did something about it. They went over to Warners and got the rights, and finally made the film.

JAG: Sylvester Stallone is a director as well as a superstar actor. How were your dealings with him?

TK: He was very good. He came up to me and said, "Listen, I'm a director but I'm telling you I'm just here as an actor. I don't want to hear anything about where the cameras should be placed or how we should stage a scene. It's your film. You tell me what you want and I will do it." He was as good as his word. I don't know how anybody acts and directs at the same time anyway, because both jobs seem to be all-consuming. I think Sylvester is an under-used actor. I think he's as good an actor as DeNiro or Pacino, and he's got all the equipment. He had an extremely tough time climbing up the ladder of success, and he told me the long, painful story of how he got there and the humiliations involved. Nobody believed in him except himself, nobody believed in *Rocky* (1976) except himself. He somehow managed to get through and his feelings about it were right and everybody else was wrong. So when you came to work with Sylvester, he doesn't trust anybody, certainly not the director. He has to build that trust and that was the hard thing in the beginning. I had to win his trust. There was a scene in which the deputy sheriff falls out of the helicopter and dies, the only dead man, actually, in the picture. Rambo runs over to get his gun and his jacket because it's freezing cold and he's stripped to the waist. He comes up to the body and there's blood everywhere. I said to Sylvester, "When you see that body, almost freak out like you had a traumatic experience, because it reminds you of all those dead people in Vietnam, all those things are flashing through your head. The audience may not understand why you're doing this but that's what we want. I want that at this moment." He wasn't sure about it but he did it, and the next day at the dailies he came and said, "That's one of the best pieces of acting I've ever done." From then on in we got along very well.

JAG: Rambo is such a demanding role for Stallone.

TK: He was incredibly physically brave, and I mean brave, because he was stripped to the waist in that freezing weather for most of the picture. He was very clever. I used to look like Mr. Michelin Tire, covered up with three down coats. I'd say to him, "Sylvester, get out of the cold." He said, "If I get out of this cold I'm going to get pneumonia. It's easier to stay out here." That was one thing. For the scene where we put rats on his bare back, I said, "Here's where you earn $3 million." For $10 million, I wouldn't let anybody put rats on my bare back! He's got tremendous guts, I will say.

JAG: Kirk Douglas was originally cast in *First Blood* as Rambo's former commanding officer.

TK: Kirk was not happy with his part. I tried to please him and so did Sylvester, who did all the final rewrites together with myself. We just couldn't please him. Kirk really wanted to make the picture about himself, which I can understand. He was a big star and he felt there should be more revelation about his character, but there was no room for it. Finally I had to say to him, "Kirk, this is a wonderful part. Please do it the way it is, but I understand if you're unhappy about it and I'll let you go back to California and we'll recast." He decided not to do it, and at the last minute Richard Crenna stepped in.

JAG: What were some of the problems you had to deal with working in the forest?

TK: Of all the pictures I've made, John, I think *First Blood* is by far the most difficult in terms of the conditions and the weather. We shot for five months. We chose completely the wrong time of year, November to March in British Columbia. It was supposed not to snow there, ha ha. I wanted that wet look because it rains a great deal there. You get this strange mixture up there of evergreen forests with these lichens hanging from trees, as if you were in New Orleans. The picture was done under sometimes very dangerous situations. We were always shooting scenes from the edges of precipices. I had a rope tied around my waist and tied to a tree 150 feet away from the precipice. The camera was always tied off. One day when we were shooting, a whole section of the canyon dropped, about a hundred feet away from us. It sounded like an A-bomb going off. There were helicopters flying down canyons, and it snowed in areas where it hadn't snowed in years. We had to steam and melt the snow for a whole valley. We had helicopters blowing the snow off trees. We had three steaming trucks melting the snow. We had workmen putting dirt on the snow in the background so you wouldn't see it. It was wet and cold, and not very firm footing, but if you want to get that look, that's the price you pay.

JAG: Andrew Laszlo was your cinematographer.

TK: The great difficulty for Andy was that we were shooting in great evergreen and fir forests. The branches would meet at the top, so even on the brightest day very little light would get down where we were. We wouldn't start shooting until about ten o'clock in the morning and we used to finish around 2:30. We had the shortest days. I'd find myself back in the hotel mid-afternoon wondering what had happened. As a result, even on the short shooting time we did have, he was forced to shoot at very low light levels. We practically shot the whole of that picture at f–1 with a fast 50mm lens. There are only two lenses that have an f–1 stop, and that was one of them, and Andy was still forcing the material one and two stops. I think Andy Laszlo is very underappreciated for what he did on that film. When Sylvester is buried in the mine, they blow him up and he's entombed in the mine, he has a match, he lights it and looks around. *That* was the lighting, the total lighting, two matches stuck together. He needed the illumination from two matches. On that stuff with the torch where Rambo's going underground to find another opening out of the mine, I'd say, "Andy, are you lit?" He'd reach for the torch, pull out his lighter, light the torch, hand it to Sylvester, and say, "Yep, we're lit." I think he's one of our great cameramen.

JAG: Do you have a particular philosophy about staging action scenes?

TK: I don't think I have a particular philosophy, except that you have to keep it moving. That's what motion pictures are anyway. They're called "motion" pictures, and when the cameras are rolling I don't say, "Speak!" I say, "Action!" I remember an old character actor, a comedian from silent film days, came on the set once and asked, "OK, what do I do?" I gave him the lines. He said, "No, not what I say, what do I do?" That's the essence of it. In action pictures, because you have nothing going for you except the action that's happening in front of you, you keep it moving, keep the camera moving, keep the story moving at a fast pace.

JAG: Some weaponry was stolen from the set of *First Blood*.

TK: It was a big theft. We had M–16 rifles and M–60 machine guns, the one that Sylvester carries that you feed bullets into. They were supposed to be guarded by the Canadian army, but someone got in on the weekend and stole all the guns. They were real guns. The Royal Canadian Mounted Police came in, the Canadian version of the F.B.I., since it's a federal offense, and we were all grilled. I said to the man, "You know, half an hour after these guns were stolen, they were in Lebanon or Northern Ireland." These are all contract jobs, so the guns were gone, never found.

JAG: To what do you attribute the phenomenal popularity of *First Blood*?

TK: Your guess is as good as mine. It was even popular in places like the Far East, as was *Rambo: First Blood Part II* (1985). Some people said the sequel was racist because he's murdering all these Oriental people, but they loved it in the Orient as well. One can rationalize all you like, but we'll never know why the Rambo character has this mythic quality. When I made *First Blood*, I felt that his contact with nature almost made him a Tarzan figure. I felt this noble savage quality to him, a man totally in touch with life in the forests. I think that's one of the appeals. I think basically *First Blood* has the appeal of a man who's being traduced by authority and finally hits back, which we all want to do. When I did *Fun with Dick and Jane* I did a little research and met this hold-up man through the L.A.P.D. He said, "You know one place you could rob with impunity? The telephone company. If you walked in there and there are a hundred people lined up to pay their bills, they wouldn't move a finger to stop you from taking money." I put the scene in the picture and every showing I ever attended, people stood up in the theatre and applauded, because everyone has been skewered by the telephone company at one time or another. They loved it when the telephone company got robbed! So I think it's always a deep element within all of us. The Establishment, authority, the government, in one way or another, is always abusing us and there's nothing we can do about it. We feel impotent. Well, John Rambo is not impotent. He struck back. One of the ironies of the story is that he comes into town and he says, "I just want to get a hamburger," and the sheriff says, "No, you move on." The denial of this hamburger led to all the chaos and mayhem that followed. I think what appeals to audiences is the initial feeling of anger that this man shouldn't be allowed to treat you in this way. They immediately identify with the Rambo character.

JAG: What was your toughest challenge in directing *Uncommon Valor*?

TK: As a director I'm really most interested in characters. That gives me the most satisfaction, the creation of characters. To properly develop a character you need certain amounts of cinematic time. One of the challenges of *Uncommon Valor* is you have seven men, seven quite separate characters, and also quite a number of permutations and relationships among these seven men. The balancing of all those elements, creating each one so you know each person quite vividly and saw something of his relationship with at least one other person in the group was for me the biggest challenge. As I say, I find the action part easiest.

JAG: Gene Hackman is the spine of *Uncommon Valor*, leading these young actors like Reb Brown, Fred Ward, and Tex Cobb. How was his relationship with the action ensemble?

TK: That was the first time I worked with Gene, and I hadn't known him prior to that. We've become very good friends since and I have tremendous admiration for him both as an actor and a person. He's a very generous and kind man, almost too kind. He gives of himself tremendously because like all good actors they realize if you don't give, you don't get when you're acting. On my latest film, *The Winter People*, I worked with Kelly McGillis and Kurt Russell, both extremely generous to other actors working with them. Kelly would be off camera and take after take she would weep because that's what her character was doing on camera. She wants the other actor to respond in the proper way, and she feels the only way he can properly respond is for her to be weeping off camera. I've never seen anything like it. Sometimes we'd do that ten takes and five different set-ups. She'd cry fifty times! That's the kind of giving that Gene Hackman has, along with the understanding that you must give generously in order for the picture to work.

JAG: John Milius was a producer on *Uncommon Valor*. Did he do any writing on the script?

TK: He didn't do much direct writing. We had a young writer whose idea it was originally, Joe Gayton, along with Wings Hauser, but John is obviously very experienced and made a number of very creative suggestions. He did directly write two or three scenes himself. I said to him, "John, you've gotta write this scene." There's that wonderful speech that Gene Hackman gives towards the beginning of the film when he finally collects the seven of them together in a barn and he tells them why. He says, "No one is interested in the Vietnam war because it's like a company that's gone bankrupt." It was a wonderful speech and John wrote that. He did write under pressure but mainly he functioned as a producer.

JAG: With *Switching Channels*, you were dealing with a classic piece of material, Ben Hecht and Charles MacArthur's *The Front Page*, which had been filmed three times before.

TK: One enters any remake with a great deal of trepidation because you know you're going to suffer in comparison with the original. In this case, the originals are both classic of the American cinema, Lewis Milestone's *The Front Page* (1931) and Howard Hawks' *His Girl Friday* (1940). The Hawks film was a trend-setter in terms of its fast-paced verbal pyrotechnics. You know the critics are waiting for you and they're going to make these invidious comparisons. I'm also not very fond of doing remakes or sequels. I did *Life at the Top* but I turned down the sequel to my own film *First Blood*. But I thought *The Front Page* was a great story with perennial appeal even though it's been done before. The Elizabethan dramatists continually kept borrowing plots and used it to their own ends to say what they wanted to say, and I think that's exactly what we did. We took the old plot of *The Front Page*, and transferred it to the world of television news where it fitted perfectly. As a result, I was able to satirize the subjects I wanted to satirize. I came into the project once Jonathan Reynolds had written the first draft, and I never screened any of the previous pictures. I remembered them very well, but I took the story further afield. You know the prescription Ezra Pound made for all art is to make it new. So in the case of *Switching Channels* we tried to make it new.

JAG: What was your approach to working with the actors?

TK: I tend to rehearse quite a bit. You have to be very careful with comedy, depending on what kind of comedy it is. Don't try to rehearse farce comedy too much because you'll finally kill it. By the time you get to put it on film it becomes a wooden imitation of itself because everybody knows what's coming. You've got to get it rehearsed enough so there'll be no technical mistakes which would damage a good take, but you don't rehearse it so much so there's always room for that improvisation that comedy needs, reacting spontaneously to anything that occurs at the moment. In general, one of the things about comedy or about anything you direct is that it has to have an atmosphere free of inhibition. When I was a kid, I used to listen to a marvelous American radio program called *Let's Pretend*. That's what I try to do on the set, create an atmosphere of children at play, let's pretend, so that the actors never feel any pressure that impedes the free flow of comedy. If the actors don't have a sense of humor, you're dead, and I was fortunate in *Switching Channels* because Kathleen Turner, Burt Reynolds, and Chris Reeve all have great senses of humor.

JAG: Kathleen Turner was pregnant during the filming.

TK: We discovered she was pregnant just before we started to shoot. It didn't make itself manifest until the last couple of weeks of shooting. Slowly and slowly the camera got closer and closer to her face as we were shooting! Since it's scattered throughout the film I can't remember to this day in what parts of the film it's beginning to show. Kathleen was the very first person cast in the film. I always saw her in the part. I think she's in the tradition of the great comediennes of the Thirties and Forties, like Carole Lombard, one of my heroines as a boy. She always reminded me of Lombard in her energy and feistiness, her quick tongue, funny, tough, intelligent. My wife was totally in awe of the fact that Kathleen was pregnant because my wife was pregnant at nearly the same time and she was prostrate on her back. We were amazed how Kathleen worked twelve hours a day and generated this incredible energy.

JAG: Burt Reynolds made a return to comedy in the film. He's been compared in the past to Cary Grant, and here he actually plays the Grant role from *His Girl Friday*.

TK: Burt's a big admirer of Cary Grant and was also a friend of his. He always aspired to be that kind of light comedian, and he's proved it in the past and on this film that he can do it. I think recently he's made a mistake in saddling himself with all these police parts and private eye detective roles, because I think he's a natural comedian. He has a great sense of humor, natural timing, he's very quick on his feet, and he's a very amusing man, always sees the ironic comedy of situations, and that ironic outlook is what constitutes sophisticated comedy.

JAG: Chris Reeve, the screen's Superman, has an amusing role as a man afraid of heights.

TK: That was an ironic by-product of having cast him. Some people thought that I introduced that glass elevator sequence where he has a total collapse because of his fear of heights after I cast him, as some kind of reference to *Superman* (1978), which isn't the case. That was always in the picture. I've seen Chris in the theatre and he's another impeccable comedic artist.

The thing with Chris is that he has extraordinarily perceptive powers. He can look at people and borrow little mannerisms to create a three-dimensional character out of this mosaic of characteristics. In the picture he's playing a total Yuppie idiot, a man completely obsessed with his outward appearance, his hair, his clothing, his food. He carries it to an excessive degree. We were discussing his character and he said, "Look, I know a lot of these people in New York and I'll borrow a bit from here and a bit from there."

JAG: Your new project is *The Winter People*.

TK: It was a very fine novel by a North Carolinian named John Ely, and it was brought to my attention by a producer friend of mine, Bob Solo. I immediately fell in love with the property. It's a period love story set in North Carolina in 1934 with Kelly McGillis and Kurt Russell, and Lloyd Bridges playing Kelly's father. I've wanted to do a love story for many years, and this is a powerful and moving story. Kurt plays an outsider who stumbles into this remote hill community and becomes involved with this woman played by Kelly who has a whole history he's not aware of. It's like a *Romeo and Juliet* story gone wrong beforehand. It's a story of moral accountability too, full of interesting sidelights and resonances. It's something I've wanted to do for four or five years and finally I was able to do it.

(1988)

Adrian Lyne

Adrian Lyne's *Fatal Attraction* became one of the indisputable film sensations of 1987. The Stanley Jaffe-Sherry Lansing production, starring Michael Douglas and Glenn Close, grossed over $150 million in rentals in its first year of release, copped a *Time* magazine cover with the headline "The Thriller is Back," and earned Lyne an Academy Award nomination as Best Director. Lyne eschewed the ultra-slick style of his earlier *Flashdance* (1983) and *9½ Weeks* (1986) for a more realistic look at the sexual machinations of a philandering husband and the nightmarish results of his affair with a psychotic.

Lyne was born in Peterborough, England, raised in London, and attended the Highgate School. He worked for the J. Walter Thompson Agency in London, directed award-winning TV commercials (which he continues to direct), and made two short films, *The Table* and *Mr. Smith*, which were official entries in the London Film Festival. *Foxes* (1980) marked his feature directing debut, a critically well-received drama about teenagers in Southern California, but it was the smash hit *Flashdance* that established Lyne as one of the hottest directors in Hollywood. His next film *9½ Weeks* was a sexually charged psycho-drama, based on the Elizabeth McNeill novel, with Mickey Rourke and Kim Basinger. While disappointing at the U.S. box-office, it performed well overseas and went on to become a huge homevideo success in America.

The following interview was conducted in September 1987, the week before *Fatal Attraction* opened in New York.

FILMOGRAPHY

Foxes (1980, United Artists). HV: Key.
Flashdance (1983, Paramount). HV: Paramount.
9½ Weeks (1986, MGM/United Artists). HV: MGM/UA.

Adrian Lyne (courtesy of Mr. Lyne).

Fatal Attraction (1987, Paramount). HV: Paramount.

LYNE INTERVIEW

JOHN A. GALLAGHER: *Fatal Attraction* is a very credible thriller. What was your attitude in handling this kind of material?

ADRIAN LYNE: I think the most terrifying things are those that are closest to home, and I certainly have known more than one person who bears a resemblance to Glenn Close's character. It's very scary dealing with this kind of obsessive when you realize that anything you tell them makes no impact. They have tunnel vision. Glenn's character tells Michael Douglas in the film, "I won't be ignored," and he says, "You don't get it." It's a scary moment because then the potential for disaster is enormous. I think a lot of people know people like this, and there but for the grace of God they could have gone.

JAG: The Douglas character cheats on his wife, yet you still feel sympathy for him.

AL: Your sympathy has to swing between Michael and Glenn. Well into the second act of the movie you understand what Glenn is going through. This man screwed her not once but twice during the course of a weekend and it would be all too easy to wash your hands of it and go back to your wife and kid and pretend it never happened, but the truth is it *did* happen. We're human beings and to a degree there's an emotion woven in when you make love to somebody. I felt very sympathetic with her point of view for a long while, and less sympathetic with his, truthfully. It changes as she plunges deeper into a psychosis and then patently you have to sympathize with him and the family.

JAG: How much of this balance was in James Dearden's screenplay?

AL: It was a very good script. I read so few that you really can't put down and I was reading this thing like there was no tomorrow. I was dying to know what else would this woman do, and when would the wife find out? The screenplay had huge in-built tension and energy, which so few scripts have. In the end, the script is just a framework and you have to make the family breathe. Hopefully I added a lot to it in terms of texture that makes a movie relationship, if you like, into a real relationship, a real family. It was a fabulous script, though. One thing I particularly like is when you have a fairly simple expositional scene, for example, early on when the family is leaving the lobby of the apartment. Anne Archer, the wife, is talking to Michael about going up to the country and he's sort of arguing with her, and at the same time he's talking to Anne, the kid is talking to the father and saying, "Dad, Dad, will Grampa be up there?" So you've got two threads going on, and a third thread at the same time with Anne asking the girl if she's got chewing gum in her mouth. So you have three concurrent dialogues, and I love those kind of layers, because you think, "Gee, this is real."

JAG: You've got a fourth thread in that scene with the dog at their heels.

AL: Exactly! It's a full feeling, and very satisfying, even though it's a relatively undramatic scene.

JAG: You also use the production design in the film to help delineate character.

AL: Glenn's apartment is rather cold and featureless, and lacks the domesticity of Michael's home. In terms of props, I wanted Glenn's to be really rather sparse, just a pile of manuscripts by the bed, which is sort of right for a book editor. I saw a number of editors' apartments and tried to find out what was the common denominator. As an opposite to that, Michael and Anne's apartment was busy and full of Polaroids, all the clutter of a family, and I tried to keep browns and beiges in the apartment, warmish colors as compared to Glenn's apartment, which was white and cold.

JAG: Did you use real locations?

AL: Yes. I always shoot on real locations. I much prefer that. In a way, it's one less thing to worry about. If you work in a studio you're always worrying about whether you're going to float the ceiling or a wall, and how long it will take. What's nice on location is "This is it."

JAG: I think the audience feels it subliminally.

AL: I think they do as well, because an art director never quite gets that sort of clutter, the dust in the corner. I love that shit. I think it makes it breathe, and I think it helps the actor when they're not a stage removed from reality. They're actually in a real kitchen where the gas *really* works.

JAG: How does that affect your location sound?

AL: It can be a nightmare. Afterwards everybody screams blue murder at the sound recordist, but in the end I think it's worth it. For example, Glenn's apartment was really in the meat market district, so it was tough with trucks outside, but it was nice for Glenn to be able to look out a real window and see what was out there.

JAG: How did you get involved with *Fatal Attraction*?

AL: I've got a place in Provence in the South of France, and I was there when I was sent the script. I read it and just couldn't put it down. Having just finished *9½ Weeks* and taken a battering at the hands of practically everybody, the last thing I wanted to do was another movie. But I thought this had the potential for really strong performances, and also I think I learned, hopefully, from the mistakes I made on *9½ Weeks*. I'm much more pleased with the way the visual side of *Fatal Attraction* backs up the performances rather than swamps them. It's a lot less stylized than *9½ Weeks*, which was too glossy. If I was doing *9½ Weeks* again, I'd do it much more like the way I did *Fatal Attraction*.

JAG: How was your relationship with the producers of *Fatal Attraction*, Stanley Jaffe and Sherry Lansing?

AL: We argued a lot and I think that's really healthy. The moment you start behaving like you're the oracle and start believing that you're right, is when you're wrong, basically. I think all the best decisions I've made have come out of massive arguing, screaming, and yelling. Quite often you arrive at something that is better than either of you thought initially. It comes out of justification and conflict. I believe in a certain extent in conflict, because I think better stuff comes out of that. I worked very closely with Glenn Close vis-à-vis her part because it was such a departure for her, playing somebody who for a long while is unlikeable. That was a bit of a pill for her to swallow because she's always played rather nice people. She was very anxious to avoid being a one-note villainess, so we spent a lot of time exploring this woman's psychiatric makeup.

JAG: It's a much more sexual role than she's done before.

AL: Yes, and she's very sexy. I think quite often the sexiest people are those you least expect to be. The ones who wear it on their sleeve are quite often less so. My first feeling was to go with Isabelle Adjani because I'd just seen her in a French film called *Deadly Summer* (1986). The part she played in that was not dissimilar to this. She's terrifically erotic and telegraphs it from way off, whereas Glenn doesn't. I think in the end it's more interesting to go that route where you suddenly unearth this craziness, this sensuality, this woman who eventually has all these demons.

JAG: How about working with Michael Douglas, an actor who is also an accomplished producer?

AL: Scary. Now and then the producer's hat appears and he'll say, "You're lit this way, why don't you shoot from that way and you'll have the same lighting." It was this sort of thing. It was good in a way because it kept you awake. You have to do your homework with Michael. I was astonished at how good an actor he was. I'd never realized it. I'd known him as a producer and I'd obviously liked him in *Romancing the Stone* (1984), so swashbuckling and heroic, but I never knew he could play so well a man who's weak and vulnerable. I think it was a brave decision on his part. Being Kirk Douglas' son I think it's tough to play this particular part.

JAG: Ellen Hamilton Latzen, who plays the daughter of Douglas and Anne Archer, had never acted before, but she is very natural.

AL: She was five or just six years old, and she was a very impressive child, eccentric, off the wall. I've never met a child like her. She couldn't read, and I'd paraphrase everything rather than give her the dialogue, because I wanted it to be her speaking rather than the script. She would say, "Let me see the script," so I'd give her the script, but I'd know she couldn't read it! I'd go along with it. She wanted a mark on the floor because Michael wanted a mark. She was fascinating. You'd give her the lines and she would start to extemporize, just a very creative kid. I've got a daughter of eleven who used to teach me these awful card tricks, except they'd never work out and she'd have to start again and again for hours, and we used that. The card game wasn't in the script. The scene was very expositional, with Anne wanting Michael to go up to the country to see this house, and there again I wanted to add another layer to the scene. I wanted to have the basis of the card game and the interruptions from the kid making him look at the row of cards. It immediately makes it real, 'cause that's what life is. We're always being interrupted, talking at once, the TV on in the background. I love that. It makes the thing live.

JAG: It's like the three-cushion dialogue in Howard Hawks movies, people stepping on each other's lines.

AL: All of a sudden it's hailed as a novelty when Woody Allen does it in *Hannah and Her Sisters* (1986), but it's not. In that particular movie I felt it became a bit mannered because you were aware of this cacophony the whole time, everybody talking at once.

JAG: Have you seen *Fatal Attraction* with a large audience yet?

AL: It's real gratifying seeing it with a proper audience rather than a critic's audience. The audience shouts and yells. In the last twenty minutes of the film, there's bedlam. I honestly can say I don't think I've ever seen it, personally, in a movie. I like that, because I don't think you're making the movie for yourself, you're making it for the people who pay the six bucks.

JAG: You really manipulate the audience in the final reel of *Fatal Attraction*.

AL: They know something's going to happen. It's the old Hitchcock maxim. You see the guy putting the bomb under the table and you know it's going to go off sometime but you don't know when, so you create an indeterminate jeopardy.

JAG: How did the release version of *9½ Weeks* differ from your cut?

AL: They were different films. There was the film that was shown in the United States that I really hated and felt didn't work. The film that was shown in Europe was better, and included the only S&M scene in the movie. It was an S&M relationship, so it had to be in. It's three different films, because the cable version has elements of the European film, but not all of them because it had to be an "R," so the best version so far is the European version. There are long cuts of three and four hours that were infinitely better than anything that's been seen because there was a background to the relationship. It never saw the light of day and it's partly my fault, partly the studio's. The other thing is I chose a rather visual, stylized route with the film. It was distracting. I made it glossy and I think the visual took over. I regret that now. Having said all that, I know in the footage I shot there's a hell of a movie. One day I'll recut it.

JAG: What cut is the American homevideo version?

AL: It's more the European version, better than the American theatrical.

JAG: *9½ Weeks* was plagued from the beginning with problems. Tri-Star was about to produce it, then the project passed on to MGM/UA.

AL: There were three or four different studios involved at different points. I'd just done *Flashdance* and that was a huge commercial success. I was

offered *A Chorus Line* (1985) and that was such an obvious move to make
that I didn't want to do it. When you have a commercial success it means
you get a chance to do something more esoteric, so I decided to do *9½
Weeks*. I'd read Elizabeth McNeill's novel previously and loved it. I'm
not sure the novel is makeable because it's so internal. Immensely erotic,
but it was her thoughts so much. The problem with the story really is
that your heroine, in popular terms, is a deviant. This is a woman who
enjoys pain in the process of getting fucked. She enjoys being hurt physically, and mentally as well. She's a masochist, and that's a hard pill for
an audience on Third Avenue to eat. I mean, in the book, he would
handcuff her to the wall, then watch TV for two hours, and somewhere
into the second hour she would start to whimper. He would ignore her,
keep watching the ballgame, and then he'd fuck her viciously. The way
McNeill wrote it, the pain and the sexuality mingled, and it was immensely erotic for this woman, and I have a sneaking suspicion, for the
people who read the book. But how do you put that on the screen?

JAG: How do you approach the lovemaking scenes in your films?

AL: The worst thing is before you do it. You never stop talking about it
two weeks prior to the scene. The moment you bring it up you think,
"Oh God, I wish I hadn't brought it up because now they'll be thinking
about it." In talking about it, though, you try to make light of it. You
don't know if it's going to be erotic. All you can do is guess. On *Fatal
Attraction*, I had known Michael well but not Glenn, so I read her with
him on scenes that involved sexuality early in the casting process. I didn't
want to do their sex scene in bed because it's so dreary, and I thought
about the sink because I remembered I had once had sex with a girl over
a sink, way back. The plates clank around and you'll have a laugh. You
always need a laugh in a sex scene. If you don't, they'll laugh *at* you.
The audience needs a release. You also get a laugh later in the scene when
his pants are down around his ankles. The faucet is also a laugh, and it
has erotic possibilities too, since her hands are wet and she splashes the
water over him. So it's a gradual process, and when I came to shoot it,
it was very easy. I did it all hand-held so there was no problem with the
heat going out of the scene while you had to move the tripod or the
dolly. By this time I knew Michael and Glenn very well, so you're doing
the love scene as a ménage-à-trois in a weird sort of way. I was very
vocal—"Good, good, that's great! Do that again!" If they know that
they're turning you on, it builds their confidence, rather than just clutch-
ing at each other in silence. In the editing, I was cutting my voice out
of everywhere.

JAG: How about the sex scenes in *9½ Weeks*?

AL: There again, you're casting chemistry, you're not casting two individuals, you're casting a pair. I spent an afternoon with Mickey (Rourke)
and Kim (Basinger). I saw so much fear and excitement and danger,

everything the movie needed, in that afternoon with them. Again, we would use the script as a basis and improvise things. I'd throw surprises, things Kim wasn't expecting, and see how she'd react.

JAG: Can you give me an example?

AL: This is going to sound a little crass, but it wasn't exploitive, it really wasn't. In the scene where she crawls across the floor to Mickey, Kim thought she was going to do the scene as we'd planned. Before the scene started, I said, "I want you to take your underwear off," and she wasn't ready for this. It was fascinating, the mixture of fear, then suddenly erotic, then back to fear, which was what the movie was about. In Kim's case, rage too, which we used in the scene. Those sort of surprises help make it real for an actor. That was quite different than *Fatal Attraction*, because Kim really had to live the part.

JAG: That was a very daring role for her.

AL: Absolutely, and even now, she talks endlessly about the movie. We're very frustrated that we've seen the longer versions of the film and know what it could be. At the time, it was very popular to beat up on *9½ Weeks*. People's public posture is very different from their private one when watching it on the video. There are areas of the film that don't work and that enrages me because I think I would know how to do it now.

JAG: What do you think of *Flashdance*?

AL: I think it moved the musical along a bit. Whether it moved the genre in good ways is debatable. At the time, to look at the dances in terms of video imagery was different. The dances weren't just a flight of fancy that one couldn't possibly do on a stage. It was all technically feasible. Ironically, it looked much more glamorous than it really was. We just had a little bit of neon around the stage, the strobe light was easily done, a hollowed-out TV with fans to make the smoke come out. *Flashdance* was just a bit of fluff, and at the time it was massacred critically because people took it very seriously. I thought it was like a Busby Berkeley movie, and about as important as that. Hopefully there's room for a bit of fluff next to a Bergman movie, or a movie like *Fatal Attraction* which has a lot of guts to it. I didn't want to do *Flashdance*. I was offered it but turned it down, then there wasn't any movie in the foreseeable future so I did it.

JAG: How were the songs in *Flashdance* chosen?

AL: We just endlessly listened to music. Giorgio Moroder is always credited with the music but he only did two tunes out of a dozen. A lot of them were unknown groups. With "Maniac," I heard a rhythm that I liked with the bell sound.

JAG: *Flashdance* was produced by Don Simpson and Jerry Bruckheimer

AL: They're very stimulating people. Don is like a child with all the faults and pleasures of a child, incredibly enthusiastic. Jerry is more of an art director, with very good visual taste.

JAG: With such an inexperienced actress as Jennifer Beals, how much did you have to hold her hand?

AL: I think you always have to. In the end, I don't think it's that much different with Jennifer Beals than it is with Glenn Close. Any director's job is to make an actor understand that you're giving everything of yourself to a part. When you do that, they tend to give it back to you, when they see that what you see is what you get, and there's no attitude. It's kind of a love affair, it really is. You get very close doing movies. It sounds really corny but it's true. There's not a lot that's left unsaid when you go in the trailor with them. They're naked, they're stark fucking naked. We all are. As long as you break down the barriers, and are in it together, then out of that nakedness will come something good. That's always the point of view that I come from, rather than coming from the position of jackboots and the whip (LAUGHTER). Although that sounds fun (LAUGHTER).

JAG: The Cecil B. DeMille School of Directing (LAUGHTER).

AL: Truffaut was always my idol. What a waste his death was. Incredible man. I went to his grave, burst into tears. It's in Montmartre, in Paris, flowers all over it. I got the sweetest note from his wife, Fanny Ardant, a great actress.

JAG: What do you admire about Truffaut's work?

AL: I'm attracted to those sorts of movies. I'd love to do a movie in French, actually. My French is fairly good. I like relationship pieces. Truffaut said once that the Europeans are attracted to movies about people with weakness and vulnerability whereas Americans tend to make movies about heroes. I think it's true. I think in the end, though, that Bertolucci is the master. I think *The Conformist* (1970) is probably the best single film ever made, for me. It's the perfect blend of visual and performance. I was talking before about layers of dialogue. Bertolucci does that with his decor and locations. They have such depth. Something will be going on in the foreground but you'll also be seeing through the kitchen and through that you'll be seeing somebody working in the pantry, and beyond *that* you'll see outside into the courtyard.

JAG: How did you get the chance to direct your first film, *Foxes*?

AL: I was doing a commercial for Levi's in the desert in Palmdale, California, and I met David Puttnam, whom I'd known in England. He gave me the script and said that he was sure they'd want an American director 'cause it's an American subject. I liked it quite a lot. I thought it was an honest, documentary-style look at these kids in the San Fernando Valley trying to grow up and be independent. David asked me to direct the film with him producing for United Artists. Unfortunately, UA threw it away. About eight people saw it. I thought it was quite a good movie. It got good reviews, but nobody really went to see it. It was one of the first movies about "Valley Girls."

JAG: How did you like working with Jodie Foster?

AL: She's a very tough, strong girl. It was the first movie she cried in, and I was quite proud of her in that scene because it was difficult.

JAG: You've directed many commercials.

AL: I still do them now and then. I think they're a good learning process.

JAG: Do you prefer working in the United States?

AL: Yes. I don't really like the English too much. I hate the whole class system there. I don't want to live in it. It's alright looking at it from here, amusing and kind of quaint, but there it percolates everywhere. I spend as much time as I can in New York but also live in L.A. as well. Actually, I'd rather be at Paramount! It's a real studio, still romantic in that sense. Stanley Jaffe's office, for example, is the old Howard Hughes office on Romaine Street in Hollywood. I find that much more exciting than walking up and down Water Street in London.

JAG: What's your next project?

AL: Hopefully I'll be able to do *Silence*. It's set in Chicago, and it's a very bizarre, interracial love story between a white middle-aged man and a black hooker who is mute. It's from a James Kennaway novel. There's a race riot background, controversial, and it's a wonderful love story. It's not set up at a studio yet, but I'm in it with Allan Carr, the producer. I'm co-producing it with him, and directing it from a David Rayfiel script.

(1987)

John Milius

The great American tradition of larger-than-life narrative filmmaking best embodied by John Ford, Howard Hawks, and John Huston lives on in the screenplays and films of John Milius. Like these veteran directors, Milius favors full-blooded characterizations, vigorous action, and a moralistic code of honor, rooted in his love for history and traditional story-telling. John Milius was born on April 11, 1944, in St. Louis, Missouri, and raised in California. and attended Los Angeles City College and the USC Film School, where he won an International Student Film Festival Award for an animated short, and bonded with another future filmmaker, George Lucas.

Milius is above all a spinner of yarns, and after breaking into the business co-scripting *The Devil's Eight* (1969) with Willard Huyck and doing some uncredited work on the screenplay for *Little Fauss and Big Halsy* (1970), he rose to become one of Hollywood's top screenwriters. He contributed to *Dirty Harry* (1971) and wrote its sequel, *Magnum Force* (1973), as well as the original screenplays *Jeremiah Johnson* (1972), directed by Sydney Pollack, and *The Life and Times of Judge Roy Bean* (1973), directed by John Huston. In 1979, Milius shared an Academy Award nomination with Francis Coppola for *Apocalypse Now*, based on a script he had written ten years earlier.

As Milius became one of the industry's highest priced screenwriters, he was able to parlay his status into the opportunity to direct his first feature, the low-budget gangster film *Dillinger* (1973). His second directing effort, *The Wind and the Lion* (1975) was high adventure in the vein of *Gunga Din* (1939) and *Lawrence of Arabia* (1962), and enabled the writer-director to dramatize an incident in the presidential career of one of his long-time heroes, Theodore Roosevelt. *Big Wednesday* (1978) was an underrated surfing saga, *Conan the Barbarian* (1982) a tremendously popular adventure-fantasy based on the Robert E. Howard pulp character, *Red Dawn* (1984), a cautionary action drama about a Soviet attack on the United States, and

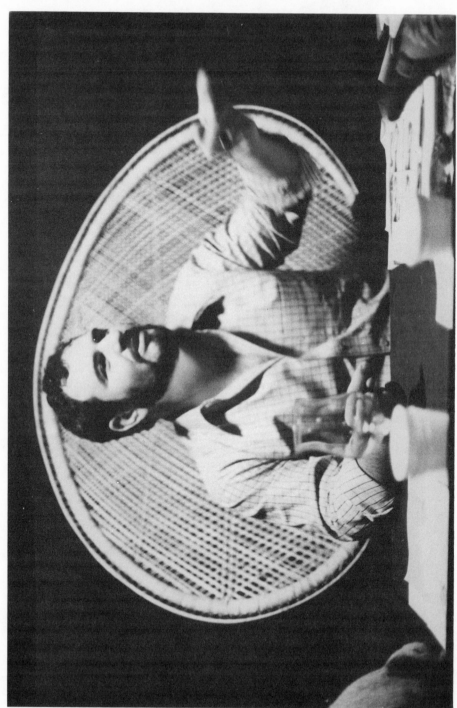

John Milius (photo by Sam Sarowitz).

Farewell to the King (1989) a return to the heroics of *The Wind and the Lion* in a jungle setting reminiscent of *Apocalypse Now*.

I first interviewed Milius in January 1978, while still an undergraduate at Emerson College. With my fellow classmates, Sam Sarowitz and Marino Amoruso, I spent the day at Milius' A-Team offices in Burbank, California, where he was editing *Big Wednesday*. I updated the interview in 1982 after the release of *Conan the Barbarian*.

FILMOGRAPHY

Dillinger (1973, American International). HV: Vestron.
The Wind and the Lion (1975, MGM). HV: MGM/UA.
Big Wednesday (1978, Warner Bros.). HV: Warners.
Conan the Barbarian (1982, Universal). HV: MCA.
Red Dawn (1984, MGM-United Artists). HV: MGM/UA.
Farewell to the King (1989, Orion).

MILIUS INTERVIEW

JOHN A. GALLAGHER: What sparked your interest in films?

JOHN MILIUS: I watched television and went to movies, and the idea that certain people made movies I liked to see got across to me at a very young age. Steven (Spielberg) has such a consuming interest in films. When he was a little kid he tried to make movies. I didn't have that so much. I had a paper route, and for an entire week after I finished I went to see *The Searchers* (1956) every day. I didn't see it again until I got one of my first writing jobs, and they let me get a film to watch. I was sure that I had imagined this film. I was enormously relieved to find it was better than I'd remembered it. I gradually got onto the idea that if a movie was made by John Ford, it was going to be something I liked, something that really moved me. Then I got the idea that if the movies had John Wayne in them, they'd probably be pretty good too, because a lot of those John Ford made. I assumed that Ford made *Red River* (1948), for example, because they were similar. Finally I got the idea that there were a group of directors who made movies I liked, including Howard Hawks, who really made *Red River*, John Huston, and Raoul Walsh. By the time I was eighteen I was aware there was such a thing as a movie director. I was also very influenced at the time by literature. I was a lousy student but I got through school by being a good writer.

JAG: What authors in particular did you admire?

JM: I read everything that Hemingway and Faulkner ever wrote. I was obsessed with Herman Melville and *Moby Dick*. To this day I still think we need no other novel. It's the greatest work of art. I would rather have written *Moby Dick* than painted the Sistine Chapel or made *Citizen Kane* (1941), or made *Citizen Kane* while painting the Sistine Chapel! I would rather have written *Moby Dick* than walked into the Mother Ship at the end of *Close Encounters* (1977), which is really going far because everyone wants to walk into that Mother Ship and walk off with Rick Dreyfuss. I was always interested in history and got good grades in it. I loved the idea of history because it was like stories being told around a campfire. Even if you had a bad history professor and he required you to read *Plutarch's Lives*, what a wonderful thing to do! I couldn't imagine how anyone could *not* read *Plutarch's Lives*. I couldn't get through *The Great Gatsby*, but I consumed Gibbons' *Decline and Fall of the Roman Empire* and H. G. Wells. Living as a kid for two years in Colorado, I became enormously interested in Western American history, and the expansion and industrialization of the country. America is a wonderful country for someone who's interested in history because it all happened in two hundred years. It's all right here to see. You can identify with it quickly.

JAG: What was the turning point for you in terms of moviemaking?

JM: More than anything else at the time, I was a surfer. When I was eighteen I went to the Hawaiian Islands on a pilgrimage, as every surfer who is worth his salt does. We'd go to the north shore of Oahu, particularly Sunset Beach, and attempt to ride the big waves. Sunset Beach is one of those magical places for me. It's like Mecca. Having been to Sunset Beach changes your life. You can never look at anything the same way again. During that period I walked into a movie theatre in the depths of depression. When you're eighteen, you're always either exhilarated or depressed. I don't think I had enough girls or *a* girl. Just one would have been enough. It was a Japanese movie theatre and I saw a couple of Kurosawa films and that did it. It just blew me out. I said, "This is what I have to do."

SAM SAROWITZ: What was it about Kurosawa?

JM: The Ford films were interesting and I had known there was this thing of making movies, but that was Hollywood. You had to know someone to get in. At that time, really, you had to be born in Hollywood. When I saw these Kurosawa films I was determined to die trying to assault the walls of whatever Establishment there was. That's all I really wanted to do. That's really all I still want to do is make movies just like his. To me those are the finest movies that have ever been made and as far as I can tell ever will be made. I have such admiration for Kurosawa as a human being. That's what really got me going about film. I never loved film. Like I say, I was never like Steve or George Lucas. They loved film, they loved the history of it, they loved putting it together, they loved the gimmicks. I'm not really a filmmaker in the sense that they are. I'm a storyteller.

JAG: You attended University of Southern California for film.

JM: I quit actually. I decided to go back to being a lifeguard. I couldn't pass French. But I wasn't able to get a job that summer because I was a lousy lifeguard. I was irresponsible. I got a job as a story assistant to Larry Gordon at American International Pictures. Willard Huyck and I lasted two weeks. I was fired for insubordination and he was fired for surliness. After that we wrote a script for AIP, *The Devil's Eight*. I always had good writing jobs after that.

JAG: Is writing the best way to enter the industry?

JM: If you're a writer. Everybody tries to be a writer, because it's the easiest thing. All you need is a nineteen-cent pen and a bunch of legal pads and you're a writer. One of the executives was commenting how few young writers have made the grade. There just aren't that many people who are natural writers that can really write. Occasionally these guys'll sell a screenplay for a lot of money and they'll be hot for a week, but they are not storytellers and writers. If you're a writer, you know you're a writer. You can't stop yourself. People always say to me, "Gee, I wish I could write." It reminds me of Tennessee Williams. He had a day job in a steam laundry, at night he was a clerk in a hotel, plus he had incredible emotional problems as only Tennessee Williams can have. Yet during this period he wrote *The Glass Menagerie* and *A Streetcar Named Desire*. He had to write. If you're a writer, you write. As far as people coming into the movie industry, you don't find that. It's probably the easiest thing to do if you can do it well, which is the catch.

JAG: You did an uncredited rewrite on *Dirty Harry*.

JM: I enjoyed the work on *Dirty Harry* more than I did on *Magnum Force*, which I did all of. By the time I got to *Magnum Force* I was pretty burned out on police shootings. That was a hard one to write because I lost my edge on it. I didn't like the movie terribly.

JAG: *Dirty Harry* was really an urban Western.

JM: Harry is a gunfighter much more so than any of those guys in Westerns. There weren't any gunfighters in the Old West. They were robbers. For anybody who knows a lot about gunfighting, many Westerns become ludicrous. If you look at *Dirty Harry*, Clint Eastwood handles the gun properly. I stretched it insofar as the gun he's using. The Magnum is not a practical gun. If *Dirty Harry* was accurate he'd use a .45, because that's the best gun for a gunfighter. It's the easiest to shoot. It does just as well as anything else, flattens the opposition, and you can reload it quickly.

JAG: What's your reply to the critics that branded *Dirty Harry* a "fascist" movie?

JM: They're coming from a very Eastern, liberal Establishment point of view. That sort of thing upsets them. They call it "fascist" the same way people in the Fifties called something "communist." It's an hysteria. Anything that is really indigenous to the West Coast, slightly out of control with a lot of energy, is dangerous to critics unless they can get a handle on it. Regardless of what movies I make, I think I will always be disliked by the Eastern critical Establishment, because the type of things I do are indigenously Western.

JAG: Did you write *The Life and Times of Judge Roy Bean* first, then solicit it?

JM: I wrote it first. I wanted to direct it, but circumstances came about in which it got into the hands of Paul Newman, and he of course didn't want me to direct it. So he bought it from me.

SS: Did you work with John Huston on the project?

JM: Yeah. I learned a lot. I don't think that it helped the screenplay at all. As a matter of fact, I consider that film a casualty. The screenplay is still probably one of the best I ever wrote. I really wish I could do that movie again. You have to lose somewhere along the line, but I did learn an awful lot from Huston.

JAG: On *Jeremiah Johnson* you shared co-credit with Edward Anhalt. How did that collaboration work?

JM: That was alright. At that point in my career I didn't know how to get along too well with people. (Robert) Redford and (Sydney) Pollack thought I was crazy and they would fire me and hire another writer. Then they'd hire me back because the other writer couldn't write that stuff. Finally, the only guy that did contribute anything was Edward Anhalt. He did it while I wasn't there, but they hired me again after they used him.

JAG: Are you pleased with the way *Jeremiah Johnson* came out?

JM: I like that movie a lot. I think it's a very fine movie.

JAG: It's not a very typical Sydney Pollack film.

JM: He's very good in that movie. I had an interesting talk with him the other day. I fought with him and didn't like him at all during that film. Now I find that I like him a lot. He has a pretty good attitude about things. I suppose that they saw me, once again, as being different than they were. They were politically more liberal than me, so I was some sort of unreconstructed sabre tooth tiger that had to be contained. I think in time I have matured, so I don't go around saying a lot of things I did, although I still have exactly the same beliefs I did then. They've accepted me—"He's not going to come to the office with a machine gun!"

JAG: What was the evolution of your script for *Apocalypse Now*?

JM: That started at cinema school. Lucas and I were great connoisseurs of the Vietnam war. As a matter of fact, I wanted to go to Vietnam but I had asthma and couldn't get in anything. I was the only person I knew who *wanted* to go in the army. George and I would talk about the battles and what a great movie it would make. He loved it because of all the technology, the helicopters, air strikes by Phantoms, the night vision scopes and devices to detect people walking around at night, and I loved the idea of a war being fought that way. Of course, we hadn't lost it then, so it was a little easier to be interested in it. We wanted a scene where the guys are doped out of their minds and they call in an air strike on themselves. We'd come up with all these things. They'd filter into my head and we always wanted to do it. I had the title, *Apocalypse Now*, because the hippies at the time had these buttons that said "Nirvana Now." I loved the idea of a guy having a button with a mushroom cloud on it that said "Apocalypse Now." You know, let's bring it on, full nuke. Ever hear that Randy Newman song, "Let's Drop the Big One Now"? That's the spirit that it started in right there.

JAG: How did the script actually come to be written?

JM: When George got to make *THX–1138* (1971), Francis (Coppola) made his American Zoetrope deal with Warner Brothers. Part of the deal was to develop projects and they gave me money to write *Apocalypse Now*. It was a big turning point in my life, because just before that I had been offered a chance to go to work for Universal for seven years as a writer. The two people they were taking in on their seven-year program were Spielberg and me. It worked for Steve because he got the chance to learn how to direct. It would have destroyed me writing television, and I didn't do it. I was very lucky Francis gave me the opportunity to write what I wanted to write. I thought it would be interesting to do Conrad's *Heart of Darkness* in Vietnam because it made a statement in itself. I felt it was interesting to take Conrad's idea of the end of the nineteenth century with merchants selling Christianity to the heathens and setting themselves up as God, and equate that with Special Forces units being dropped in and sent up to the river to sell democracy to the heathens, again setting themselves up as God. I worked from there. I don't think the script was ever political, really. I think Francis had sentiments about the war and how horrible it was as someone who lives in San Francisco and listens to the political ramblings of the people around him. When Francis started talking to the people who'd been there, the soldiers who fought in the war, he began to study the war very thoroughly. He took more of an historian's attitude.

JAG: How did you get a chance to direct your first film?

JM: I got very expensive as a writer, so I was able to make a deal with AIP. They would never have been able to buy one of my scripts, and I said, "I'll write whatever you want if I can direct it." I would have paid *them* to direct. They said, "These are the movies we're gonna make— *Blacula* (1972), *Black Mama, White Mama* (1972), and a gangster thing with Pretty Boy Floyd or Dillinger." I looked at the gangsters of the early Thirties, and the one that had the most appeal was Dillinger. It was a subject I never would have chosen myself, but it allowed me to show how good I could do a gunfight. It was a showcase to show everyone I could make it cut together, make the story hold and the actors act. So *Dillinger* was the first one, although I consider *The Wind and the Lion* my first real movie.

JAG: You're a well-known Theodore Roosevelt buff.

JM: Teddy was terrific. I always wanted to make a movie about the two years he spent in the Dakotas as a rancher, and I always wanted to do a play about the end of his life. He was going up the Amazon and each night he'd ask them to leave him behind. He was slowing up the party because he was sick and dying. He was reminiscing about his life. Before he went on the trip, someone told him, "You can't go. You have responsibilities." He was still a very vital political force, and he said, "It's my last chance to be a boy again." I love that remark. That's what I said to myself on Sunset Beach when I was making *Big Wednesday* and I was staring at this terrifying wave coming at me.

JAG: How do you stage a battle scene, for example, the climax of *The Wind and the Lion*?

JM: I stage it militarily. I take the place and I stage the battle first on paper. Say I have so many Arabs defending this place against a company of mounted heavy cavalry, and I have certain amounts of artillery and infantry. I figure a logical way that these obstacles would be overcome. Since you're doing it yourself you can invent things. You can have a ditch that goes down, but they can bring their horses reasonably close to make the charge.

JAG: It's like playing with toy soldiers.

JM: Yeah, and you design the whole battle that way. Once you've planned what is to happen in the battle, you just go shoot it. A lot of people make a mistake about the action by designing the shots and trying to get the battle out of the shots. That's backwards. If you design the battle, then just shoot it, the shots are always going to fit in. You'll know whose side everybody is on, why this guy is shooting that guy. In *The Wind and the Lion* I think you know who the different soldiers are.

SS: What was the budget on *The Wind and the Lion*?

JM: About $4.2 million.

JAG: What was it like directing John Huston in that picture?

JM: That was fun. He was real easy. I just told him what to do. He practically taught me to direct anyway. He taught me what to say to actors and taught me how to run a set. You don't talk to actors, you don't tell them what they're feeling. You just tell them what to do. I never discuss the actor's character with them. I have an hour before the movie starts in which we sit down in a room like this and I ask them what they want to say about the character and how they feel about the movie. Then what I try to do is create an atmosphere in which they can't help but do it that way. They have to react to it. They have to do what's required in the thing. I don't like to rehearse. I think you lose something. It becomes too actorish.

JAG: What was your approach to *The Wind and the Lion*?

JM: As a David Lean film, to do it in that style on a large epic canvas, to see if I could pull off great movements of troops. The story is even written that way, two guys, Teddy Roosevelt and the Raisuli yelling at each other across oceans. On *Big Wednesday* I did it much more Kazan-like, an extremely emotional film.

JAG: Is *Big Wednesday* autobiographical?

JM: It's a very personal picture, not autobiographical. There are things in there that happened to me. None of the characters really resembles me. They're their own characters with feelings that were important to me that I always wanted to write about when they were happening. *Big Wednesday* is about the test of people, call it rites of passage. It's important to go out and do something in your life with tremendous commitment and dedication, maybe even commit your life on the line to do it. It makes you a bigger and larger person. We've gotten away from this. What I really mean is the pursuit of excellence. I find this is gradually disappearing from society, especially kids growing up. They're not asked to pursue excellence. They're not asked to try and do well. That's really one of the values that I try to get into all the movies I do. These are people, whatever they're doing, they're doing it well. They'll take it to the end.

JAG: What are your feelings about *Big Wednesday* in retrospect?

JM: I like it because it takes a lot of risks. It has a lot of heart in it. I was really hurt when it was so viciously attacked by the critics. But it was good to be destroyed and to come back. I didn't like *Big Wednesday* for a while. I thought maybe I'd done it wrong.

JAG: *Apocalypse Now* was released a year later, and you and Coppola were nominated for an Oscar for the script.

JM: I love *Apocalypse Now*. That one movie justified my career. I feel I really did something worthwhile by writing it. Even though I share a credit and I didn't direct it, it's a real piece of me.

JAG: How did you get involved in directing *Conan the Barbarian*?

JM: I started reading the Conan books and the Oliver Stone script, and I said, "I was born to do this movie." I wanted to do a story of his becoming a complete man. The movie's really about strength—physical strength, moral strength, character strength, and the consequences of strength. I didn't find in any of the Robert Howard books any one story that would make a good Conan movie, so I had to create a story of my own. I studied a tremendous amount of research about various cults and barbaric cultures. I settled on two cults, the cult of the assassins, the Hashishim, and the cult of the Thuggee in India, Kali. I make the cult in the movie similar to those, with a little Jim Jones and a little Charlie Manson.

Manson was very influenced by the Hashishim. He set up his family very close to the way they were set up, and his crazed ideas were right out of the mouth of Hassim, the Old Man of the Mountain.

JAG: *Conan the Barbarian* has a dynamic opening raid in the forest.

JM: That took a lot of arduous toil. It was extremely cold. There was a blizzard while we were shooting most of that scene, and the snow would literally melt in a day. We'd have to go shoot something else and come back. When we finally burned that village everybody was really happy.

JAG: The movie's special effects are also quite elaborate.

JM: I still wanted a certain reality to it. *Kwaidan* (1964) has effects that are also dream-like, but the film still has a reality. I've always felt that the most strange and wondrous movies are *Apocalypse Now* and *Aguirre, The Wrath of God* (1972), and they have no effects in them at all.

JAG: You worked very closely on *Conan the Barbarian* with Ron Cobb, the production designer.

JM: Ron was the only person with whom I'd discuss the story initially, because he is so well read and graced in history. Ron has wonderfully original ideas with philosophical concepts to them and a wry sense of humor that goes with them. I got him to read tremendous volumes about the Mongols. Of all the barbarian cultures, the Mongols affected us the most, though Ron's architecture has an Aztec look. We went to Mexico several times and looked at the Aztec architecture. We wanted everything to be anthropologically correct, consistent, and logical. For example, we wanted the Wheel of Pain to be made of materials that would have likely been there. I'm quite proud of *Conan* in that it had a real good physical look.

JAG: Arnold Schwarzenegger became a huge action star from that film.

JM: Arnold is one of the great people of the world. His whole philosophy is based on the fact that you have to push so much weight before the muscle grows, and that resistance is good for you. The thing that was terrific about Arnold, Sandahl Bergman, and Gerry Lopez is that they were all open, kind of blank slates, but they're all extremely disciplined in that they're all professional athletes. Sandahl is a dancer used to extraordinary pain just to get a little step right. She was willing to put up with great amounts of training that a regular actress wouldn't have done. Gerry is a tremendously disciplined surfer who probably has more arduous workouts than the other two. The three of them gave themselves totally to the training. The other part of the casting was to surround them with wonderful actors like James Earl Jones, Max Von Sydow, and Mako, to give them confidence.

JAG: You've worked with Steven Spielberg on pictures like *1941* (1979) and *Used Cars* (1980) as co-executive producers.

JM: I don't know if you'd call it work. We joke and laugh. He and I have been really good friends for a long time. Same with George Lucas and

I. George and I went to school together, so I hardly think of it in terms that it's all become. It's hard to imagine the whole thing becoming so big. I can believe it that Francis is a big director. I still can't believe Steven and George are big directors. It's hard to believe. I think Francis is the best of the "New Wave," so to speak.

JAG: Do you all get together and look at each other's films-in-progress?

JM: Oh yeah, all the time. Especially Steve and me. George too, but he lives up in San Francisco so he doesn't come down as often.

JAG: You wrote the U.S.S. *Indianapolis* scene in *Jaws* (1975).

JM: Steve needed a scene to tell why Quint hated sharks and we just came up with most of it over the phone.

JAG: It's a powerful sequence.

JM: I have a scene like that usually in all of my movies where people tell of some hair-raising thing that happened to them, or a turning point in their life. In *The Wind and the Lion* it's when Raisuli is sitting around the fire telling of how he was put in the dungeons of Mogador by his brother and how he escaped. In *Big Wednesday*, a character called the Bear tells this harrowing, *Jaws*-like story, a true story actually, about two guys who were trapped out at Sunset Beach. The surf started to come up very quickly and got to thirty feet. Before they could get back in to shore they were trapped out there.

JAG: Do you have any particular writing habits, like so many pages a day?

JM: I do six pages of handwritten a day. No less than that. If I like going further and finishing it, I go as far as I need.

JAG: Do you write à la Hemingway, standing up?

JM: No, I sit down and talk on the phone all day to people and play with my guns. Anything to avoid writing. Then I finally sit down. It's not so bad when I do it, but I never learned that. I always seem to think that it's going to be horrible.

JAG: How have your dealings been with the studios?

JM: Not that bad. Sometimes they're terrible. They've never really screwed me over on anything too much. That's just part of the game. That's the current in the water. You have to swim against it. It's there all the time. It's the rip at Sunset Beach. If you wipe out you get caught in the rip. If you don't want to swim in the rip you don't go swimming there.

JAG: How do you feel about screen violence?

JM: I think it's great when it's well done. I liked the violence in *Dillinger* because it's real. There are consequences in *Dillinger*. You rob a bank, people are going to start shooting and people are going to get hurt and shot. They run over a woman leaving the bank because that's what they did. They were desperate. But you don't dwell on the bullet hole and blood pulsing out. *Big Wednesday* was violent, but there were no guns.

It was a man and a wave, and that's scary. A movie I thought was really sick was *Black Sunday* (1977), oppressively violent in an exploitative way.

JAG: What did you think of the violence in *Bonnie and Clyde* (1967)?

JM: Good, but not as good as *The Wild Bunch* (1969). When you see *Bonnie and Clyde* it's very good, but it goes away in a little while, whereas *The Wild Bunch* stays with you. I wouldn't want to see *Bonnie and Clyde* right now, but I'd love to see *The Wild Bunch*. Peckinpah's just a much better director than Arthur Penn.

JAG: Do you watch many current films?

JM: I don't really see many, because they're not often about very much. You don't get your money's worth. In old movies, a lot happens. Ideas were communicated. Sure, *The Searchers* is a story about a guy searching for his niece, but it's also a movie about the family and pioneering, and what it is to put yourself out on a limb. It's a movie about doing your job. A lot of movies today are "so what?" movies, and they're the ones I dislike the most, like *Dog Day Afternoon* (1975). How does that make my life better? What values are shown in this movie? What is the point of it? Directors today carefully tread that line where they don't get too emotional. They don't risk. I like Marty Scorsese. I don't like the way he moves his camera always, but I love his risk. All his movies are movies of great personal risk. *New York, New York* (1977) and *Raging Bull* (1980) are enormous risks. Every scene is taking a chance, and I think he's an exceptionally good director for that.

JAG: You've done a little bit of teaching at film schools.

JM: Yeah, I'd just go and bullshit, show Japanese movies. The class was very strange. All the kids didn't want to see those movies. They wanted to see *The Godfather* (1972), the movies that made a lot of money. They were always asking questions like, "How much do you get for a screenplay?" or "How do you get an agent?" In my day, if we saw a movie we really liked such as *Dr. Strangelove* (1964), we never sat there saying, "What are this film's grosses?"

JAG: What do you think about the way the press has built you into this Hemingwayesque character?

JM: That's why I don't do interviews. Whatever I say sounds OK when I say it, but when it's printed it's awful. I end up being this terrible guy that has guns and likes to shoot hippies. They always take the humor out of what I say. It's always, "Milius in Jack Boots and Leather Coat Says Fascism is on the Rise!" or "Para-Military Group Led by Director." The first thing they ask is, "How many machine guns have you?" I say, "How many cannon has the Pope?" That's a wonderful quote. Napoleon was going to take Spain, and he told the Pope, who didn't approve. Napoleon's other line was, "God is on the side of those with the most cannon."

JAG: Many of the old virtues expressed in films by directors like Ford and Hawks seem to be missing from movies today.

JM: People are more inwardly concerned, more concerned with what they can get. It's all summed up so well in a surfer term—"Go for it." That's why I like surfing and surfers. If you read Hemingway, it's all macho—"Ahhh, it was a good lion." That's all posturing as opposed to the exhilaration of going for it. That's really a good thing. In moviemaking too. Pull out all the stops.

(1978, 1982)

Alan Parker

Alan Parker is in the forefront of a group of distinguished British directors who started their careers at the BBC and/or in commercials, then went on to achieve success making movies for the majors. This unofficial "school" of filmmakers includes Ridley Scott, Franc Roddam, Adrian Lyne, Hugh Hudson, and Roland Joffe; Parker was the first to make his mark and continues to excel in film after film.

Born on February 14, 1944 in Islington, London, Parker worked as a writer and director in the advertising business, and directed a BBC telefilm (*No Hard Feelings*) and two shorts for EMI (*Our Cissy* and *Footsteps*). His 1975 BBC movie *The Evacuees*, about Jewish children during World War Two, won an International Emmy Award and honors from the British Film Academy, and led to his first theatrical feature, *Bugsy Malone* (1976), a musical satire on Thirties gangster films with an all-children cast. He secured his reputation with the riveting *Midnight Express* (1978), based on the true story of Billy Hayes, an American youth arrested in Turkey for possessing hashish who was forced to do time in a brutal, inhumane prison. Parker earned an Academy Award nomination for *Midnight Express*, and the freedom to make films of his choice.

The director has chosen his material carefully—the musical drama *Fame* (1980); the intimate family drama *Shoot the Moon* (1982); the surrealistic musical extravaganza *Pink Floyd—The Wall* (1982); the brilliant *Birdy* (1984), based on William Wharton's drama; and the controversial detective horror story *Angel Heart* (1987). All of Parker's films are meticulously crafted, technically superb, and boast notable performances from such actors as Brad Davis and John Hurt (*Midnight Express*), the young ensemble cast of *Fame*, Albert Finney and Diane Keaton (*Shoot the Moon*), Matthew Modine and Nicholas Cage (*Birdy*), and Robert DeNiro and Mickey Rourke (*Angel Heart*), and Gene Hackman and Willem Dafoe (Mississippi Burning).

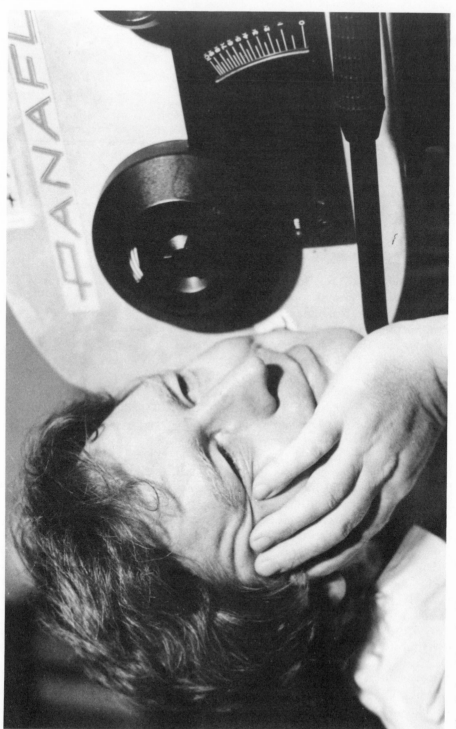

Alan Parker (photo by Terry O'Neill).

The following interview with Alan Parker took place in New York on February 17, 1987, as *Angel Heart* was beginning its theatrical run.

FILMOGRAPHY

The Evacuees (1975, BBC).
Bugsy Malone (1976, Paramount). HV: Paramount.
Midnight Express (1978, Columbia). HV: RCA/Columbia.
Fame (1980, MGM/United Artists). HV: MGM/UA.
Shoot the Moon (1982, MGM/United Artists). HV: MGM/UA.
Pink Floyd—The Wall (1982, MGM/United Artists). HV: MGM/UA.
Birdy (1984, Tri-Star). HV: RCA/Columbia.
Angel Heart (1987, Tri-Star). HV: IVE.
Mississippi Burning (1988, Orion). HV: Orion.

PARKER INTERVIEW

JOHN A. GALLAGHER: How did you break into the feature film business?
ALAN PARKER: I wanted to write originally. To be honest, I had no aspiration to be a director. It was always writing that most interested me. I grew up in a working class background in London, which makes it quite difficult within the very rigid English class system. I didn't go to university, but what I did do was get into advertising. The important thing about advertising in England is that it's very egalitarian, so if you've got a few bright lines they'll let you do it. I was fortunate enough to be able to start as a copywriter. It was the early days of television commercials in England. They'd just begun. They'd either fly over American directors or you'd get rotten commercials. Somebody gave us some money to experiment in the basement of the advertising agency where I worked. With a 16mm camera we just did lots of commercials. Suddenly there was somebody who could work a spectral light meter, somebody could work a Nagra tape recorder, somebody could operate the camera. I was actually the only one who couldn't do anything, so I said, "What shall I do?" and they said, "You better say action." Everybody knows that's the easiest job on a commercial, so I said "Action" and "Cut," and suddenly I was a director. It sounds like a glib story but it's perfectly true! Michael Seresin and David Puttnam were in the same advertising agency. One day David said to me, "Let's try and get into films." I said, "Don't be ridiculous." He said, "Write a screenplay," which I did, and it became his first film and my first film. It's a film we don't have on our resumes, thank God.
JAG: How did *Bugsy Malone* come together?
AP: Pragmatic exercise, really. Most of the things that I'd written at that point were parochial, about me, about growing up in England, about things I understood. The scripts kept coming back with a rubber stamp

on them saying "parochial," which was irritating. It was a very depressed period of filmmaking in England. I really didn't know anything about making American subjects, but what I did know a little was American movies, so *Bugsy* was really a parody of the American gangster film and the American musical. I'd worked a lot with kids and I had four very young children of my own at the time. When you do have young children like that you're very sensitive to the kind of material that's available for them. This was pre-*Star Wars* (1977) and *Raiders of the Lost Ark* (1981). The only kind of movies they could see were Walt Disney movies, and you knew when you were in a Disney movie then because all the adults were tilted at an angle, asleep. I thought it would be nice to make a movie that would be good for the kids, and also the adults that had to take them. So to be absolutely honest, *Bugsy Malone* was a pragmatic exercise to break into American film. It was financed in England, and Paramount picked it up for distribution in America.

JAG: How did *Midnight Express* happen?

AP: David Puttnam was about to take a job in Los Angeles at a company called Casablanca. Almost simultaneously, I had come over. They wanted me to do a thing called *The Wiz*, which Sidney Lumet eventually did (1978), but I didn't like the project very much. I was walking along Fifth Avenue, and somebody came out of Columbia Pictures with this book manuscript and asked if I'd like to read it. It was *Midnight Express*. I read it on the plane going home and I spoke to David quite independently. He said he was taking this job at Casablanca, and it turned out that Casablanca owned the book. He said, "If you do the film, I'll take the job," so it worked out very well. I wanted to do something that was different from *Bugsy Malone*. I wanted to do something that showed the other side of me, because I didn't want to be put in a pigeon hole of what kind of director I was, so it was a definite reaction to that.

JAG: At what point did Oliver Stone join the project?

AP: Oliver had been employed by Casablanca. He came to England and sat in the back office of our offices in London, popping away. Every so often we would send in sandwiches and beer, and at the end of it came this fantastic screenplay. He did a terrific job.

JAG: You used the island of Malta to double for Turkey.

AP: We'd gone to Italy, Israel, and North Africa looking for a prison. We found this old fort in Malta, which was exactly right. It was a combination of two locations actually, because there are in fact two prisons within the film. In the film it looks like there's one prison, but there are two halves to it, because he does go in to Section Thirteen, the insane part of the prison. That was a different location but they were both there in Malta only one hundred yards from one another. It was very convenient. Malta is an English-speaking place, which was easy. Obviously I wasn't going to be allowed to make *Midnight Express* in Istanbul, although I'd been there a few times. Not a lot of people know this, but I did a second unit shot of a car, which I intercut at the very beginning of the film with something I'd shot in Malta. I needed a shot of the car going over the bridge in Istanbul. Hugh Hudson did that shot for me before he'd directed a film, but he never wanted any credit for it because he thought if the studios knew he was doing second unit he might never get a movie. He's done enough now—*Chariots of Fire* (1981), *Greystoke* (1984), *Revolution* (1985)—that he can own up to the fact that he did that shot!

JAG: You had your pick of projects after the success of *Midnight Express*.

AP: I did *Fame* immediately after *Midnight Express*, and again, that was a reaction to doing something very dramatic and serious, although *Fame* has its serious side. I wanted to do something with music again. After that, I did *Shoot the Moon*, which was a personal story. I call it the first grown-up film that I'd done. After I'd made two American films, *Fame* and *Shoot the Moon*, I'd gone back to England and found it a very angry and violent place. I'd always liked Pink Floyd's music and when I did *The Wall* I tried to put a lot of that anger into the film. Looking back on it, I think the film is almost too angry. I'm very proud of it technically and creatively. It was Roger Waters who wrote the original music. He was screaming when he wrote the music and I was screaming when I made the movie.

JAG: What was the genesis of *Birdy* from novel to film?

AP: I was sent the William Wharton book very early on as a manuscript. I remember writing on top of the *Birdy* manuscript, "Wonderful story. Have no idea how to make it as a movie," because so much happened in the boy's head, so much poetry. I didn't know if you could take the poetry of the book and make it cinematic poetry, or if an audience would actually want it. I was then sent a script that Jack Behr and Sandy Kroopf had written and I thought it was actually quite interesting. They hadn't entirely solved the problems, but it was a very interesting way of doing it and I got interested again. We went back to the book again and it developed from there.

JAG: Did Wharton have any creative input in the project?

AP: No. He sent me a videotape of canaries. I think he wanted us to get on with it. A film has to take on a life of its own, although the book was obviously the beginning of everything. I was intrigued with the experience of the book. It *had* to be a film, it had to be its own thing. You can be too intimidated by a novel. I think he understood that, and he didn't have to be there.

JAG: How did you achieve the flying sequences in *Birdy*?

AP: The secret ingredient was going to be a new camera called the Sky-Cam, which was invented by Garrett Brown, who also invented the Steadicam, which was an enormous advantage from the point-of-view of tracking, since you could strap it on to a man's body. Sky-Cam was meant to be an even greater evolution of that in that it could fly, and therefore I could actually show the flight of the bird from the bird's point-of-view, which would be very exciting. As it turned out, we were probably a bit too soon in the evolution. It crashed into the ground more often than it should have, and finally, it didn't fly again. So a lot of the flying sequences that you see, 95%, were achieved with the Steadicam rather than this wonderful new invention, with a lot of cheating and a lot of thinking on your feet.

JAG: What was the process of adapting the William Hjortsberg novel *Falling Angel* and turning it into *Angel Heart*?

AP: Similar to *Birdy* in that I was originally sent the book when it was first published. The thing about being in England is you always get things last, so by the time you try to get it, it's lost in the Hollywood machinery. Different people owned the rights at different times, including Robert Redford. I think they found it was a rather tough nut to crack as a novel, as most first person novels always are, since so much happens inside the person's head. From the point-of-view of exposition you *have* to put it into dialogue, and to make the lead character sympathetic considering what has happened. Those were the difficulties, and I suppose the reason why people like Redford probably couldn't find their way around it. I'd always liked the book. I hadn't written an original screenplay for a long time. By original I mean even an adaptation. I'd always sort of rewritten other people's things. I thought it would be rather nice to get back to doing that. I've tried to do different genres with each film, and this was a classic Raymond Chandler detective story, but it was also about the supernatural, so in a way, I had two genres in one. The fusion of the two was what intrigued me.

JAG: What kinds of changes did you make from the novel?

AP: Characterization—most important. I moved the story away from being all in New York to being half in New York and half in New Orleans. That was for very selfish reasons. It's difficult to give something a cinematic edge in New York now. Everywhere you look there's gaffer tape where somebody's put their camera! You find a wonderful location here and suddenly you find the Polaroid film from the picture that's been there before. Also, a lot of the leads within the novel itself went down to New Orleans, and I thought it was a way for me to open it up and give it a different look. Those are basically the things I changed. I kept the heart of it, though I did change the title.

JAG: In *Angel Heart* you use a recurring visual motif of fans.

AP: That wasn't in the book. I used the fan as the portent of death each time. It was just an image that I kept seeing everywhere in New Orleans and I used it even here in New York. I've always been interested in the graphic images you get when you put light behind fans and it just happened to be in a couple of times in a couple of the murders within the story and it developed from there. Sometimes you do things subconsciously without knowing why you're doing them. I knew it was an image I was repeating and there was something quite macabre about it, and I couldn't say why. In the end it's totally an aesthetic thing, really. There's no real intellectual justification for it, except that cinematically it works. Sometimes you never quite know why.

JAG: All your films have striking visual and aural designs.

AP: A lot of people do that other than me, of course. I'm the one who gets all the credit for it since the French invented the *auteur* theory, and of course directors are the ones who do the interviews, so we get all the credit. But a lot of very good people do it, wonderful editors and sound editors. Every tiny little element had a lot of care put into it. It's nice when people notice the difference. Often people don't. Critics never do of course because they're stuck in trade's words. I think that's why they prefer foreign films with subtitles because they prefer a good read to seeing a good movie. But it's nice when the sheer craft that's gone into the films is appreciated.

JAG: *Angel Heart* was put together independently by Carolco.

AP: Yes. I wrote the script in England independently before even Carolco was interested in it. It went to them and they said, "Yes." They had made rather a lot of money from *Rambo* (1985), so I'm not proud. I'll take anybody's money! There's no such thing as clean money in Hollywood anyway.

JAG: Mickey Rourke's performance in the film is very internal in comparison with the external mannerisms of some of his other work.

AP: He's very much his own man. He hates you to even think that he cares. It's charade in a way because he really does care. He has a lot to offer. As a director, in the end, it's often taking things out rather than putting things back in. No director can actually create a performance. All he can do is provide an atmosphere and environment where the actor can be at their best, and I think that's all I did for Mickey, for him to trust us to really do as well as he could do.

JAG: His revelation sequence at the film's climax is powerful.

AP: We did that towards the end of the shot. I always try to shoot in sequence anyway. As an actor starts to develop within the role they're obviously comfortable because of work that's been done in previous scenes. They understand where they are at any given point, so we did that scene right at the end. He was quite confident about the work that he'd done, particularly the scenes he'd done with Robert DeNiro, so I think he was quite happy with himself and therefore ready to give a little more. It has to do with trust. If an actor trusts a director, and, more importantly trusts the crew around him, they they'll give of their best.

JAG: DeNiro plays Louis Cyphre, the human embodiment of Satan, with every detail in place—makeup, hair, the long nails. In *The Godfather Part*

Two (1974) he learned Sicilian, in *New York, New York* (1977) he learned the saxophone, and in *Raging Bull* (1980) he became Jake LaMotta. How did he prepare for his part in *Angel Heart?*

AP: All I know is when we were working we always knew when he was on the set because suddenly we all felt kind of strange. He became very creepy. Most of the tiny things in his character which in the end add up to the overall performance came mostly from him. He thinks a great deal about everything. Before he'd even said "Yes," he went through every single line and every single idea that he had from the point-of-view of the character. It's very hard to get inside the head of that particular character the same way it would be to get inside Jake LaMotta, for instance. So we always knew when Bob was around. You'd feel his presence. Somebody would say, "Bob must be here," and you'd turn around and there he was.

JAG: His beard seemed to be patterned and cut like Martin Scorsese's.

AP: Yeah, maybe that's how he sees the devil, I don't know!

JAG: Lisa Bonet also gives a mature performance, and she seemed to shed her television mannerisms.

AP: She's extremely intelligent. I hadn't seen her in *The Cosby Show*, so in a way my judgments of her were only as the actress who came in to the audition and the actress that I worked with on the set. She's much older than her years in a way. I spoke to her sometimes as someone who'd done twenty films, instead of someone making her first film. With regard to television technique as opposed to film technique, I never quite know, and I don't know how other directors work. In the end, the things I say are always intuitive to me, to what I believe. In the end, it's terribly simple, in that you're always looking for truth, so if caricature or mannerism get in the way of the truth that you're trying to show onscreen, that's the first thing I will point out. Sometimes it was necessary to do that with her. I'll come back to what I said about Mickey. You create a situation which is special in itself, an environment for the film, and the actors will be at their best. There's nothing magical about it really. Because I wasn't familiar with Lisa's television program, I wasn't nervous about taking those things out. I took it on face value.

JAG: *Angel Heart* gained a great deal of notoriety with the controversy surrounding the lovemaking scene with Mickey Rourke and Lisa Bonet. You were originally given an "X" rating.

AP: We had an appeal and won six to five that it should be an "R" and not an "X." Apparently you need two-thirds majority to overturn their original "X" decision. The six to five majority means I had the right to appeal again, so the process carried on. It's very general what they wanted me to do. There were no details as to what particular shot had to be cut. The film was made with maximum integrity. It's not an exploitation picture, and there's nothing really from a sexual or violence point-of-view that hasn't already been seen in some film. It's *how* it's been done or the combination of the two. It's very difficult to tell.

JAG: The sex scenes in *An Officer and a Gentleman* (1982), for example, were much more explicit.

AP: It's strange. It's a cumulative effect of the kind of a film that it is, I think. It's probably what they responded to. It's very hard because in the end if it's this shot or that shot, one can understand the difference but the criticisms of why it was made an "X" were very general. It's hard enough making the movie without having to go through that as well. It's almost commercial blackmail because it's very hard to release a major film as an "X," very difficult indeed.

JAG: Did you storyboard *Angel Heart*?

AP: I'd written it quite graphically. Knowing that you're going to direct it, you write it for one's style. We had done an enormous amount of photographic research. It was more that research that became the storyboard. I do draw quite a lot at times, but I try to avoid it because my theory is that storyboarding is how they'd make movies in Detroit. Sometimes you cannot be that specific. On certain things like special effects or very big action scenes you have to storyboard because there are too many people who have to know exactly what's going on. But in an emotional, dramatic scene, it does take on a life of it's own. I think however much you block it out in your head, there's always something that you do differently. So I try not to be too specific. On the other hand, you do have a storyboard in the back of your brain and when you go on to the set in the morning the shot is much better than how you imagined it. A line can be read not quite how you hear it in your head, and other times it's totally changed because of a particular situation. Sometimes for the good, often not as good as you've imagined it.

JAG: How did you approach the period detail of 1955 New York and New Orleans?

AP: Locations were found, but also in a sense created. Everything was filmed where it should have taken place. We probably did as much work on the street in Harlem and the Lower East Side as we would have if we had done the whole thing on a back lot. There's a lot of detail that goes into it from the production designers and the set dressers if you're doing a period piece. In a way, 1955 is quite difficult. Sometimes it's easier to do 1855 than it is 1955. I remember when we did *Birdy* in Philadelphia, set in the early Sixties, things had changed, but not much. It's easier when you recreate one hundred years ago because the errors stick right out. When it's recent history it's more difficult.

JAG: Most of your films have been done on locations rather than soundstages—*Midnight Express* in Malta, *Shoot the Moon* in Marin County, California, *Fame* and *Angel Heart* in New York, *Birdy* in Philadelphia.

AP: It would be a lot more convenient to shoot in a studio but I've never been able to overcome the phoniness of a studio situation. I did do *The*

Wall at Pinewood Studios and it's nice to have that kind of control. As a filmmaking process it's more comfortable and more civilized, but that might be it. There's something about the masochism of being in some horrible street in Philadelphia that makes you feel the film a little more. You can be in a tiny back alleyway or a back room and think, "Why are we here and not on a soundstage in Burbank?" Truthfully, it never looks the same. I personally can't do it that way. I have a brilliant art director, Brian Morris, but to me it's more than that. I have to feel it. I have to smell it in order for it to be real. Then it makes the make-believe, which is what we're doing, believable. I always feel more comfortable in real locations, even though it's infinitely more difficult to do than being in the comfort of a controlled set.

JAG: You've worked with the same team of people for years.

AP: I've worked together with my producer, Alan Marshall, my cinematographer, Michael Seresin, my production designer, Brian Morris, and my editor, Gerry Hambling, for twenty years. If I film in England, it's many other people within the crew. I'm comfortable with all those people. It's nice to make films with people you know to be the best at what they do, but also those people are your friends. Often we're away from home and you need that kind of support. I've always thought that film directing is a crash course in megalomania anyway, and it's hard because everybody looks at you and you have to get it right every time. Of course you don't. The trick is to appear to be getting it right! It's nice to have people around you who are able to say things to you that you might not get from other people. I believe Alan Marshall is so good as a producer because he cares about the film aesthetically and creatively as much as I do. His job is logistics. He doesn't interfere with creative decisions that I have to make. He's brilliant at organizing the films so I never have to worry about that side of things. He's also an extremely good editor in his own right, and in post-production he's very good for me to have, someone else that I can actually refer to. It's not just Alan, it's all of them. Whatever the French say, the film process is made up of a lot of people doing good work, not just one person. I'm very fortunate to work with the people I do. I think the identity of my work is as much theirs as it is mine. Michael Seresin is about to direct on his own now, *Homeboy* (1988), which is inevitable. I'll encourage him to do so, but deep down you think, "Well, it's strange to make films for so many years with the same person," and he'll probably have that same problem. Gerry, my editor, never fails to astonish me every single time. He'll always add something that I haven't actually put there to begin with. He always says, "Nonsense, you film it and it's either there or it's not." In a way he always adds some tiny little thing which is exciting because it means the creative process goes on and on, and it isn't just the director. There are many other people. A lot of directors are grateful that an editor hasn't messed it up. They've just put it together maybe as you've intended. Sometimes directors like myself who do shoot an enormous amount of film present a lot of options to an editor, and often it ultimately has to do with the editor's choices and taste as much as their actual skills and dexterity. After that, it's in the attitudes within the individual scenes. You can sit at the moviola at the editor's shoulder and cut every frame with the editor. Sometimes it's necessary to do that, and sometimes it's nice to leave the cutting rooms for a couple of hours then go back, and maybe he's taken it further or somewhere I've not thought about. Sometimes it's not right. Sometimes it's not how I intended it at all, but a lot of times there's an addition to what one's done. I find that very important. That's how I work anyway.

JAG: You're still based in England.

AP: I live in London and work in America. In fact, they call me the first of the jumbo jet directors, which sounds terrific, but it's not a lot of fun.

JAG: In the Sixties, the British cinema was thriving with filmmakers like Stanley Kubrick, Richard Lester, Bryan Forbes, Tony Richardson, Tony Harvey, but then there was a lull until David Puttnam started producing films with you, Adrian Lyne, Roland Joffe, Hugh Hudson.

AP: I don't think it's been very different actually through the years. We had actually generated many wonderful directors, and always have from the beginning of film. What was not evident is that no one ever wanted to be a producer, mainly because in England that's kind of a rotten thing to do. Puttnam was the first one who was smart enough to think that he actually could be a producer and could also have creative integrity being a producer. You didn't just have to have a posh car and a big cigar. It's also not often made clear that because of the strength of our television, which is very good compared to American television, a lot of the good people go into television, particularly people who have a political point-of-view to make. It's very hard to make, for instance, a very political left-wing film within the Hollywood studio system, almost impossible. I think there are a lot of very talented directors in England who do not want to go into the Hollywood system. That doesn't mean to say they can't work on film. They do work on film. Alright, it's 16mm film, but it's still film. In any other country in the world it would be called film because the audience would see it in the movies. But in England it's on television. I think that's always been the backbone of what's happened in England.

JAG: Do you have a particular philosophy in your films, an aim beyond providing entertainment?

AP: I work within the commercial cinema framework. I want my films to be seen by the maximum number of people. I don't want them to be seen by film critics and six intellectuals at a cinématheque. That doesn't interest me. By the same token, I want to say more than just sit down and laugh or cry. You want the film to stay with people afterwards. There are images in films that you remember when you leave the cinema, and maybe you remember them for longer than that. I try to give a cinematic experience that is not just another movie. Sometimes I succeed, sometimes I don't succeed, but I always try for it. It just seems to me that the greatest crime is to make just another movie.

(1987)

Franc Roddam

British director Franc Roddam has earned a reputation in the last ten years as a talented and outspoken young director. His creative vision is evident in his first three theatrical movies—*Quadrophenia* (1979), *The Lords of Discipline* (1983), and *The Bride* (1985), films with consistently imaginative visuals and interesting casting choices. Roddam was born on April 29, 1947, in Norton, a small town in northern England. An avid moviegoer as a child, he traveled extensively in Africa, India, and the Middle East when he came of age, and landed a job as a film extra in Greece. His appetite for filmmaking whetted, he returned to England and went to film school before embarking on a career as one of the British Broadcasting Company's top documentary directors.

His first feature, *Quadrophenia,* was based on the rock opera by The Who, and was an impressive debut that resulted in a flood of offers from Hollywood. After a tenure at Francis Coppola's Zoetrope Studios, Roddam directed *The Lords of Discipline,* a powerful indictment of racism set in a Southern military academy in 1964, based on the Pat Conroy novel. *The Bride* was a retelling of the Frankenstein story, unsuccessful at the box-office, but praised for the sumptuous visuals and Gothic atmosphere.

I interviewed Roddam twice, just prior to the New York openings of *The Lords of Discipline* in 1983, and *The Bride* in 1985.

FILMOGRAPHY

Mini (1975, BBC).
Dummy (1977, ATV).
Quadrophenia (1979, World Northal). HV: RCA/Columbia.
The Lords of Discipline (1983, Paramount). HV: Paramount.
The Bride (1985, Columbia). HV: RCA/Columbia.

Franc Roddam (courtesy of Mr. Roddam).

Aria (1988, Miramax). Roddam directed "Tristan und Isolde"; other seg-
ments directed by Robert Altman, Bruce Beresford, Bill Bryden, Jean-Luc
Godard, Derek Jarman, Nicolas Roeg, Ken Russell, Charles Sturridge, and
Julien Temple. HV: Academy Entertainment.
War Party (1988, Tri-Star).

RODDAM INTERVIEW

JOHN A. GALLAGHER: What attracted you to film initially?

FRANC RODDAM: What I like about film is it embodies all the art forms—
composition, music, drama, dance, color—all the art forms in one art
form. I'm interested in writing, in storytelling, in philosophy, and in
camera. I like to keep outside of it so I can use it all. I come from a small
town in the north of England. I always loved the cinema and as a kid I
went three times a week and saw a lot of American films in the Fifties
with Bogart and Cagney. I came from such a small town, I'd no idea I
could possibly enter the film industry. I was travelling in Greece and got
a job as an extra on a Michael Cacoyannis film, *The Day the Fish Came
Out* (1967). When I came back to England in 1968 I realized film was
available to me and entered film school. I'd always been a traveller, and
I liked writing and poetry, but after that I shut everything out and it
became film totally from that point on.

JAG: What was it like for you at film school?

FR: It was the London Film School in Covent Garden. It was a very wild
time in London. The class was 60% Americans who were understandably
running away from the Vietnam war, draft dodgers, or conscientious
objectors as we called them in England. It was a very liberal era. A lot
of young Americans were taking on the government. When I came back
to America it was a bit of a surprise for me. I thought all these people
were liberals, with a liberal mentality, but in fact most of them just turned
out to be draft dodgers. It was very disappointing for me that a lot of
the young guys active in that period were really only active on their own
behalf. Not all of them, but quite a few came back and ignored their
social responsibilities.

JAG: You went to work making documentaries for the BBC.

FR: I enjoyed my time in television. Working for the BBC was wonderful.
It's a huge corporation, with 22,000 people working throughout the
country. They have a fantastic newspaper clipping library. They can get
you any research book, and they have the best record collection in the
world. There's a whole group of young British intellectuals working
there for very little money, all trying to produce quality programming.
No hype, just work. If you work for the networks in America, you're
dictated to, told what to make and how to make it. They worry about

ratings, but at the BBC they allow you a free hand. They make films for what they are, so it was a very encouraging time.

JAG: What were some of your BBC films?

FR: I did a thing called *Mini* about a little boy that's a psychopathic arsonist. I did an interesting film about Joe Frazier and Joe Bugner called *The Fight*. For *Family*, made in '73 and '74, we lived with a real family for six months and filmed their every action. We did twelve episodes. It took over from my real life for a while. The last thing I did in television was a play called *Dummy*, which won the Prix Italia Drama Prize for the best drama in Europe. It was a film about a deaf girl who was also a prostitute and killed somebody. It was a very moving film. It was shown on prime time television on a Wednesday evening in England between 8:30 and 10 o'clock. People went crazy. Our Jerry Falwell equivalent tried to get me sued. A lot of people switched their sets off afterwards because they were so upset. All the kids were talking about it at school the next day. The wonderful thing about England is if you have something on TV, it's such a small country, and there were only three channels in those days, that the whole country would see it. One in every two adults in the country saw that film.

JAG: What prompted the move into feature film directing?

FR: I'd always wanted to, but I had to bide my time. I had to build a strong enough platform to enable me to get into features. In TV, since I couldn't go straight into dramas, I went into documentaries and that was a really good training. You have to develop a good ear. You have to listen to people. You have to develop a good eye because you have to be an opportunist. Finally I convinced them I should do a drama, *Dummy*, which was more expensive, much more expensive, and a lot harder work. I remember writing about myself in *Screen International*, which is the English film magazine. I wrote an article about how there are certain directors in television who would make good feature directors, and in fact, some of the films they were making were as good as the German cinema that was getting so much praise. I wrote the piece, sent in a photograph of myself and a headline, and they printed the whole lot just as *Dummy* came out on TV. I started getting feature offers!

JAG: *Quadrophenia* was your first feature.

FR: I was offered that on the basis of *Dummy*. It was perfect for me, because there was no acceptable screenplay. We wrote the script in ten days, got an immediate go-ahead, and then I brought in a writer from film school and did a rewrite in seven days. I started the film on June 16th, started shooting on September 30th, and finished on December 7th. We even had some money left at the end. It was quite unusual. I thought all movies were like that, but then I went to Hollywood, where I found that it takes six months to get somebody to read a script.

JAG: *Quadrophenia* must have been a difficult film to make.

FR: I used a large number of extras. That gives the whole film a sense of reality, and a lot of texture. I love Kurosawa and Ford. I love the rich texture in their films.

JAG: How involved was Pete Townshend of The Who?

FR: Strangely enough, he wasn't, in a way. He was really involved in that he wrote the concept album, the score, and therefore made a major contribution. When the film got started we met twice. He'd seen some of my work in England and liked it a lot. He was really gracious. He said, "Look, I know the difference between music and film. I made the album, you make the film." He completely left me alone. Of course, there was some guidance at the end on the soundtrack from him and John Entwistle. I really admired him for that, the fact that he said, "OK, this is your movie, you do it."

JAG: Where did you find the actor Phil Daniels, who plays Jimmy?

FR: Even though he was quite young, he was one of the few actors in the film who was quite known in England. He'd done some splendid theater parts and Shakespeare. It was his first lead in a film. A lot of those young actors have become very famous in England in their own right, like Sting, head of The Police.

JAG: How did Sting come to be cast in the film?

FR: If memory serves me right, I'd already cast the part of Ace Face. One of the girls in the office said, "There's a very interesting guy who lives in my apartment building. He's quite good-looking and I think you should see him." I brought him in and he was perfect for Ace Face, very cool. I gave the original actor another part and cast Sting. I got two really tough actors, guys from the street, and I said to them, "OK, I want you to intimidate him, really put pressure on him, make him crawl." I told Sting, "I want you to absorb it and make them afraid." That was the simple brief. I left them alone for a few minutes and came back and he did it very well. They didn't know how to operate and Sting scared them, so he was perfect for the part.

JAG: You later directed him in *The Bride*. Would you comment on his growth as an actor?

FR: His major growth has been his wealth. The guy is stinking rich, though I think he's getting better as an actor. He's becoming calmer. He's always had a great visual presence, which is important for film. Beyond that, he's better read now and I think he's taking acting more seriously. I don't think he's the actor he wants to be yet, and that's a good thing. He has to work on his voice more, but he works very hard and he's a very disciplined actor.

JAG: How do you approach camera movement?

FR: I have a basic theory that the real tension in a film comes not from juxtaposition of shots, but the tension within the frame. I move the camera a lot, the camera goes in, comes back, leans over, etc. Unless it's a studio floor with a very smooth surface, I have to build a floor for the camera dolly. I use very strange shapes; they have to follow the line of my camera. I rehearse first, then get the carpenters to build this very smooth, flat surface. They build two-by-two wooden frames and they put a hard plank of wood on top of it. They have to balance it out and make it smooth. While they're doing that, the cameraman can light, and I spend my time with the actors and extras. You don't notice the camera movement because they're always motivated by the movement of characters, yet it gives the film tremendous energy and a sense of reality. The camera operator has to be like an acrobat.

JAG: A cinematographer loves that kind of challenge.

FR: Yeah, but it drives the producers crazy, because I sometimes don't turn over until four o'clock, but then I get the whole thing in twenty minutes. It's particularly true in *Quadrophenia*. I often incorporate stillness and movement in the same shot. In *The Lords of Discipline* there's a shot where the Ten come down the corridor, a shot I used quite a lot in *Quadrophenia*. You're waiting for the action, so you have what would normally be a static shot, but there's a certain point when you don't notice that you're suddenly moving together. In *Quadrophenia,* I did it with the scooters in the street. You have to have precisely the same movement. We had this little Citroen we used instead of a camera car, and we're waiting with the engine on. We had eight people pushing it so the car gets off smoothly when the scooters come around the corner, and then we're away. We dash across a main road into a huge market and a crash takes place, and a fight with this rocker. The whole thing becomes quite dramatic.

JAG: The British film industry was inactive for many years, and English directors like Alan Parker, Ridley Scott, and yourself have come to Hollywood.

FR: Thank God for Hollywood. *Quadrophenia* was a big critical success in America, but not a big financial success, but the major reviewers really liked the picture. I was getting hundreds of offers from Hollywood. All the studios asked me to do deals here, but I got not one offer from England. The same happened with Ridley Scott and Alan Parker. We had to come to America, because the English producers, apart from David Puttnam, who has his own little niche, don't take a gamble, don't understand cinema. They don't understand the potential as an investment, and what a great business it can be if you make it. The whole industry there is quite lame. So that's one reason why one would leave. The other thing is that going to Hollywood for a director is like going to the Olympics. We may have done finer things elsewhere, but Hollywood is the home of the cinema and that's where you want success. It's the last big step. Even though it's a real fight working with the major studios in Hollywood, it's the place on earth where they'll give you ten million dollars for an idea and let you spend it in ten weeks. The major difference is that in England when you have an idea, they say, "Great. Go and write and come back." In Hollywood you can get the money for development. You know who to go to, the people at Paramount, the people at Fox. It's very hard to know who to go to in England. These guys are invisible. It's a major city for investment and banking, but film is a very small part of it. In Hollywood, if they're ambitious, they'll even seek you out.

JAG: After the success of *Quadrophenia,* when you were looking for just the right property, what kinds of things were you being sent?

FR: They're very hungry for new talent, always have been. When a script comes out, they always approach the top ten guys and the ten new guys, and they forget about everybody in the middle. I was one of the ten new guys so I was offered everything. In the first two years, I suppose I was sent three hundred screenplays. Of those, I'd say at least thirty have been made, all of them bad movies, unsuccessful, and no positive reviews. It was very tempting to come to Hollywood, get offered a picture, big stars, big director's fees. But the scripts were no good and I knew they were not going to make great movies, so I turned them down, which is a hard thing to do.

JAG: What appealed to you about *The Lords of Discipline*?

FR: I discovered a theme in my work, through my BBC work and continuing with my features—that I like to make films about people who challenge the status quo, because if you do that you become in conflict with the status quo, and from that conflict you get drama. I like to have people challenge the moral, sexual, or social climate, who refuse to accept the limitations of their environment. *Quadrophenia* was somebody attacking the social-economic restrictions of his environment. In *Lords of Discipline* it's somebody refusing to accept the moral limitations of his environment. David Keith's character sees something he doesn't like and even though it doesn't directly involve him, he says, "I'm going to do something about it." In *The Bride,* it's going to the very heart of it. Here's a man who challenges his Maker, if you like, and he decides that he will create life in the true Promethean sense. The other thing I liked about *Lords of Discipline* was that it was about America and I wanted to make a very American picture. I saw many symbolic and allegorical qualities in the script. It wasn't just a film about a military school, it was a film about a corporation. It was a film about America, a film about individual courage and integrity. These are the ideas that traditionally the great American films always had in them. *On the Waterfront* (1954), *The Grapes of Wrath* (1940), *High Noon* (1952), and *Shane* (1953) are all about the individual rising above the circumstances and taking a risk, personal courage, integrity, and growth. So in that sense, I found *Lords of Discipline* very optimistic, even if the setting of a military academy is somewhat bewildering.

JAG: It's interesting that you found a theme emerging from your work. It's not as though you said, "I'm going to choose this theme to work from."

FR: It was something that was always inside me. I think too many directors don't really know what they want to do. They're very able technicians, a lot of them better than myself, but they have no point of view. The thing that distinguishes an artist from a technician is a point of view. What distinguishes a good and lasting film from just a piece of celluloid is a point-of-view with philosophical undertones. Of course, it also has to be dramatic and entertaining.

JAG: How did you initially get involved with *The Lords of Discipline*?

FR: The producers Gabriel Katzka and Herb Jaffe bought the Pat Conroy novel, took it to Paramount, and started to look for a director. The then president of Paramount, Jeffrey Katzenberg, wanted to make a film with me and asked me to do it. There was a screenplay in existence, which I didn't like, so I brought in Lloyd Fonveille, a writer I work with, and we produced a draft that was acceptable and went into production. It's a slow business, a long haul, and you have to be very persistent.

JAG: You must have had some apprehensions about tackling such a thoroughly American film.

FR: Indeed. A lot of directors come here from England and make a film immediately. I've lived here a few years now and I'm quite absorbed in America. I like to travel, so I know quite a bit about America. Traditionally, we've been brought up on American culture to a great degree. America has a big influence on England, and vice versa. Apart from the common tongue, we've been brought up on American movies and TV. Nevertheless I think you have to be very careful when you're making a film that you don't misrepresent somebody. In America, there are a lot of people in the West and the Northeast who don't know the South. I think I'm a keen observer, so I can pass that information to the rest of America.

JAG: In an historical sense, the South has always been close to England, far more than the rest of the United States. In fact, during the American Civil War the South went to Great Britain for financial assistance.

FR: They feel comfortable with us. Sometimes it's easier for an English actor to do a Southern accent than it would be for somebody from New York. I think there's a closeness in certain parts of the culture between England and the South. I felt comfortable there.

JAG: Yet *The Lords of Discipline* was filmed primarily in England.

FR: I filmed 80% of it in England and 20% of it in Charleston, South Carolina. You can't tell the difference between the two locations. I was very careful to make sure that happened. The vegetation and the coloring of England in the summer is very similar to the South. The production designer, John Graysmark, who did *Ragtime* (1981), and myself did a lot of research. I brought sixteen actors over from America to England, and then as many young Americans in England as possible, and as many young English people who looked American. I had Southern actors, and Lloyd Fonveille is a Southerner himself. So I had a little guidance. The thing about directing is you've got to be very strong willed, as you know, but you have to make sure that you listen to the best of advice from people.

JAG: In both *Quadrophenia* and *The Lords of Discipline,* you worked with young actors who were relatively unknown to audiences.

FR: Even if they're unknown, they have to be good actors, or have the potential to be good. In *Lords,* some of them were not actors at all. Mark Breland was a boxer. There are several advantages for me. I like to have all my actors with me one month before the shooting. Actors get paid on a weekly basis. That's very expensive, and so if they're unknowns, they're not that costly and I can have them a month. I like to create an ensemble, have us all get to know each other. All the actors work out their histories and their futures in character, so they know about the character before the film started and after the film finished. It takes a long time. I make them wear their costumes in public, and they've got to really live and breathe the film. The "goodies" lived in one house and the "baddies" in another. They were all trained by master sergeants in the Marines for three weeks. By the time I started the film they were totally immersed, and they could almost guide *me.* That allows me to concentrate on my camera technique, which is slightly different from the way a lot of people direct. In Europe we tend not to place our actors as much in the foreground as American directors do. We place them in the middle, amongst and through the background. The extras can't just be out of focus or mumble. It means you really have to cast and direct the extras. That takes a lot of time. When I come to direct on the first day, the main actors know completely what is going on. I concentrate on my camera and my background, and I have great support from the actors. In that sense, having unknowns is essential for me. It doesn't matter if they're unknown, but they have to be totally cooperative. The other advantage is I like to direct in a realistic fashion. I want an audience to totally believe in a film. I don't do anything that breaks the emotional impact of an audience. If the audience believes in a character, then they get really anxious or happy for that person. If it's someone that they've seen many times, it's just entertainment. I like people to leave the cinema laughing and crying.

JAG: That's an interesting point about American directors giving you everything up front. In the old days, a director like John Ford only gave you a closeup if it was absolutely necessary.

FR: I love John Ford. There's a scene in *The Quiet Man* (1952), and a very important scene, where he plays a whole scene on John Wayne's back.

You try doing that with a studio today. I'd do it, but it's a real battle to get the studio to perceive that and understand that dramatic impact of shape.

JAG: Republic wanted to change the title of *The Quiet Man* to *The Prize-fighter and the Lady*.

FR: No! *The Third Man* (1949) was going to be changed to *Nights in Vienna*.

JAG: You worked with the writer Lloyd Fonveille on *The Lords of Discipline* after Thomas Pope had done a previous draft.

FR: Pope did a good job. He broke the back of the novel, and then Lloyd turned it into a makeable screenplay. Lloyd's very smart and good with dialogue. We were at a point with Paramount where we were trying to get them to commit to make the film. It's very hard for even the best-willed executive to commit to spend eight million dollars, and with prints and advertising, fifteen million. You really have to push them. I got to the point where I thought they'd had enough of this project. Either the script was going to work now or it's going to fail, so Lloyd and I worked closer than usual. We didn't have the time to be polite with each other. Most of the work was done in the first three weeks. We were losing our energy and we had a final push to make it happen. When it comes to spending that kind of money, people are always looking for reasons not to do it. It's understandable. You have to push them over the edge.

JAG: What are some of the practical considerations you make in reading a screenplay?

FR: Things that work on the written page don't necessarily work on film. There's the classic example of the script that says, "Then the Arabs take the town." Well, what the hell does that mean? Does it mean ten million dollars, or does it mean a telex from Cairo? Like on *Lords of Discipline,* there were six parades in the first draft. In the film, we have half a parade. Six parades are phenomenally expensive, and also very dull. I've just been reading a very good screenplay from a very famous writer, and he's making the same mistake. He mentions thousands of little bits of action that would cost a fortune. Every line or description he makes might take a day to shoot.

JAG: What kind of support did you get from the producers?

FR: Herb Jaffe and Gabriel Katzka had the passion to get this film made. Truthfully, it's hard for someone who actually doesn't work on the floor to know what goes into the making of a film. I think the major thing a producer does in this day and age is actually acquire the property, get it started, and put things in place. My English producer on *Quadrophenia* said, "Look, if I get you the money, I'm done." I believe that. If a producer gets the director the money, then it's up to me, because nobody can put the film together better than the director.

JAG: David Keith has the kind of face that can be very hard, yet also register sensitivity.

FR: He does have that combination. There is a coarseness in his face. The Bear (Robert Prosky) used to call him "Potato Face." You're right, he can work on the other levels. I think the best asset he has is that he comes across with great sincerity. The New York faces had their day, the Al Pacinos. Everybody on the West Coast wanted to look like that. David represents Middle America, so in a way, now they're having their day.

JAG: Brian Tufano photographed both *Quadrophenia* and *The Lords of Discipline*.

FR: We work very closely. He also did my very first BBC film. He was a BBC cameraman for seventeen years. He would travel all over the world to film. He did wars, he went with David Attenborough to film turtles. Since he's been forced to film in incredible circumstances and has seen a great deal of real life, he has a feel for reality, as well as a real love of cinema. When you work on a feature, everyone is telling you to do so-and-so. The person who has to be most convinced is me. I have to make the picture. I have a very clear vision of what to do to make a film have a sense of unity. You have to have people around you who really sympathize, understand, and support that vision. It's a question of imposing your view.

JAG: You worked for a while with Francis Coppola.

FR: I was working at Zoetrope, which was a nightmare. I was there during the making of *One from the Heart* (1982). It was very unfortunate. We all had great hopes for Zoetrope. It would be the most wonderful place on earth, where a director could go and make the film that he wanted to make, since we all had this love/hate relationship with the studios. But Francis turned out to be worse than anybody at a studio. And the worst of it was that he didn't have any money, so we were all wasting our time. It was a bad dream being there. It was like being at Jonestown.

JAG: At what stage of development did you get involved with *The Bride*?

FR: Late for me. The script had already been written. Usually I try and instigate the idea. In this instance, the script had been written by a friend of mine, Lloyd Fonveille, who was also writing a script for me at United Artists. He disappeared for two months because he couldn't finish my script. He turned up very apologetically, said he had a writer's block and came up with *The Bride*. We shelved the other project and did *The Bride*.

JAG: Was the other project *Women, Money and Restaurants*?

FR: That was really Lorne Michaels' title. We wanted to call it *Foolish Things*. It was a love story about New York after midnight.

JAG: So Lloyd introduced you to *The Bride*.

FR: Lloyd had an obsession with the Frankenstein theme from the age of twelve. His rationale is that young guys feel awkward at that age. You feel your arms are too skinny, your legs are too long. You feel you're a bit of a monster. He identified with the creature and felt that the creature's difficulty relating to women was a starting point. Lloyd went to Victor

Drai the producer to get some money, and Victor contributed some ideas to the script. Lloyd felt duty bound to include him in the package and the three of us went off to the studio to try and get the money.

JAG: You gave the Frankenstein story a feminist sensibility.

FR: In a period film or a futuristic film, you have the opportunity to state some very basic truths. If you say those ideas in a contemporary film, like women should be treated equal, it comes out corny. But if you go backward or forward in time, you can say something very simple and honest. When I read the script I felt it was very entertaining and had great visual potential, and at the same time it related to modern ideas because it was about the freedom of a woman, one of society's major preoccupations at the moment.

JAG: *The Lords of Discipline* was set in the Sixties, but *The Bride* is your first real period film, set in 1830. What kind of problems did that present?

FR: More joys than problems. When you do a period film you have fantastic opportunities to do creative things. When you start any film, you create a life out of a blank piece of celluloid. In a period film, you recreate a total world. It felt like I was making a real film, like the ones I'd seen as a child. There were horses, castles, strange people, exotic locations, and explosions. I really enjoyed making *The Bride* much more than the others. I wanted to make a film in the grand style. I'm perceived as a young filmmaker because both *Quadrophenia* and *The Lords of Discipline* were about young people, but stylistically I very much admire Orson Welles and Kurosawa, the grandeur of their filmmaking, so *The Bride* was a great opportunity for me.

JAG: What kind of pressure did you feel in terms of people relating to James Whale's classic *The Bride of Frankenstein* (1935)?

FR: To be honest with you, I don't think today's audiences, the generation of filmgoers from fifteen to twenty-five, have seen that film. We're very conscious of the past Frankenstein films, but I don't think today's audiences are. I viewed the making of the film the way a director would restage an opera or a Shakespeare play. You can continually redo it because the themes are classic enough to restate them for a different generation.

JAG: Sting as Baron Frankenstein is unusual casting.

FR: I didn't think that he could carry the film, but he was in the back of my mind. It's a classic director story. I flew in from London to Chicago for a day to see him for half a day, test him with an actress, and fly back. He gave a very good reading and really wanted to do it. Visually I felt he was perfect. Once I cast him, I had a stylistic cornerstone, then went to Jennifer Beals because she is a great visual contrast to Sting. Then I found my monster, Clancy Brown, and the dwarf, David Rappaport.

JAG: *The Bride* is Jennifer Beals' second picture. Since she's not a very experienced actress, how did you approach working with her?

FR: You have to approach every actor differently. Clancy and David are very well trained and easy to direct. Jennifer and Sting were harder because they were less experienced. I brought Jennifer in a month ahead of time and taught her some skills like riding. She got very involved in the film. In between casting and checking the sets, I would do a couple of hours with them and make them interact, so they got over their nervousness and anxieties. I did it like a theater director. I do disciplines outside of the film itself. I make them shout. I do a little piece with them. I make something up and say, "OK, you've come home from school, you got a very bad report. He's the father, let's see what you can do." Eventually their confidence grows.

JAG: Stephen Burum did a magnificent job on the cinematography. He has a long list of outstanding credits, *The Black Stallion* (1979), *The Outsiders* (1983), *Rumble Fish* (1983).

FR: I think he's one of the best cameramen in the world today. He's very disciplined. Sometimes the cameraman is very precise because ultimately they're technicians. I've found that if they're that type, they caution you every day and push you. Stephen was like that. He pushed me. It was a relationship full of dialogue which worked in favor of the film.

JAG: You shot *The Bride* in England and France.

FR: I do prefer filmmaking in Europe. *The Bride* cost $13 million, but in the States it would have been at least $25 million. You get very good value in Europe, but you have to go to Hollywood to get financed. Hollywood has always been a very tough place for creative people, actors, directors, writers. A few hearts have been broken there. You go there and you think it's all wonderful. There's flowers in your hotel room and you lie there and it all seems great. But it's all talk. The ratio of scripts written in Hollywood to scripts made is about a hundred to one, so there's a lot of people dying there. In order to get through and get the movies made, you have to be very persistent and very bold.

(1983, 1985)

Mark Rydell

Mark Rydell has a contagious enthusiasm for making films that matter, and an understanding and compassion for the actor's task. He has demonstrated these qualities in such films as *The Fox* (1968) from D. H. Lawrence's novella; William Faulkner's *The Reivers* (1969) with Steve McQueen; *The Cowboys* (1972), featuring one of John Wayne's finest performances; *Cinderella Liberty* (1973), a love story between a sailor (James Caan) and a prostitute (Marsha Mason); *The River* (1984), a passionate drama of a farm family's struggle to survive through economic upheavals, with Mel Gibson and Sissy Spacek; and especially the sensitive *On Golden Pond* (1981), a powerful portrayal of old age, starring Katharine Hepburn and, in his final film, Henry Fonda, who won an Academy Award as the cantankerous but lovable Norman Thayer.

A native New Yorker, born on March 23, 1934, Rydell studied at the Julliard School of Music and played jazz piano in Manhattan nightclubs. His desire to act led to classes at the Neighborhood Playhouse under Sanford Meisner and at Lee Strasberg's Actor's Studio. Following a stint on the television soap opera *As the World Turns,* Rydell landed the role of a juvenile delinquent in Don Siegel's *Crime in the Streets* (1955) before making a name for himself in the Sixties as a top television director on such shows as *The Reporter* (1964), *I Spy* (1964–1965), *The Wild, Wild West* (1965), *Slattery's People* (1965), *Gunsmoke* (1965), and *The Fugitive* (1965). He has also acted in Robert Altman's *The Long Goodbye* (1973) and David Seltzer's *Punchline* (1988).

This interview took place in New York prior to the opening of *On Golden Pond,* and focuses on the making of that film and the director's reflections on the craft of acting.

Mark Rydell (courtesy of Mr. Rydell).

FILMOGRAPHY

The Fox (1968, Claridge).
The Reivers (1969, National General). HV: Key.
The Cowboys (1972, Warner Bros.). HV: Warners.
Cinderella Liberty (1973, 20th Century-Fox). HV: CBS/Fox.
Harry and Walter Go to New York (1976, Columbia). HV: RCA/Columbia.
The Rose (1979, 20th Century-Fox). HV: CBS/Fox.
On Golden Pond (1981, Universal). HV: MCA.
The River (1984, Universal). HV: MCA.

RYDELL INTERVIEW

JOHN A. GALLAGHER: What attracted you to *On Golden Pond*?

MARK RYDELL: As a director you know that the pursuit of material is never ending. I look for something where the values are equally meaningful ten years from now, something where the values transcend immediacy. A picture about facing the final years in one's life is relevant at any time. It's hard to find material like that. When Jane Fonda called me and said that she was going to buy this play for her father, and she had told Ernest Thompson to try a first draft screenplay, I was immediately hooked by the idea of Henry, Jane, and material of substance. It took me about five seconds after I read the script to know that this was going to be my next two years. Kate Hepburn's involvement was almost simultaneous. This picture has been a genuinely magical experience that clicked from word one. Everybody fell right in. Every member of the crew—and you never find this—literally pleaded for the job. Dave Grusin begged to write the score, Billy Williams came from London and begged to shoot the picture. Jim Contner, a fine New York cinematographer agreed to step down and become the operator because he very much wanted to be involved on what everybody felt was an historic moment in time. The film never had a rocky road or a moment's difficulty once they agreed to finance it. The past two years of my life have been elegant, deeply involved in substantial material with first class artists in every department. Where do you go from here in terms of the pleasure of an experience? I can't see it being equalled.

JAG: The emotion you're talking about is also on the screen.

MR: Everything agitates from the material. Ernest Thompson is a magician. He's an exquisite, sensitive, talented writer with a real literate sense and a great humane compassion for human abrasion and the problems that result from that. It's one of those rare instances where the material is so strong that it transcends and dominates even our most powerful personalities, Hepburn, Jane, and Henry Fonda.

JAG: Frances Sternhagen and Tom Aldredge played the leads on Broadway.

MR: They're indeed talented actors, but I don't think they could fully realize the material because they're both twenty years too young. Norman

Thayer, Jr., is on the eve of his eightieth birthday, and his wife, Ethel, is seventy. In the Los Angeles production of the play, Julie Harris and Charles Durning played the roles, and all four of them are truly wonderful actors, but there was no way they could make an equivalent contribution to Fonda and Hepburn. The minute you cast them, it becomes somewhat similar to a Bergman film because you have a small group of people in an enclosed place, like Bergman's people, who are not only unpacking their baggage, but also emotional baggage, resolving relationships, and in this case, facing the last years of their lives.

JAG: It hits home because in a sense we've all grown up with Fonda and Hepburn, seeing their films through the years.

MR: Someone said recently that if we could vote for the grandparents of America, the winners would likely be Hepburn and Fonda. Who more likely than Henry to be our great individual American grandfather, the man who played Lincoln, Tom Joad in *The Grapes of Wrath* (1940), who's been President half a dozen times and Secretary of State half a dozen times, and who is the absolute embodiment of noble, moral strength. Kate's the same way. She's legendary.

JAG: Had you met them before this film?

MR: I knew Henry. He had expressed his admiration for my work in the past. He loved *The Reivers* and *The Cowboys,* and said so on several occasions. I had never met Kate. Kate knew some of my films and ran the rest.

JAG: What was your professional training?

MR: First I was a musician, then an actor. I went to the Neighborhood Playhouse in Manhattan, where I was trained by the best existing acting teacher, Sanford Meisner. I spent many years as his assistant. I was trained by Harold Clurman, Lee Strasberg, Elia Kazan, Bobby Lewis, so that my education as a director and actor is based on an understanding, sympathy, and compassion for the actor's chore.

JAG: How do you feel about the term "actor's director"?

MR: I don't mind. As a matter of fact, I'm delighted I've been thought of that way. There's no better label, because the actor is the most vulnerable human being in a piece when you direct it. You as a director understand that actors are very brave people. They stand there unguarded if they're any good. They peel away all those layers of insulation that most people develop in order to take the assaults of life and the horrors of society. They remain children in a sense, child-like in their availability to the ravages of human existence, because that's their stock and trade. They have to be vulnerable to injury, and to interchange and exchange. They have to be vulnerable to emotional invasion. If actors trust me to do what is maybe the most single significant contribution you can make as a director, which is to create an atmosphere in which they can flourish, in which they can expose themselves without fear of injury, in which they can allow themselves to be brutalized by circumstances, the play, or another actor, or reach into that magic box of emotion to create some behavior, if they think of me as a director who encourages that to happen, I'm grateful.

JAG: How do you create that atmosphere on a film set?

MR: It starts when you walk on the set in the morning. It's how people respond to you. First of all, it has to do with the selection of the people. You don't want somebody who drags you down. I make a real effort to bring not only talent onto the set, but also a healthy attitude, so that there's a genuinely optimistic spirit about the work that's about to be done. I don't believe that chaos is necessary on a film set. If people are skilled and really know their job, and are eager to do their job and know it will be appreciated, there's a sense of constructive energy. It's a really critical element for a director to be aware of the contributions, to pat the back of the guy who's made a good dolly move, or to acknowledge somebody who's built a little platform for a light way up on the ceiling where nobody could get to, the proper handshake at the proper moment. All of a sudden that spirit permeates the set. It's an absolutely essential thing to do. At least it's so on my sets. I like it to be fun, to have a good time. I don't mean it's not religious when you shoot, because it is. There's a religiosity, absolute concentration and commitment. It all comes from the director. The director sets the tone. The people on this picture knew they were on something that mattered, and as a result it shaped their day-to-day attitudes towards other people. That's the job.

JAG: How much articulation do you give to Fonda and Hepburn?

MR: There's no question in my mind that Henry Fonda is the greatest living actor. I have great admiration for Robert DeNiro and a number of great actors. I don't want to make the list because I'm bound to leave someone out, but there's something very special about Henry Fonda. He is the actor's actor, and I worship his skills. Kate Hepburn is incomparable. Who is like Kate Hepburn? She is absolutely inimitable. Somebody said to me the other day, "That's what they should do, 'The Kate Hepburn Story.'" I said, "Who's gonna play her? Not possible." She's special. She's jubilant, alive, vital, emotionally resonant and deeply skilled. It's an awesome proposition. I had to work very hard to be ahead of them. I stayed up every night for hours working on the material until I knew exactly what I thought each moment had to do with. Then you have to remain elastic within the confines of those plans so that these great talents can make all the contributions they can make. One of the things that helped is that I knew they wanted me. My reputation for making actors' performances reasonably good had preceded me. They reached out to me. They said it very early on—"Don't be afraid, please, Mark." Not that I would have been, I must confess, because I'm a constructively arrogant person. You need that to be a director because you have to operate from the hypothesis that what you like is good. That's already a very arrogant position, but that's really a critical position for the artist. You cannot design things for audiences and studio heads. You really have to please yourself. You're the guy who watches the moment and says, "It's fine. Print. That's what I want." There's an implicit arrogance in that, not negative, but constructive. I wouldn't have backed down anyway. They gave me many opportunities early on in the material to back down. They tested me. They wanted to see if I was going to take the reins.

JAG: Can you give me an example?

MR: The first day of rehearsal, Kate seated herself at the head of the table in the director's chair. I said, "Gee, that's a lovely rehearsal place that you've set up for us in your home, but I don't like the seating arrangements, so if you'd be so kind as to move where the other actors are. That's where I sit." She looked at me, pleased, because she didn't want to run the show. What she was saying is, "Are you going to do it? Because if you don't, I'll do it." She was absolutely certain someone was going to direct this picture, and she wanted to know whether or not I was scared of her. While I was, I didn't show it! Man, how can you not be uneasy in the presence of such figures?

JAG: How did you deal with those feelings?

MR: Underneath these legends and myths are flesh and blood human beings, and like most actors, they are eager for guidance and direction. It was difficult for the first few days, difficult to say, "This is wrong, Henry, what you're doing. I think maybe we can do it better if we look in this area," or "Kate, this is wonderful but it needs some adjustment. What do you think of this idea as a way of going?" One had to be gentle, and obviously they were measuring what you had to say, measuring its worth. Once they felt that the suggestion made sense and was helpful, it was OK. What does a director do? A director turns people on, among other things.

JAG: A catalyst.

MR: Exactly. He literally must lubricate the talents that are present, turn on those engines and get them rolling, get them purring, point them in the right direction. Guide them down the path that has to be run toward an objective that's decided upon, usually by the director, and aim everybody at that target. Once he communicates that target to everybody, he turns them on and makes them want to go there. Once you do that with those actors, they're thrilled, they're relaxed, and they let go. They want to do their job.

JAG: How long was the rehearsal process on the film?

MR: Approximately two weeks. We sat around a table, examined the values in the material, moment by moment, and made sure the specific objectives of each character were clearly set. They understood how I was going to shoot the movie, not in terms of the shots, but they knew what I was about. I discussed what I thought were the most prominent values in the script, the issues, and how I thought each relationship dovetailed into the spine of the script. I explained those things gently, step by step, and they responded. They saw that I was planning to do something of moment and that turn-on process happened. Of course, they also brought their own enthusiasms. Henry *loved* his part. He said to me, "It's the crowning moment of my life." When he saw the picture he fell into my arms, sobbed, and he's a very modest man emotionally, with a kind of Puritan ethic. The problems were few. The music was soaring from the beginning. A lot of it has to do with holding in those thoroughbreds. Kate is like a prancing colt. You have to hold her back, because she'll run out too quick if you don't keep her easy and tell her when to run.

JAG: She contrasts with Fonda's reserve.

MR: It works, doesn't it? It works because it's well cast. She's a woman who's trying to breathe life into a man who's drying up, and that's ideal for her. She loved that role.

JAG: How do you keep the performances fresh after you rehearse?

MR: When you select the material to direct, you'd better damn well make sure that the material has sunk into some area of your unconscious and has the resonance to take you on a two-year trip. You cannot have an infatuation with material, because infatuation is over in six months and suddenly you're in the middle of a picture and you have no juices from which to draw your creative strength. So select material that stays deep, that can cook into areas that last. It's like working on Shakespeare. The more you work on it, the more you reveal to yourself, the more you understand, the more it turns you on. *On Golden Pond* is a terrific piece of material, so I didn't have a problem staying stimulated. You only have a problem when you don't like the material, and I just cannot do material I don't like.

JAG: Is it true that Hepburn and Fonda met for the first time on the picture?

MR: It's true. I introduced them. To this day it astonishes me that these two people who were the leading lights of their profession for fifty years had never met. I was uneasy about it. I thought, "Jesus, what if they don't like each other?" I mean, who knows, the chemistry is critical. So I said, "Miss Hepburn, this is Henry Fonda, Henry, this is Kate Hepburn." She looked at him in the eye and said, "Well, it's about time." He laughed, they embraced. He's very taciturn and economical. She, on the other hand, has a great spirit. They were very intimate very quickly. There was an immediate mutuality of respect, of history, of time, of achievement. Kate and Jane were much more wary of one another. There was a sense of animals circling one another, of potent tigresses. We didn't know whether they would be friends or enemies.

JAG: They seem so much alike.

MR: They are alike. But that's what caused it. Here is Jane, at the peak of her powers, certainly an individual who has run against the grain. Kate recognizes that because that was and still is Kate. Kate is an individual, not likely to fall into a conventional mold. She knows what it's like to be rebellious. Kate took hold of her life very early, bought her own play and insisted they make it a certain way, negotiated her own deals. She recognized that individuality in Jane. Jane, of course, revered Kate, although Kate didn't know that yet. Kate was waiting. She wanted to be respected by Jane. Jane *worshipped* her. But those first moments were very guarded and wary. It took a very short time for them to recognize something common in each other's talents and personalities. Halfway through the picture Kate was hiding in the bushes watching Jane work, cheering her on like a mother. It was quite touching, because as most people have acknowledged, this material is very reflective of Jane and Henry's relationship. Everybody was aware of that. I think in a sense Jane purchased this material ostensibly for Henry, but perhaps unconsciously she purchased it to give herself an opportunity to resolve some of the distances that existed between her father and herself before the end, which is really what the play is about.

JAG: When I interviewed Henry Fonda, I asked him about the old studio school attitude of acting practiced by Ford and Wellman, where there is little motivation—"What's my motivation?" "Your paycheck." Was there any conflict of styles between that and Jane's Actors Studio training?

MR: For Henry to—as I've seen him in the past—deny an Actors Studio method of acting is ludicrous. He does it, too. A lot of these guys do it instinctively. So does Kate. I've directed Duke Wayne. *The Cowboys* was a picture in which in the entire crew there was not one person who had ever worked with him before. I hired only Actors Studio people around him. That was necessary for me because I didn't want him to be comfortable doing his old kind of John Wayne thing. I hired young, talented crew members.

JAG: It wasn't Harry Carey and Paul Fix and Bruce Cabot. . . .

MR: Exactly. There was nobody there who were his comfortable drinking partners. The actors were all Actors Studio people, Roscoe Browne, Bruce Dern. The woman who played his wife, Sarah Cunningham, was a left-wing, blacklisted actress, but he didn't know that. He would've died! She was trained as I was at the Actors Studio. John Wayne was so challenged. He *knew* that he was in alien territory. He was the first guy on the set in the morning, he was the last guy to leave at night. He watched everybody work. He insisted that he and Gary Cooper had been doing Actors Studio stuff all their lives and nobody hadda teach 'em how to do it, you know, and it's true. It just means . . . what does it mean . . . it's a real problem. This is an important question you've brought up, by the way. There's been a lot of prejudice and stupid, uneducated commentary about the Method, the Actors Studio, all the conventional clichés that are discussed about actors who are "difficult" or "They want to know everything about everything and you don't really need to know all that. They mumble," all of that nonsense. Let's put it to rest here, once and for all. What is the Method? What does it mean? What did Stanislavsky do when he developed the Moscow Art Theatre? What did he do when he wrote *An Actor Prepares* and other magnificent works about the acting profession? What he did was document what had been done for centuries by all of the best actors. Not only did he document it, he set down a series of exercises, technical craft definitions, that permitted people to pursue proper work, not declamatory work, not artificial work. I think reality is the absolute root and core of any real achievement in art. It has to have verisimilitude or it doesn't work. It has to relate to you as a human being in some way you can understand and identify with, then you can move to any area. You can be fantastic, you can be impressionistic and theatrical beyond belief, but the core must be real. If it's not real, you won't believe it. Something has to be real. If an actor walks on stage sobbing, really sobbing, you'll believe any line he speaks. You'll believe, "My father is dead," you'll believe "I lost my comb," you'll believe anything he says if the behavior is real. So the Method is merely a mode to create a series of well-observed characteristics that help you to create genuine behavior, real behavior.

JAG: It's articulating something that has to be felt.

MR: Of course! It's a craft, like a musician must have. I went to Julliard in New York City, and Chicago Musical College and I trained as a pianist and a composer. You can't pretend to be a musician. Someone says "Play!" Unfortunately you can pretend to be an actor because people think that if you talk, you're acting. Well, speech has very little to do with acting. It's the final filigree on the creation of behavior. The text is the blueprint for that creation. The Method is a way of going about the creation of that life, a series of exercises just like a pianist studies scales and arpeggios and trains his fingers. The actor too must train his instrument. His instrument is trained in a number of fashions because he *is* his instrument. You have to work on yourself as a human being, make yourself emotionally fluid, sensitive, responsive. You can't be thick-skinned and insensitive and be an actor. You can and still be a person, but not an actor, and not an artist, at any rate.

JAG: How about the thin line between comedy and drama? In *On Golden Pond,* when Fonda has the heart attack, you have us laughing and crying.

MR: The wonderful thing about Henry Fonda's part is that his defense against his anxiety is humor. The line is a careful one. In a moment of extreme pain and physical illness in this film, Henry Fonda is able to be funny. Isn't that reflective of moments in life all the time, at the oddest moments? In drama, isn't that what you reach for all the time? You want a moment where people are crying and suddenly they're laughing and then they're crying again. That's what makes it worthwhile. I don't think it's difficult to achieve that, but you need fine material, resonant actors, and clarity of purpose. *On Golden Pond* is full of laughs. Audiences are roaring at the movie, yet it deals with absolutely ultimate issues—how does one face death, how does one resolve relationships with parents, how does a boy achieve manhood, how does an old man whose loss of manhood certainly is disturbing him make a relationship with a kid who's not yet a man—a lot of genuine and fundamental issues that seem dramatic.

JAG: In the boating accident scene, Fonda is in the water and Hepburn really dove in after him.

MR: I particularly didn't interrupt that shot so you would know she did it. Kate dives off the boat, in the middle of the night, and swims to rescue Henry Fonda, who's hanging onto a rock after an accident. They did it! We did everything we could to protect them. Henry was in a wet suit underneath his clothing. We kept him in the water only for the time necessary to take the shot. We had boats there with brandy. Everybody was drunk by the time we were halfway through the shooting! There were heaters there. We were all deeply concerned for the health of our actors, but there was no way to deter them from doing it themselves. If I had hired a stunt double for Kate Hepburn to dive into the water, she'd have had me beheaded. There's no way you can keep her from that. She's a woman of extreme vitality and pride. One month before we started shooting this picture she separated her shoulder from serving too hard in tennis and had to have an operation in which pins were placed in her shoulder. The doctor said there was no way she could do this movie. She looked at them and laughed and showed up on the set. In pain, by the way. That kind of determination to live a full life is what makes her something fabulous.

JAG: Jane Fonda learned how to do a backflip for the picture.

MR: She was concerned about it. She learned how to do it much better than the take I showed in the picture. There's a take in the picture that's not a very good backflip. She spent all summer with an expert diver, practicing day by day. She was determined to do it properly. She was terrified, and Kate challenged her. Kate is very clever. Kate asked her in rehearsal, "Do you know how to do a backflip well?" Jane said, "No," looked Kate in the eye and said, "You do, don't you?" Kate said, "Yes, I do," and that minute you knew that the moment was engaged. That day, Jane hired a teacher and practiced. She learned how to do an expert backflip, but I had to make her do a bad one because it seemed more real that the backflip be executed awkwardly and that she be delighted that she even went over. It seemed more human.

JAG: How did you open up the play in transposing it to film?

MR: I think the screenplay is maybe fifty percent new. Everything that's outside the house is new. Henry's painful loss in the woods—when he goes to pick strawberries and gets lost, is helpless—is a scene of which I'm really proud. You don't see that in the movies, someone lost in the woods and being in terror.

JAG: Not unless there's a guy with an axe chasing him.

MR: Yes, exactly! There are no axes or car chases in this movie, and I hope very seriously it helps bring our focus back to the fact that there's enormous drama in human interchange and that you don't need hardware. There's nothing wrong with outer space pictures, but there are inner space pictures, too. That's where my interest lies.

JAG: *On Golden Pond* is a very affirmative film.

MR: I'm a hopeful person. I'm not a cynic. I believe that cynicism is cancer for an artist. It's a way of insulating yourself from experience. If you're cynical about something, it somehow becomes removed and can't invade you. If you believe that life has to do with the engagement of issues and personalities, it makes you young and vital, and it's hard to be anything but hopeful. The cynicism that lurks in all of our intelligences, which points out the horrors that exist in the world and reminds you of them, has to be defeated. I don't mean to be a Pollyanna, but I believe that we are in charge of ourselves and our lives. We *can* make a difference. It has to do with determination and will.

(1981)

Susan Seidelman

Shot in 16mm for a mere $80,000, *Smithereens* was a powerful feature film debut for the then thirty-one-year-old Susan Seidelman. The New York University graduate school alumna produced, directed, edited, and co-wrote the movie, and guided young actress Susan Berman in a tour-de-force performance as Wren, a desperate groupie trying to break into the rock world any way she can. When *Smithereens* opened in late 1982, it was greeted with critical raves and a cult following, and broke the box-office records at New York's Greenwich Village Waverly Theatre One.

The film's success led to the "hip" hit *Desperately Seeking Susan* (1985), the picture that made Madonna a movie star, and that shares with its predecessor the director's feel for New York's Lower East Side. *Desperately Seeking Susan* was a leap for Seidelman into the mainstream, and the distributor, Orion, rewarded her with *Making Mr. Right* (1986), an enjoyable, if less successful, entertainment.

But it was *Smithereens* that signalled the arrival of a talented young director, and Seidelman's account of the film's problem-plagued production is a casebook of an ultimately winning independent motion picture. This interview was held on February 22, 1983, during the movie's resounding run at the Waverly.

FILMOGRAPHY

Smithereens (1982, New Line Cinema). HV: Media Home.
Desperately Seeking Susan (1985, Orion). HV: Thorn-EMI/HBO.
Making Mr. Right (1986, Orion). HV: HBO.
Cookie (1989, Lorimar/Warner Bros.).

Susan Seidelman (photo by Andy Schwartz).

SEIDELMAN INTERVIEW

JOHN A. GALLAGHER: What prompted you to make *Smithereens*?

SUSAN SEIDELMAN: I'd made three short films, each one getting a little longer than the one before. Around 1979, I decided to attempt a feature. I was living in the East Village at that time, and I noticed there was a new group of people who had moved into the Village and that fascinated me. I decided I wanted to make a film about that milieu. A lot of it came from the musical scene. I was at NYU Graduate School from 1974 to 1976 when the East Village was really dead. The hippies from the Sixties had moved out and there was nothing really happening. Somewhere around '76, my last year in film school, the neighborhood started to change, and there was a new burst of energy. A lot of that was coming from the rock 'n' roll movement.

JAG: How did the story and screenplay evolve?

SS: Basically I started with a character. I knew there was a kind of person I wanted to make a film about, a character I've known in various forms throughout my life. I'm sure there's a little bit of me in that character although it's not exactly autobiographical. It's a person who, in both male and female forms, has a lot of energy but doesn't stop to think how to channel that energy. A character that's always running after something. That intrigued me immensely. So I knew the character, and I knew I wanted to set her in that East Village environment, and the narrative developed out of the character. There were two people involved in the writing, Ron Nyswaner and Peter Askin. Over a period of two years I was writing notes to myself on the backs of napkins, on scraps of paper and index cards about this character, and I knew in my mind the kinds of things she might do and bits of dialogue she might say. I kept throwing these scraps of paper into a drawer and after about two years I sat down to try and write a screenplay based on all that information. I was just too close to it and got very confused, so I called in Ron and Peter and we sorted through the notes to see what was really there. We discussed it and figured out the storyline.

JAG: How did you approach the visual aspect of the film?

SS: I had a pretty clear idea of what I wanted the film to look like. I knew it was a film about pop culture and its influences on the main character, so I knew I wanted to give the film a very pop, almost cartoon-like look, but I also wanted it to be gritty. The image I had in mind was a gritty street cartoon. A lot of the visuals have a graphic look, with a lot of cartoon pop art.

JAG: In addition to being a very low-budget film that has performed tremendously in New York and at the various festivals, *Smithereens* is also unique in that Wren, the lead character, is an anti-heroine who is allowed to make the same mistakes as men do, as Carrie Rickey aptly put it in *The Village Voice*.

SS: It's funny, because most of the female characters you see are often put into various categories. There's the sex symbol and there's the maternal type. But I wanted to make a character that had a lot of energy but wouldn't necessarily always be nice. For some strange reason, female characters *aren't* allowed to make the same mistakes as men. Wren is in some ways similar to the Ratso Rizzo character in *Midnight Cowboy* (1969), manipulative. She's charming but also a liar, and I think some people might have trouble seeing a woman like this onscreen. I think it makes her an interesting character that she doesn't always have to be nice.

JAG: Susan Berman manages to make Wren appealing. How did she come to be cast?

SS: We put an ad in the trade papers, *Backstage* and *Show Business*. We had no money to make the film with, really, so we put in this horrendous ad—"No Pay. No Food. No Sleep." I was shocked that anyone responded to it but we must have gotten about a thousand photos and resumes. We started to audition people, and I knew I wanted somebody who seemed like a street person but was also a professional actress. We must have auditoned one hundred people and still couldn't find anybody who had the right mix. Yossi Segal, the assistant director, happened to go to an Off-Off Broadway play one night and saw Susan Berman sitting in the audience. He liked the way she looked and walked over to her, told her about the audition, and after the fact, asked her, "By the way, are you an actress?" When she came in, I just knew she was right.

JAG: How would you describe your working relationship with her?

SS: It was difficult in the beginning because you get very close to the people you work with, and like all marriages, when you're really close to somebody you fight. You love them and you hate them, so you're sort of battling. Out of knocking heads together, some real interesting stuff happens. The character was one thing on paper, and I think when Susan Berman was cast, Wren took on a totally different dimension. She made the character very real.

JAG: Where did you find Brad Rinn, who plays the boy from Montana?

SS: Brad's character is supposed to be this naive, optimistic guy from Montana who travelled in a van to New York. I was looking for somebody who seemed naively Midwestern, as though he'd just arrived in New York. We auditioned a lot of actors who were originally from the Midwest, but for some reason after living in New York a little while they seemed too cosmopolitan and we couldn't find somebody who was authentically naive. Again, the same guy, Yossi Segal, was walking through Washington Square Park in Greenwich Village and saw this tall kid sitting on a park bench reading an acting book. He walked over to

Brad and invited him to an audition. When I saw him he was exactly the character I was looking for.

JAG: How about Richard Hell?

SS: Originally we had another actor. In fact, that character was a little different in the original screenplay. Susan Berman broke her leg in the middle of shooting and we had to stop filming for four months. We rewrote the script at that point and started rethinking the rock star character, Eric. We were throwing out names and somebody suggested Richard Hell. We called him up and sent him the script. I think he had been in one film before, *Blank Generation* (1979), which was never released in this country. He always liked film and wants to be an actor. I think he was real excited about the opportunity to work.

JAG: All low-budget films are problem-ridden just by the fact they're low-budget. What would you say was your biggest problem?

SS: Because of Susan Berman's broken leg, the shooting was spaced out over the period of a year. It gets real hard when you're trying to hold together a group of twenty cast and crew when no one's getting paid and you're working under horrendous conditions a lot of the time, long hours, working in really dingy surroundings sometimes. To the credit of everyone involved, there was an overriding belief in the project.

JAG: How much did the film cost to make?

SS: For the 16mm version it cost $80,000, and another $25,000 to blow it up to 35mm. Originally I started the film for $25,000 and I thought I could shoot the whole film for that. It was supposed to be a five-week shoot, but by the end of the second week we'd used up about $18,000. That's when Susan broke her leg. At the time I thought it was a disaster, but the advantage of her breaking her leg was I was able to re-learn what it takes to make a feature film, because I was pretty naive to it at the time. Also, I was able to raise additional money. Since I had some footage in the can it was easier to raise money since I could show people footage.

JAG: How was the experience of shooting on the streets of downtown New York?

SS: At times it was really fun, because some unexpected thing would happen sometimes in the background that would be interesting. At other times it was a pain in the neck, because not only did you have to be constantly aware of what the actors were doing, but I was always nervous some jerk walking down the street would look in the camera and wave to his mother or his girlfriend. Often that *did* happen. Sometimes people would come by with big radios in the middle of a great take, and suddenly the sound would be ruined because some disco was blaring in the background.

JAG: And shooting in the subway?

SS: The problem was I knew I needed to shoot in the subway for one or two days. When I called up the MTA to get permission, I was told I needed something like a half a million dollars worth of insurance to shoot.

That means a couple of thousand dollars to get a half a million of insurance. When you're working with an $80,000 budget, there's no way you can put out $2,000 for insurance. We were told we weren't allowed to shoot on the subway without insurance, and yet I needed to shoot there. So five of us went down, two actors, the cameraman, the assistant cameraman, and myself, and we just snuck into the subway at midnight. It was the Memorial Day weekend, and we just rode the subway the entire night for two nights, stealing shots here and there. The problem with stealing locations is you're always nervous about continuity, because you'll get a shot one day then go back the next to finish it and everything's different. If you look at the film you'll notice a few continuity mistakes. Hopefully not too many!

JAG: At what point did you bring in your musicians, Glenn Mercer and Bill Million of The Feelies?

SS: Not until I had what I thought was a fine cut. I found out later that I was actually about twenty minutes away from a fine cut. I thought I had finished the film and brought them in to do the background music. At that time the film was about two hours long. One night I was in the editing room and another director, Jonathan Demme, came in with a friend of mine and watched the film. He made some real good comments, but what I found real interesting was watching it with somebody who I respected sitting behind me. I could feel myself squirming at different parts, wanting to speed up the editing machine. Judging by my own body reactions, I could tell it was a signal as to where I should start chopping. After he left, I chopped out an additional twenty minutes the following week, and that was the final version. Glenn and Bill had already started scoring. I gave them a video copy of the film and they brought that back to their studio and played around with different things. When the film was recut I was able to edit their music down to fit the new version.

JAG: What happened next?

SS: It took me two years to get *Smithereens* into the can, but things started to happen rather quickly at that point. I got an answer print at the lab and the next day I brought it to a screening room where the guy from the Directors' Fortnight at the Cannes Film Festival was scheduled to look at it. I had never really shown it to anyone, outside of a few actors who had worked on the film, so I had no real feedback. I didn't know what to expect. I brought it over to the screening room, where this gentleman saw it, and the next day I got a message on my answering machine that he'd like to meet me for breakfast. I didn't know what it meant. I got real nervous. I met him for breakfast and he told me that he liked the film very much and was considering putting it in the Directors' Fortnight at the Cannes Film Festival. I had applied to Cannes because I figured I'd send the application form and waste a dollar on an airmail stamp, but I really didn't know what Cannes meant for a film. At breakfast I was told that I couldn't put *Smithereens* in the festival unless I had a 35mm print. I was totally broke and didn't have another $25,000 to blow it up. As it turned out, as I was telling him my situation and he was saying, "Sorry, maybe another time," it just so happened that sitting a table away from us was the head of Janus Films, sitting with Joy Pareths, a foreign sales agent. They were having breakfast with the director of *Gal Young Un* (1979), Victor Nunez. The guy from Cannes called over the guy from Janus Films, said something in French, turned to me and said, "Would you mind showing them your film tomorrow?" I said, "Why not?" The next day they saw the film and four days later I got a phone call from Joy Pareths saying she would lend me $25,000. That guaranteed it would be in the Directors' Fortnight. What was even more shocking was about a week later I got a phone call from Paris saying Gilles Jacob, the head of the entire Cannes Film Festival, was going to be in New York and wanted to see the film. He did, and asked me if he could take it out of the Directors' Fortnight and move it into the main competition.

JAG: When did you get a distributor?

SS: Once it was in the main competition, getting distribution was a lot easier because the film was so different from the other films, and it got a good amount of attention in France. Rather than having to hustle to find a distributor, they were coming to us, which was real surprising. While it was still in 16mm, I had shown it to the people at New Line Cinema. I had heard from Sara Risher there that she liked it but they were unwilling to put money into blowing it up. I had the feeling that they were going to release it on the college market in 16mm. Before they'd made their final decision, and before I'd agreed to go with New Line, I heard the news about Cannes. At that point we withdrew from the New Line Cinema deal, had it blown up to 35mm, and then they came back to us at Cannes and made a better offer.

JAG: Why do you think *Smithereens* has been so successful?

SS: I think people are getting sick of these over-produced $40 million Hollywood extravaganzas. *Sophie's Choice* and *Tootsie* have been successful, but before that there were a lot of big flops, and I think audiences were fed up with being served that kind of pabulum. *Smithereens* tries to be honest about its subject matter. Also, because it's cheap, people respond to its grittiness.

JAG: Thematically, *King of Comedy, Starstruck,* and *Smithereens* all have something in common—an unknown wanting fame. But while *King of Comedy* and *Starstruck* are almost fantasies, *Smithereens* is ultra-realistic.

SS: I think people want characters they can identify with, whether in themselves or in other people. Although Wren is not a nice character, she is a recognizable, real character. I know a lot of people have seen the film and come out saying, "Yeah, I know somebody like that."

JAG: Have you encountered any difficulty because you're a woman director in a business dominated by male directors?

SS: I haven't really, because working independently you generate your own work, and I choose to work with people who are pretty open-minded. The more I have dealings with the industry, the more that becomes an issue.

JAG: How have you dealt with the major studios since the success of *Smithereens*?

SS: I've been talking with them about projects and so far they've been pretty nice. I'm a little skeptical about working with the studios. It would be nice to be able to work with more money and to be able to pay myself, but on the other hand I'm sure there are trade-offs. You have to ask yourself, "What are you giving up?" I think one of the problems and one of the fears I have is that as a woman working in the business, there are so few female directors making studio films. Often as a woman you do something independently that achieves some degree of success, then you get your shot to work with the big boys and if you blow it, you don't get a second shot. There have been a lot of women who make something independently, then make one studio film and you never hear from them again. I'd like to make more than one more film in my life. I don't want to be thinking, "If I don't pull the next one off, that may be the end of a studio career." I think it's somewhat unfair, because there are a lot of male directors who make mediocre film after mediocre film. Maybe they're part of some boy's club and are able to continue working!

JAG: *Smithereens* is a breakthrough film for what one can loosely categorize as the New York independent feature filmmaking scene.

SS: Over the last several years there has been a real energy in the New York independent film community. I was at the Seville Film Festival in Spain and they have a category called "New York Independents." They had about thirteen films there. In Europe these films seem to be much more of a force than they are here in New York. Fortunately for *Smithereens* it was able to get a relatively commercial distribution. I think distribution is the problem with some of the other films. Often they play in cinemas that don't get a wider audience, or they play in midnight shows or on weekends. Unfortunately, the people who control distribution also determine the taste, so there are probably some independent films that would appeal to a wider audience if they could find distributors willing to bank on them.

JAG: What kind of film background did you have?

SS: I'm from Philadelphia originally, and went to school at Drexel Institute of Technology, which is sort of a poor man's M.I.T. It was basically an engineering school but they had a small School of Design. The School

of Home Economics had three categories—nutrition, household management, and design. I was in design school, and the second year I was
there you had to pick a major. I chose fashion design, and they quickly
assign you to eight hours a day of sewing and tailoring classes. I was
about nineteen years old and I just couldn't see sitting behind a sewing
machine all day, so I started cutting my classes and going to the movies.
It was around that time that I started taking movies more seriously.

JAG: What was your film orientation when you were growing up?

SS: I came from a small suburb of Philadelphia so I grew up on the shopping
mall variety of cinema. When I was real young it was Hayley Mills and
Doris Day movies. I didn't see too many foreign films until I hit college,
and it was then that I started cutting class and hanging around the school's
very small film department. I think the first film I saw was Godard's
Breathless (1959). It was just so different from any I had seen before and
it opened up a lot of thoughts in my head. I hadn't thought that was the
kind of movie one could make. I started getting intrigued with cinema,
and since I had always been involved with graphics and visuals, and always
liked storytelling, it seemed a natural move to go from design to film.

JAG: You attended New York University.

SS: I started at NYU Graduate School in 1974. I had never made a film
before. The first year you got to know the basics like "This is an editing
machine," "This is how the camera works." The second year you got
to make a film with sound. My film *And You Act Like One Too* turned
out much better than I had anticipated. In fact, it won a student Academy
Award. What was shocking to me when I went to NYU was I felt so
inferior to everyone in the class because they had made films before and
I knew relatively nothing about it. Technically I had very little experience.
Making that film showed me that if you trust your instincts, you'll learn
the technical things along the way. The most important thing is figuring
out what you want to say, and then listen to your guts.

(1983)

Joan Micklin Silver

Joan Micklin Silver has successfully managed the transition from independent feature filmmaker to major studio director. Her first three low-budget films demonstrated an acute understanding of people in a variety of *milieus*—the turn-of-the-century Jewish ghetto of *Hester Street* (1975); the Back Bay Boston of *Between the Lines* (1977); and the Rocky Mountain love story of *Head Over Heels* (1979), based on Ann Beattie's novel *Chilly Scenes of Winter*. She followed with another unorthodox love story for HBO, *Finnegan Begin Again* (1985), starring Mary Tyler Moore and Robert Preston, and the hit *Crossing Delancey* (1988), a contemporary romantic comedy starring Amy Irving.

Born in Omaha, Nebraska, on May 24, 1935, and educated at Sarah Lawrence, Silver became involved in film when she moved from Cleveland to New York City in the late Sixties. She began with educational and children's films for Encyclopaedia Brittanica and Learning Corporation of America, and also served a stint as a writer with *The Village Voice,* an experience she put to good use on *Between the Lines.* She first achieved recognition for writing and directing three shorts for LCA (*The Case of the Elevator Duck, The Furcoat Club, The Immigrant Experience*). While researching *The Immigrant Experience,* Silver read "Yekl," a story by Abraham Cahan that became the source for her screenplay *Hester Street.* Her husband Raphael Silver raised the financing, Joan directed, and the couple distributed the film themselves throught their own company, Midwest Films. Joan Micklin Silver's feature career was launched as *Hester Street* won international praise and earned actress Carol Kane an Academy Award nomination. With her version of F. Scott Fitzgerald's *Bernice Bobs Her Hair* (1976), produced for a notable series of short story adaptations, she confirmed her chemistry with young actors and a genuine concern for the human condition that has marked all of her work.

Joan Micklin Silver (photo by Jean Pagliuso).

In August, 1977, while we were film students at Boston's Emerson College, Janet Wortendyke and I interviewed the director at her office at Midwest Films in New York City.

FILMOGRAPHY

Hester Street (1975, Midwest Films). HV: Vestron.
Between the Lines (1977, Midwest Films). HV: Vestron.
Head Over Heels/Chilly Scenes of Winter (1979, United Artists). HV: MGM/UA.
Finnegan Begin Again (1985, HBO Premiere). HV: Thorn-EMI/HBO.
Crossing Delancey (1988, Warner Bros.). HV: Warners.
Lover Boy (1989, Tri-Star).

SILVER INTERVIEW

JOHN A. GALLAGHER: Were there any filmmakers that you really respected or were influenced by?

JOAN MICKLIN SILVER: Well, I'll tell you about one of the films that's clearest in my mind. I saw it when I was a little girl in Omaha, and to this day I could tell you where I was sitting in the theater, and who I was sitting next to. That was Hitchcock's *Shadow of a Doubt* (1943). For some reason I carried for a very long time the memory of Joseph Cotten trying to push Teresa Wright off the train, and I was almost afraid to see that film again as an adult. I thought, "Oh, it will be like a lot of films that you loved when you were a kid." That was such a good film. I think I was influenced by any of the films I saw when I was a little girl in the Forties. Not to say that my taste was always so elevated. I also loved *Presenting Lily Mars* (1943) with Judy Garland and *Song of the Islands* (1942) with Betty Grable, just whatever I got to see. Television didn't come to Omaha until I was thirteen, so I always spent Saturday afternoons in the movies. There's a lot of filmmakers I admire. I think Truffaut's just a terrific director. I guess the director whose work I feel close to is Satyajit Ray. I don't quite know why, but whenever I see his films, even though what he's describing is certainly very far away from anything that I know about, I just feel, "I want to make films." I like the richness of detail in his films. I like his approach toward characters because they're presented really in the round. It isn't just a simple division into good people and bad people.

JAG: *Limbo* (1972) was one of the first films to deal with the reality of the Vietnam war. How did your conception of the screenplay differ from the finished product?

JMS: My screenplay was developed from interviews with P.O.W. and M.I.A. wives I have met. Some of them were interesting women who had been changed a great deal by their experience. One in particular was an absolutely superb character. She was Irish Catholic, very conservative, with a number of children, and she was going to wait for him for seven years. But she was really radicalized by the war, and she was the core of the script. The director, Mark Robson, thought she was totally a bitch, and his secretary read it and she thought the character was a bitch, too. He did what he had every right to do, which was to make the film that he wanted to make. He was exceedingly generous to me because he let me come down on the set, and that was my first chance to watch a movie being made from a close position. I got to look through the camera. They were very nice to me because they thought I was pretty unhappy. I'd been replaced by another writer, and he knew that I really didn't agree with what he'd done to the screenplay. It sort of turned into a slick soaper. I think if it had been done in a gritty, more honest way, it would have been, as you say, an early film talking about how people had been changed by the war. As it happened, nobody ever saw it and it disappeared from view.

JAG: It pops up occasionally on television.

JMS: Yeah, and believe me, I'm very fast to cash my royalty checks! But I'm very grateful to the whole experience in retrospect because it started me directing. It really propelled me out of this little plan I'd had of writing screenplays. It just made me say, "I can't do this anymore." So in the end, some of those bad experiences can be helpful to you.

JAG: On *Hester Street,* how did you come up with the financing?

JMS: My husband raised the money, and we also put some of our own into it.

JAG: How did you go about recreating the period locations on Morton Street and turn the block into turn-of-the-century New York?

JMS: The scenes on Morton Street took four-and-one-half days. They would be propping a part of the street while we were shooting. The street consisted of both a number of retired people and a number of students, and they wanted us to make the film there. Some streets they wouldn't have been as nice, but the people on Morton Street were just great. I had an excellent designer named Stuart Wurtzell. New York has been a very easy place to film since the days of the Lindsay administration, comparatively speaking. They'll give you police and they'll help you do anything you need to do, so from the point-of-view of utilizing the resources of the city, they're great. It was a matter of a lot of hard work and sweat. If it had rained, I don't know what we would have done because we left the props out for the days we shot there.

JAG: How did Carol Kane come to be cast in *Hester Street*?

JMS: I had seen her in a Canadian film called *Wedding in White* (1972). She played a very different role, a sixteen-year-old Scotch Protestant girl, kind of slow, who is raped by her brother's friend and then forced by her family to make a marriage to an old, discouraging kind of fellow. I was just very interested in her work. I thought she was very fresh and different, and she had a unique quality. In the original story "Yekl," the wife is described as being dark, swarthy, and peasant-like, and Carol obviously doesn't fit those things.

JAG: Your adaptation of *Bernice Bobs Her Hair* for public television is very straightforward. Fitzgerald's work has proven difficult to adapt for many filmmakers.

JMS: The trouble with most Fitzgerald adaptations is that everybody gets too reverential and too awestruck. Certainly, if I'd had *The Great Gatsby* to do, I would have felt the same way because you've got a masterwork. But the story of *Bernice* is really a charming early story of Fitzgerald's, but it's hardly one of the great stories of all time. I think that helped me feel a little less awestruck and therefore it didn't have that waxworks quality that a lot of Fitzgerald adaptations have. Also, I think some of them drown in period detail. In the case of *Bernice,* the narrative line was there and it was merely a matter of enriching it with incident that was it keeping with the thing. It really came very easily to me. It had to do with adolescent girls and I not only have been one, but I'm the mother of some.

JAG: I understand that Fred Barron presented his screenplay for *Between the Lines* to you during an interview.

JMS: He was doing a roundup on the Cannes Festival for the *Boston Real Paper,* and *Hester Street* had played in that particular festival. We met him then, and he did an interview with us. Six months later when *Hester Street* opened in Boston, we met up with him again and he happened to mention that he'd written a screenplay. I didn't know that he had ambitions along that line and he asked us to look at it and we did. So that's really how it came to us.

JAG: How was your experience shooting in Boston?

JMS: We just loved it. In fact, if we had been a studio-backed film we would have shot the whole thing there. I mean, when we shoot on location we have to pay everyone's hotel and food for the whole duration of the shoot. We really couldn't afford that because we were financing *Between the Lines* out of our share of *Hester Street*'s earnings. We only shot in Boston for two weeks. I thought that we got some terrific stuff. I loved the light. The day we shot in the subway we had one of those misty gray Boston days and I thought it really had a beautiful look to it.

JAG: Why did you choose Southside Johnny and the Asbury Jukes for the party sequence?

JMS: I didn't want a heavy metal group because I knew that I wanted to integrate the dialogue into the scene. I wanted a group that lived on the East Coast so I wouldn't have to spend the money to bring them to New York and put them up, right? I mean, these are all the decisions. Then it had to be a group that had already recorded and whose recording company was behind them and would help us pay some of the expenses. That reduced the field. We wanted especially somebody from the East Coast, because an awful lot of them are out on the West Coast now. We met that group, heard them sing down in Asbury Park and we liked them.

JAG: They were a fine choice.

JMS: I love them. Johnny was tremendously helpful to us in the filming. He took charge of them so they were there and did what they were supposed to do. They're very nice.

JAG: What was your reaction to some of the media criticism of *Between the Lines*? Some alternative press people like David Denby seemed to really take it personally. They seemed to miss the point that it was a comedy.

JMS: I felt that way, too, but you know, I don't consider it my responsibility to do a documentary study of the alternative press. I was telling my particular story and it was a fictional paper. As you say, it was a comedy. Some of the criticism we could have anticipated and we did, but not quite the degree of it. It's funny, it's the people who still work on them that felt we were trying to denigrate their work, which was really untrue. If there's anyone who likes the alternative press and feels affection towards it, it's me, because *The Village Voice* was where I worked when I was trying to get into film, and they were great to me. After *Between the Lines,* I had lunch with my old editor from the *Voice* and he really loved the film and thought it was quite true.

JAG: You have a real penchant for bring out the best in young actors.

JMS: I've had good luck.

JAG: Do you have any particular theories about working with young actors?

JMS: I think it's an advantage to use an actor who has not had his chance yet because they're just as eager as you are. They don't give you the tired rendition you sometimes get from very experienced actors. There's an expression in Hollywood—"He just phones it it"—which means somebody comes up there and gives you the same performance he gave in the last twenty films he was in. You don't get that from young actors. They aren't experienced, of course, and oftentimes have not had a lot of training. What seems to be a problem with young actors, now at least, is that a lot of them are coming from television acting, if you can call it that. In most cases it is something very specific and they learn to deliver an acceptable line on the first take. If they don't, they don't get hired on television. They go off the lists, so therefore they aren't giving you anything very surprising. I think shooting that way does encourage that sort of thing. Part of the problem is to just make them feel relaxed, make them feel they can make mistakes. When they stop saying "I'm sorry," I feel that I've gotten somewhere.

JAG: Do you encourage improvisation?

JMS: Whenever it's useful. I certainly did on *Between the Lines*. But not on camera improvisation. Improvisation during rehearsal, then I script from improvs. Basically they're doing their own lines, but it's been scripted, typed, and they've learned the scenes. I don't actually care for improvisation on camera, even if I could afford it.

JAG: How did you like working with Shelley Duvall in *Bernice Bobs Her Hair*?

JMS: She's excellent. I've worked so far with two very trusting, instinctive actors, Shelley and in *Between the Lines* Jeff Goldblum. Most actors are tremendously self-conscious. They always have part of themselves sitting outside watching them and afterwards they come to you and say, "On the first take I thought I did my turn better but on the second take I thought I handled the lines better." Jeff and Shelley are just very trusting. Jeff would finish up a take and say. "Was it wonderful?" I'd say yes or no, and he'd say, "OK, what shall I do?" They trust the director. They aren't worried about it all the time and it gives a different purpose to their performances. Which isn't to say that they don't think about what they're doing. It's just that once they've established that relationship with the director, they are just *there*.

JAG: There seems to be a real warmth that comes through in your films.

JMS: I'll tell you what I think. I think that people express in films their own personalities. It may be a function of my age or the way I was raised, but I don't have nearly as depressed or pessimistic a view of human beings as some people do. It may have something to do with the era I grew up in. Somebody said to me about *Between the Lines* that I was too nice to the characters. I said, "What do you mean?" They said, "You end up liking them all, even the awful ones." I don't think that's a criticism. I think that's pretty nice. I tend to see people as a mix, you know, the Jewish view is that people have the potential for good and evil and I really agree.

JAG: Could you talk about self-distribution?

JMS: We've succeeded in getting some very good houses for *Between the Lines*. It depends on the material, the situations in the city, and on the exhibitors and what they're looking for. Some exhibitors have unwritten commitments. They'll take the product of say, Columbia or Paramount, and it varies from city to city. The Orson Welles Cinema in Boston has been great to us, so the ideal thing is to get an exhibitor who cares about the film and doesn't just throw it up on the screen. I think what booking is all about is having people who really understand the whole circuit and what's going on in various cities. They understand how that's constantly shifting. Two years ago a theatre might have been very good and now it's a porno house, so it constantly changes. It's very specific from town to town. We have a man who works for us named Jeff Lipsky, who also worked for us on *Hester Street*. He'd come to us from John Cassavetes' organization, which has very successfully distributed *A Woman Under the Influence* (1975). Jeff is very young and very knowledgeable, and he's made it his business to find out what's going on in the various cities. I think exhibitors are beginning to realize now that we're a fairly predictable source of product, but it doesn't come very often, whereas the majors make enough films so that it behooves the exhibitor to say, "OK, I'll play your dog for you because I'll get your next one and that'll be a good one." On *Between the Lines,* we started distribution and then we had to taper off a little because all these big summer films came out. The studio films tend to suck-up hundreds of theaters at a time, so when there are six big studio films out there and they've got eight hundred theaters each, there isn't very much left for you. You have to wait for some of those films to "fall out of bed," as they say, and then you can move in because exhibitors are looking for product again. You're not going to get much play in a city that has three theaters when there are things like *The Other Side of Midnight* (1977) and *The Deep* (1977) out. Those movies are going to come before yours in exhibition.

JAG: Why have roles for women in the Seventies been so one-dimensional? They go from one extreme to the other.

JMS: I think the people who make decisions for the most part are middle-aged men who live in California. Those are the ones who have the power to say, "Yes, we're going to make this; no, we're not going to make that." I think that women have had an impact. They've said, "Hey, we don't want to see that stuff. We want to see something about women, not somebody's girlfriend." I think it's begun to change. In Hollywood they respond to things that satisfy them personally and things that they think are going to make money. If you had more women in executive positions, they would get more personal satisfaction out of other kinds of stories and maybe you'd see greater variety. That's just speculation, but I think it would help.

JAG: What kind of prejudice, if any, did you face in getting to make films?

JMS: I would say that the worst prejudice for women to overcome is getting work. Obviously there's nothing about directing that requires you to be a man. In my opinion, a woman could direct anything including a battle scene. After all, men have directed childbirth scenes. The act of directing doesn't require one form of sexual orientation or the other. It's really a matter of getting work, although women are slowly trickling their way in. It's very slow. You could say there's been a 100% improvement because now two women directed Hollywood films this year and only one did last year. I mean two, you know, out of all the ones that make it. No studio is going to take a woman who hasn't directed anything and say, "Here's two million dollars." You've got to be able to say, "I've done this and this." When I talk to women, I tell them to do what I did, and a lot of them do. They're just getting it together somehow and making independent films. No one is going to give them the chance to do it, but at the same time it's really not fair. Little by little, it's getting better, but it's not happening fast enough. I expect that it will eventually.

JAG: Do you think that writing is the best entree?

JMS: Yeah, because you can write a feature film and never have done anything before. Freddie Barron would be a perfect example. Fred was a journalist but had never written a screenplay. It's probably the best way to break in at the moment.

JAG: What advice would you have for film students hoping to realize their ambitions?

JMS: Toughen up would be first. In the end, I think those who succeed will succeed probably because of their talent, but perhaps even more because of their persistence, their ability to withstand rejection, their ability to keep hold of the fact that what they want to do is a good thing to do. I'd say character traits in the end are probably the most important thing to a filmmaker who wants to make it. There was an article in California a few weeks ago in *New West* magazine with a list of directors. Most were twenty-eight-year-old men, and me. It said, "Silver isn't as young as the others, but since women have so recently entered feature films . . . " I felt like I was the grandmother of the crowd! Besides short pieces on these various young directors and me, there was a longer piece on Brian DePalma. His career is such an example of the value of persistence and just keeping at it. He's been up and down and up and down, and now he's finally up.

JAG: That's tenacity.

JMS: It's the ability to say what you're doing is right when a lot of people are saying, "I don't think that's such a good idea." Believe me, nobody thought *Hester Street* was a good idea. But what are you gonna do? You have to just believe in what you're doing and not constantly subject yourself to criticism, as well meant as it is, and the advice of others, because you lose sight of what you want to do.

JAG: Just stick to your own convictions?

JMS: If you can. It takes a lot of gumption. It really does. It takes people to say "No" to you a thousand times before you get someone to say "Yes." You just have to keep at it.

(1977)

James Toback

The Gambler, Fingers, Love and Money, Exposed, The Pickup Artist, The Big Bang!—the titles of James Toback's movies reflect his themes and obsessions. Toback's films are off-beat, visceral, and highly original, with characters who constantly confront their own contradictions, and generally split critics and audiences right down the middle. People seem to either love or hate Jim Toback movies.

Born in New York City in 1944, Toback graduated *magna cum laude* from Harvard, did graduate work at Columbia University, and taught literature at the City College of New York. He wrote for such magazines as *Esquire* and *Harper's,* and in 1971 published a book, *Jim,* based on his relationship with football hero-turned-actor Jim Brown. Toback's original screenplay, *The Gambler* (1974), directed by Karel Reisz, set the tone for his subsequent film work with its riveting portrayal of a compulsive gambler, played by James Caan. In 1978, Toback made an astounding directorial debut with *Fingers,* a brilliant and violent drama about an aspiring concert pianist (Harvey Keitel) who lives a double life as a collector for his loan shark father. *Fingers* was poorly distributed, but was highly praised by such film-makers as R. W. Fassbinder and François Truffaut, who selected it as one of his all-time favorite films in a 1979 American Film Institute poll, the only current film to make his list.

Championed by Warren Beatty, Toback followed with *Love and Money* (1982), memorable for a performance by veteran director King Vidor; *Exposed* (1983) a quirky melodrama with Nastassia Kinski as a high fashion model embroiled with a European terrorist (Keitel); and *The Pickup Artist* (1987), starring Molly Ringwald and Robert Downey, Jr., a comedic departure for the director. Toback's next film, *The Big Bang!*, is a self-financed, low-budget documentary examining the attitudes of males and females towards such subjects as sex, love, money, politics, and religion.

James Toback (courtesy of Mr. Toback).

My interviews with Jim Toback took place in New York City in 1983, before the release of *Exposed*; and in 1988 as he was preparing to film *The Big Bang!*

FILMOGRAPHY

Fingers (1978, Brut). HV: Media Home.
Love and Money (1982, Lorimar).
Exposed (1983, MGM/United Artists). HV: MGM/UA.
The Pickup Artist (1987, 20th Century-Fox). HV: CBS/Fox.

TOBACK INTERVIEW

JOHN A. GALLAGHER: Your films have been better appreciated in Europe than in the United States.

JAMES TOBACK: I have a convoluted theory about this which revolves around the implications of World War Two and the special closeness to death that people felt all over Europe during and just after the war. It was a totally different experience from the American one, with the direct bombing of European cities, while Americans—as with the Vietnamese war—were sent off *to* a war while their homeland was protected. Being bombed forces a population *en masse* into an awareness of death, an awareness which people usually like to shelve. The films I've done force themselves towards death, make one aware of the randomness of extinction, the closeness of danger and terror, and the nightmarishness of finality. In Europe, death is just beneath the surface of consciousness. In America, it's impolite. But even in Europe, it's now a full generation removed, and the younger generation is less responsive. It's the generation in their thirties and forties that are most excited by my films and the films of people whose films stay close to death. I gave Jimmy Caan some lines in *The Gambler*. He's teaching D. H. Lawrence's *Studies in Classic American Literature* and he quotes Lawrence: "Americans are the great dodgers. They dodge their own very selves." Americans by and large like to think that they love the truth and they tell the truth. Jimmy Carter got elected by one of the great manipulations in American political history. He took 200 million people and in effect treated them like a bunch of five-year-olds by saying, "I'm never going to lie to you, so vote for me. I'll be a good father and I'll be a good President. You be good children. Elect me." They went for it because they like to think of themselves as truth tellers when in fact there is a fundamental evasiveness of the real truth, which is not awful so much as it is inevitable—the truth being death. People like to think they can prepare themselves. They have insurance policies. They have wills. Death is an event somewhere off in the future, which maybe they can avoid altogether if they behave. One can never underestimate the American need to control the future. But no one has that control. Life can end at any moment. You and I are sitting here talking. We'll probably both get out of this room, but maybe we won't. The only thing we know is not that we're going to get out of this room alive, but that at some point, which will not be of our choosing, we will die. That's the only thing anybody ever knows about his life. Once one accepts that, knows it, feels it, and thinks about it a bit, one is paradoxically *free* from the fear of it.

JAG: Your screenplay for *The Gambler* opened the door for you. Is there anything you'd do differently if you had directed it?

JT: The essential thing to capture in any film is the dream/nightmare intensity you've written. Karel Reisz got it.

JAG: *Fingers* was released by Brut, but had a very limited run. Siskel and Ebert included it in their television program on forgotten films.

JT: *Fingers* ended up making money because it only cost one million dollars. Although a good 50% of the people who saw it wanted to stab me. They hated it. It offended and upset them. But there was a hard core 25% that I get letters from even now—*Fingers* freaks. Unfortunately, at the time it was released, Truffaut hadn't written about it, Ebert and Siskel hadn't come out with what they said, David Thomson hadn't called it a masterpiece in a book that he did, Fassbinder hadn't gone around proselytizing. So its opening preceded most of the strong and potentially influential reactions. It's much easier to write something difficult off than it is to champion it. There are a lot of minor league minds who need somebody else's stamp of approval before they will accept any strange movie as serious; a year or two later, those same people get very excited after the proper patina of "seriousness" has been attached to it. One reviewer hated *Fingers* and wrote vile stuff about it, and then when *Love and Money* came out bemoaned the loss of intensity and abandonment of the thrilling qualities of *Fingers*.

JAG: What happened with the domestic distribution?

JT: *Fingers* did not get legitimate domestic distribution but it did quite well considering that $150,000 was spent to sell it. That's a speck of dust. Usually you spend a million to open a movie in New York alone, and they spent $150,000 to open it in fifteen cities *including* New York. There was a head of distribution at Brut at that time named Morry Lefko, a feisty little guy with a fringe of orange hair, who'd been head of MGM distribution for thirty years. He had just been hired to run Brut's distribution. Now, I will be eternally grateful to George Barrie, who was head of Brut, until my dying day, because he gave me the shot with *Fingers* when no one else would have. I would not be a director if it weren't for George Barrie. But this head of distribution saw the movie and obviously didn't know what to make of it. I went into his office with my ideas on distribution. I said, "I don't want to impose on your terrain, but I think this movie needs special handling. Let me give you a few of my ideas." He yawned and let me talk for five minutes. Then he said, "OK, you finished?" I said, "Yeah." He said, "Alright, let me tell you something. A few years ago at MGM there was a piece of shit movie called *Blow Out*"—he meant *Blowup* (1966)—"by some wop named Tony Oni"—he meant Antonioni—"and I sold that piece of shit. I put it over on the American public, and if I could put that piece of shit over on the American public, I can put your piece of shit over on the American public too." I don't think people realize how totally a movie can be poisoned in terms of its response if it is badly distributed, or how far you can go with a mediocre film if it is sold with zeal, intelligence, and a lot of money. But fuck it. What's important is the movie. If you make the movie you wanted to make, all you should be is ecstatic. If Morry Lefko were here now, I would just say, "Hi, Morry."

JAG: Harvey Keitel is so powerful in *Fingers*.

JT: It's almost difficult to remember back to this time in 1976 when we didn't know each other. We've become second nature companions since then. But there was suspicion at first. The first time I met him was in Los Angeles. Jack Clayton, the British director, was talking to him about doing a movie. I knew Jack and I said, "I'd really like to meet Harvey Keitel. I want to use him in *Fingers*." He introduced me briefly, then I called Harvey later that day and said, "Hi, I'm Jim Toback, I wrote *The Gambler*." He had a bad vibe from that because I had wanted Bobby DeNiro, who is Harvey's best friend, to play the lead. Bobby wanted to play it and Karel Reisz had used Jimmy Caan instead, so to Harvey, *The Gambler* was this movie that his buddy Bobby had wanted and didn't get. He kept me at arm's length. He said, "What do you want to talk about?" I said, "*Fingers*." He was very cautious, and I, being somewhat expansive and insistent by nature, said, "This part is the reason you're an actor." It was a bit fatuous but I was a bit naive. After I finished what I considered to be a knockout one-hour rap, Harvey said, "Let me read it and I'll think about it." I said, "Say yes now. It'll be in the spirit of the relationship we're going to have. Say yes now and *then* read it. Say yes on instinct." He said, "I don't know if I have the instinct yet." I said, "Then you don't have instincts. Instinct means spontaneity. Say yes or no right now." He started to laugh. He said, "You've gotta give me a little breathing room. You can't approach me this way. It's not gonna work." It started to get tense. It almost reached the point where he was going to say "Forget it" and walk out. Finally I said, "OK, look. I don't want to cross your rhythm. You do it your way. But if you don't feel that something special has happened between us right here, then my intuition about you is wrong." He said, "Well, to tell you the truth, the last few minutes I have been feeling odd myself. No one's ever talked to me this way before. It *is* intriguing to me but I still want to read the script and I'm not going to say no or yes until I've thought about it for a while." Two days later he called me up, we met again, and he started to get more and more interested. We got closer and closer. By the time we were shooting we were like a couple of communicants. Three or four days after we finished shooting *Fingers,* I ran into Harvey on the street. He said to me, "How can you stand to be you?" I said, "What do you mean?" He said, "I just realized now that the film is over that I've come out of this cloud of total dread, tension, and despair that I was in when I was shooting. It's like having an awful weight lifted off me. You must feel like that all the time." I said, "I don't. You took it past me. Another actor wouldn't have taken it that way, so part of that was you." We knew we'd work together again. I tried to use him in *Love and Money* but David Picker wouldn't make the movie with him. On the other hand, I was dumb. I really shouldn't have made *Love and Money* without Harvey, but I'd been desperate to do it after two years of frustration. I probably would have made it with the doorman of the Trinidad Hilton.

JAG: You cast the great director King Vidor in *Love and Money* as the grandfather.

JT: King was one of the noblest human beings I've ever known, but he was not my first choice. He was my third. First I'd gone to George Cukor, who was an old friend of mine and who said, "I did not spend forty years *behind* the camera *not* making a fool out of myself all of a sudden to *make* a fool out of myself at the age of eighty in *front* of the camera." Then I went to Harry Ritz of the Ritz Brothers. He was a diabetic and went into insulin shock after the first day of shooting and had to quit. Dick McWhorter, the production manager and an old friend of King's, suggested King. He said, "I think King would be great for this part. He's not doing much. He's eighty-two years old. We had to shoot at seven o'clock the next morning and it was then eight o'clock at night. Dick called King upstate, a five-hour drive away from Hollywood. King said, "Have the fellow call me." I called King. He had read something Truffaut had written about *Fingers,* and he said, "Oh, I wanted to see *Fingers* from what he said. I like Truffaut. What's this part like?" I described it to him. He said, "Let me hear a little of it." I read him two or three pages and he said, "I'll do it. When do you need me?" I said, "We're supposed to shoot at seven tomorrow morning but obviously that's impossible. This is Tuesday, we can shoot around you for the rest of the week." He interrupted me and said, "No, it's 8:30, I need an hour to pack. I just want to get some dinner. I could leave by midnight. I'll be there by five, take an hour nap, and I'll be ready by seven." I thought he was kidding, but he was there at seven o'clock in the morning, having driven down himself at the age of eighty-two with his friend Kate Finley. He showed up and he worked thirteen hours! Never complained. One day he had food poisoning but didn't tell me because he was afraid that on a rushed budget it would cost me time. He never imposed his advice. He often would say to me, "Remember, I'm the actor, not the director. If you ever want suggestions from me, just ask. I won't impose them on you." When I did ask he always had something interesting to try. He was a phenomenal man. I'll tell you a story about him and Cukor. They were friendly and that weekend they had lunch together at Cukor's house. King said he was in L.A. to act in this film *Love and Money* that Jim Toback was directing. Cukor said, "Oh, Jim offered me that part and I turned it down." The next Monday King said to me, "You didn't tell me you offered this part to Cukor? Harry Ritz was bad enough, but I was your third choice!" and gave me his wry San Antonio smile. There was a very sad moment some time later. He'd been on the MGM lot from the Twenties through the Forties, shooting movies. He was coming to have lunch with me and I left his name at the front gate. The man at the gate said, "Who are you?" "I'm King Vidor. I'm having lunch with Jim Toback." The guard looked down at his list and said, "I don't have your name down here." King said, "Well, it should have been left by Jim Toback, but I was a director on this lot for thirty years and I had an office in the Thalberg Building before you were born." The guy said, "Your name is not on this list and you cannot get on the lot." King's heart was pounding. He said, "My name should be there. It's King Vidor." The guard said, "How do you spell that?" "V-i-d-o-r." The guard said, "I have a Viter here on my sheet, V-i-t-e-r. Why didn't you tell me in the first place?" Then he let King through. King was so upset he couldn't think of anything else. Cornel Wilde was also in the commissary. He came over to say hello and King said to him, "Have they forgotten you, too?" Cornel said, "Sure, here and there there's one, but most of them have never heard of me." King told Wilde the story. He was hurt. He was also hurt because he felt he was quite good in *Love and Money* in portraying senility, but that no one had seen the movie. He knew he was good, but he was hearing nothing. Just before he died I sent him some reviews from *Positif* and *Le Monde* in France saying how great he was in it. He called me up and said, "See, I knew I was good in this movie." I miss him.

JAG: In *Exposed* you combined the world of high fashion, which like film and television perpetuates immortality, with the mortal, dangerous world of terrorism.

JT: I like polarities and extremes in every aspect of life, in character, in subject matter, in style. *Exposed* begins with a character, a post–Women's Lib figure who has an unconscious nose for trouble, who attracts it almost in spite of herself, who takes for granted the things that Neanderthals endlessly debate, both in movies and out, about Women's Lib. What I tried to do in *Exposed* was start with a character who takes the women's movement for granted and let her, through her own qualities of restlessness, curiosity, compulsive risk-taking, love of danger, adventure, excitement, and general horniness, go wherever she will. Set her up in circumstances that are restrictive at the beginning with a school she doesn't like, a teacher she's been involved with and is trying to break away from, a family that's repressive, and let her break away and go to New York. From then on, it was open-ended. All the things that came up once she got to New York and then to Paris in *Exposed* came up because they seemed inevitable next steps. The juxtaposition of terrorism and high fashion grew almost accidentally out of that progression of events. Of course, I was in a kind of collusion in getting the story to go in those directions. Both Nastassia (Kinski) and her character, Elizabeth Carlson, were similarly intrigued, even infatuated with those worlds. Nastassia was a model, so she knew the worlds, and the terrorist idea would appeal to many restless, curious, radical young women.

JAG: Paul Schrader mentioned that in working with her in *Cat People* (1982), her premature stardom made her insecure. That quality seemed to work for you in *Exposed*.

JT: What happened is that, for the first time, Nastassia had a chance to show all of her contradictions, which in the past she'd been forced for the most part to hide. *Cat People, One from the Heart* (1982), and *Tess* (1979) lace her up quite a bit. An earlier film directed by Alberto Lattuada, *Stay As You Are* (1979), lets her loose a little more. It was in that film much more than the others that I saw this range of qualities even before I knew her. She isn't just a Garbo/Dietrich figure, glamorous and cold, the stark European *femme fatale,* which is the fashion model of image, but rather an awkward, horny, crazy, uncontrolled, passionate, volatile, explosive woman. I tried to put the two together. I wanted to start with this restless intelligence and curiosity and let it go in both directions, which is why she could never be happy just being a model either in real life as Nastassia or in *Exposed* as Elizabeth Carlson. She would be looking for some kind of breakaway from it through romance, adventure, and danger. On the one hand Nastassia is ambitious, but also impatient with the fruits of ambition on the other. I once told her that Jefferson said, "Show me a man who's satisfied and I'll show you a failure," and she loved the remark. I try to create characters who want to know "What's next?" the minute there's been any fulfillment of ambition. There is both ambition and a subversion of ambition. Ambition self-destructs as soon as it is realized. No sitting, patting one's own back, a trait which is the enemy of organic development in art or in life. Being involved in movies or modeling or any exciting, highly sped up, glamorous world you are faced with all these temptations that try to seduce you away from the restless energy and dissatisfied temperament that got you involved in the activity in the first place. It's very easy for an actor, an actress, a writer, a director to sit by a pool in Hollywood, lay out five projects, withdraw from the dreary chaos of the world, get a business manager, an agent, a publicist, and talk your life away on a car phone. I think that's one reason that so many talented directors, actors, and writers who were so good when they were young got so dull as they got older; and Hollywood rewards them for their timidity. Can you imagine Scorsese or Bertolucci or Coppola having made *The Color of Money* (1986), *The Last Emperor* (1987) or *Peggy Sue Got Married* (1986) earlier in their careers? Look at Robert Redford in *The Chase* (1966), or in *Downhill Racer* (1969), or in *This Property Is Condemned* (1966) or *Inside Daisy Clover* (1965), and then you go to Redford today and it's a complete flattening out of what was interesting and raw in him. There are any number of writers and directors one could speak of. It isn't that these people are used up or have lost talent, it's that as success sets in and ambition is realized, the pressures of convention can seduce into suffocation. Nastassia Kinski will be interesting in that regard. I think she'll do both. She'll do some mainstream films like *Unfaithfully Yours* (1984), but I think she'll continue to do films like *Exposed,* which really challenge her and reach those people in the audience who are finally like her, people who are not hiding from themselves, and then again she may, like any interesting person, flip out.

JAG: You wrote *Exposed* specifically for Kinski.

JT: Yeah. I find that my best luck has come when I've had an actor in mind even if that actor doesn't end up playing the part. The focus is clearer for me. *In Love and Money* I ended up with an actor in the lead, Ray Sharkey, who while perfectly good for more rodential characters like the ones in *The Idolmaker* (1980) and *Who'll Stop the Rain* (1978), was simply unsuited to the character. Although I was lucky to have great work from King Vidor, Klaus Kinski, Armand Assante, Ornella Muti, and Tony Sirico, the result with Ray is a hole in the middle of the film. It's not that he's bad. He's just not good. It made me know that I could not make that mistake again, that I am not an alchemist who can turn base metal into gold, or an inappropriate actor into a right one in the wrong role. In *Exposed* I was not going to make that mistake again. Nastassia seemed to me a great model for the part. There were a couple of cases where financing was offered if I used other actresses who were more attractive to exhibitors, but I wasn't going to bend. I hoped the money would just come through and in fact a year later it did, but there was a great deal of delay, humiliation, and rage along the road.

JAG: You had the opportunity to cast Harvey Keitel again in *Exposed.*

JT: I saw a way to use him as the terrorist. I'd seen photographs of Carlos, the prototype of the character, and read a lot about him. Even though Harvey is an actor and he's not like Carlos in any ostensible way, I thought there was a real personality connection there. There's also something in the eyes and nose that's similar. He started reading about Carlos and thinking about him and we created the part together. I got hold of a long interview with Carlos, the only interview he ever gave, in an Arab paper in Paris. We got it translated and a lot of great dialogue was suggested by it. His rap in response to Kinski's telling him that he likes destruction is, "I'll tell you what I like. Hot showers, fresh sheets in Hilton Hotels, poker, blackjack, dancing, Clint Eastwood Westerns." The only line I added was "Clint Eastwood Westerns," but here this terrorist was giving all the junior executive bourgeois values imaginable as his goals. I thought, "What a terrific, ambiguous way to do this character." It gave Harvey and me a real handle. It's ironic that three or four of the dumber reviewers pointed to that dialogue as unbelievable and even "ludicrous," when it is precisely that dialogue that came out of the character on whom the part is based, and which gives it some truth and takes it away from being a stock cliché. Finally, that's what a lot of people are not ready for. They're not ready to face up to the complexity of characters they don't like. Orson Welles has a moment like that after another in every movie he made. *Touch of Evil* (1958), my favorite movie of all time, is nothing but moments of that kind. I'm not crazy about Altman, but one of the great moments in recent years is the Mark Rydell Coke bottle number with Elliott Gould in *The Long Goodbye* (1973). It's even better than the Roman Polanski knife-in-the-nose routine with Jack Nicholson in *Chinatown* (1974). It's during moments like those, highly unpleasant, where half of the straight audience tends to walk out. But those notes are really hit to establish a character. The thing that's great about Keitel is he has this sense of impacted rage that seems always about to spurt out. No matter what he's saying, you feel it could come out at any time. It's why a lot of people are attracted to him and a lot of people hate him.

JAG: In *Exposed*, during your scene as the English teacher, you have *Touch of Evil* written on the blackboard as a screening for the class.

JT: That's my first sort of *hommage* and it might be a sign of senility but I put it there because it seemed integral to *Exposed* in many ways. The teacher I was playing would have had it up there. It was legitimate for the movie. I also couldn't resist giving the movie a plug. The older I get the angrier I get that certain great films have not been seen by enough people. The fact that *Touch of Evil* is probably unknown to 98% of the American public is an obscenity. The movie, if not the greatest film ever made, is very close to it, and yet millions of people who see every dreary piece of trash and every pseudo-serious piece of empty claptrap somehow don't even know that *Touch of Evil* exists let alone that it's there for the viewing, that they can see it five or six times a year finally after years of its being hidden and bowdlerized.

JAG: Did you write the part of the English teacher for yourself?

JT: No, and I read a bunch of other actors, but finally I was the only person I could find, and I promise to end my acting career with this part. I needed two qualities together which were very hard to find, an arch literary sensibility with a finesse at literary language and a loutish, oppressive, demanding, possessive violent streak. To combine the two is difficult, and not to cheat, not to try to make yourself look a little bit better in your evil is a difficult temptation to resist. People want to look good on the screen. I don't think I spared myself. In the scene with Nastassia in the dorm, I come off in a pretty odious light.

JAG: That scene has a very improvisatory, spontaneous feel to it. How did you work with her in this scene where she's looking at you as both director and co-player?

JT: I love to shoot scenes in one shot for a lot of reasons, stylistic mainly, but one of the side virtues is that you can afford all kinds of improvisation because you don't have to match shots. Half the scenes in the movie are done in one shot. You can just let the scene happen. You don't *only* improvise, but what I did in this scene and several others was to write dialogue, have a basic plan about what each character was going to do, and then in the course of the scene allow each of the two actors, in this case Nastassia and myself, the leeway to surprise the other. The better the actors know each other, the stronger their feelings, the better it works. The take that's in the movie is the last of six that we did. During the first five the improvisation felt forced, but we were getting there. Nastassia and I, great friends before shooting and very close now, were having a lot of trouble then. Like Elizabeth Carlson, she was rebelling against the father, me, and we had a lot of tense, rough stuff. I felt it was ideal that the antagonism would come across in the scene. On the last take we got it. I think the key was getting into the challenge—did I bore her? We hadn't used that before. The rhythm started going at that point and there was no question that something was going to happen. It wasn't planned but I thought, "I can't fake it. I'm going to smack her." I had not smacked her in any of the previous takes. It was the language that led me into it. I said, "You know what you need? A good smack." You make a statement and you either have to call your own bluff or back off from it. I called my own bluff and smacked her. She was shocked. She poked her finger in my eye and hurt me. She got it straight in the open eye. I think you can feel that pain. So I bent over, my eye bloodshot, and then with great relish I called her a cunt, which is for most women that I've known, including very hip, loose, liberated women, *the* most offensive word you can use because you're choosing a word to define them biologically as a woman that is always derogatory in other contexts. I knew Nastassia hated the word and its use in any context, let alone in a nasty way. That got her going and she yelled me out of the room and slammed the door. It was a riff which gave the scene the punch and coda that it needed.

JAG: You taught at City College and have compared working with actors to teaching.

JT: There are many different ways of teaching. I'm talking about my experience. I got to know my students and dealt with their personal lives.

My goal was to bring out the best in each. Let each find where his talents are if he has any, develop them, let me help him in the best way for him. Seven or eight of my students are now published writers, people who were plumbers and electricians doing nothing literary at the time, and that's a great satisfaction. With actors it's similar. I never understand directors who say they have this or that method of working with actors because you cannot impose your method on actors. Six different actors have six different sets of needs. You find out what those needs are and you cater to them. You need their best, which is sometimes easier said than done. So the approach is similar to teaching and an actor's point-of-view is similar to a student's point-of-view. Whether he wants to be told or wheedled or cajoled or egged on or yelled at or catered to, he wants *something* from you. They are demanding something from you, some responsiveness to who they are, what they are, and what they can do.

JAG: You wrote a screenplay with Michael Cimino about mob boss Frank Costello.

JT: I wrote a screenplay that Michael Cimino has been passing around with his name on it and I don't understand why he's doing it because we're friends. I registered mine with the Writer's Guild. He may have made a few changes but 95% of the dialogue is mine. It got lost in the shuffle at 20th Century-Fox. Gordon Stulberg had commissioned it. He was fired the day before I finished it. Alan Ladd's first gesture as head of Fox was to turn down this script that had been commissioned by his predecessor. Since then Cimino has gone around everywhere with it. I'm always hearing rumors it's about to start, he's going to use Dustin Hoffman, Robert DeNiro, Jack Nicholson, he's going to resuscitate Frank Costello's corpse. I think it could be a terrific film. I'd love to direct it myself and I think Cimino would do a great job as well. But it does irk me that he's running around with his name on a script he didn't write. There's a word for that and it's not something I could do anything about or would do anything about until the time came. I grew up in the building that Costello lived in, the Majestic at 72nd Street and Central Park West. His wife used to walk their little French poodle in front of the Majestic every day. He and my father used to go downtown in Costello's limousine. He was a sort of model gangster, a gentleman gangster who kept his hands clean after he was twenty-five years old. He was the businessman's gangster, "Uncle Frank." He was also the model for Brando's character in *The Godfather* (1972). Brando got that gravelly voice from Costello, who had something wrong with his vocal chords and his whole adult life spoke in that gravelly voice. Brando got that from listening to tapes of Frank Costello's voice.

JAG: *The Pickup Artist* started in development at Paramount.

JT: Originally, *The Pickup Artist* was, if you can believe it, *Beverly Hills Cop* (1985), which was Don Simpson's idea when he was a production executive at Paramount. Barry Diller had made a deal with me to do a movie, but he did not want to make *Exposed*. He said, "I'm dying to make a movie with you, but I don't want to make *Exposed*." I said, "Well, that's the same as saying you don't want to make a movie with me because that's the movie I want to make." He said, "Make it on your own. I'm not playing with you—I want to make a movie with you. Just give me something else." I said, "That's all I have right now, that's what I want to do." He said, "Then make a deal with us for something we want to make." He called Don Simpson and said, "Get together with Jim Toback and tell him what you know we're going to do." Simpson said, "The movie we're going to make which is going to be our biggest hit yet is *Beverly Hills Cop*. Why don't you write it and direct it?" He gave me the basic idea, and, perverse as I am, I immediately suggested changing it to *Beverly Hills Outlaw*. With my astounding commercial prescience I predicted that *Beverly Hills Cop* would be a bore for people. Who wanted to see another cop movie, even if it was someone from the Midwest coming to L.A.?

JAG: Was this when Stallone was slated to star?

JT: Nick Nolte was going to be the actor at the time, and of course they were going to ask Warren Beatty if he wanted to do it. I couldn't get into it or get excited about it, so finally I changed movie history, because had I continued and done *Beverly Hills Cop,* believe me, it wouldn't have been anything like it was, which is probably to Paramount's great relief. I wrote a hundred pages, which Simpson and Michael Eisner liked very much and were encouraging me to finish. By then, Jeff Katzenberg was the production executive and I suggested *The Pickup Artist,* which he found an intriguing idea and allowed me to substitute for *Beverly Hills Cop.* When I finished *The Pickup Artist* I showed it to Warren Beatty before I showed it to anybody and he liked it. I didn't get into any details with him, I just told him that I was eager to see what he would think. He doesn't speak lightly. I knew that if he hadn't liked it he would have told me. Armed with that enthusiasm I wasn't about to play the suitor with Paramount if there was any problem whatsoever. It was put in turnaround, and rather than do my usual charge forward with hope in my heart and light at the end of the tunnel, I simply went to Beatty and said, "If you like it, why don't you buy it from me and set it up," and he did. It was not quite so simple. He had quite a lot to say about it and we talked a lot. Finally he took it to Diller who was by now at 20th Century-Fox, and it was set up there. In essence, Warren husbanded the project, and his cousin David McLeod, who had been the associate producer on *Reds* (1981), *Heaven Can Wait* (1978), and *Ishtar* (1987), an extremely bright, knowledgeable, and witty film fellow, was made the producer. Beatty was intimately involved all along. He also brought Robert Towne in for a while.

JAG: In what capacity?

JT: Towne gave me a number of ideas, some of which I think were quite good, and he also wrote two scenes, the first time I've ever shot anybody else's scenes. It was hard for me to adjust to because I'm so used to shooting my own language and vision, and these were two not so insignificant scenes. I rewrote them and worked on them, but basically they were his scenes. One was the blowup in the casino when Bob Downey says, "What is this shit?" in front of everybody and carries on. The other was the rather emotional scene at the end on the boardwalk when Downey tears up the list and walks away. I got into trouble in those two areas of the script. I didn't quite think or feel my way through to my own satisfaction, and Towne came up with those two scenes. Also, he was in on reading most of the thirty or forty drafts over a period of time.

JAG: *The Pickup Artist* is a schizophrenic movie, dark elements mixed with humor.

JT: It's a comedy about subjects which more easily lend themselves to tragedy. I think comedy is serious. I think it's a serious film, but not in the way *Fingers* or *Exposed* is. It is not a film that forces its audience to face death and suggests that people are evading it, whose main character leads the audience into death and then says, "Stay there and look." This is a film that lies in a sense and says, "You can get away with it for a while." Well, it's not a total lie. Many people do get away with it. We're getting away with it. We're still sitting here. But it is a comedy with a cast of lead players that are in that vein. Downey and Molly Ringwald are both comfortable in roles like the ones they're playing. The material could have been treated in a different way. I wanted to try something new. *The Pickup Artist* shows characters with a dark side in their lighter vein with an acknowledgment of a dark side, but you don't feel it viscerally in the way my other movies try to get you to feel it. The rich, dark look of the film could just as easily have served as the look for a dark movie. There's a restrained, contained, detached stately feel to the film with certain dark, somber visual qualities. The look is so handsome I find it seduces me. A lot of that was Gordon Willis' thinking. He's very good at assimilating material, coming up with a vision which expresses the material. It was a collaboration based on his understanding of the material. He's very eager to get your point-of-view. Gordon interviews you about your own script to learn what your deepest intentions are, and then given certain principles that he feels bound to, he tries to invent a look which will express those intentions.

JAG: *The Pickup Artist* was Bob Downey, Jr.'s, first starring role.

JT: Two people suggested him to me simultaneously—Brian Hamill, who had worked as a still photographer on *First Born* (1984), which Downey had a scene in, and David McLeod, who saw him in *Weird Science* (1986). Both said, "This is your guy," and since I'm very close with both and trust their judgment, I felt right away there was a good chance they'd be right. As soon as Downey came into my office I was certain it was right because of his quickness and grace of movement, intelligence in the eyes, a kind of erotic charge unencumbered by narcissism and a quick verbal facility, a love of words and a comfort with language, which ironically, given the profession, most young actors don't have. Language is the enemy of many young actors, and Downey loves words and you feel it and know it. That was essential for this script because it's built around its words. Jack Jericho is a character whose life is built around his words. His words are his dick. Let's put it this way—without words, all he has is a dick. He talks his way into existence. In the first three minutes I was with Downey I decided this is the guy. We spent a lot of time together working on the part and the script, got to know each other, became very close. If I had the movie to recast I wouldn't hesitate to use him again.

JAG: How was your experience with Molly Ringwald?

JT: I have never gotten along better with any actor or actress than I did with her. If there is such a thing as an ideal relationship between actor and director, this was it. She was smart, inventive, reliable, self-contained, independent, humorous, cooperative. She was really eager to do the part. Apparently she'd sneaked a look at the script a year before Beatty officially showed it to her, when she was up at his house. She didn't tell him she'd seen it and told me she was just waiting for him to suggest it. She has her own ideas and is much too smart to just accept something without understanding it. She's probably the most impressive nineteen-year-old, male or female, I've ever met. I am maybe now approaching half the maturity in certain areas that Molly had at nineteen. It's almost intimidating.

JAG: How about Dennis Hopper?

JT: He's a great film presence, very intense with a wild sense of humor. As far out as you can go, he's there. He's one of the few people I've met in my life whom I can say nothing that goes by him. It's as if he's as far out as space will stretch. He also made everybody else feel good. He's a real actor's actor, and an actor's director. He relaxes and helps other actors. In fact, he's using Tony Sirico, who played Riccamonzo in *Fingers* and was in *Love and Money, Exposed,* and *The Pickup Artist,* as a co-lead with him in his new movie, *Backtrack* (1988).

JAG: To what extent are *you* Jack Jericho, *The Pickup Artist*?

JT: I've always liked meeting people on the street. When I was three I used to go up to boys and girls in the park and say, "I like you," and I think it's a habit that's continued pretty much to the present. I like the idea of starting with the premise that a guy in New York met most of the people, in particular women, who appealed to him by saying hello on the street. There's something affirmative and exuberant and risky and attractive to me about somebody who in an unthreatening way, with a readiness to

make a U-turn if needed, is ready to open himself to whatever experiences
are potentially around him on the street.

JAG: What kind of research did you do with Downey?

JT: It's funny. He had never done much cruising. Despite his openness and
goofiness once he gets going, he was rather shy with strangers on the
street as many ultimately gregarious people are. We did a lot of cruising.
It started out with me doing most of the approaching and then he got
into the rhythm and did quite a bit himself. I don't think he ever got to
the point where he was quite so shameless about it as I was.

JAG: How did *The Pickup Artist* do at the box-office?

JT: It ended up doing about $16 million. It's doing phenomenally world-
wide, which to me is a big surprise simply because Molly, who is the
main selling point here, is not known as well in other countries. It's done
well in Europe, Brazil, Japan, Australia, everywhere except Sweden for
some reason. It set house records in the Philippines and Puerto Rico.

JAG: It's your most overtly commercial film to date. Did you get any
backlash that Toback is going Hollywood?

JT: Yes, not to my face, but I read it. It doesn't ring entirely true with me.
There are a hundred different ways of doing every movie, none of them
single-minded and independent. *The Pickup Artist* was more of a collaboration than any other film by far, but my original intentions were clear
throughout, changed throughout, so I would not for a second pass it off
as not my own. I'll just say that I got more help than I probably did in
the past.

JAG: It was also your most expensive movie to date.

JT: I think it was about $13 million, and believe it or not, $19 million is
now considered average for a major studio. *Exposed* cost about $9 million,
Love and Money was around $2 million, *Fingers* about $1 million, and
now I'm going to do a movie for a couple of hundred thousand dollars
called *The Big Bang!* I'm doing it through a company I'm forming with
Joe Kanter, the president of the Bank of Florida, who was an executive
producer on *Ironweed* (1987), who in his sixties has decided to get involved
in film financing and production. It's a film that's unlike anything I've
ever seen before, let alone done. I'm taking women and men of different
backgrounds, professions, personalities, and looks, and getting to the
bottom of all of them so that some kind of notion of what's going on
with women and men today will come through. It'll either be a really
inventive, wild, revolutionary work or it'll be an incoherent fiasco. I like
being an observer in my own life and here I'm an observer in a rather
mad enterprise. I've drawn a really interesting group of people—professional basketball player Darryl Dawkins; former light heavyweight champion Jose Torres, who is now the State Athletic Commissioner of New
Jersey; Barbara Traub, a novelist and a survivor of Auschwitz; Fred Hess,
an astronomer; concert violinist Eugene Fodor; a nun named Sister Ann-

Marie Keyes who teaches philosophy at Marymount; a black teen rap group named The Float Committee; Veronica Geng, published writer; saxophonist Julius Hemphill; Sheila Kennedy, a former Penthouse Pet of the Year; a med student at Columbia named Marcia Oakley; and Tony Sirico, who spent a fair amount of time in jail before he became an actor. I'm approaching this movie the way I approach all the others, as an open-ended revelation of personalities, except in this case there's no line between player and role. I don't want anybody to meet each other until we actually start shooting. I'm not averse to finding somebody on the way up to the set the first day, jumping out of the car, pulling that person in and including that person in the film. I actually did that in *Fingers* with Carol Francis, who plays with Tisa Farrow and Jim Brown in the scene at the Pierre Hotel. We'd already chosen an actress who I wasn't really happy with, and the only person in the movie who I felt wasn't right. I met Carol on my way down to film the scene that day. I was in my car on Fifth Avenue, said, "She'd be great," and went charging out of the car and said, "You've got to be in this scene we're shooting at the Pierre Hotel in about a half an hour." She said, "What does the scene involve?" I described the scene to her in which she and Tisa are licking Jim Brown's nipple, and then Jim gets angry and bangs their heads together. She looked at me as if I was bordering on psychotic and said, "Is he really going to hit our heads together?" I said, "No way, this is a movie." She said, "Well it sounds crazy. OK." Unfortunately, Jim actually did whack their heads together, so there was a lot of added tension one didn't anticipate. But the idea of including strangers at the last minute in an organic whole is exciting to me. In the case of *The Big Bang!*, the process of finding them will be a part of the film. I am fair game for everybody and I can be called on, challenged, attached, deposed, depending on the actions that occur during shooting. I'm very much a subject as well as the director in this film. I'm on and off camera throughout.

JAG: So you will truly be *Exposed*.

JT: That's right. Exposed and defrocked. I sort of beg for assault on the titles I choose. When I wrote *The Gambler* I was waiting for somebody to write, "He gambled and he lost," and it took me a week to find a critic to write that. When I did *Fingers* I was waiting for a critic to say, "*Fingers* is all thumbs," and Frank Rich immediately did that. I was waiting when *Love and Money* came out for somebody to say, "I wouldn't see this movie again for love *or* money." That took about a month. In *Exposed,* not only did I know that someone would write, "The only person who is exposed in *Exposed* is Jim Toback," but I knew it would be Stanley Kauffman, and he greeted me with that in a review.

(1983, 1988)

François Truffaut

François Truffaut was truly the Man Who Loved Movies, a quintessential filmmaker who wrote and directed his pictures with a consistency of quality and artistic conviction that placed him firmly among the greatest *auteurs* in international cinema, right beside Federico Fellini, Ingmar Bergman, and Stanley Kubrick. He wrote about movies with great love, and celebrated life in his own films with a poetic and often romantic realism.

Born in Paris on February 6, 1932, Truffaut endured an unhappy childhood, drawn both to cinema and trouble. Rescued from delinquency by the critic Andre Bazin, he cultivated his passion for film by viewing thousands of movies, interviewing directors, and writing brilliant articles for the influential film journal *Cahiers du Cinema*. It was only a matter of time and money before he started making films himself, and after a brief apprenticeship with Roberto Rossellini, he directed several shorts, *Une Visite* (1954) and *Les Mistons* (1957). He provided the story for Godard's *Breathless* (1959), and with his directorial debut *Les Quatre Cents Coups/The 400 Blows* (1959), helped spearhead the "New Wave" of French filmmaking. *The 400 Blows* introduced cinematic alter-ego Jean-Pierre Leaud as Antoine Doinel, and audiences watched Leaud/Doinel progress from childhood to maturity in a remarkable series of films—*L'Amour à Vingt Ans/Love at Twenty* (1962), *Baisers voles/Stolen Kisses* (1968), *Domicile conjugal/Bed and Board* (1970), and *L'Amour en fuite/Love on the Run* (1979).

Internationally acclaimed after his first feature, Truffaut went on to astound filmgoers with his virtuosity on *Tirez sur le Pianiste/Shoot the Piano Player* (1960) and *Jules et Jim/Jules and Jim* (1961), films that reflect the influence, respectively, of Truffaut's spiritual mentors Alfred Hitchcock and Jean Renoir. Hitchcock's manipulative suspense and Renoir's poetic lyricism helped formulate the Truffaut style in some of the finest films of the Sixties— *La Peau Douce/The Soft Skin* (1964), *Fahrenheit 451* (1966), *La Mariee etait*

François Truffaut on the set of *Small Change* (from the author's collection).

en Noir/The Bride Wore Black (1968), *La Sirene du Mississippi/Mississippi Mermaid* (1969), and *L'Enfant Sauvage/The Wild Child* (1970). After a brief hiatus from filmmaking to pursue his other loves, reading and writing, Truffaut made a triumphant return with *La Nuit americaine/Day for Night* (1973), his portrait of the making of a film, in which he played a director, and won an Academy Award for Best Foreign Language Film. He continued to mature with such films as *L'Histoire d'Adele H./The Story of Adele H.* (1975), an intimate character study; *L'Argent de Poche/Small Change* (1976), a warm tribute to adolescence; *L'Homme qui aimait les Femmes/The Man Who Loved Women* (1977), an homage to love, remade in Hollywood by Blake Edwards (1983); *Le Dernier Metro/The Last Metro* (1980), about a theatrical troupe in wartime Paris; and his last film, a sophisticated thriller in the Hitchcock vein, *Vivement Dimanche!/Confidentially Yours* (1983). Truffaut's death from brain cancer on October 21, 1984, was a shock to movie lovers the world over.

I wrote to François Truffaut while I was a film student at Emerson College in 1977 publishing a journal called *Grand Illusions*. I requested an interview, and to my delight, received a letter from the director complimenting the magazine and asking me to contact his New York publicist John Springer. During the last days of September, 1977, Sam Sarowitz and I had the opportunity to interview M. Truffaut during his brief stay in Manhattan for the New York Film Festival, where he was premiering *The Man Who Loved Women*. We met with him in his suite at the Sherry Netherlands Hotel, with his long-time associate Helen Scott providing the translation. As we spoke, a copy of Herman Weinberg's revised *The Lubitsch Touch* was close at hand, demonstrating Truffaut's affection for classic cinema.

FILMOGRAPHY

Les Quatre Cents Coups/The 400 Blows (1959, Les Films du Carrosse/SEDIF). HV: Key.

Tirez sur le Pianiste/Shoot the Piano Player (1960, Les Films de la Pleiade). HV: French Film House.

Jules et Jim/Jules and Jim (1961, Les Films du Carrosse/SEDIF). HV: Key.

L'Amour à Vingt Ans/Love at Twenty (1962, Embassy). Other segments directed by Renzo Rossellini, Shintaro Ishihara, Marcel Ophuls, Andrzej Wajda.

La Peau Douce/The Soft Skin (1964, Les Films du Carrosse/SEDIF). HV: Key.

Fahrenheit 451 (1966, Anglo-Enterprise/Vineyard/Universal). HV: MCA.

La Mariee etait en Noir/The Bride Wore Black (1968, Les Films du Carrosse/Dino de Laurentiis Cinématografica/United Artists).

Baisers vole/Stolen Kisses (1968, Les Films du Carrosse/United Artists). HV: RCA/Columbia.

La Sirene du Mississippi/Mississippi Mermaid (1969, Les Films du Carrosse/United Artists).

L'Enfant Sauvage/The Wild Child (1970, Les Films du Carrosse/United Artists).

Domicile conjugal/Bed and Board (1970, Les Films du Carrosse/Valeria Films/Fida Cinématografica).

Les Deux Anglaises et le Continent/Two English Girls (1971, Les Films du Carrosse/ Cinetel). HV: Key.

Une Belle Fille comme moi/Such a Gorgeous Kid Like Me (1972, Les Films du Carrosse/ Columbia).

La nuit americaine/Day for Night (1973, Les Films du Carrosse/Warner Brothers). HV: Warners.

L'Histoire de Adele H./The Story of Adele H. (1975, Les Films du Carrosse/New World). HV: Warners.

L'Argent de Poche/Small Change (1976, Les Films du Carrosse/United Artists). HV: Warners.

L'Homme qui aimait les Femmes/The Man Who Loved Women (1977, Les Films du Carrosse/United Artists). HV: RCA/Columbia.

La Chambre verte/The Green Room (1978, Les Films du Carrosse/United Artists). HV: Warners.

L'Amour en fuite/Love on the Run (1979, Les Films du Carrosse/New World). HV: Warners.

Le Dernier Metro/The Last Metro (1980, Les Films du Carrosse/United Artists). HV: Key.

La Femme à Cote/The Woman Next Door (1981, Les Films du Carrosse/United Artists Classics). HV: Key.

Vivemant Demanche!/Confidentially Yours (1983, Les Films du Carrosse/International Spectrafilm). HV: Key.

TRUFFAUT INTERVIEW

JOHN A. GALLAGHER: What attracted you to the Hollywood films of the Forties when they were being taken for granted in the United States?

FRANÇOIS TRUFFAUT: I saw the first American films shown at the time of the Liberation in '45. These were new films and some old films, but no older than 1938. For instance, I hardly know the first talking pictures of Frank Capra, who is a very important director. But in this period I've mentioned, I adored American pictures. They were more professional than they are today. Their scripts were more childish, but the care and the execution of the films turned them into more coherent works than those that are turned out today, in general. The Hollywood system didn't work as well with important personalities like Eric Von Stroheim and Orson Welles. For the others, it enabled them to give the best of themselves. There were many directors whom we admired, and whose work was inferior when they became free and independent. So finally, the system worked. This became obvious to us from 1955 on. Today, they speak a great deal of Thalberg, particularly because of *The Last Tycoon,* but if you look at the list of his pictures, there is no masterpiece within his credits. There are rather good pictures, and his work must have consisted of improving them. But aside from that, he crushed

Von Stroheim, and he may have crushed other Von Stroheims that we don't know of.

JAG: What impact did *Citizen Kane* (1941) have on you the first time you saw it?

FT: *Citizen Kane* is probably the best film of talking American pictures, one of the rare pictures in which there is almost unanimous agreement that it is a masterpiece. It is, at the same time, the picture which gave young people the desire to become filmmakers. That's what is so paradoxical about this picture. It should have been very forbidding, and in fact it was an encouraging picture, perhaps because historically it was the first anti-Hollywood picture. It was a different product from the rest of the Hollywood product that we saw. You might even say that it was the first film of the New Wave. That is, it fits the impression of being the work of a young man speaking in the first person, as if he was writing his first novel. This makes this picture so special.

JAG: How do you feel today about your Antoine Doinel films, particularly *The 400 Blows*?

FT: There is no problem with *The 400 Blows*. It's a coherent picture. I think the same thing of *Love at Twenty*. I began to have some problems with *Stolen Kisses,* because I had this marginal character outside of life, and I had to bring him into life. It was even more difficult with *Bed and Board*. It's difficult to discuss it.

SAM SAROWITZ: After the commercial success of *The 400 Blows,* what drew you to *Shoot the Piano Player*?

FT: When I saw the completed film of *The 400 Blows,* I was surprised myself that it had been such a French film. I had been a film critic for five years and I used to insult French cinema all the time, and I thought I was bred on American filmmaking. When I saw the finished *400 Blows,* I said, "It doesn't reflect the fact that I adore American filmmaking." I adored David Goodis, so I took his novel *Down There* merely for the pleasure of treating an American theme—the man who was a great piano player and is now a nobody, working in a bar, with three women in his life, one being a prostitute, the other a waitress, and lastly his wife, who throws herself out of a window, plus the gangsters who come at the end to the house in the snow. I must tell you that in France there was a whole group of people who had admiration for that type of literature by Charles Williams, David Goodis, and William Irish. I know these writers are not so well known in the United States, but in France we have a collection of thrillers called *Le Serie Noir.* The fans of these books call each other up and say, "You've got to read this one, you've got to read that one." And I had a long-standing theory, very personal, but in which I believed strongly. That is, there was a relationship between the *Serie Noir* thrillers and children's fairy tales. And the meeting point between *Serie Noir* and fairy tales was the spirit and literature of Jean Cocteau. So you see, that is a very special kind of theory. But even today, I feel it makes sense. You might say that *Shoot the Piano Player* was a result of this reflection. Instead of making a picture in which I would try to imitate Jean Cocteau, I decided to take the *Serie Noir* thriller and treat it like a children's fairy tale. I made a picture which was a big flop in France, and even in America it took some time before it had some recognition.

JAG: Is it true that when you finished reading the novel *Jules and Jim,* you decided that your vocation was cinema?

FT: No, the vocation was always there. But it is true that I had met the writer, Henri-Pierre Roche, and I had said to him, "If I can ever become a filmmaker I will make a film of this book." Unfortunately, he died while I was shooting *400 Blows.*

JAG: On *Fahrenheit 451,* your first English-language film, you engaged Alfred Hitchcock's favorite music composer, Bernard Herrmann, who also scored *Citizen Kane* for Welles.

FT: It came off very well. On occasion I was a little concerned because I felt that the music was more lyrical than the picture itself. The spirit of *Fahrenheit 451* was very ambiguous, and I think that even the people who worked with me didn't really understand the story of the film, probably because I was working instinctively, and I didn't take the trouble to clearly explain what I was trying to do. I didn't really want it to be a science fiction film. I wanted it to be a picture that would be an homage to books in general, in the generic sense. The result was not what I hoped for, but the music was extraordinary. It was also music that should have been for another picture, for a picture that would have been more serious.

SS: Do you have any desire to direct a Hollywood film?

FT: Not yet.

JAG: You were actually offered the script for *Bonnie and Clyde* (1967) to direct.

FT: At that time my mind was full of *Fahrenheit 451.* At the same time, I was also offered *The Day of the Locust,* but I had my mind set on *Fahrenheit. Bonnie and Clyde* was an excellent script but it was 100% American material. There was no reason to ask a Frenchman to do it.

JAG: In *Day for Night,* you played a film director. Why did you have your character wear a hearing aid?

FT: Because I have a great deal of sympathy for the deaf mutes and also because that was the only character in the whole film who had no private life. That's because I had a lot of work. I didn't have time to go into the makeup room and yet I didn't want to be completely myself. I wanted some difference with François Truffaut, some distinction.

JAG: What was the main problem in telling *The Story of Adele H.*?

FT: The main problem was that the story has no twists or dramatic progression. There are not many events, not many things happening in it. The picture could have been made in a certain way, which would have been to make the audience feel or hope that the love story would work out in the end. But I don't think it would have been a good idea, because in any case, the people would have been disappointed in the end. So I thought it was important to show from the very beginning that it was a lost cause as far as she was concerned. In that way, the only way to retain the public's attention was to employ some variations on the girl's eccentricities and odd behavior, establishing at the same time a certain progression of the story. So that normally, while the picture unfolds, the public should be asking itself, "What is this girl going to think of next?" For the audience that likes the picture, that's the way it works. But for the people who refuse to go along with it, who refuse to become interested in the girl's problems, I think the picture is simply a bore.

JAG: What appeals to you about working with children, which you've done so successfully in *The 400 Blows, The Wild Child,* and *Small Change*?

FT: The principal reason is that working with children you have many more surprises than in working with adults. You go through more violent emotions. There are certain days when the whole day is wasted because what you've done can't be embodied into the picture. But the next day, what you may do may be far superior to the screenplay. It is very exciting and very stimulating.

JAG: Then it's more improvisational.

FT: On the part of the children. There are certain things they can't do that are in the script, but other things they do much better. To use a formula, I would say that with adult actors, you film the screenplay. Certain days, it's better than the screenplay and other days it's not as good. With the children, the screenplay loses its importance. You have to constantly change it, improvise. You have the impression that you are being more creative when you're working with children.

JAG: How was your experience acting in Steven Spielberg's *Close Encounters of the Third Kind* (1977)?

FT: It was very slow shooting even for a big American production. On occasion, we only did two shots in a day. We were on call at eight o'clock in the morning even if we didn't start shooting until five in the afternoon. But I feel that I didn't waste my time because I wrote the script of *The Man Who Loved Women* during the shooting, and the shooting was very interesting to observe. I always dreamed of being able to watch the shooting of a film without being in the way. Directors don't dare to go to another director's shooting. It's not done. But here, I had a perfectly rational reason for being there, to be sitting on a chair with nobody paying attention to me.

JAG: What compelled you to make *The Man Who Loved Women*?

FT: I make a picture a year in any case, but it was an old project, like practically all of my work. Almost all of my projects are stories that I've had in mind for a very long time. I undertake them after having thought of them for many years. They are not overnight projects. Occasionally, I only think of them once a week, but essentially, I compile notes into a file and one day the time comes when you feel that this file might become a film. It often happens when I find that there are two ideas that can be blended, which at first I didn't know could make one film. There is a coincidence. For instance, in the case of *The Man Who Loved Women,* I wanted to tell a story which visually presented one man and many women. I undertook it on the day I realized that I could embody an idea which appealed to me, to film the idea of the manufacture of a book from the moment of its writing until the time it is published and in the bookstores. That was the case of this picture. I combined both in the film. The picture was completely conceived around Charles Denner, the principal performer. He played one of the characters in *The Bride Wore Black,* and his part was almost a trailer for *The Man Who Loved Women.* He had a four-minute monologue on his feelings on women in general, and *The Man Who Loved Women* is an extension of what he did in *The Bride Wore Black.*

JAG: Can you tell me about your new production, *The Vanished Fiancée?*

FT: The title has been changed to *The Green Room.* I will play the lead role, and the girl will be Nathalie Baye, who played the script girl in *Day for Night.* She has a very small part in *The Man Who Loved Women.* *The Green Room* is not inspired by any specific story by Henry James, but rather by his spirit and his faithfulness to his dead fiancée. I would situate the story between *Adele H.* and *The Wild Child.* There are very few characters, very little decor, very little action. For the time being, I believe in this form of filmmaking because in the past when television didn't exist, a picture had a great deal of variety. You saw different scenery, there were interior and exterior scenes, and while you looked at a picture you might be travelling with the picture, and one might enjoy a chase scene, for example. The more variety there was in a picture, the happier the audience was. Since people have been viewing television in their homes, there is too much variety in our eyes and in our minds. So the Hollywood films have resolved the problem by going back to the origin of silent movies, that is, in giving physical shocks to the viewer. I am trying to resolve a problem by trying to cast a spell over the public, by the contrary of variety. Right or wrong, I believe that if a picture gives an impression of unity through one single color, place, dramatic situation, or a unique character, one can interest the public even more than by a spectacle of variety. In any case, in one quarter of an hour on television, you have the variety. There is news, fiction, there are guns, advertising, all that.

JAG: How have your attitudes about filmmaking changed over the years?

FT: To sum it up, I would say at the moment of the birth of the New Wave, we felt that it was necessary to give a great deal of reality. We had to shoot in real places, real decors. For the pictures to be made cheaply, we made them with cameras that were very noisy, and we didn't take sound. We did it in the dubbing afterwards. I did my first four pictures that way, and most of my friends worked the same way, Godard, Chabrol, Rivette. From '64 to '65 on, we finally understood what Jean Renoir had been trying to make us understand for five or six years, that our pictures would be better with direct sound and that the dubbing, particularly in exterior scenes in the countryside, was really a cheap process. From that time on, pictures were made with direct sound. Two or three years later, the color films arrived, Technicolor. Initially, I think I made very ugly pictures with Technicolor, because we didn't care about color. We went into real places, as we had before, and we weren't aware that color not only made the picture uglier, but even detracted from the meaning of the picture by providing a great deal of useless information. At that time a sort of awareness set in. Realistic subjects shot in real places with direct sound and color, without changing it, added up to very bad pictures. So we became aware that one way or another, we had to return to artifice. Ideally, the perfect artifice would be to do everything in the studio, even street scenes, even a scene within a forest like Hawks' *Sergeant York* (1941), for instance. But we can't do that. However, we *are* careful now about color, so we've gotten back to the conversation about unity and variety. Since color provides too much useless information, we come back to unity, rather than having three different scenes taking place in three different places. If these three scenes can take place in the same place, it's better for the picture.

JAG: Do you have any theories about camera movement?

FT: The best director of the invisible, non-obtrusive camera is probably Howard Hawks. But that doesn't mean that's the only way to make films, because Hitchcock often has a very visible, very obvious camera movement. He's not wrong because at certain moments you use the camera to take the public by the hand and say, "Come, I want to show you something."

JAG: You've published the definitive book on Hitchcock, the interview book *Hitchcock/Truffaut*.

FT: I'm sorry somebody didn't do a similar book with Howard Hawks★, because something I feel that's very interesting with Hawks is that in all those interviews he always criticizes, he raps the intellectuals, and in my opinion, he is one of the most intellectual filmmakers in America. He often speaks in terms of film concepts. He has many general theories. He doesn't belong to the school of instinctive filmmakers. He thinks of everything he does. Everything is thought out. So somebody ought to

★*Hawks on Hawks* by Joseph McBride was eventually published in 1982 by the University of California Press.

tell him one day that despite himself, he is an intellectual and that he has to accept that!

JAG: Are there any current American directors that you admire?

FT: For the time being, my favorite is Woody Allen, because I adored *Annie Hall* (1977), which I've seen three times so far. But otherwise, I admire rather separate pictures. If you questioned a Frenchman about my work, he would tell you that I am now part of the system in France, and it's rather true. But in American pictures for the past few years, I'm always attracted to offbeat pictures, strangely enough, pictures like *Johnny Got His Gun* (1971) and *The Honeymoon Killers* (1970), marginal pictures which are not part of the industry. There is no doubt about the fact that I had more admiration for the Hollywood pictures when I didn't know America at all.

JAG: Have your views on the *auteur* theory altered at all since your days at *Cahiers du Cinema*?

FT: Not really. I still go to see an Ingmar Bergman film the day of its release, and there are many filmmakers who've made twenty pictures and I haven't seen one of theirs. So in this sense, I continue to apply the *auteur* theory. On the other hand, I might concede more readily than I did in the past that on occasion a good director will make a picture that isn't so good. At the time of the *Cahiers du Cinema,* we in bad faith would insist on defending any picture by a good director, but today, I believe that is not necessary.

(1977)

Wim Wenders

Wim Wenders' former Gray City, Inc., office overlooks 11 East 14th Street, one of the most famous addresses in film history, the site of D. W. Griffith's American Biograph studio. Wenders was delighted when I informed him of the proximity of Gray City to Biograph: "You're kidding! Whooh!" He stood and looked out the window at the carnival of street vendors and discount stores on 14th Street between Union Square and Fifth Avenue. The old Biograph brownstone has long since been replaced by a sprawling, dirty white condominium, obliterating the birthplace of film grammar. There used to be a plaque, but vandals ripped it down.

It's fitting that seventy years after Griffith used Manhattan as his personal back lot, Wenders and producer Chris Sievernich established Gray City near this historic location, for Wim Wenders appreciates our film heritage like few contemporary directors. Like the best of Bogdanovich, his movies can pay *hommage* to the masters yet remain fresh and original in their own rights. In his native Germany, Wenders was drawn by American "B" movies, and he has enjoyed creative associations with Sam Fuller and the late Nicholas Ray.

Born in Düsseldorf, Germany, on August 14, 1945, Wenders' educational background was in medicine and philosophy before moving to Paris to study painting. Back in Germany to attend Munich's Academy of Film and Television from 1967 to 1970, he also wrote film criticism. After winning some acclaim for a series of shorts, he and fourteen other young filmmakers formed Filmverlag Der Autoren in 1970 to produce and distribute their films. Through the Seventies, Wenders was an integral part of the New German Cinema, along with Werner Herzog, Volker Schlondorff, R. W. Fassbinder, and Wolfgang Petersen. His features *Summer in the City* (1970); *The Goalie's Anxiety at the Penalty Kick* (1972), from the Peter Handke novel; Nathaniel Hawthorne's *The Scarlet Letter* (1973); and the remarkable trio of

Wim Wenders (left) with Sam Fuller (courtesy of Gray City, Inc.).

features, *Alice in the Cities* (1974); *The Wrong Move* (1975); and *Kings of the Road* (1976) established Wenders as a major international talent. For his first English language film, he chose Patricia Highsmith's thriller novel *Ripley's Game,* and shot it under the title of *The American Friend* (1977), starring Bruno Ganz and Dennis Hopper. Wenders also cast two of his favorite directors, Sam Fuller and Nicholas Ray, in key roles.

Wenders developed a special relationship with Ray, the director of *Rebel Without a Cause* (1955), *Johnny Guitar* (1954) and *They Live by Night* (1949), that lasted until Ray's death from cancer in 1979. Together, they directed a pseudo-fictional film, *Lightning Over Water* (1980), made in New York while Wenders was on hiatus from the troubled *Hammett* (1982), his first big budget American movie, based on the Joe Gores novel about Dashiell Hammett, the real-life detective writer who drew from his Pinkerton experience to create works such as *The Maltese Falcon, The Thin Man,* and the Contiental Op stories. *Hammett* was a stylish 1920's period film *noir,* produced by Francis Coppola's American Zoetrope, initially held up for release by the distributor, Warner Brothers. It was a frustrating experience for Wenders, who learned his craft under low-budget, spontaneous conditions.

I interviewed Wenders after the release of *The State of Things* (1983), a film about filmmaking. We focused on his work with Fuller and Ray, and his feelings about *Hammett,* which at that time had still not received a New York premiere. Since this interview, Wenders won accolades for *Paris, Texas* (1984), departed Gray City, and won the Best Director Award at the 1987 Cannes Film Festival for *Wings of Desire* (1987).

FILMOGRAPHY

Summer in the City (Dedicated to the Kinks) (1970).
The Goalie's Anxiety at the Penalty Kick (1972, Bauer International). HV: Pacific Arts.
The Scarlet Letter (1973, Bauer International). HV: Pacific Arts.
Alice in the Cities (1974, New Yorker Films). HV: Pacific Arts.
The Wrong Move (1975, New Yorker Films). HV: Pacific Arts.
Kings of the Road (In the Course of Time). (1976, Bauer International). HV: Pacific Arts.
The American Friend (1977, New Yorker Films). HV: Pacific Arts.
Lightning Over Water (1980, Pari Films). HV: Pacific Arts.
Hammett (1982, Warner Bros.). HV: Warners.
The State of Things (1983, Gray City). HV: Pacific Arts.
Paris, Texas (1984, 20th Century-Fox). HV: CBS/Fox.
Tokyo-Ga (1985, Gray City). HV: Pacific Arts.
Wings of Desire (1987, Orion Classics).

WENDERS INTERVIEW

JOHN A. GALLAGHER: Have you ever been in a situation where you've run out of money on a film?

WIM WENDERS: It happened once on *Kings of the Road*. We had money to shoot for eight weeks, and the film went fifteen. After eight weeks we had an interruption of three weeks in order to get more money. It was a different case on *The State of Things*. Someone wouldn't show up with the money and it was slowly very obvious that we'd have to stop because we couldn't pay the crew anymore. We really started underfinanced. Chris Sievernich had enough money for two or three weeks of shooting only because the project happened so spontaneously. He kept traveling around and getting us more money. Sometimes we were sitting there in Portugal hoping that Chris would fly in the next day.

JAG: *The State of Things* came about very quickly. I understand you were visiting the set of Raul Ruiz' *The Territory* (1983) and decided to stay and make a film.

WW: I fell in love with the scenery, and also the kind of filmmaking that allows you to work peacefully with a small crew. I knew that way of filmmaking from Germany. *The State of Things* was planned, written, cast, and financed in two weeks. When we started we only had three pages about a film crew shooting a science fiction film, then running out of money. The belly of the film would be the crew waiting for money, and then at the end the director would go to Hollywood. That's all we had. Three pages. I had two writers on location, Robert Kramer and Joshua Wallace. Joshua left after a week and Robert was there until the end of the shoot. We sat in the hotel and wrote every day. The next day I would come back and tell him how everything worked on the set. I'd tell him how I felt we should continue, and he'd show me what he'd written, so he was always a day ahead. Sometimes we passed him with the shooting, but it worked out nicely.

JAG: The science fiction movie in *The State of Things,* the film-within-a-film called *The Survivors,* was inspired by Allan Dwan's *The Most Dangerous Man Alive* (1961).

WW: Yeah, though there isn't much of that Dwan connection left, except for the style. I only thought it would take us two days to shoot this little piece of science fiction, and we could go on and switch to the people who are shooting it. But it took a week because we started in day-for-night. We had to wait for the sun, and we had cloudy days. After a week, I seriously considered continuing with *The Survivors* and dropping the idea of a movie about the making of film.

JAG: How did you come to work with the cinematographer Henri Alekan?

WW: He was shooting *The Territory* when I came to Portugal. I'd never met him, but I knew his work, especially his black and white stuff. For years he was Eugene Shuftan's assistant and operator on Cocteau films like *The Beauty and the Beast* (1945).

JAG: Sam Fuller is great in the film playing the cameraman.

WW: Sam had played a tiny part as the mafioso in *The American Friend,* but there it was more of a joke. I knew that Sam had enjoyed the few pieces of acting that he'd done, like with Dennis Hopper in *The Last Movie* (1971). He was usually just playing Sam Fuller, like in the Godard film *Pierrot Le Fou* (1965). The part of the old cinematographer in *The State of Things* was based a bit on Joe Biroc. Joe had shot four films in a row for Sam, including *Forty Guns* (1957).

JAG: Fuller also plays a part in *Hammett.*

WW: Again, that was a tiny part that was more of a joke than anything else. When Joe Biroc was in a real good mood on *Hammett,* he'd give us a hilarious, mind-blowing Sam Fuller imitation. He'd take a cigar and play Sam directing. When I wrote the character of the cinematographer, I thought, "Maybe Sam can imitate Joe," and Sam liked the idea. Sam looks the experience of all his films. You almost recognize Richard Widmark and Lee Marvin in his face. I didn't actually have high hopes that Sam would come to Lisbon. He said, "I have a week, I can't give you any more. You have to pay me with a box of Cuban cigars every day." We did, and it turned out to be very expensive. Since we had to shoot all his scenes in a week, they're the only pieces that are out of continuity. Otherwise, the film was shot entirely chronologically.

JAG: For the Hollywood sequences you were literally shooting the whole time out of a mobile home.

WW: We shot one week of Friedrich riding across Hollywood until he finds Gordon, and then another week in the mobile home back and forth Sunset Boulevard. We wrecked that goddam mobile home entirely. At the end of that week, I knew every corner of Sunset Boulevard from beginning to end, all the hookers, all the cops. We had to stop every two minutes to collect the lighting or do something.

JAG: In Hollywood you asked Roger Corman to play a bit.

WW: Roger had helped me in the beginning when I was looking for a film to use as the model for the science fiction film. I had another movie in mind first called *The Day the World Ended* (1956), which Roger had directed. I called up Roger and explained the situation, and he suggested Allan Dwan and *The Most Dangerous Man Alive.*

JAG: Some critics commented that *The State of Things* was your reaction to working with Coppola on *Hammett.*

WW: It's obvious that people would think that, but I think seeing the film might upset their thoughts about it. Of course, it is about Hollywood, American filmmaking as opposed to European filmmaking. But you can't really say this is autobiographical. It's really generalized and it's really not about American Zoetrope. Gordon is really not Francis Coppola. I don't think you can find any traces of *Hammett* or Coppola in it. Those people who see the film and still insist it's my comment on making *Hammett* must realize that the only two people in *The State of Things* who are friends are the producer and the director. The film is not about *Hammett*.

JAG: What are your feelings about Zoetrope and Coppola?

WW: I always respected Francis' idea enormously. It was a very daring enterprise. The vision never really turned into reality. Zoetrope never became that family of filmmakers he dreamed of because the idea had so much resistance from Hollywood. That could well be the reason it didn't work. Obviously inside Hollywood, with his position and power, Francis saw himself in the tradition of the studio producers of the Forties. That's the kind of dream you might have in Hollywood, but not the dream somebody like me would have in New York. I believe very much in overseeable budgets and films where the money involved allows you a freer expression. It's not so big that people will be breathing down your neck all the time to look at what you're doing. The movies that I enjoy throughout the whole history of Hollywood were never the big pictures. They were the underbelly, like Allan Dwan, Edgar Ulmer, Sam Fuller, Tay Garnett.

JAG: On *Hammett,* you had two great old-time cameramen, Joe Biroc and Phil Lathrop.

WW: I knew Joe's work with Robert Aldrich. No diffusion, no indirect lighting, but really shadows. He was one of the few who had kept up this style of photography that I always liked better than anything else. He also goes for depth of focus. It was so chic in the Seventies to work with open lenses, where the focus would just be on the tip of the nose and the earth would be out of focus. Joe had always worked in a different style than that. I had dreamt for some time of making *Hammett* in black and white, but of course it was impossible. Warners wouldn't go for it. Francis was in favor of the idea, but it was just impossible to override the studio. I told Joe my initial idea and asked him if he could come up with some of the effects that you usually only get in black and white for our color film. We came up with the term "black and color." Joe went quite far. You'd probably have a hard time finding a color film with these kind of black shadows. You see somebody with a hat on, and if he lowers his head a little, you don't see the eyes anymore. No fill, which is daring.

JAG: When did Lathrop come on?

WW: Joe shot for ten weeks and with Phil we only shot for four weeks. Still, more of Phil's stuff is in the movie than Joe's. In Phil's four weeks we shot two-thirds of the movie. In the ten weeks we only shot one-third. I don't think anybody could tell who shot what. Very often we went from one shot that we did with Joe in 1980 to a shot we did with Phil in 1981. They were both incredibly efficient and professional.

JAG: Your film *Lightning Over Water* is a very moving experience for anyone who loves movies. How did you meet Nicholas Ray?

WW: I met Nick on *The American Friend*. We'd never met before. I only knew him through his work. I was in New York to shoot five or six scenes between Dennis Hopper and Sam Fuller. Part of the background plot had Sam representing porno film production under Mafia influence. We were in New York waiting for Sam, who was scouting locations for *The Big Red One* (1980). Nobody knew where he was. Some said Yugoslavia, some said Israel. We had already done some scenes with Sam in Hamburg, Germany. We just didn't know how to get in touch with him. I met Nick, and since I couldn't shoot, we were sitting around every night playing backgammon. We were both avid players and we liked each other. I told Nick the story of *The American Friend* and also of the other two Ripley novels by Patricia Highsmith that preceded this one. There was reference in our film to a painter who was believed to be dead but was really forging his own work and selling them to Europe via Ripley. Nick liked this character a lot and as we couldn't shoot, together we came up with the idea to substitute the plot of the porno film mafiosi and replace it with the story of this painter. Nick and I wrote the scenes together and we shot them with Nick and Dennis Hopper. Only on the very last day of shooting did Sam finally show up, and since we had to leave the next day, we shot one scene with Sam in New York.

JAG: How did *Lightning Over Water* come about?

WW: I stayed in touch with Nick over the years. He sent me a few of his scripts, but I was never able to raise the money. At some point Nick had the idea that someday we could make a film together, since the biggest problem for him to get a contract was the insurance. He was too sick. He asked me if I could back him so the production could go ahead knowing that if he couldn't go on, I would take over. The film never took place, and Nick underwent surgery several times. The surgery was successful, but it was obvious that it wouldn't cure the cancer. It was only helping him to live longer but not survive in the long run. He was really suffering that he was not able to work for so long. Though he was sick with cancer, he was otherwise in better shape than he'd been in years because he didn't drink anymore. That had been a problem for him getting work in America in the Sixties. Mentally he was able to work, but not physically, and it was obvious that he wasn't going to get another movie.

JAG: You were involved in preparing *Hammett* at this point in time.

WW: Joe Gores, who had written the novel and the first drafts, had to go on with something else, so we brought in another writer, Thomas Pope. Tom had to get familiar with the material and he also wanted to write his draft alone, so I had six weeks where I wasn't really needed. Nick called up and said, "If we can ever work together, it's now or never." Also at the same time, a director named Jon Jost had proposed a film to

Nick in 16mm, but Nick felt there wasn't the basis for a collaboration, and that financially they weren't ready to go. On the phone, I said maybe I could raise some money in Germany from a film prize I had won for *The American Friend*. I flew to New York and hired a crew in five days' time, not really knowing in which direction the film would go. We knew from the beginning that it was going to have something to do with Nick's reality. His idea was to go with his painter character from *The American Friend* and he wrote a twenty-page script about this painter and an old Chinese friend of his, both sick with cancer. In another draft they robbed a bank, in another they stole some paintings from a museum and sold them, and bought a Chinese junk and together went out on a slow boat to China. We never got into any of these different fictionalized ideas because Nick was decaying very fast. We wanted to, but the reality was always too quick. What we did was have a conversation in the evening about what happened between the two, tape record it, have it transcribed the next day, and work on it. We'd shoot the situation like our own reality, but lit in 35mm like you would do any fictional film. People usually see the film and take it as a documentary, which it isn't. The documentary is only the video stuff inside. The rest, unlikely as it may seem, is really quite artificial.

JAG: You formed Gray City Films to distribute your films and produce. How did that happen?

WW: I wanted to stay in New York and I wanted to work in America. Chris Sievernich was the production manager on *Lightning Over Water,* and then turned out to be much more and became the producer of the film. We got along well so we said, "Let's make a company." I was very unhappy with the way my old films had been distributed in America, except for *The American Friend,* on which New Yorker Films had done a good job. The others were thrown away, or had not been shown at all. I got the rights to these films back. We thought to have an office in New York and make a film a year, we'd have a more solid base by distributing these old films to carry the rent and the overhead. We found Tom Prassis for distribution, and we realized we had the potential to do a bit more and distribute a few other films, for example Jim Jarmusch's *Permanent Vacation* (1982) and Alain Tanner's *In the White City* (1983). We're going to be very careful because I want the films to fit in with the size of this little company.

JAG: You had been involved a little with distribution in Germany.

WW: In the early Seventies we founded a directors' company called Film-verlag, with fifteen directors. This enabled each of us to independently produce our films within the framework of the company. All the others would back the one who was making his film. After the first couple of films we realized that producing was not really the problem, it was distribution. If you wanted to have control of your films and produce, yourself, you had to be very serious about distribution. It didn't make sense to be fussy about your production and then hand it over to somebody who would do whatever they wanted with it. As everybody began to produce more and more, Filmverlag became only a distribution company. With Gray City, it's on a real small scale, and even if it means investing everything that comes in for a couple of years into distribution, in the long run it's worth it.

(1983)

Bibliography

A number of American periodicals regularly feature interviews with film directors, including *Premiere, Millimeter, Cineaste, Films in Review, Film Comment, American Film* (especially its regular "Dialogue on Film" entry), and *Interview. Fangoria, Starlog,* and *Cinefantastique* feature interviews with filmmakers in the horror, science fiction, and fantasy genres.

The following books are highly recommended:

Baker, Fred, with Ross Firestone. *Movie People.* New York: Douglas Book Corp., 1972.

    Includes interviews with Sidney Lumet and Francis Coppola, as well as composer Quincy Jones, writer Terry Southern, actor Rod Steiger, editor Aram Avakian, and producer David Picker.

Garnett, Tay. *Un Siècle de Cinema.* Paris: Hatier, 1981.

    This is an outstanding volume, unfortunately unavailable in English. Veteran Hollywood director Garnett (*The Postman Always Rings Twice*) sent detailed questionnaires on the craft of directing to Hal Ashby, Alessandro Blasetti, Clarence Brown, Rene Clair, Jack Clayton, Luigi Comencini, George Cukor, Allan Dwan, Blake Edwards, Federico Fellini, Bryan Forbes, Milos Forman, Samuel Fuller, Howard Hawks, George Roy Hill, Jan Kadar, Elia Kazan, Henry King, Stanley Kramer, Alberto Lattuada, J. Lee Thompson, Claude Lelouch, Mervyn LeRoy, Louis Malle, Lewis Milestone, Satyajit Ray, Jean Renoir, Alain Resnais, Tony Richardson, Dino Risi, John Schlesinger, Martin Scorsese, Don Siegel, Steven Spielberg, Leopoldo Torre Nilsson, François Truffaut, King Vidor, Raoul Walsh, Robert Wise, William Wyler, Serge Youtkevich, and Fred Zinnemann. Garnett compiled their answers into an extraordinary book that lives up to its author's original title, *Learn from the Masters.*

Gelmis, Joseph. *The Film Director as Superstar.* Garden City, New York: Doubleday and Company, 1970.

    Interviews with Jim McBride, Brian DePalma, Robert Downey, Norman Mailer, Andy Warhol, John Cassavetes, Lindsay Anderson, Bernardo Bertolucci, Milos Forman, Roman Polanski, Roger Corman, Francis Ford Coppola, Arthur Penn, Richard Lester, Mike Nichols, Stanley Kubrick.

Oumano, Ellen. *Film Forum: Thirty-Five Top Filmmakers Discuss Their Craft*. New York: St. Martin's Press, 1985.

Subjects such as cinematography, sound, the actor, structure and rhythm, film and reality, the process—writing, shooting, and editing the film, the viewer, film and society, movie business—production, distribution, and exhibition are commented upon by Chantal Akerman, Nestor Almendros, Robert Altman, Emile de Antonio, Bernardo Bertolucci, Claude Chabrol, Jacques Demy, R. W. Fassbinder, Milos Forman, Jean-Luc Godard, Perry Henzel, Henry Jaglom, Benoit Jacquot, Barbara Kopple, Sidney Lumet, Dusan Makavejev, Al Maysles, Philip Messina, Ermanno Olmi, Elio Petri, Michael Powell, Mark Rappaport, Eric Rohmer, George Romero, Jean Rouch, Werner Schroeter, Martin Scorsese, Joan Micklin Silver and Raphael D. Silver, Jean-Marie Straub, Andre Techine, Lina Wertmuller, Billy Williams, Yves Yersin, Krzysztof Zanussi.

Pye, Michael, and Lynda Myles. *The Movie Brats: How the Film Generation Took Over Hollywood*. New York: Holt, Rinehart and Winston, 1979.

Chapters, including interviews, with Francis Coppola, George Lucas, Brian DePalma, John Milius, Martin Scorsese, Steven Spielberg.

Sherman, Eric, and Martin Rubin. *The Director's Event*. New York: Atheneum, 1970.

Interviews with Budd Boetticher, Peter Bogdanovich, Samuel Fuller, Arthur Penn, Abraham Polonsky.

Singer, Michael. *Film Directors: A Complete Guide*. Beverly Hills, California: Lone Eagle Publishing, 1983—the present.

An indispensable directory, published yearly, listing directors, credits, and contact numbers. Each volume also features several interviews with directors.

Thomas, Bob. *Directors in Action*. Indianapolis: Bobbs Merrill, 1973.

Selections from *Action,* the defunct, sorely missed magazine of The Directors Guild of America, including interviews with Stanley Kubrick, Alfred Hitchcock, Roger Corman, Don Siegel, John Frankenheimer, John Schlesinger, Robert Altman, George Stevens, Richard Lester, Gordon Parks, Mel Brooks, John Cassavetes, Paul Newman, Jack Lemmon, Carl Reiner, Paul Henreid, Sam Peckinpah, Henry Hathaway, Paul Williams, Bill Norton, James Bridges, Cy Howard, Hal Ashby, Lawrence Turman, Gilbert Cates, Dick Richards, Michael Ritchie, Richard Colla, an article by William Friedkin on staging the chase in *The French Connection,* and an interview with the master, John Ford, by director Burt Kennedy.

Of related interest:

Brady, John. *The Craft of the Screenwriter*. New York: Simon and Schuster, 1981.

Interviews with Paddy Chayefsky, William Goldman, Ernest Lehman, Paul Schrader, Neil Simon, Robert Towne.

Chell, David. *Moviemakers at Work*. Redmond, Washington: Microsoft Press, 1987.

Interviews with film technicians, including cinematographers Allen Daviau and Chris Menges, editors Carol Littleton and Thom Noble, production designers Patrizia von Brandenstein and Eiko Ishioka, makeup artist Michael

Westmore, costume designer Kristi Zea, sound recordist Chris Newman, re-recordist Bill Varney, animators Sally Cruikshank and Jimmy Picker, computer graphics experts Robert Abel and Gary Demos, and special effects technicians Roy Arbogast (mechanical effects), Dennis Muren (visual effects), Chris Evans (matte paintings), Mike Fulmer (miniatures), and Jonathan Erland (scientific and technical development).

Schaefer, Dennis, and Larry Salvato. *Masters of Light*. Berkeley, California: University of California Press, 1984.

Interviews with cinematographers Nestor Almendros, John Alonzo, John Bailey, Bill Butler, Michael Chapman, Bill Fraker, Conrad Hall, Laszlo Kovacs, Owen Roizman, Vittorio Storaro, Mario Tosi, Haskell Wexler, Billy Williams, Gordon Willis, Vilmos Zsigmond.

Index

Abdication, The, 123
About Last Night, 89
Actors' Studio, 130, 209, 216
Adamson, Chuck, 55
Adjani, Isabelle, 163
Adler, Stella, 132
Aerosmith, 53
Agatha, 108
Aguirre, the Wrath of God, 178
Ahlberg, Mac, 92, 94
Aiello, Danny, 68
AIP (American International Pictures), 135, 173, 175
Albertson, Frank, 106
Aldredge, Tom, 211
Aldrich, Robert, 274
Alekan, Henri, 272–73
Alice in the Cities, 271
Alien, 91–92
Aliens, 91–92
Allen, Dave, 96, 97
Allen, Woody, 101, 111, 164, 267
All Quiet on the Western Front, 130
All the President's Men, 79
Altman, Robert, 81, 83, 209, 250
America, America, 31
American Biograph, 269
American Buffalo (play), 101, 110
American Film Institute, 26, 241
American Friend, The, 127, 130, 271, 273, 275, 276

American in Paris, An, 19
American International Pictures (AIP), 135, 173, 175
American Ninja, 75, 80, 81, 82, 84
American Zoetrope, 129, 175, 195, 205, 271, 273–74
Anders, Luana, 87
And You Act Like One Too, 229
Angel Heart, 183, 185, 188–91
Angry Silence, The, 119
Anhalt, Edward, 174
Annie Hall, 267
Anspaugh, David, 129
Antioch College, 57
Antonioni, Michelangelo, 3, 245
Apartment, The, 150
Apocalypse Now, 43, 63, 127, 135–36, 137, 169, 171, 174–75, 177, 178
Apprenticeship of Duddy Kravitz, The, 141, 144, 145, 146–48
Archer, Anne, 161, 162, 163
Ardant, Fanny, 167
Ashby, Hal, 21, 27, 106
Askin, Peter, 223
Asquith, Anthony, 119
Assante, Armand, 249
As the World Turns (TV show), 209
Astrologer, The (Suicide Cult), 57, 59–61, 72
Attenborough, David, 205

Attenborough, Richard, 118, 119
Audran, Stephanie, 123
Autry, Gene, 136
Avco Embassy Pictures. *See* Embassy
   Pictures
Avildsen, John G.: interview, 1–20;
   photo, 2; filmography, 3
Avildsen, Jonathan, 19
Aykroyd, Dan, 15

Babenco, Hector, 81
Bach, Steven, 37
Back Stage, 224
Backtrack, 129, 255
Badlands, 134
Balsam, Martin, 79
Bancroft, Anne, 104
Band, Albert, 96
Band, Charles, 95–96
Barbarella, 95
Barrie, George, 244
Barron, Fred, 235, 239
Barry, John, 120
Basinger, Kim, 159, 165–66
Baye, Nathalie, 266
Bazelli, Bojan, 49, 52
Bazin, Andre, 259
BBC (British Broadcasting Corpora-
   tion), 183, 195, 197–98, 205
Beals, Jennifer, 167, 206–7
Beatles, The, 33
Beattie, Ann, 231
Beatty, Warren, 138, 241, 253, 255
Beauty and the Beast, 273
Bed and Board, 259, 260
Begelman, David, 14
Behr, Jack, 187
Belson, Jerry, 148
Belushi, John, 15
Berenger, Tom, 54
Berger, Thomas, 15
Bergman, Ingmar, 19, 166, 212, 259,
   268
Bergman, Sandahl, 178
Berkeley, Busby, 166
Berman, Susan, 221, 224, 225
Bernice Bobs Her Hair, 231, 235, 237
Berridge, Elizabeth, 32

Berserker, 98
Bertolucci, Bernardo, 167, 249
Bettelheim, Bruno, 96
Between the Lines, 231, 235–38
Beverly Hills Cop, 166, 252–53
Beverly Hills Cop II, 69
Bible, The, 95
Big Bang!, The, 241, 243, 256–59
Big Brawl, The, 68
Big Red One, The, 275
Big Wednesday, 169, 176, 177, 179–80
Bill, Tony: filmography, 21, 23; inter-
   view, 21–35; photo, 22
Bill-Phillips Productions, 21, 26
Billy Two Hats, 141, 145–46
Birdy, 183, 187–88, 191
Biroc, Joseph, 273, 274
Blacula, 175
Black Hole, The, 63
Black Like Me, 3
Black Mama, White Mama, 175
Black Roses, 72
Black Stallion, The, 207
Black Sunday, 180
Blank Generation, 225
Bleacher Bums, 89
Blondell, Joan, 98
Bloom, John, 122, 124
Blowup, 245
Bluejean Cop (Shakedown), 57, 67, 68,
   69–71, 72
Blue Velvet, 129
Blumenthal, Andy, 33
Bode, Ralf, 11
Bogarde, Dirk, 115, 124
Bogart, Humphrey, 81, 82, 124, 197
Bogdanovich, Peter, 60, 86, 269
Bonaparte, Napoleon, 180
Bonet, Lisa, 190
Bonnie and Clyde, 180, 264
Boston Real Paper, 235
Boulting, John, 115, 118, 120
Boulting, Roy, 115, 118, 120
Boyle, Peter, 1, 5, 19
Brando, Marlon, 14, 132, 135, 136,
   252
Breakin', 81
Breathless, 229, 259

Brecht, Bertolt, 71
Bregman, Martin, 7
Breland, Mark, 203
Breslin, Jimmy, 14
Breughel, 121
Bride, The, 195, 201, 205–7
Bride of Frankenstein, 91, 206
Bride of Re-Animator, 91, 196
Bride Wore Black, The, 261, 266
Bridges, Jeff, 37, 46
Bridges, Lloyd, 158
Brighton Rock, 118
Briley, John, 123
British Broadcasting Corporation
    (BBC), 183, 195, 197–98, 205
British Film Academy, 183
Bronson, Charles, 63, 83
Brown, Clancy, 206
Brown, David, 27, 80
Brown, Garrett, 11, 187
Brown, Jim, 241, 257
Brown, Reb, 155
Browne, Roscoe Lee, 216
Brownlow, Kevin, 119
Brubaker, James, 103
Bruckheimer, Jerry, 166
Brut, 244
Buchanan, Jack, 117
Buddy Holly Story, The, 61
Buechler, John, 92
Bugner, Joe, 198
Bugsy Malone, 183, 185–86
Buntzman, Mark, 65
Burr, Raymond, 138
Burum, Stephen, 207

Caan, James, 9, 10, 209, 241, 243, 245
Cabot, Bruce, 216
Cacoyannis, Michael, 197
Caesar and Cleopatra, 115, 117
Cage, Nicholas, 183
Cagney, James, 81, 197
Cahan, Abraham, 231
Cahiers du Cinema, 259, 268
Calley, John, 25, 26, 108
Campbell, Robert, 87
Campbell, William, 87

Canadian Broadcasting Corporation
    (CBC), 143
Canadian Film Development Corpora-
    tion (CFDC), 146
Cannes International Film Festival, 53,
    61, 63–64, 68, 69, 82, 88, 89, 115,
    139, 226, 227, 235, 271
Cannonball Run, The, 68
Cannon Group, The, 5, 19, 65, 75, 78,
    80–84, 86, 88, 124
Can She Bake a Cherry Pie?, 136, 137
Capotorto, Carl, 32
Capra, Frank, 12, 262
Capra, Frank Jr., 65, 67
Carelli, Joann, 39, 41
Carey, Harry, 216
Carlton-Browne of the F. O., 118
Carmichael, Ian, 118
Carney, Art, 9
Carr, Alan, 168
Carter, Jimmy, 243
Casablanca, 40
Casablanca Pictures, 186
Case of the Elevator Duck, The, 231
Cassidy, Bill, 12
Castle, John, 121
Castle Keep, 21, 25–26
Cat People, 248
CBC (Canadian Broadcasting Corpo-
    ration), 143
CCNY (City College of New York),
    1, 75, 86, 211, 251
CFDC (Canadian Film Development
    Corporation), 146
Chabrol, Claude, 267
Chan, Jackie, 67–68
Chandler, Raymond, 188
Chaplin, Charles, 119, 143
Chariots of Fire, 187
Charlot, Andre, 117
Chartoff, Robert, 9, 103, 104, 108
Chase, The, 249
Cherry Lane Theatre, 120
Cheyenne (TV show), 130
Chicago Musical College, 217
Chilly Scenes of Winter, 231
China Girl, 49, 51–53
Chinatown, 250

Chong, Rae Dawn, 54
Chorus Line, A, 165
Chow, Raymond, 68
Cimino, Michael, 252; filmography, 39; interview, 37–47; photo, 38
Cinderella Liberty, 209
Cinecitta, 95
CinemaScope, 119
Cinematheque Francaise, 134
Citizen Kane, 172, 263
City College of New York (CCNY), 1, 75, 86, 211, 251
Clan of the Cave Bear, The, 69
Clarke, Arthur, 94
Clayton, Jack, 144, 245
Cleopatra, 95
Clift, Montgomery, 132
Close Encounters of the Third Kind, 172, 265
Close, Glenn, 159, 161, 162, 163, 165, 167
Clouse, Robert, 168
Cobb, Lee J., 10
Cobb, Ron, 178
Cobb, Tex, 155
Cobra, 86
Cochran, C. B., 117
Cocteau, Jean, 263, 264, 273
Color of Money, The, 249
Colors, 129
Colossus of Rhodes, 59
Columbia Pictures, 16, 82, 83, 186, 237
Columbia University, 241
Combs, Jeffrey, 98
Come Blow Your Horn, 21, 23–24, 26
Coming Home, 63, 137
Conan the Barbarian, 169, 177–78
Confidentially Yours, 261
Conformist, The, 167
Conrad, Joseph, 175
Conroy, Pat, 195, 202
Conti, Bill, 11, 13
Conti, Tom, 34
Continental Op, 271
Contner, James, 211
Cooke, Alistair, 95
Cooper, Gary, 81, 82, 216

Cooper, Ray, 33
Coppola, Francis Ford, 1, 21, 24–25, 27, 42, 43, 44, 46, 60, 86, 87, 127, 129, 135–36, 169, 175, 177, 179, 195, 205, 249, 271, 273–74
Corman, Roger, 59, 72, 75, 78, 86–87, 98, 135, 273
Cosby Show, The (TV show), 190
Costello, Frank, 252
Cotton, Joseph, 233
Coward, Noel, 117
Cowboys, The, 209, 212
Crampton, Barbara, 96, 98
Crenna, Richard, 153
Crime in the Streets, 209
Crime Story (TV show), 49, 55
Cristofer, Michael, 111
Crosby, Floyd, 87
Crossing Delancey, 231
Crown Film Unit, 118
Cry Uncle!, 6, 11
Cukor, George, 43, 123, 246, 247
Cunningham, Sarah, 216
Curve of Binding Energy, The (book), 165
Czech Film School, 52

Dalton, Timothy, 121
Daly, Bill, 124
Dangerfield, Rodney, 15
Daniels, Phil, 199
Davis, Bette, 115, 123
Davis, Brad, 183
Dawkins, Darryl, 256
Day, Doris, 229
Day for Night, 261, 264, 266
Day of the Locust, The, 264
Day the Fish Came Out, The, 197
Day the World Ended, The, 273
Deadhead Miles, 21, 26
Deadly Summer, 163
Dean, James, 127, 129, 130, 131, 132, 133
Dearden, James, 161
Death of a Salesman (play), 132
Death Wish, 84
Death Wish 3, 82
Deauville Film Festival, 49

Decline and Fall of the Roman Empire, The (book), 172
Deep, The, 238
Deer Hunter, The, 37, 39–46, 137
DeLaurentiis, Dino, 7, 95
Delerue, Georges, 34
Delta Force, The, 75, 77–80, 87
Delta Force II: Operation Crackdown, The, 87
Dementia 13, 25, 87
DeMille, Cecil B., 167
Demme, Jonathan, 226
Denby, David, 236
Denham Studios, 117
DeNiro, Robert, 43, 45–46, 60, 101, 109–10, 111, 112, 152, 183, 189–90, 213, 245, 252
Denner, Charles, 266
DePalma, Brian, 239
Dern, Bruce, 47, 60, 216
DeSica, Vittorio, 82
Desperately Seeking Susan, 221
Devil's 8, The, 169, 173
Didion, Joan, 108
Dietrich, Marlene, 248
Diller, Barry, 253
Dillinger, 41, 147, 169, 175–76, 179
Dillon, Matt, 28, 136
Dinocitta, 95
Director's Guild of America, 17, 115
Dirty Harry, 37, 169, 173
Disappearance of Aimee, The, 115, 123
Disney, Walt, 186
Dodge City, 127
Dog Day Afternoon, 180
Dolls, 89, 95, 96, 97
Doublin, John, 92
Douglas, Kirk, 153, 163
Douglas, Michael, 159, 161, 162, 163, 165
Downey, Robert, Jr., 241, 254–55, 256
Downhill Racer, 249
Down There, 263
Dr. Stangelove, 115, 119, 120, 180

Face of Fire, 96
Fahrenheit 451, 259, 264
Fairie Tale Theatre, 34

Falk, Peter, 16, 17
Falling Angel (book), 188
Falling in Love, 101, 103, 104, 111–12
Falwell, Jerry, 198
Fame, 183, 187, 191
Family, 98
Farewell to the King, 171
Farina, Dennis, 55
Farrell, Glenda, 98
Farrow, Tisa, 257
Fasano, John, 72
Fassbinder, Rainer Werner, 241, 244, 269
FBI (Federal Bureau of Investigation), 154
Fear City, 49, 52, 154
Federal Bureau of Investigation (FBI), 154
Feelies, The, 226
Fellini, Federico, 3, 44, 82, 94, 259
Ferrara, Abel: filmography, 49, 51; interview, 49–50; photo, 50
Ferris Bueller's Day Off, 54
Fieldston School, The, 59
Fiddler on the Roof, 87
52 Pickup, 84
Fight, The, 198
Filmverlag der Autoren, 270, 276, 277
Final Cut (book), 37
Fingers, 241, 244–46, 254, 255, 256, 257
Finley, Kate, 246
Finnegan Begin Again, 231
Finney, Albert, 118, 183
First Artists, 26, 108
First Blood, 85, 141, 149, 151–55
First Born, 254
F.I.S.T., 85
Fitzgerald, F. Scott, 143, 231, 235
Five Corners, 21, 29–34
Fix, Paul, 216
Flap, 21, 25
Flashdance, 159, 164, 166–67
Fleming, Victor, 46
Float Committee, The, 257
Floating Light Bulb, The (play), 101, 111
Flood, Barbara, 137

Flynn, Errol, 127
Fodor, Eugene, 256
Fonda, Henry, 209, 211, 212, 213, 214, 215, 216, 217, 218
Fonda, Jane, 141, 148–49, 211, 212, 215, 216, 218
Fonda, Peter, 60, 134
Fonveille, Lloyd, 202, 203, 204, 205–6
Fool for Love, 81
Footsteps, 183
Forbes, Bryan, 115, 119, 120, 193
Ford, John, 44, 135, 138, 169, 171, 181, 199, 203, 216
Fore Play (The President's Women), 8
For Keeps, 17–18
Formula, The, 14
Forster, Robert, 79
Fort Apache, The Bronx, 67
Fortune Cookie, The, 150
Forty Guns, 273
Foster, Jodie, 31, 168
Fountainhead, The, 40
400 Blows, The, 259, 263, 264, 265
Fox, The, 209
Foxes, 159, 167–68
Fox Magnetic Video, 73
Francis, Carol, 257
Frank, Anne, 88
Frank, Robert, 44
Frankenheimer, John, 80, 84, 130, 143
Frazier, Joe, 198
Freeman, Al, Jr., 120, 121
Friedkin, William, 84
Friedman, Bruce Jay, 8
From Beyond, 89, 92, 93, 94, 95, 96, 98
From Hell to Texas, 127, 133
Front Page, The (1931), 56
Fugitive, The (TV show), 209
Fuller, Samuel, 53, 269, 271, 273, 274, 275
Fun with Dick and Jane, 141, 144, 148–49, 154–55
Furcoat Club, The, 231

Gal Young Un, 277
Gambler, The, 241, 243, 244, 245, 257
Ganz, Bruno, 271
Garbo, Greta, 248

Gardner, Herb, 106, 108
Garland, Judy, 233
Garner, James, 130
Garnett, Tay, 274
Gayton, Joe, 156
Geng, Veronica, 257
Gent, Peter, 150
George, Christopher, 62, 63
Georgy Girl, 122
Germi, Pietro, 82
Giant, 127, 129, 131, 133
Gibbons, Edmund, 172
Gibbs, Gary, 72
Gibson, Mel, 209
Giler, David, 148
Gill, David, 119
Gilmore, Gary, 66
Gilroy, Frank, 105, 106
Ginty, Robert, 62, 63
Glass Menagerie, The (play), 173
Glass Menagerie, The (1973), 115, 122–23
Glickenhaus, James: filmography, 59; interview, 57–73; photo, 58
Glickman, Paul, 137
Gleason, Jackie, 24
Globus, Yoram, 75, 82, 83, 88
Goalie's Anxiety at the Penalty Kick, The, 269
Godard, Jean-Luc, 44, 81, 129, 229, 259, 267, 273
Godfather, The, 43, 46, 180, 252
Godfather Part II, The, 43, 111, 189–90
Golan, Menachem: filmography, 77; interview, 75–78; photo, 76
Goldblum, Jeff, 237
Golden, Matt, 52
Golden Harvest, 67–68
Goldman, Bo, 40
Goldman, James, 121, 122
Goldwym, Samuel, 83
Gone with the Wind, 46
Goodis, David, 263
Gordon, Larry, 173
Gordon, Stuart: filmography, 89; interview, 89–99; photo, 90
Gores, Joe, 271, 275
Gould, Elliott, 250

Grable, Betty, 233
Grace Quigley, 84, 115, 124
Grant, Cary, 124, 157
Grapes of Wrath, The, 201, 212
Gray, Tom, 67–68
Gray City, Inc., 269, 277
Graysmark, John, 202
Green, Guy, 119
Greenberg, Dan, 8
Greenberg, Jerry, 124
Green Room, The, 266
Greenwich Village Story, The, 3
Greystoke: the Legend of Tarzan, Lord of the Apes, 187
Griffiths, Melanie, 54
Grosbard, Ulu: filmography, 101, 103; interview, 101–114; photo, 102
Grusin, Dave, 211
Guardian Angels, The, 19
Guber, Peter, 151
Guess What We Learned in School Today?, 5
Gulf and Western, 139
Gunga Din, 169
Gunsmoke (TV show), 130, 209

Hackman, Gene, 109, 123, 141, 155–56
Haley, Michael, 124
Halloween, 54
Hambling, Gerry, 192
Hamill, Brian, 254
Hammer, Armand, 14
Hammett, 271, 273–74, 275
Hammett, Dashiell, 271
Handke, Peter, 269
HandMade Films, 30, 33
Hannah and Her Sisters, 164
Hanna's War, 75, 77, 87–88
Hansel and Gretel, 96
Happy New Year (1973), 16–17
Happy New Year (1986), 16–17
Harman, H. Boyce, Jr., 66, 71
Harper, Jessica, 28
Harper's, 241
Harris, Julie, 212
Harrison, George, 33
Harvard University, 241

Harvey, Anthony, 193; filmography, 117; interview, 115–25; photo, 116
Harvey, Morris, 117
Hathaway, Henry, 127, 133–34, 135
Hauser, Wings, 156
Hawks, Howard, 156, 164, 169, 171, 181, 267
Hawthorne, Nathaniel, 269
Hayes, Billy, 183
Hayes, Gabby, 136
Hays Office, 94
HBO (Home Box Office), 232
Head Over Heels, 231
Healy, Katherine, 29
Heart of Darkness, 136, 175
Hearts of the West, 21
Heaven Can Wait, 253
Heaven's Gate (The Johnson County Wars), 37
Hecht, Ben, 156
Hell, Richard, 225
Hell's Kitchen (Paradise Alley), 9
Hemingway, Ernest, 143, 171, 179, 180, 181
Hemphill, Julius, 257
Henry, O., 33
Hepburn, Katharine, 84, 115, 121, 122, 123, 124, 209, 211, 212, 213, 214, 215, 216, 218
"Herbert West, Ren-Animator," 93
Herrmann, Bernard, 264
Herzog, Werner, 269
Hess, Fred, 256
Hester Street, 231, 234–35, 237, 239
Highgate School, The, 159
High Noon, 87, 201
Highsmith, Patricia, 271, 275
Highway Queen, 80
Hildyard, Jack, 119
His Girl Friday, 156
Hitchcock, Alfred, 164, 233, 260, 261, 264, 267
Hitchcock/Truffaut (book), 267
Hitler, Adolf, 88, 101
Hjortsberg, William, 188
Hoffman, Dustin, 79, 101, 106–8, 252
Holocaust, 63
Home Box Office (HBO), 232

Honeymoon Killers, The, 267
Hoosiers, 129
Hopkins, Anthony, 121
Hopper, Dennis, 60, 255, 271, 273, 275; filmography, 129; interview, 127–39; photo, 128
House of Usher, 59
Howard, James Newton, 33
Howard, Robert E., 169, 177
Hudson, Hugh, 183, 187, 193
Hudson, Rock, 129
Hughes, Howard, 168
Hurry Sundown, 3, 10
Hurt, John, 183
Hustler, The, 101, 104
Huston, John, 96, 169, 171, 174, 176
Huyck, Willard, 169, 173

IATSE (International Alliance of Theatrical Stage Employees), 1
I Bury the Living, 96
Ice Station Zebra, 21, 25
Idolmaker, The, 249
Ienner, Jimmy, 53
I'm All Right, Jack, 115, 118
Immigrant Experience, The, 231
"In My Life" (The Beatles), 33
Inside Daisy Clover, 249
International Alliance of Theatrical Stage Employees (IATSE), 1
International Student Film Festival, 169
In the White City, 276
Invasion of the Body Snatchers (1956), 99
Irish, William, 263
Ironweed, 256
Irving, Amy, 231
Ishtar, 253
I Spy (TV show), 209
It's a Wonderful Life, 19

Jacob, Gilles, 227
Jackson, Glenda, 115, 124
Jackson, Michael, 33
Jaffe, Herb, 202, 204
Jaffe, Stanley, 159, 162, 168
Jaglom, Henry, 127, 135, 136
Jakubowicz, Alan, 80
James, Henry, 266

James, Steve, 62–63, 80
Janus Films, 227
Jarmusch, Jim, 276
Jaws, 179
Jeremiah Johnson, 169, 174
Jesus Christ, Superstar, 145
Jewison, Norman, 145
Jim (book), 241
Jinxed!, 67
Joe, 1, 5–6, 11, 19
Joffe, Roland, 183, 193
Johnny Got His Gun, 267
Johnny Guitar, 271
Johnson, Don, 55
Johnson, Lyndon B., 8
Johnson, Pat, 16
Johnson County Wars (Heaven's Gate), The, 37
Jones, Evan, 145
Jones, James Earl, 178
Jones, Jim, 177
Jones, Leroi, 120
Jones, Tommy Lee, 66
Joplin, Janis, 40
Jory, Victor, 25
Joshua Then and Now, 144
Jost, Jon, 275
Joypack, 64
Juilliard School of Music, 209, 217
Jules and Jim, 259, 264
Junior Bonner, 44
J. Walter Thompson Agency, 159

Kamen, Robert, 15–16
Kane, Carol, 231, 234–35
Kane, Mary, 52
Kanter, Joe, 256
Karate Kid, The, 1, 13, 15–16
Karate Kid Part II, The, 1, 16
Kassar, Mario, 152
Kastner, Peter, 24, 25
Katzenberg, Jeffrey, 202, 253
Katzka, Gabriel, 202, 204
Kauffman, Stanley, 257
Kaye, Simon, 124
Kazablan, 80
Kazan, Elia, 31, 101, 104
Kazurinsky, Tim, 34

Keaton, Diane, 183
Keitel, Harvey, 123, 241, 245–46, 249–50
Keith, David, 201, 204–5
Kennaway, James, 168
Kennedy, George, 79
Kennedy, Sheila, 257
Kertman, Leonard, 4, 10
Keyes, Sister Ann-Marie, 257
Khadafy, Muammar, 65
King of Comedy, The, 227
King of New York, The, 55
Kings of the Road, 271
Kinski, Klaus, 249
Kinski, Nastassia, 248, 249, 250, 251
Kirkwood, Gene, 9
Kishon, Ephraim, 87
Knight, Shirley, 120
Koch, Howard, 23
Konchalovsky, Andrei, 81, 83, 84
Kotcheff, Ted: filmography, 141, 143; interview, 141–58; photo, 142
Kramer, Robert, 272
Kranze, Don, 104
Kroopf, Sandy, 187
Kubrick, Stanley, 115, 119, 120, 193, 259
Kurosawa, Akira, 84, 172, 199, 206
Kwaidan, 178

Ladd, Alan Jr., 252
Ladyhawke, 94
Lafayette Escadrille, 130
LaMotta, Jake, 190
Langlois, Henri, 134
Landsbury, Edgar, 105, 106
Lansing, Sherry, 159, 162
LAPD (Los Angeles Police Department), 155
Last Emperor, The, 249
Last Metro, The, 261
Last Movie, The, 127, 138, 139, 273
Last Tycoon, The, 262
Laszlo, Andrew, 153–54
Lathrop, Phil, 274
Lattuada, Alberto, 248
Latzen, Ellen Hamilton, 163
Law, John Phillip, 4

Lawrence, D. H., 209, 243
Lawrence of Arabia, 169
LCA (Learning Corporation of America), 231
Lean, David, 177
Lear, Norman, 23, 24, 26, 67
Learning Corporation of America, 231
Leaud, Jean-Pierre, 259
LeCarre, John, 120
Lefko, Morry, 244–45
Leigh, Janet, 55
Leigh, Vivien, 115, 117
Lelouch, Claude, 16
Lemmo, James, 52
Lemmon, Jack, 1, 7
Le Monde, 247
Leonard, Elmore, 84
Leone, Sergio, 59, 94
Lester, Richard, 193
Lethal Pursuit, 72
"Let's Drop the Big One Now" (Randy Newman), 175
Let's Pretend (radio show), 157
Lewis, Paul, 138
Life at the Top, 144
Life and Dreams of Frank Costello, The, 40, 252
Life and Times of Judge Roy Bean, The, 169, 174
Lightning Over Water, 130, 271, 275–76
Limbo, 232
Lincoln, Abraham, 212
Lindsay, John F., 120, 234
Lion in Winter, The, 115, 121–22
Lipsky, Jeff, 237–38
Little Fauss and Big Halsy, 169
Little Shop of Horrors (1960), 78
Little Shop of Horrors (1986), 78
Lolita, 115
Lombard, Carole, 157
London Film Festival, 89, 159
London Film School, 197
Long Goodbye, The, 209
Lopez, Gerry, 178
Lords of Discipline, The, 195, 200, 201–3, 204, 205, 206
Lords of Flatbush, The, 9
Loren, Sophia, 119

Los Angeles City College, 169
Los Angeles Police Department
    (LAPD), 155
Lost Weekend, The, 149
Love and Money, 241, 244, 246, 247,
    249, 255, 256, 257
Love at 20, 259, 263
Lovecraft, H. P., 89, 93, 94, 97, 98
Love on the Run, 259
Love Streams, 83
Love Thy Neighbor, 21
L-Shaped Room, The, 115, 119
Lubitsch, Ernst, 149
Lubitsch Touch, The (book), 261
Lucas, George, 104, 169, 172, 174–75,
    178–79
Lumet, Sidney, 101, 111–12, 143, 186
Lupino, Ida, 44
Lurking Fear, 97
Lustig, William, 72
Lynch, David, 129
Lyne, Adrian, 183, 193; filmography,
    159, 161; interview, 159–68; photo,
    160

MacArthur, Charles, 156
Macchio, Ralph, 1, 15
Mad Max, 97
Magician of Lublin, The, 80
Magnificent Seven, The, 24
Magnum Force, 37, 41, 169, 173
Maguire, Charles, 104
Makepeace, Chris, 28
Making Mr. Right, 221
Mako, 178
Malick, Terence, 26
Maltese Falcon, The, 271
Mamet, David, 89, 101
"Maniac" (Michael Sembello), 166
Maniac Cop, 172
Mann, Anthony, 54
Mann, Michael, 49, 54, 55, 107
Manson, Charles, 177, 178
Man Who Loved Women, The (1977),
    261, 265–66
Marriage on the Rocks, 23
Marshall, Alan, 192
Marvin, Lee, 79, 80, 273

Mason, James, 144
Mason, Marsha, 209
Massachusetts Institute of Technology
    (MIT), 228
Masterpiece Theatre, 95
Maverick, 130
McCarey, Leo, 23
McGillis, Kelly, 155–56, 158
McIntyre, John, 52
McLeod, David, 253, 254
McNeill, Elizabeth, 159, 165
McPhee, John, 65
McQueen, Steve, 24, 209
McWhorter, Richard, 246
Mean Streets, 134
Meatballs, 28
Meisner, Sanford, 132, 209, 212
Melville, Herman, 171
Melvin Simon Company, The, 28
Mercer, Glenn, 226
Meredith, Burgess, 4, 10
Merrow, Jane, 121
Metro-Goldwyn-Mayer (MGM), 13,
    14, 82, 119, 244, 245
Metro-Goldwyn-Mayer/United Artists
    (MGM/UA), 164
MGM (Metro-Goldwyn-Mayer), 13,
    14, 82, 119, 244, 245
MGM/UA (Metro-Goldwyn-Mayer/
    United Artists), 164
Miami Vice 49, 54–55
Michaels, Lorne, 205
Mickey One, 3, 4
Milder, Bette, 67
Midnight Cowboy, 7, 224
Midnight Express, 183, 186–87, 191
Midwest Films, 231, 233
Miles, Joanna, 123
Milestone, Lewis, 129, 156
Milius, John, 47, 147, 156; filmogra-
    phy, 171; interview, 169–81; photo,
    170
Miller, Arthur, 101, 105
Miller, Jason, 84
Million, Bill, 226
Millionairess, The, 119
Mills, Hayley, 229
Mills, John, 144

Mini, 198
Minnelli, Liza, 34
Minnelli, Vincente, 44
Miracle Worker, The, 101, 104
Missing in Action III: Braddock, 87
Mississippi Mermaid, 261
MIT (Massachusetts Institute of Technology), 228
Moby Dick, 171–72
Modern Times, 143
Modine, Matthew, 183
Moonstruck, 33, 124, 149
Moore, Dudley, 28, 29
Moore, Mary Tyler, 231
Moore, Roger, 84
Moriarty, Cathy, 15
Moriarty, Michael, 115, 123
Morita, Pat, 15
Moroder, Giorgio, 167
Morrell, David, 151
Morris, Brian, 192
Moscow Art Theatre, 217
Most Dangerous Man Alive, The, 272, 273
Mostel, Zero, 8
Motion Picture Association of America (MPAA), 61–62, 94–95
MPAA (Motion Picture Association of America), 61–62, 94–95
Mr. Smith Goes to Washington, 159
Ms. 45, 49, 52, 54
Mull, Martin, 28
Murray, Forrest, 30
Muti, Ornella, 249
My Bodyguard, 21, 27–28, 29, 34

NABET (National Association of Broadcast Employees and Technicians), 30
Naha, Ed, 97
Naked Face, The, 84
Naked Spur, The, 55
Natalucci, Giovanni, 94
National Association of Broadcast Employees and Technicians (NABET), 30
National Broadcasting Company (NBC), 66, 67

National Film Theatre, 46
Naulin, John, 92
NBC (National Broadcasting Company), 66, 67
Neal, Patricia, 101, 106
Neighborhood Playhouse, 209, 212
Neighbors, 15, 17
Nelson, Ralph, 21, 24, 27
New Land, The, 123
New Line Cinema, 227
Newman, Paul, 19, 174
Newman, Randy, 175
New West, 239
New York Film Festival, 261
New Yorker Films, 276
New York, New York, 180, 190
New York Times, 70
New York University, 221, 223, 229
Nicholson, Jack, 60, 86, 134, 135, 138, 250, 252
Nickelodeon, 10
Night Moves, 145
9½ Weeks, 159, 162, 164–66
Noah Films, 75
Nobody Waved Goodbye, 25
No Hard Feelings, 183
Nolte, Nick, 84, 115, 124, 141, 150, 253
None But the Brave, 23
Norris, Aaron, 87
Norris, Chuck, 79, 83, 84, 87
North Dallas Forty, 141, 144, 150–51
Norton, Kenny, 10
Notre Dame University, 21, 23
Nunez, Victor, 227
Nyswaner, Ron, 223

Oakley, Marcia, 257
O'Connell, Jack, 3
Officer and a Gentleman, An, 191
Okay, Bill (Sweet Dreams), 1, 16
Old Dark House, The, 96
Old Vic, 75
On Camera (TV show), 143
Once Upon a Time in America, 52, 94
O'Neal, Patrick, 25
O'Neal, Ryan, 10
One from the Heart, 205, 248

On Golden Pond, 209, 211–12, 213–16, 217–19
On the Waterfront, 201
Operation Bandersnatch, 9
Operation Thunderbolt, 75, 77–78, 80
Ordinary People, 107
Organic Theatre Company, 89, 91, 98
Orion Pictures, 221
Orson Welles Cinema, 237
Osterman Weekend, The, 127, 137
Otello, 75, 81, 83
Other Side of Midnight, The, 238
O'Toole, Peter, 115, 121, 122, 124
Our Cissy, 183
Outback, 141, 145
Out of the Blue, 127, 129, 133, 137–39
Outsiders, The, 207
Over the Edge, 28
Over the Top, 75, 84, 85, 86
Ox-Bow Incident, The, 81

Pacino, Al, 152, 205
Page, Anthony, 124
Panebianco, Richard, 52
Paoli, Dennis, 95, 98
Paper Chase, The (TV show), 63
Paradise Alley (Hell's Kitchen), 9
Paramount Pictures, 40, 82, 104, 138, 139, 168, 201, 202, 204, 237, 252, 253
Pareths, Joy, 227
Paris, Texas, 271
Parker, Alan, 200; filmography, 185; interview, 183–94; photo, 184
Parsons, Estelle, 8
Pat Garrett and Billy the Kid, 44
Paths of Glory, 119
Patricia Neal Story, The, 115, 124
Patrick, Vincent, 19
Patty Hearst, 52
Pawnbroker, The, 101, 104
Pearl, 40
Peck, Gregory, 145–46
Peckinpah, Sam, 44, 67, 127, 137, 180
Peggy Sue Got Married, 249
Penn, Arthur, 3, 4, 101, 104, 143, 180
Perenchio, Jerry, 67
Peres, Shimon, 78

Perfect Strangers, 40
Permanent Vacation, 276
Persson, Gene, 120
Petersen, Wolfgang, 269
Phillips, Julia, 21, 26
Phillips, Michael, 21, 26, 27
Pickens, Slim, 44
Picker, David, 40, 246
Pickup Artist, The, 241, 252–56
Pierrot Le Fou, 273
Pilma, Pilma, 24
Pinewood Studios, 192
Pink Floyd—The Wall, 183, 187, 191–92
Pit and the Pendulum, The, 59
Pizer, Larry, 124
Plutarch's Lives, 172
Poe, Edgar Allan, 98
Polanski, Roman, 250
Pollack, Sydney, 21, 25, 26, 27, 169, 174
Polygram Pictures, 28
Pope, Thomas, 204, 275
Pope of Greenwich Village, The, 19
Positif, 247
Pound, Ezra, 156
Powell, Michael, 117
Prassis, Tom, 276
Preminger, Otto, 3–4
Presenting Lily Mars, 233
President's Women, The (Fore Play), 8
Presley, Elvis, 81, 138
Preston, Robert, 44, 231
Price, The (play), 101, 105
Price, Vincent, 98
"Princess and the Pea, The" (*Faerie Tale Theatre*, TV show), 34
Private's Progress, 115, 118
Prix Italia, 198
Prosky, Robert, 205
Protector, The, 57, 68–69, 71
Psycho, 91
Pumpkinhead, 52
Punchline, 209
Puttnam, David, 16, 167, 185, 186, 193, 200

Quadrophenia, 195, 198–201, 203, 204, 205, 206

Quiet Man, The, 203–4
Quinn, Anthony, 25

Rafelson, Bob, 134, 135
Raging Bull, 15, 109, 111, 180, 190
Ragtime, 202
Raiders of the Lost Ark, 186
Rambo: First Blood Part II, 85–86, 91,
  154, 156, 189
Ramos, Vic, 28
Rank Organization, 117
Ransom of Red Chief, The, 33
Rappaport, David, 206
Ray, Nicholas, 127, 129, 130, 269,
  271, 275–76
Rayfiel, David, 168
Reagan, Ronald, 77
Re-Animator, 89, 92–95, 98
Rebel Without a Cause, 127, 129, 130
Red Badge of Courage, The, 96
Red Dawn, 169
Redford, Robert, 26, 79, 174, 188, 249
Red River, 171
Reds, 139, 253
Red Sonja, 95
Reed, Carol, 21, 25, 27
Reed, Jerry, 9
Reeve, Christopher, 157–58
Rehme, Robert, 67
Reisz, Karel, 241, 244, 245
Reivers, The, 209, 212
Renoir, Jean, 259, 267
Renzetti, Joe, 61
Return of the Jedi, The, 92
Revolution, 187
Reynolds, Burt, 9, 10, 141, 156, 157
Reynolds, Jonathan, 156
Rich, Frank, 257
Richardson, Tony, 193
Richard's Things, 123
Richler, Mordecai, 141, 144, 146–47,
  148
Rickey, Carrie, 224
Rickman, Tom, 9
Rifleman, The (TV show), 137
Ringwald, Molly, 17, 241, 254
Rinn, Brad, 224–25
Ripley's Game (book), 271

Risher, Sara, 227
Ritt, Martin, 120, 151
Ritz, Harry, 246, 247
Ritz Brothers, The, 246
River, The, 209
Rivette, Jacques, 267
Robinson, David, 124
Robojox, 89, 95, 96, 97
Robson, Mark, 234
Roche, Henri-Pierre, 264
Rocky, 1, 9–13, 16, 19, 85, 152
Rocky Horror Picture Show, 112
Roddam, Franc, 183; filmography,
  195; interview, 195–207; photo, 196
Romancing the Stone, 163
Romeo and Juliet (play), 49, 51, 158
Romeo and Juliet (1968), 95
Room at the Top, 144
Roosevelt, Theodore, 169, 176, 177
Rossellini, Roberto, 259
Rossen, Robert, 101, 104
Rourke, Mickey, 136, 159, 165–66,
  183, 189, 190
Royal Academy of Dramatic Arts
  (RADA), 115, 117
Royal Canadian Mounted Police, 154
Rozakis, Gregory, 31–32
Ruiz, Raul, 272
Rumble Fish, 127, 136, 207
Runaway Train, 75
Run-DMC, 53
Russell, Kurt, 155, 158
Russo, James, 52
Rydell, Mark, 250; filmography, 211;
  interview, 209–19; photo, 210

Sable, Dan, 17
Safe Place, A, 136
St. John, Nicholas, 52, 53–54, 55
Sallah, 87
Sarah Lawrence College, 57, 231
Sargent, Alvin, 107
Saturday Night Fever, 13
Savage Club, The, 117
Save the Tiger, 1, 6, 7, 9, 11
Scarlet Letter, The, 269
Schaffner, Franklin, 143
Schatzberg, Jerry, 81

Scheider, Bert, 134, 135
Scheider, Roy, 19
Schepisi, Fred, 145
Schlondorff, Volker, 269
Schrader, Paul, 27, 52, 248
Schwarzenegger, Arnold, 98, 178
Scorsese, Martin, 19, 86, 180, 190, 249
Scott, George C., 14, 115, 122
Scott, Helen, 261
Scott, Ridley, 183, 200
Screen Actors Guild, 30
Screen International, 198
Searchers, The, 171, 180
Segal, George, 148, 149
Segal, Yossi, 224–25
Seidelman, Susan: filmography, 221;
    interview, 220–29; photo, 222
Sellers, Peter, 118, 119, 120
Selznick, David O., 83
Senesh, Hanna, 75, 87–88
Seresin, Michael, 185, 192
Sergeant York, 267
Serie Noir, Le, 263, 264
Serpico, 7, 10
Serpico, Frank, 18
Seven Days to Noon, 118
Seville Film Festival, 228
Sexual Perversity in Chicago, 89
Shadow of a Doubt, 233
Shagan, Steve, 14
Shakedown (Bluejean Cop), 57, 67, 68,
    69–71, 72
Shakespeare, William, 199, 206, 215
Shampoo, 21, 27
Shane, 201
Shanley, John Patrick, 21, 29, 33
Shapiro, Lenny, 65, 67, 71
Shapiro, Robert, 151
Shapiro Entertainment, 57
Shapiro Glickenhaus Entertainment,
    57, 71–72
Sharkey, Ray, 249
Sharp, Alan, 145
Sharpe, Cornelia, 7
Shaw, George Bernard, 119, 148
Sheen, Martin, 101, 106, 115, 123
Sheldon, Greg, 53
Shepperton Studios, 118

Shire, Talia, 10
Shoot the Moon, 183, 187, 191
Shoot the Piano Player, 259, 263–64
Show Business, 224
Shuftan, Eugene, 273
Sicilian, The, 37
Siegel, Don, 209
Sievernich, Chris, 269, 272, 276
Silence, 168
Silent Running, 40, 46–47
Silver, Joan Micklin: filmography, 233;
    interview, 231–39; photo, 232
Silver, Joe, 147
Silver, Raphael, 231, 234
Silvestri, Alan, 80
Simon, Neil, 21
Simpson, Don, 166, 252, 253
Sinatra, Frank, 21, 23–24
Singer, Isaac Bashevis, 75, 80
Sirico, Tony, 255, 257
Sitting Ducks, 136
Six Weeks, 21, 28–29, 34
Ski Bum, The, 121
Sky-Cam, 187–88
Slattery's People (TV show), 209
Sliwa, Curtis, 19
Sliwa, Lisa, 19
Slocombe, Douglas, 121, 124
Slow Dancing in the Big City, 11, 12,
    13–14
Small Change, 261, 265
"Smile" (Charles Chaplin), 143
Smiles, 19
Smith, Eugene, 44
Smithereens, 221, 223–28
Smokey and the Bandit, 60
Soft Skin, 59
Soldier, The, 57, 65–67, 68, 69, 71, 72
Soldier in the Rain, 21, 24
Solo, Robert, 158
Song of the Islands, 233
Sons of Katie Elder, The, 127, 133, 135
Sophie's Choice, 227
Southern, Terry, 8
Southside Johnny and the Asbury
    Jukes, 235–36
Spacek, Sissy, 209

Spielberg, Steven, 171, 172, 175, 178, 179, 265
Spinell, Joe, 33
Splendor in the Grass, 101, 104
Split Image, 141, 151
Springer, John, 261
Spy Who Came in from the Cold, The, 120, 122
Stairway to Heaven, 19, 117
Stallone, Sylvester, 1, 9, 10, 11, 12, 13, 19, 75, 84, 85, 86, 141, 152–53, 154, 253
Stalmaster, Lyn, 147
Stanislavsky, Konstantin, 132, 133, 217
Stanton, Harry Dean, 33
Starstruck, 227
Star Wars, 84, 86, 92
State of Things, The, 271, 272–74
Stay as You Are, 248
Steadicam, 11, 187
Steel Helmet, The, 53
Steelyard Blues, 21, 26, 27
Sternhagen, Frances, 211
Sterile Cuckoo, The, 26
Stevens, George, 127, 129, 133, 135
Stewart, James, 55
Stigwood, Robert, 13
Sting, 199, 206–7
Sting, The, 21, 26–27, 29
Stolen Kisses, 259, 263
Stone, Oliver, 177, 186
Stoolie, The, 1
Story of Adele H., The, 261, 264, 266
Straight Time, 101, 106–8
Strasberg, Lee, 100, 131, 132, 209
Strasberg, Susan, 79
Stravinsky, Igor, 45
Streep, Meryl, 45, 111, 112
Streetcar Named Desire, A (play), 173
Studies in American Literature (book), 243
Studio One, 130
Stulberg, Gordon, 252
Sturges, John, 21, 24, 25, 27
Sturhahn, Larry, 104
Subject Was Roses, The, 101, 103, 105–6
Sugarfoot (TV show), 130
Suicide Cult (The Astrologer), 60

Summer in the City, 269
Superman, 157
Suschitzsky, Peter, 112
Sweet Dreams, (Okay, Bill), 1, 6
Switching Channels, 141, 156–58
Syson, Michael, 123

Table, The, 159
Tamerlis, Zoe, 49
Taming of the Shrew, The (1968), 95
Tanner, Alain, 276
Taormina Film Festival, 49
Tapeheads, 52
Taxi Driver, 21, 26, 27, 111
Taylor, Elizabeth, 129
Taylor, John Russell, 124
Technicolor, 56, 267
Territory, The, 272
Terry, Nigel, 121
Tess, 248
Texas Chainsaw Massacre, The, 54
Thalberg, Irving, 262–63
That Championship Season, 84
They Live by Night, 271
They Might Be Giants, 115, 122
Thing, The, (1951), 99
Thin Man, The, 271
Third Man, The, 204
This Property is Condemned, 249
Thomas, Phillip Michael, 55
Thomas, Terry, 118
Thomson, David, 244
Thompson, Ernest, 211
Thunderbolt and Lightfoot, 37, 40, 46
THX–1138, 175
Tiara Tahiti, 144
Time, 159
"Times They Are A-Changin', The" (Bob Dylan), 33
Toback, James, 40; filmography, 243; interview, 241–257; photo, 242
Tootsie, 227
Top Gun, 166
Topol, Chaim, 87
Touch of Evil, 250
Towne, Robert, 86, 253–54
Townshend, Pete, 199
Tracks, 127, 136, 137

Tracy, Spencer, 124, 129
Trancers, 96
Traub, Barbara, 256
Tri-Star Pictures, 164
True Confessions, 101, 103, 108–11
True Grit, 127, 135
Truffaut, François, 129, 167, 241, 244, 246; filmography, 261–62; interview, 259–68; photo, 260
Trumbull, Douglas, 116
Tufano, Brian, 205
Turner, Kathleen, 141, 157
Turn on to Love, 4–5
Turpin, Gerry, 120, 122
Turturro, John, 31
20th Century-Fox, 28, 40, 82, 201, 252, 253
21st Century Pictures, 60
Twickenham Studios, 120, 121
Twilight Zone—The Movie, 61
2½ Dads, 21, 34
Two Gentlemen Sharing, 141, 144–45
Two Minute Warning, 12

UCLA (University of California, Los Angeles), 26
Ullmann, Liv, 115, 123
Ulmer, Edgar, 274
Uncommon Valor, 141, 155–56
Unfaithfully Yours (1984), 249
United Artists, 40, 82, 103, 145, 167–68, 205
Universal Pictures, 26, 27, 57, 67, 122, 175
University of California, Santa Barbara, 57
University of Chicago, 101
University of Southern California (USC), 172, 179
University of California, Los Angeles (UCLA), 26
Unknown Chaplin, The, 119
Unsworth, Gregory, 124
USC (University of Southern California), 172, 179
Used Cars, 178
Uses of Enchantment, The (book), 96–97

Vajna, Andrew, 152
Variety, 63, 72
Venice Film Festival, 145
Ventura, Lino, 16
Vestron Pictures, 53
Vidor, King, 241, 246–47, 249
View from the Bridge, A (play), 101, 105, 110
Village Voice, 224, 232, 236
Visconti, Luchino, 44
Von Stroheim, Eric, 262–63
Von Sydow, Max, 178

Wagon Train (TV show), 130
Wahl, Ken, 67
Walker, Clint, 29
"Walk This Way" (Run-DMC/Aerosmith), 53
Wallace, Bill, 80
Wallace, Joshua, 272
Walsh, Raoul, 129, 171
Walt Disney Pictures, 34, 63, 82
Wanderers, The, 67
Ward, David, 26
Ward, Fred, 55
Warner Brothers, 6, 41, 69, 82, 86, 108, 127, 129–30, 135, 151, 152, 175, 271, 274
Washington Post, 72
Wasserman, Lew, 27
Waters, Roger, 187
Waterston, Sam, 123
Waugh, Evelyn, 144
Waverly Theatre, 221
Wayne, John, 127, 135, 203, 209, 216
Wayne, Michael, 135
Wayne, Patrick, 135
Weathers, Carl, 11
Wedding in White, 234
Weinberg, Herman G., 261
Weir, Peter, 145
Weird Science, 254
Weller, Peter, 70
Welles, H. H., 172
Welles, Orson, 29, 206, 250, 262
Wellman, William A., 81, 129, 135, 216
Wells, Frank, 108

Wenders, Wim, 127, 130; filmography, 271; interview, 269–77; photo, 270
West Side Story, 51, 101, 104
Wexler, Norman, 5
Whale, James, 206
Wharton, William, 183, 187
Whisperers, The, 115, 119, 120
Who, The, 195, 199
Who'll Stop the Rain, 249
Who is Harry Kellerman and Why is He Saying Those Terrible Things About Me?, 106, 108
Who is Killing the Great Chefs of Europe?, 149
Widmark, Richard, 273
Wild Bunch, The, 180
Wild Child, The, 261, 265, 266
Wilde, Cornel, 247
Wilde, Oscar, 149
Wilder, Billy, 123, 211
Wild, Wild, West (TV show), 209
William Morris Agency, 23
Williams, Billy, 123, 211
Williams, Billy Dee, 54
Williams, Charles, 263
Williams, Tennessee, 173
Willis, Gordon, 46, 254
Wind and the Lion, The, 169, 171, 176–77, 179
Wings of Desire, 271
Winkler, Irwin, 9, 103, 104, 108
Winter People, The, 141, 155, 158
Winters, Shelley, 179

Wise, Robert, 101, 104
Wiz, The, 186
Wizard of Oz, The, 46, 94
Woman Under the Influence, A, 237
Women, Money and Restaurants, 205
Woods, James, 151
Woodward, Joanne, 115
Wright, Teresa, 233
Wrong Move, The, 271
Wurtzell, Stuart, 234
W. W. and the Dixie Dance Kings, 9
Wyler, William, 123

Yale Drama School, 101
Yale University, 37
Yates, Steve, 23
Year of the Dragon, The, 37
"Yekl" (story), 231, 235
Yorkin, Bud, 21, 23, 24, 26, 27
Young, Burt, 10
Young Racers, The, 75, 86–87
Young Sherlock Holmes, 96
You're a Big Boy Now, 21, 24–25
Yuzna, Brian, 92

Z, 40
Zanuck, Darryl, 81
Zanuck, Richard, 27, 80
Zefferelli, Franco, 81, 83
Zinnemann, Fred, 129
Zinner, Peter, 43
Zsigmond, Vilmos, 39, 41–42, 43, 112

About the Author

John Andrew Gallagher is a film director, screenwriter, producer, and historian. His directing credits include two feature films, the action comedy *Beach House* (1982, New Line Cinema) and the documentary *One Life Is Not Enough* (1985, Theatre Lab Productions). He also directed and adapted Kurt Vonnegut's *Long Walk to Forever* (1982), nationally broadcast on Arts and Entertainment Network; wrote and directed the short *Other Men's Wives* (1983), a 1920s comedy of manners; and directed the made-for-homevideo documentary *Secrets of Pro Wrestling* (1988, Diamond Entertainment).

John wrote the screenplay for *Blue Highways,* based on the William Least Heat Moon best-seller, for producer Jean DeNiro; and a dozen commissioned screenplays for such producers as Forrest Murray, J. Boyce Harman, Jr.; Raphael Shauli and Arnon Milchan; and Lewis Allen and Peter Newman. In various production capacities, he has worked on Henry Jaglom's *Can She Bake a Cherry Pie?* Robert Downey's *America,* Jack Sholder's *Alone in the Dark,* Lorne Michaels' *Superman's 50th Anniversary,* and Ira Gallen's *Ronnie Dearest.*

John also produces the Manhattan Cable movie magazine show *Video Airwaves* for Video Resources New York, Inc., and in 1982 produced and co-wrote the National Board of Review's David Wark Griffith Awards at Lincoln Center, hosted by Robert Preston and featuring James Cagney, Martin Scorsese, Warren Beatty, Myrna Loy, Lauren Bacall, and Lee Strasberg.

He is the author of *Tay Garnett* (1989), an authorized biography of the director with a foreword by Greer Garson; the monograph "Victor Fleming" in *Between Action and Cut* (1985), and has contributed to *World Film Directors* (1988), *International Encyclopedia of Films and Filmmakers, Volumes III & IV* (1987–1988), *Speelfilmencylopedie* (1986), and *International Film Periodicals* (1984, Greenwood Press). His articles on cinema and interviews with filmmakers have appeared in *Rolling Stone, Millimeter, Films in Review, Starlog, Fangoria, Cinemacabre, American Classic Screen, The Velvet Light Trap, Classic Images, Film Bulletin, Film Industry Gazette,* and *Quirk's Reviews of Motion Pictures.*

John is a 1978 graduate of Emerson College in Boston, with a Bachelor of Fine Arts Degree in Film. At Emerson, John founded and edited the film journal *Grand Illusions,* cited for excellence in *American Film, The Boston Globe,* and *The Real Paper.*

John lives in New York City, where he continues to work on screenplays and feature film projects.